THE
REVELATION
OF
Law
IN
Scripture

Considered with respect both to
its own nature, and to its relative
place in successive dispensations.

Patrick Fairbairn, D.D.

Write for a complete title list:

ALPHA PUBLICATIONS
P. O. Box 655
Winona Lake, Indiana 46590

T. & T. Clark *1869*
Zondervan *1957*
ALPHA PUBLICATIONS *1979*

Published by ALPHA PUBLICATIONS
Winona Lake, Indiana.   1979

PREFACE.

THE subject handled in the following Lectures enters so deeply into the whole scheme and objects of Divine Revelation, that no apology can be required for directing public attention to it ; at any period, and in any circumstances of the church, it may fitly enough be chosen for particular inquiry and discussion. But no one acquainted with the recent phases of theological sentiment in this country, and with the prevailing tendencies of the age, can fail to perceive its special appropriateness as a theme for discussion at the present time. If this, however, has naturally led to a somewhat larger proportion of the controversial element than might otherwise have been necessary, I have endeavoured to give the discussion as little as possible of a polemical aspect ; and have throughout been more anxious to unfold and establish what I conceive to be the true, than to go into minute and laboured refutations of the false. On this account, also, personal references have been omitted to some of the more recent advocates of the views here controverted, where it could be done without prejudice to the course of discussion.

The terms of the Trust-deed, in connection with which the Lectures appear, only require that not fewer than six be delivered in Edinburgh, but as to publication wisely leave it to the discretion and judgment of the Lecturer, either to limit himself to that number, or to supplement it with others according to the nature and demands of his subject. I have found it necessary to avail myself of this liberty, by the addition of half as many more Lectures as those actually delivered; and one of these (Lecture IV.), from the variety and importance of the topics discussed in it, has unavoidably extended to nearly twice the length of any of the others. However unsuitable this would have been if addressed to an audience, as a component part of a book there will be found in it a sufficient number of breaks to relieve the attention of the reader.

The Supplementary Dissertations, and the exposition of the more important passages in St Paul's writings in reference to the law, which follow the Lectures, have added considerably to the size of the volume; but it became clear as I proceeded, that the discussion of the subject in the Lectures would have been incomplete without them. It is possible, indeed, that in this respect some may be disposed to note a defect rather than a superfluity, and to point to certain other topics or passages which appear to them equally entitled to a place. I have only to say, that as it was necessary to make a selection, I have endeavoured to embrace in this portion what seemed to be, for the present time, relatively the most important, and, as regards the passages of Scripture, have, I believe, included all that are of essential moment for the ends more immediately contemplated. But several topics, I may be allowed to add, very closely connected with the main theme of this volume, have been already treated in my work on the ' Typology of Scripture ;' and though it has been found impracticable to avoid coming here occasionally on the ground which had been traversed there, it was manifestly proper that this should not be done beyond what the present subject, in its main features, imperatively required.

GLASGOW, *October* 1868.

CONTENTS.

EXPOSITION OF THE MOST IMPORTANT PASSAGES ON THE LAW IN ST PAUL'S EPISTLES.

THE REVELATION OF LAW IN SCRIPTURE.

LECTURE I.

INTRODUCTORY.

PREVAILING VIEWS IN RESPECT TO THE ASCENDENCY OF LAW
(1) IN THE NATURAL; (2) IN THE MORAL AND RELIGIOUS SPHERE;
AND THE RELATION IN WHICH THEY STAND TO THE REVELA-
TIONS OF SCRIPTURE ON THE SUBJECT.

AMONG the more marked tendencies of our age, especially as represented by its scientific and literary classes, may justly be reckoned a prevailing tone of sentiment regarding the place and authority of law in the Divine administration. The sentiment is a divided one; for the tendency in question takes a twofold direction, according as it respects the natural, or the moral and religious sphere—in the one exalting, we may almost say deifying law; in the other narrowing its domain, sometimes even ignoring its existence. An indissoluble chain of sequences, the fixed and immutable law of cause and effect, whether always discoverable or not, is contemplated as binding together the order of events in the *natural* world; but as regards the *spiritual*, it is the inherent right or sovereignty of the individual mind that is chiefly made account of, subject only to the claims of social order, the temporal interests of humanity, and the general enlightenment of the times. And as there can be no doubt that these divergent lines of thought have found their occasion, and to some extent also their ground, the one in the marked advancement of natural science, the other in the progress of the Divine dispensations, it will form a fitting introduction to the inquiry that lies before us to take a brief review of both, in their general relation to the great truths and principles of Scripture.

I. We naturally look first, in such a survey, to the physical territory, to the vast and complicated field of nature.   Here a twofold disturbance has arisen—the one from men of science pressing, not so much ascertained facts, as plausible inferences or speculations built on them, to unfavourable conclusions against Scripture ; the other from theologians themselves overstepping in their inter-pretations of Scripture, and finding in it revelations of law, or supposed indications of order, in the natural sphere, which it was never intended to give.   As so inter-preted by Patristic, Mediæval, and even some compara-tively late writers, the Bible has unquestionably had its authority imperilled by being brought into collision with indisputable scientific results.   But the better it is under-stood the more will it be found to have practised in this respect a studious reserve, and to have as little invaded the proper field of scientific inquiry and induction, as to have assumed, in regard to it, the false position of the nature-religions of heathenism.   It is the moral and religious sphere with which the Bible takes strictly to do ; and only in respect to the more fundamental things belonging to the constitution of nature and its relation to the Creator, can it be said to have committed itself to any authoritative deliverance.   Written, as every book must be that is adapted to popular use, in the language of common life, it describes the natural phenomena of which it speaks according to the appearances, rather than the realities, of things.   This was inevitable, and requires to

be made due account of by those who would deal justly
with its contents.   But while freely and familiarly dis-
coursing about much pertaining to the creation and providence of the world, the Bible does not, in respect to the
merely natural frame and order of things, pronounce upon
their latent powers or modes of operation, nor does it
isolate events from the proper instrumental agencies.   It
undoubtedly presents the works and movements of nature
in close connection with the will and pervasive energy of
God ; but then it speaks thus of them all alike—of the
little as well as the great—of the ordinary not less than
the extraordinary, or more striking and impressive.
According to the Bible, God thunders, indeed, in the
clouds ; but the winds also, even the gentlest zephyrs,
blow at His command, and do His bidding.   If it is He
who makes the sun to know his going forth, and pour
light and gladness over the face of nature, it is He also
who makes the rain to fall and the seeds of the earth to
spring, and clothes the lilies of the field with beauty.
Not even a sparrow falls to the ground without Him.
And as in the nearer and more familiar of these operations everything is seen to be accomplished through
means and ordinances bound up with nature's constitution ; so, it is reasonable to infer, must it be with the
grander and more remote.   In short, while it is the
doctrine of the Bible that God is *in* all, and in a sense
does all, nothing is authoritatively defined as to the *how*
or *by what* they are done ; and science is at perfect
liberty to prosecute its researches with the view of discovering the individual properties of things, and how,
when brought into relation, they act and react on each
other, so as to produce the results which appear in the
daily march of providence.

Now, let this relation of the Bible, with its true

religion, to the pursuits of science, be placed alongside
that of the false religions of Greek and Roman polytheism which it supplanted, and let the effect be noted—
the legitimate and necessary effect—of the progress of
science in its clearest and best established conclusions on
the one as compared with the other. Resting on an
essentially pantheistic basis, those ancient religions ever
tended to associate the objects and operations of nature
with the immediate presence and direct agency of some
particular deity—to identify the one in a manner with
the other ; and very specially to do this with the greater
and more remarkable phenomena of nature. Thus Helios,
or the Sun, was deified in Apollo, and was not poetically
represented merely, but religiously believed, to mount
his chariot, drawn by a team of fiery steeds, in the morn-
ing, to rise by a solid pathway to mid-heaven, and then
descend toward the western horizon, that his wearied
coursers might be refreshed before entering on the labours
of another day. Selené, or the Moon, in like manner,
though in humbler guise, was contemplated as pursuing
her nocturnal course. Sun, moon, and stars, it was
believed, bathed themselves every night in the waves of
ocean, and got their fires replenished by partaking of the
Neptunian element. Eclipses were prodigies—portentous
signs of wrath in heaven—which struck fear into men's
bosoms, as on the eve of direful calamities, and sometimes
so paralysing them as to become itself the occasion of the
sorest disasters. Hence, the philosophy which applied
itself to explore the operation of physical properties and
laws in connection with natural events, was accounted
impious ; since, as Plutarch remarks,[1] it seemed ' to
ascribe things to insensate causes, unintelligent powers,
and necessary changes, thereby jostling aside the divine.'

[1] Life of Nicias.

On this account Anaxagoras was thrown into prison by the Athenians, and narrowly escaped with his life. Socrates was less fortunate; he suffered the condemnation and penalty of death, although he had not carried his physical speculations nearly so far as Anaxagoras. At his trial, however, he was charged with impiety, on the ground of having said that the sun was a stone, and the moon earth; he himself, however, protesting that such was not his, but the doctrine of Anaxagoras; that he held both sun and moon to be divine persons, as was done by the rest of mankind. His real view seems to have been, that the common and ordinary events of Providence flowed from the operation of second causes, but that those of greater magnitude and rarer occurrence came directly from the interposition of a divine power. Yet this modified philosophy was held to be utterly inconsistent with the popular religion, and condemned as an impiety. Of necessity, therefore, as science proceeded in its investigations and discoveries, religion fell into the background; as the belief in second causes advanced, the gods, as no longer needed, vanished away. Physical science and the polytheism of Greece and Rome were in their very nature antagonistic, and every real advance of the one brought along with it a shock to the other.

It is otherwise with the religion of the Bible, when this is rightly understood, and nothing from without, nothing foreign to its teaching, is imposed on it. For it neither merges God in the works and operations of nature, nor associates Him with one department more peculiarly than another; while still it presents all—the works themselves, the changes they undergo, and every spring and agency employed in accomplishing them—in dependence on His arm and subordination to His will: He is in all, through all, and over all. So that for those who have imbibed the spirit of the Bible, there may appear the most perfect regularity and continued sequence of operations, while God is seen and adored in connection with every one of them. It is true, that the sensibilities of religious feeling, or, as we should rather say, the freshness and power of its *occasional* outbursts, are less likely to be experienced, and in reality are more rarely manifested, when, in accordance with the revelations of science, God's agency is contemplated as working through material forces under the direction of established law, than if, without such an intervening medium, in specific acts of providence, and by direct interference, He should make His presence felt. The more that anything ceases to appear strange to our view, abnormal—the more it comes to be associated in our minds with the orderly domain of law—the less startling and impressive does it naturally become as an evidence of the nearness and power of Godhead : it no longer stands alone to our view, it is part of a system, but still a system which, if viewed aright, has been all planned by the wisdom, and is constantly sustained and directed by the providence of God.

In this, as in so many other departments of human interest and experience, there is a compensation in things. What science may appear to take with one hand, it gives —gives, one might almost say, more liberally with another. If, for example, the revelation on scientific grounds of the amazing regularity and finely-balanced movements which prevail in the constitution and order of the material universe, as connected with our planetary system,—if this, in one aspect of it, should seem to have placed God at a certain distance from the visible world, in another it has but rendered His presiding agency and vigilant oversight more palpably indispensable. For such a vast, complicated, and wondrous mechanism, how

could it have originated ? or, having originated, how
could it be sustained in action without the infinite skill
and ceaseless activity of an all-perfect Mind ?   There is
here what is incalculably more and better than some
occasional proofs of interference, or fitful displays of
power, however grand and imposing.   There is clear-
sighted, far-reaching thought, nicely planned design,
mutual adaptations, infinitely varied, of part to part, the
action and reaction of countless forces, working with an
energy that baffles all conception, yet working with the
most minute mathematical precision, and with the effect
of producing both the most harmonious operation, and
the most diversified, gigantic, and beneficent results.
It is, too, the more marvellous, and the more certainly
indicative of the originating and controlling agency of
mind, that while all the planetary movements obey with
perfect regularity one great principle of order, they do so
by describing widely different orbits, and, in the case of
some, pursuing courses that move in opposite directions to
others.   Whence should such things be ?   Not, assuredly,
from any property inherent in the material orbs themselves, which know nothing of the laws they exemplify,
or the interests that depend on the order they keep :
no, but solely from the will and power of the infinite and
eternal Being, whose workmanship they are, and whose
purposes they unconsciously fulfil.   So wrote Newton
devoutly, as well as nobly, at the close of his incompar-
able work : ' This beautiful system of sun, planets, and
comets, could have its origin in no other way than by the
counsel and sovereignty of an intelligent and powerful
Being.   He governs all things—not as the soul of the
world, but as the Lord of the universe. . . . We know
Him only through His qualities and attributes, and
through the most wise and excellent forms and final

causes, which belong to created things ; and we admire
Him on account of His perfections ; but for His sovereign
lordship, we worship and adore Him ;'—thus in the
true spirit of the Psalmist, and as with a solemn halle-
lujah, winding up the mighty demonstration.[1]

We are informed, in a recent publication by a noble
author,[2] that modern science is again returning to this
view of things ; returning to it, I suppose, as becoming
conscious of the inadequacy of the maxim of an earlier
time, in respect to creation, ' That the hypothesis of a
Deity is not needed.'   Speaking of the mystery which
hangs around the idea of force, even of the particular
force which has its seat in our own vitality, he says, ' If,
then, we know nothing of that kind of force which is so
near to us, and with which our own intelligence is in
such close alliance, much less can we know the ultimate
nature of force in its other forms.   It is important to
dwell on this, because both the aversion with which some
men regard the idea of the reign of law, and the triumph

---

[1] On this point, Dr Whewell has some remarks in his ' Philosophy of the
Inductive Sciences,' which another great authority in natural science, Sir John
Herschel, has characterized as admirable (' Essays and Addresses,' p. 239).   ' The
assertion appears to be quite unfounded, that as science advances from point to
point, final causes recede before it, and disappear one after the other.   The
principle of design changes its mode of application indeed, but it loses none of
its force.   We no longer consider particular facts as produced by special interpositions, but we consider design as exhibited in the establishment and adjustment of the laws by which particular facts are produced.   We do not look upon
each particular cloud as brought near us that it may drop fatness on our fields ;
but the general adaptation of the laws of heat, and air, and moisture, to the
promotion of vegetation, does not become doubtful.   We are rather, by the
discovery of the general laws of nature, led into a scene of wider design, of
deeper contrivance, of more comprehensive adjustments.   Final causes, if they
appear driven farther from us by such an extension of our views, embrace us
only with a vaster and more majestic circuit ; instead of a few threads connecting some detached objects, they become a stupendous network which is wound
round and round the universal frame of things.'—Vol. I. p. 635.

[2] The Duke of Argyle, ' Reign of Law,' p. 122.

with which some others hail it, are founded on a notion, that when we have traced any given phenomena to what are called natural forces, we have traced them farther than we really have. We know nothing of the ultimate nature, or of the ultimate seat of force [that is, know nothing scientifically]. Science, in the modern doctrine of the conservation of energy and the convertibility of forces, is already getting something like a firm hold of the idea, that all kinds of force are but forms or manifestations of some central force issuing from some one Fountainhead of power. Sir John Herschel has not hesitated to say, that it is but reasonable to regard the force of gravitation as the direct or indirect result of a consciousness or a will existing somewhere. And even if we cannot certainly identify force in all its forms with the direct energies of one omnipresent and all-pervading will, it is, at least, in the highest degree unphilosophical to assume the contrary ; to speak or to think as if the forces of nature were either independent of, or even separate from, the Creator's power.' In short, natural science, in its investigations into the forces and movements of the material universe, finds a limit which it cannot overpass, and in that limit a felt want of satisfaction, as conscious of the necessity of a spontaneity, a will, a power to give impulse and direction to the whole, of which nature itself can give no information, because lying outside of its province, and which, if discovered to us at all, must be certified through a supernatural revelation.

But this is still not the whole of the argument for the pervading causal connection of God with the works of nature, and His claim in this respect to our devout recognition of His will as the source of its laws, and His power as the originator and sustainer of its movements. For, besides the admirable method and order, the simplicity in

the midst of endless diversity, which are found to characterize the system of material nature, there is also to be
taken into account the irrepressible impulse in the human
mind to search for these, and the capacity to discern and
appreciate them as marks of the highest intelligence. A
pre-established harmony here discovers itself between the
world of thought within, and the world of material order
and scientific adjustment without, bespeaking their mutual
co-ordination by the wise foresight and plastic energy of
one Supreme Mind. 'Copernicus[1] (it has been remarked),
in the dedication of his work to Pope Paul III., confesses
that he was brought to the discovery of the sun's central
position and of the diurnal motion of the earth, not by
observation or analysis, but by what he calls the feeling
of a want of symmetry in the Ptolemaic system. But
who had told him that there *must* be symmetry in all the
movements of the celestial bodies, or that complication
was not more sublime than simplicity? Symmetry and
simplicity, before they were discovered by the observer,
were postulated by the philosopher;' and by him, we
may add, truly postulated, because first existing as ideas
in the Eternal Mind, whose image and reflex man's is.
So also with Newton : the principle of gravitation, as an
all-embracing law of the planetary system, was postulated
in his mind before he ascertained it to be the law actually
in force throughout the whole, or even any considerable
part of the system—mind in man thus responding to mind
in God, and finding, in the things which appear, the evidence at once of His eternal power and Godhead, and of the
similitude of its own understanding to that of Him by
whom the world has been contrived and ordained.

There is a class of minds which such considerations
cannot reach. They would take a position above them ;

---

[1] Max Müller, 'Lectures on Language,' p. 19.

and adventuring upon what tends to perplex and confound, rather than satisfy, the reason, they raise such
questions respecting the Absolute and Infinite, as in a
manner exclude the just and natural conclusions deduced
from the works of creation concerning the Being and
Government of the Creator. But questions of that description, pressing as they do into a region which transcends all human thought and known analogy, it is presumption in man to raise, folly to entertain; for 'man is
born,' as Goethe well remarked, ' not to solve the
problems of the universe, but to find out where the
problem for himself begins, and then restrain himself
within the limits of the comprehensible.' Considered
from this point of view, the reflections which have been
submitted as to the prevalence of natural law in the
general economy of the world of matter, in its relation
to God and its bearing on the religion of the Bible, are
perfectly legitimate; and they might easily be extended
by a diversified application of the principles involved in
them to the arrangements in the natural world, which
stand more closely related to men's individual interests
and responsibilities. But to sum up briefly what relates
to this branch of our subject, there are three leading
characteristics in the teaching of the Bible respecting the
relation of God to the merely natural world, and which,
though they can only in a qualified sense be termed a
revelation of law, yet form, so to speak, the landmarks
which the Bible itself sets up, and the measure of the
liberty it accords to the cultivators of science.

(1.) The first of these is the strict and proper personality of God, as distinct from, and independent of, the
whole or any part of the visible creation. This to its
utmost limits is His workmanship—the theatre which
His hands have reared, and which they still maintain, for

the outgoing of His perfections and the manifestation of His glory. As such, therefore, the things belonging to it are not, and cannot possibly be, a part of His proper self. However pervaded by His essential presence and divine energy, they are not 'the varied God,' in the natural sense of the expression. They came into being without any diminution of His infinite greatness, and so they may be freely handled, explored, modified, made to undergo ever so many changes and transformations, without in the slightest degree trenching on the nature of Him, who is 'without variableness or shadow of turning.' Such is the doctrine of the Bible—differing from mere nature-worship, and from polytheism in all its forms, which, if it does not openly avow, tacitly assumes the identification of Deity with the world. The Scripture doctrine of the Creator and creation, of God and the world, as diverse though closely related factors, leaves to science its proper field of inquiry and observation untrammelled by any hindrance arising from the view there exhibited of the Divine nature.

(2.) A second distinguishing feature in the revelations of the Bible is, that they rather pre-suppose what belongs to the domain of natural science, than directly interfere with it. With the exception of the very earliest part of the sacred records, it is the supernatural—the supernatural with respect more immediately to *moral* relations and results—which may be designated their proper field ; and while in this the supernatural throughout bases itself on the natural, the natural itself is little more than incidentally referred to, or very briefly indicated. Even in the account given of the formation of the world and the natural constitution of things therewith connected, it is obviously with the design of forming a suitable introduction to the place of man in the world, his moral relation

to the Creator, and his special distinction as the responsible head of creation upon earth, that the narrative was
framed, rather than for the purpose of affording any
insight into the merely natural relations and properties
of things.   The physical as such, with its manifold
gradations of life and being, its history and developments,
its laws of attraction and repulsion, modes of operation,
existing forms and possible transformations,—all this is
either unnoticed in Scripture, or indicated only in its
rougher outlines.   Even the vexed question respecting
the origin and distinctions of species in the animal creation
is but partially involved here ; for, while Scripture undoubtedly represents the existing families of mankind as
originating in the formation of one pair by the immediate
interposition of God, and also represents the production
of plants, fishes, land animals, fowls, as coming at successive stages into being, and each constituted so as to bring
forth after its kind ; yet nothing is said as to the number
of kinds, or the centres, one or more, in which they
respectively originated, how far the several kinds should
remain stereotyped, or how far they might be capable,
through human art or climatic influences, of departing
from the original type, and in process of time developing
into varieties and making indefinite approaches one to
another.   On such points Scripture is altogether silent,
even in that introductory portion which most nearly
resembles a piece of natural history.   Nothing depends
on them for the higher interests which it has mainly in
view, the things which concern the moral character and
purposes of God, as connected with His crowning work
in creation—Man.   And it may well surely be regarded
as a wonderful thing in that simple primeval record, an
evidence of something more in it than a merely human
authorship, that it should, while touching but incidentally

on scientific ground, stand, as a whole, in such striking accord even now with the established results of science— exhibiting, by means of a few graphic lines, not merely the evolution from dark chaos of a world of light, and order, and beauty, but the gradual ascent also of being upon earth, from the lowest forms of vegetable and animal life, up to him, who holds alike of earth and heaven —at once creation's head, and the rational image and vicegerent of the Creator. Here, substantially at least, we have the progression of modern science; but this combined, in a manner altogether peculiar, with the peerless dignity and worth of man, as of more account in God's sight than the entire world besides of animated being, yea, than sun, and moon, and stars of light, because incomparably nearer than them all to the heart of God, and more closely associated with the moral aims, to which everything in nature was designed to be subordinate. Better than all science, it reveals alike man's general place in nature and his singular relation to God.[1]

(3.) A third characteristic of Bible teaching in this connection is the free play it allows to general laws and natural agencies, or to the operation of cause and effect; and this, not merely as bearing on simply natural results, but also as connected with spiritual relations and duties. Those laws and agencies are of God; as briefly expressed by Augustine, ' God's will constitutes the nature of things' (*Dei voluntas rerum natura est*); or more fully by Hooker,[2] ' That law, the performance whereof we behold in things natural, is as it were an authentic or original draft written in the bosom of God himself, whose Spirit being to execute the same with every particular nature, every mere natural agent is only as an instrument created at the beginning, and ever since the beginning used, to work His

[1] *See* Butler, ' Analogy,' P. I. c. 7.　　　[2] ' Eccl. Polity,' B. I. c. 3, sec. 4.

own will and pleasure withal. Nature, therefore, is nothing else but God's instrument.' Whence the various powers and faculties of nature, whether in things animate or inanimate, her regular course and modes of procedure, are not supplanted by grace, but are recognised and acted upon to the full extent that they can be made subservient to higher purposes. Thus, when in respect to things above nature, God reveals His mind to men, He does it *through* men, and through men not as mere machines unconsciously obeying a supernatural impulse, but acting in discharge of their personal obligations and the free exercise of their individual powers and susceptibilities. So also the common subject of grace, the ordinary believer, obtains no warrant as such to set at nought the settled laws and ordinances of nature, no right to expect aught but mischief if he should contravene their action, or fail to adapt himself to their mode of operation; and at every step in his course toward the final goal of his calling, reason, knowledge, cultivation, wise discretion, and persevering diligence have their parts to play in securing his safety and progress, as well as the divine help and internal agency of the Spirit. It is, therefore, within the boundary-lines fixed by nature, and in accordance with the principles of her constitution, alike in the mental and the material world, that the work of grace proceeds, though bringing along with it powers, and influences, and results which are peculiarly its own. And even as regards the things done *for* the believer in the outer field of providence, and in answer to humble prayer, there may be no need (for aught we know to the contrary) for miraculous interference, in the ordinary sense of the term, but only for wise direction, for timely and fitting adjustment. It may even be, as Isaac Taylor has said, 'the great miracle of providence, that no miracles are needed to accomplish its purposes;' that 'the *materials* of the machinery of providence are all of ordinary quality, while their combination displays nothing less than infinite skill;' and, at all events, within this field alone of divine foresight and gracious interventions through natural agencies, there is in the hand of God 'a hidden treasury of boons sufficient for the incitement of prayer and the reward of humble faith.'[1]

The three principles or positions now laid down in respect to God's operations in nature and providence, seem to comprise all that is needed for the maintenance of friendly relations between the religion of the Bible and the investigations of science ; on the one side, ample scope is left to these investigations, while, on the other, nothing has been actually established by them which conflicts with the statements of the Bible interpreted by the principles we have stated. But undoubtedly there is in them what cannot be reconciled with that deification of material forces, which some would identify with strict science—as if everything that took place were the result of the action only of unconscious law—law working with such rigid, unbroken continuity of natural order, as to admit of no break or deviation whatever (such as is implied in miracles), and no special adaptation to individual cases (as a particular providence would involve). Both miracles and a particular providence, within certain limits, and as means to the attainment of important ends, are postulated and required in the revelations of the Bible. For if, as it teaches, there be a personal God, an infinite and eternal Spirit, distinct from the works of creation, and Himself the author of the laws by which they are governed—if also this God sustains the character of *moral* Governor in regard to the intelligent part of His creation, and subordinates everything in His administration to the

---

[1] ' Natural History of Enthusiasm,' sec. vi.

principles and interests therewith connected—then the *possibility*, at least, of miracles and a particular providence (to say nothing at present of their evidence), can admit of no reasonable doubt. This does not imply, as the opponents of revelation not unfrequently assume, the production in certain cases of an effect without a cause, or the emerging of dissimilar consequents from the same antecedents. For, on the supposition in question, the antecedents are no longer the same; the cause which is of nature has superadded to it a cause which is above nature, in the material sense—the will and the power of a personal Deity. We reason here, as in other things, from the human to the divine. Mind in man is capable of originating a force, which within definite limits can suspend the laws of material nature, and control or modify them to its desired ends. And why, then, should it be thought incredible or strange, that the central Mind of the universe, by whom all subsists, should at certain special moments, when the purposes of His moral government require a new order of things to be originated, authoritative indications of His will to be given, or results accomplished unattainable in the ordinary course of nature, bring into play a force adequate to the end in view? It is merely supposing the great primary cause interposing to do in a higher line of things what finite beings are ever doing in a lower; and the right, and the power, and the purpose to do it, resolve themselves (as we have said) into the question, whether there really be a God, exercising a moral government over the world, capable for its higher ends of putting forth acts of supernatural agency—a question which natural science has no special mission to determine, or peculiar resources to explicate.[1]

---

[1] *See* M'Cosh, ' Method of Divine Government,' B. II. cap. i sec. 7. And for an admirable and conclusive exposure of the views of the chief opponents

The subject of a particular providence so far differs from that of miraculous action, that, to a large extent, its requirements may be met through the operation of merely instrumental causes, fitly disposed and arranged by Divine wisdom to suit the ever-varying conditions of individual man. To have respect to the individual in His method of government cannot be regarded as less

in the present day of all miraculous agency, even in creation and intelligent design as connected with the works of nature—namely, the advocates of natural selection and progressive development—see particularly 'The Darwinian Theory of Development examined by a Cambridge Graduate.' It is there stated, as a remarkable thing, that this theory, which professes to be based on scientific grounds, yet expresses itself in the form of a creed: the words 'We must believe,' 'I have no difficulty in believing,' etc., are perpetually recurring, and, in fact, form the necessary links in the chain of so-called deductions. Hence, while setting out with the object of avoiding the miraculous, the end is not attained. ' In the old method, the great physiologists take it for granted that their researches can only reach a certain point, beyond which they cannot penetrate; there they come to the inexplicable; and they believe that barrier to be the Creator's power, which they leave at a respectful distance. This, according to the feelings of the ancients, was "the veil of nature which no mortal hand had ever withdrawn," and, as they approached it, they felt and spoke of it with reverence. Now, the new method is to discard the belief in a Creator, to reject the omniscience and omnipotence of a Maker of all things, to charge us who believe in it with endeavouring to conceal our ignorance by an imposing form of words; and to undertake to explain the origin of all forms of life by another and a totally different hypothesis. What, then, is the result? A long list of new and doubtful assertions, some of them of surpassing novelty and wildness, and all of them unaccompanied by proof, but proposed as points of belief. The marvellous in the old method is in one point only, and that, for the most part, more implied than expressed—the belief in a paramount Intellect ordaining life and providing for its success. The marvellous in the new way is a vast assemblage of prodigies, strange and unheard-of events and circumstances that cannot be confirmed by any authentic evidence, and which, indeed, are out of the reach of evidence—a throng of aëry dreams and phantasies, evoked by the imagination, which we are called on to *believe* as realities, as it is impossible to *prove* that they are so' (p. 355). A distinguished naturalist has said, ' No one who has advanced so far in philosophy as to have thought of one thing in relation to another, will ever be satisfied with laws which had no author, works which had no maker, and co-ordinations which had no designer' (Phillips, 'Life on Earth'). The development school vainly try to satisfy themselves by making enormous drafts on their imagination and faith.

consistent with the nature of an all-wise and omnipotent Being, than to restrain His working within the bounds of general laws ; and nature itself is a witness to the infinite minuteness of the care and oversight of which even the smallest forms in the animated creation are the object. Besides, in a vast multitude of instances, probably in by far the greater number of what constitute special acts of providence for individuals, it is not the law of cause and effect in material nature that is interfered with, but the operations of mind that are controlled—the Eternal Spirit directly, or by some appropriate ministry, touching the springs of thought and feeling in different bosoms, so as to bring the resolves and procedure of one to bear upon the condition and circumstances of another, and work out the results which need to be accomplished. In the ordinary affairs of life, where secular ends alone are concerned, we see what a complicated network of mutual interconnection and specific influences is formed, by the movements of mind transmitted from one person to another, and the same we can readily conceive to exist in relation to spiritual ends ; in this case, indeed, even more varied and far-reaching, as the ends to be secured are of a higher kind, and there is the action of minds from the heavenly places coming in aid of the movements which originate upon earth. But without dilating further, the principle of the whole matter in this, as well as the previous aspect of it, is embodied in another grand utterance of Newton's, in which, after describing God as a being or substance, ' one, simple, indivisible, living, and life-giving, everywhere and necessarily existing,' etc., it is added, in these remarkable words, ' perceiving and governing all things by His essential presence, and con- stantly co-operating with all things, according to fixed laws as the foundation and cause of all nature, *except when it is good to act otherwise (nisi ubi aliter agere bonum est):'* the will of the great Sovereign of the universe being thus placed above every impressed law and instrumental cause of nature, and conceived free to adopt other and more peculiar lines of action as the higher ends of His government might require.

II. We turn now from the physical to the moral and religious sphere, the one with which in the present discussion we have more especially to do; and in doing so we pass into quite another region as regards the tendency of thought in the current literature and philosophy of the day. For here, undoubtedly, the disposition with many is to fall as much short of the teaching of Scripture in respect to the supremacy of law, as in the other department to go beyond it. But opinions on the subject are really so diverse, they differ so much both in respect to the forms they assume and the grounds on which they are based, that it is not quite easy in a brief space, and impossible without some detail, to give a distinct representation of them.

(1.) At the farthest remove from the Scriptural view stand the advocates of materialism—those who would merge mind and matter ultimately into one mass, who would trace all mental phenomena to sensations, and account for everything that takes place by means of the affinities, combinations, and inherent properties of matter. In such a philosophy there is room for law only in the physical sense, and for such progress or civilization as may arise from a more perfect acquaintance therewith, and a more skilful use or adaptation of it to the employments and purposes of life. The personality of God, as a living, eternal Spirit, cannot be entertained; and, of course,

responsibility in the higher sense, as involving subjection
to moral government, and the establishment of a Divine
moral order, can have no place.   For, mind is but a
species of cerebral development; thought or desire but
an action of the brain; man himself but the most perfectly
developed form of organic being, the highest type in the
scale of nature's ascending series of productions, whose
part is fulfilled in doing what is fitted to secure a healthful organization, and provide for himself the best conditions possible of social order and earthly wellbeing.   But,
to say nothing of the scheme in other respects, looking at
it simply with reference to the religion and morality of
the Bible, it plainly ignores the foundation on which
these may be said to rest ; namely, the moral elements in
man's constitution, or the phenomena of conscience, which
are just as real as those belonging to the physical world,
and in their nature immensely more important.   In so
doing, it gives the lie to our profoundest convictions, and
loses sight of the higher, the more ennobling qualities of
our nature, indeed would reduce man very much to the
condition of a child and creature of fate—capable, indeed,
of being influenced by sensual desires, prudential motives,
and utilitarian considerations, but not called to aim at
conformity to any absolute rule of right and wrong, or to
recognise as binding a common standard of duty.   Such
an idea is strongly repudiated by writers of this school ;
each man, it is contended, has a right or 'just claim to
carry on his life in his own way,' 'his own mode of laying
out his existence is the best, not because it is the best in
itself, but because it is his own mode ;' hence, on the
other side, Calvinism, which appears to be taken as
another name for evangelical Christianity, is decried as
comprising all the good of which humanity is capable in

obedience, and prescribing a way of duty which shall be essentially the same for all.[1]

(2.) Formally antagonistic to this sensational or materialistic school—occupying, one might say, the opposite pole of thought in respect to moral law, yet not less opposed to any objective revelation of law—is the view of the idealists, or, as a portion of them at least are sometimes called, the ideal pantheists. With them, mind and God are the two great ideas that are to rule all ; God first, indeed, whether as the personal or ideal centre of the vital forces that work, and the fundamental principles that should prevail throughout the moral universe ; but also mind in man as the exemplar of God, the exponent of the Divine, and the medium through which it comes into realization. Man, accordingly, by the very constitution of his being, is as a God to himself; or, in the language of one who, more perhaps than any other, may be regarded as the founder of the school, ' Man, as surely as he is a rational being, is the end of his own existence ; he does not exist to the end that something else may be, but he exists absolutely for his own sake ; his being is its own ultimate object.' Consequently, ' all should proceed from his own simple personality,' and should be determined by what is within, not by a regard to what is external to himself, though this latter element will usually more or less prevail, and bring on a sort of con-

---

[1] J. S. Mill ' On Liberty,' ch. iii. In referring to Mr Mill, we certainly take one of the less extreme, as well as most respectable and able of the advocates of a materialistic philosophy—one, too, who in his work on Utilitarianism has laboured hard to make up, in a moral respect, for the inherent defects of his system. But there still is, as Dr M'Cosh has shown (' Examination of Mill's Philosophy,' ch. xx.), the fundamental want of moral law, the impossibility of giving any satisfactory account of the ideas of moral desert and personal obligation, and such loose, uncertain drawing of the boundary lines between moral good and evil, as leaves each man, to a large extent, the framer of his own moral standard.

tradiction, empirically or as matter of fact, to his proper self. But he *should* be determined by nothing foreign, and 'the fundamental principle of morality may be expressed in such a formula as this, " So act, that thou mayest look upon the dictate of thy will as an eternal law to thyself."'[1] Thus the Divine becomes essentially one with the human; the law for the universe is to be got at through the insight and monitions of the individual, especially of such individuals as have a higher range of thought than their fellow-men; the heroes of humanity are, in a qualified sense, its legislators. ' What,' asks Carlyle,[2] ' is this law of the universe, or law made by God? Men at one time read it in their Bible. In many bibles, books, and authentic symbols and monitions of nature, and the world (of fact), there are still some clear indications towards it. Most important it is, that men do, and in some way, get to see it a little. And if no man could now see it by any bible, there is written in the heart of every man an authentic copy of it, direct from Heaven itself : there, if he have learnt to decipher Heaven's writing, and can read the sacred oracles, every born man may find some copy of it.' An element of truth, doubtless, is in such utterances—a most important element, which Scripture also recognises — but intermingled with what is entirely alien to the spirit and teaching of Scripture. For, it proceeds on the supposition of man being still in his normal state, and as such perfectly capable, by the insight of his own rational and moral nature, to acquaint himself with all moral truth and duty. The inner consciousness of man is entitled to create for itself a morality, and a religion (if it should deem such a thing worthy of creation) ; it is, in effect, deified—though itself, as every one knows, to a large

---

[1] Fichte, ' Vocation of Man.'   [2] ' Latter Day Pamphlets,' No. II.

extent the creature of circumstances. And thus all takes a pantheistic direction—the Divine is dragged down to a level with the human, made to coalesce with it, instead of the human (according to the Scriptural scheme) being informed by and elevated to the Divine.[1] And the general result, in so far as such idealism prevails, is obviously to shut men up to 'measureless content' with themselves, and dispose them to resist the dictation of any external authority or revelation whatever. This result is beyond doubt already reached with considerable numbers among the educated classes, and is also pressing through manifold channels of influence into the church! For it is of this that the historian of rationalism speaks when he says,[2] 'The tendency of religious thought in the present day is all in one direction, towards the identification of the Bible and conscience. Generation after generation the power of the moral faculty becomes more absolute, the doctrines that oppose it wane and vanish, and the various elements of theology are absorbed and recast by its influence.' The representation is plausibly made, and only when taken in its connection is its full import seen; for the meaning is, that the identification in question proceeds, not from the conscience finding its enlightenment in the Bible, but from the Bible being made to speak in accordance with the enlightenment of conscience. The intellectual and moral idealism of the age, if still holding by the Bible, reads this in its own light, and throws into the background whatever it disrelishes or repudiates.

(3.) This species of idealism—allying itself with the Bible, though sprung from philosophy, and in itself naturally tending to pantheism—has its representatives in the Christian church, especially among the class whose

---

[1] *See* Morell, 'Hist. of Modern Philosophy,' Vol. II. p. 611.
[2] Lecky's 'Hist. of Rationalism,' Vol. I. p. 384.

tastes lie more in literature than in theology. Of cultivated minds and refined moral sentiments, such persons
readily acknowledge the ascendency of law in the government of God, but, in accordance with their idealism, it is
law in a somewhat ethereal sense, having little to do with
definite rules or external revelations, recognised merely
in a kind of general obligation to exercise certain feelings,
emotions, or principles of action.   Hence in the same
writers you will find law at once exalted and depreciated;
at one time it appears to be everything, at another nothing.
' This universe,' says a religious idealist of the class now
referred to,[1] ' is governed by laws.   At the bottom of
everything here there is law.   Things are in this way and
not that ; we call that a law or a condition.   All departments have their own laws.   By submission to them you
make them your own.'   And still more strongly in another
place, adopting the very style of the pantheistic idealists,[2]
' I think a great deal of law.   Law rules Deity, and its
awful majesty is above individual happiness.   This is
what Kant calls the " categorical imperative ;" that is, a
sense of duty which commands categorically or absolutely
—not saying, " It is better," but " Thou shalt."   Why ?
Because " Thou shalt"—that is all.   It is not best to do
right, thou *must* do right ; and the conscience that feels
that, and in that way, is the nearest to divine humanity.'
But in other passages language equally decided is used
in disparagement of anything in the moral or spiritual
sphere carrying the form of law.   Nothing now must rest,
we are told, on enactment; if necessary, it is not on that
account, ' not because it is commanded ; but it is commanded because it is necessary'[3]—hence binding on the

---

[1] Robertson of Brighton, ' Sermons,' 2d Series, p. 114.
[2] ' Life and Letters,' Vol. I. p. 292.
[3] ' Life,' in a Letter, October 24, 1849.

conscience only so far as it is perceived to be necessary. And again, professing to give the drift of St Paul's admonitions to the Galatians respecting observance, it is said,[1] 'All forms and modes of particularizing the Christian life he reckoned as bondage under the elements or alphabet of the law;' so that, though the Christian life might, if it saw fit, find a suitable expression for itself in any particular observance, this could be defended 'on the ground of wise and Christian expediency alone, and could not be placed on the ground of a Divine statute or command.' Professor Jowett seems to carry the idealizing a little further; he thinks that, under the Old Testament itself, the period emphatically of law, there is evidence of its adoption by the more thoughtful and intelligent of the covenant people. The term 'law,' he says, is ambiguous in Scripture;[2] 'it is so in the Old Testament itself. In the prophecies and psalms, as well as in the writings of St Paul, the law is in a great measure ideal. When the Psalmist spoke of "meditating in the law of the Lord," he was not thinking of the five books of Moses. The law which he delighted to contemplate was not written down (as well might we imagine that the Platonic idea was a treatise on philosophy); it was the will of God, the truth of God, the justice and holiness of God. In later ages the same feelings began to gather around the volume of the law itself. The law was ideal still'—though he admits that 'with this idealism were combined the reference to its words, and the literal enforcement of its precepts.' A strange sort of idealism, surely, which could not separate itself from the concrete or actual, and continued looking to this for the material alike of its study and its observance! But it is the view only we at present notice, the form of thought itself respecting the law,

[1] 'Sermons,' 2d Series, p. 184.   [2] 'Epistles of St Paul,' II. p. 501.

not its consistence either with itself or with the statements of Scripture. It clearly enough indicates how idealism has been influencing the minds of Christian writers in this direction, and how, along with much that is sound, pure, and sometimes elevating in the sentiments they utter, there is also a certain laxity as to particular things, an asserted superiority for the individual over law in respect to everything like explicit rules and enactments.

(4.) There is, however, a class of Christian writers, more properly theological and also of a somewhat realistic character, who so far concur with the idealists, that they maintain the freedom of the Christian from obligation to the law distinctively so called—the law in that sense is abolished by the Gospel of Christ, or, as sometimes put, dead and buried in His grave ; but only that a new and higher law might come in its place, the law of Gospel life and liberty. This view is what in theological language bears the name of *Neonomianism*—that is, the doctrine of a new law, in some respects differing from or opposed to the old—a law of principles rather than of precepts, especially the great principles of faith and love, which it conceives to be carried now higher than before. The view is by no means of recent origin ; it was formally propounded shortly after the Reformation, was adopted by the Socinians as a distinguishing part of their system, and with certain unimportant variations has often been set forth afresh in later times.[1] Dr Whately puts it thus : The law as revealed in the Old Testament bears on the face of it that the whole of its precepts, moral as well as

[1] Zanchius, who belongs to the Reformation era, states expressly that we have nothing to do with the moral precepts of Moses, except in so far as they agree with the common law of nature, and are confirmed by Christ (Op. IV. l. i. c. 11). To the same effect, Musculus, ' De Abrogatione Legis Mos. ;' and more recently, Knapp, ' Christian Theology,' sec. 119, ' Bialloblotzky, De Abrog. L. Mos.,' &c.

ceremonial, 'were intended for the Israelites exclusively;'
therefore 'they could not by their own authority be
binding on Christians,' and are by the apostle in explicit
terms denied to be binding on them, hence as regards
them abolished.[1]   'But, on the other hand, the natural
principles of morality which (among other things) it
inculcates, are from their own character of universal
obligation ; so that Christians are bound to the observance
of those commandments which are called moral—not,
however, because they are commandments of the Mosaic
law, but because they *are* moral.'   The moral law, as
written upon man's heart, remains still, as ever, authoritative and binding, and 'is by the Gospel placed on higher
grounds.   Instead of precise rules, it furnishes sublime
principles of conduct, leaving the Christian to apply these,
according to his own discretion, to each case that may
arise.'   In a somewhat modified form, the same view has
been presented after this manner : 'Under the Christian
dispensation, the law in its outward and limited form—in
its form as given to Israel—has passed away ; but the
substance, the principles, of the law remain.   Would we
be free from that substance, these principles must be
written on our hearts.   If they are not so written, we
ourselves reduce them to an outward and commanding
law, which, not being obeyed, brings bondage with it.'
The law, therefore, in one sense has passed away, in
another not ; it is improper to speak of it as dead and
buried in the grave of Christ, for in its great principles it
never dies ; but 'the outward, the limited, the commanding form of it may be said to be dead ;' or, as otherwise
expressed, 'that law in a particular and local form has
been taken up and widened out into a higher law, in Him
who not only exhibits it in its most perfect form, but gives

[1] 'Essay on the Abolition of the Law,' secs. 1, 2.

the strength in which alone we can obey.'[1] The differ-ence between this and the other mode of representation is evidently not material: in both alike the revelation of law in the Old Testament is held to be not directly, and in its letter, binding upon Christians; but its essential prin-ciples, which constitute the basis of all morality, being recognised and embraced in the Gospel, developed also to nobler results and enforced by higher motives, these are binding, and if not strictly law, at least in the stead of law, and more effectively serving its interests.

(5.) A still farther development in the same direction is what is known under the name of *Antinomianism*—antithesis to the law, in the sense of formal opposition to it, as from its very nature destructive of what is good for us in our present state—an occasion only and instrument of death. It is the view of men, evangelical indeed, but partial and extreme in their evangelism—who, in their zeal to magnify the grace of the Gospel, lay stress only upon a class of expressions which unfold its riches and its triumphs, as contrasted with the law's impotence in itself, yea, with the terror and condemnation produced by it, and silently overlook, or deprive of their proper force, another class, which exhibit law in living fellowship with grace—joint factors in the accomplishment of the same blessed results. But it is right to add, the spirit and design with which this is done differ widely in the hands of different persons. Some so magnify grace in order to get their consciences at ease respecting the claims of holiness, and vindicate for themselves a liberty to sin that grace may abound—or, which is even worse, deny that anything they do can have the character of sin, because they are through grace released from the demands of law, and so cannot sin. These are Antinomians of the

---

[1] Milligan on ' The Decalogue and the Lord's Day,' pp. 96, 108, 111.

grosser kind, who have not particular texts merely of
the Bible, but its whole tenor and spirit against them.
Others, however, and these the only representatives of
the idea who in present times can be regarded as having
an outstanding existence, are advocates of holiness after
the example and teaching of Christ. They are ready to
say, ' Conformity to the Divine will, and that as obedience to commandments, is alike the joy and the duty of
the renewed mind. Some are afraid of the word obedience, as if it would weaken love and the idea of a new
creation. Scripture is not. Obedience and keeping the
commandments of one we love is the proof of that love,
and the delight of the new creature. Did I do all right,
and not do it in obedience, I should do nothing right,
because my true relationship and heart-reference to God
would be left out. This is love, that we keep His commandments.'[1] So far excellent ; but then these commandments are not found in the revelation of law,
distinctively so called. The law, it is held, had a specific
character and aim, from which it cannot be dissociated,
and which makes it for all time the minister of evil.
' It is a principle of dealing with men which necessarily
destroys and condemns them. This is the way (the
writer continues) the Spirit of God uses law in contrast
with Christ, and never in Christian teaching puts men
under it. Nor does Scripture ever think of saying, You
are not under the law in one way, but you are in another ;
you are not for justification, but you are for a rule of life.
It declares, You are not under law, but under grace ; and
if you are under law, you are condemned and under a
curse. How is that obligatory which a man is not under
—from which he is delivered ?'[2] Antinomianism of this
description—distinguishing between the teaching or com-

---

[1] Darby ' On the Law,' pp. 3, 4.   [2] *Ibid.* p. 4.

mandments of Christ and the commandments of the law, holding the one to be binding on the conscience of Christians and the other not—is plainly but partial Antinomianism ; it does not, indeed, essentially differ from Neonomianism, since law only as connected with the earlier dispensation is repudiated, while it is received as embodying the principles of Christian morality, and associated with the life and power of the Spirit of Christ.

(6.) Still it is clear, from this brief review, that there is a very considerable diversity of opinion on the subject of law, in a moral or spiritual respect, even among those who are agreed in asserting our freedom from its restraints and obligations in the more imperative form ; and from not a little of the philosophic, and much of the current secular literature of the age, a tendency is continually flowing into the church, which is impatient of anything in the name of moral or religious obligation, beyond the general claims of rectitude and benevolence. In respect to everything besides, the individual is held to have an absolute right to judge for himself. It cannot, therefore, appear otherwise than an important line of inquiry, and one specially called for by the present aspect of things, what place does law hold in the revelations of Scripture ? How far has it varied in amount of requirement or form of obligation, at different periods of the Divine administration ? What was the nature of the change effected in regard to it, or to our relation to it, by the appearance and work of Christ ? It is of the more importance that such questions should receive a thoughtful and considerate examination, as the confessional position of most churches, Reformed as well as Catholic, is against the tendency now described, and on the side of law, in the stricter sense of the term, having still a commanding power on the consciences of men.

At the farthest extreme in this direction stands the Roman Catholic church, which holds Christ to be a legislator in the same sense as Moses was, and deems itself entitled by Divine right to bind enactments of moral and religious duty upon the consciences of its members, similar in kind, and greatly more numerous and exacting in the things required by them, than those imposed by the legislation of Moses. There are sections also of the Protestant church, and parties of considerable extent and influence in particular churches, who have ever endeavoured to find, either by direct imposition, or by analogical reasonings and necessary implication, authority in Scripture for a large amount of positive law as well as moral precept, to be received and acted on by the Christian church. And from the opposite quarter, we may say, of the theological heavens, there has recently been given a representation of Christ, in which the strongest emphasis is laid on His legislative character. Speaking of the first formation of the Christian society, the author of ' Ecce Homo ' says,[1] ' Those who gathered round Christ did in the first place contract an obligation of personal loyalty to Him. On the ground of this loyalty He proceeded to form a society, and to promulgate an elaborate legislation, comprising and intimately connected with certain declarations, authoritatively delivered, concerning the nature of God, the relation of man to Him, and the invisible world. In doing so He assumed the part of a second Moses ;' and he goes on to indicate the specific character of the legislation, and the sanctions under which it was established, both materially differing from the Mosaic. Yet this seems again virtually recalled by other representations, in which the New Testament is declared to be ' not the Christian law ;'[2] not ' the pre-

[1] P. 80.   [2] P. 202.

cepts of apostles,' not even 'the special commands of Christ.' 'The enthusiasm of humanity in Christianity is their only law;' 'what it dictates, and that alone, is law for the Christian.' But apart from this, which can only be set down to prevailing arbitrariness and uncertainty on the subject, the Protestant churches generally stand committed to the belief of the moral law in the Old Testament as in substance the same with that in the New, and from its very nature limited to no age or country, but of perpetual and universal obligation. They have ever looked to the Decalogue as the grand summary of moral obligation, under which all duty to God and man may be comprised. Is this the true Scriptural position? or in what manner, and to what extent, should it be modified?

C

LECTURE II.

THE RELATION OF MAN AT CREATION TO MORAL LAW—HOW FAR
OR IN WHAT RESPECTS THE LAW IN ITS PRINCIPLES WAS MADE
KNOWN TO HIM—THE GRAND TEST OF HIS RECTITUDE, AND HIS
FAILURE UNDER IT.

WHEN opening the sacred volume for the purpose of
ascertaining its revelations of Divine law, it appears
at first sight somewhat strange that so little should be
found of this in the earlier parts of Scripture, and that
what is emphatically called THE LAW did not come into
formal existence till greatly more than half the world's
history between Adam and Christ had run its course.
'The law came by Moses.'[1] The generations of God's
people that preceded this era are represented as living
under promise rather than under law, and *the* covenant of
promise—that, namely, made with Abraham—in the
order of the Divine dispensations took precedence of the
law by four hundred and thirty years.[2] Yet it is clear
from what is elsewhere said, that though not under law
in one sense, those earlier generations were under it in
another ; for they were throughout generations of sinful
men, subject to disease and death on account of sin, and
sin is but the transgression of law ; 'where no law is,
there is no transgression.'[3] So that when the apostle
again speaks of certain portions of mankind not having
the law, of their sinning without law, and perishing
without law,[4] he can only mean that they were without

[1] John i. 17.   [2] Gal. iii. 17.
[3] Rom. v. 12, 13 ; iv. 15 ; vi. 2, 3.   [4] Rom. ii. 12, 14.

the formal revelation of law, which had been given through Moses to the covenant-people, while still, by the very constitution of their beings, they stood under the bonds of law, and by their relation to these would be justified or condemned.   But this plainly carries us up to the very beginnings of the human family; for as our first parents, though created altogether good, sinned against God, and through sinning lost their proper heritage of life and blessing, their original standing must have been amid the obligations of law.   And the question which presses on us at the outset—the first in order in the line of investigation that lies before us, and one on the right determination of which not a little depends for the correctness of future conclusions—is, what was the nature of the law associated with man's original state? and how far, or in what respects, did it possess the character of a revelation?[1]

I. The answer to such questions must be sought, primarily at least, in something else than what in the primeval records carries the formal aspect of law—the commands, namely, given to our first parents respecting their place and conduct toward the earth generally, or the select region they more peculiarly occupied; for it is remarkable that these are in themselves of a merely outward and positive nature—positive, I mean, as contradistinguished from moral; so that, in their bearing on man's original probation, they could only have been intended to form the occasions and tests of moral obedi-

---

[1] In discussing this subject, it will be understood that I take for granted the truth of the history in Genesis i.-iii., and the fact of man's creation in a state of manhood, ripeness, and perfection.   The impossibility of accounting for the existence and propagation of the human race otherwise, has been often demonstrated.   *See* Dr Moore's ' First Man and his Place in Creation,' and the authorities there referred to.

ence, not its proper ground or principle. Underneath those commands, and pre-supposed by them, there must have been certain fundamental elements of moral obligation in the very make and constitution of man—in his moral nature, to which such commands addressed themselves, and which must remain, indeed, for all time the real basis of whatever can be justly exacted of man, or is actually due by him in moral and religious duty. In applying ourselves, therefore, to consider what in this respect is written of man's original state, we have to do with what, in its more essential features, relates not to the first merely, but to every stage of human history—with what must be recognised by every law that is really Divine, and to which it must stand in fitting adaptation.

The notice mainly to be considered we find in that part of the history of creation, which tells us with marked precision and emphasis of the Divine mould after which his being was fashioned : ' Let us make man,' it was said by God, after the inferior creatures had been formed each after their kind, 'in our image, after our likeness (or similitude).' And the purpose being accomplished, it is added, ' So God created man in His own image, in the image of God created He him'—the rational offspring, therefore, as well as the workmanship of Deity, a representation in finite form and under creaturely limitations of the invisible God. That the likeness had respect to the soul, not to the body of man (except in so far as this is the organ of the soul and its proper instrument of working) cannot be doubted; for the God who is a Spirit could find only in the spiritual part of man's complex being a subject capable of having imparted to it the characteristics of His own image. Nor could the dominion with which man was invested over the fulness of the world and its living creaturehood, be regarded as more than the mere con-

sequence and sign of the Divine likeness after which man
was constituted, not the likeness itself; for this manifestly pointed to the distinction of his nature, not to
some prerogative merely, or incidental accompaniment of
his position.   Holding, then, that the likeness or image
of God, in which man was made, is to be understood of
his intellectual and moral nature, what light, we have
now to ask, does it furnish in respect to the line of
inquiry with which we are engaged ?   What does it
import of the requirements of law, or the bonds of moral
obligation ?

Undoubtedly, as the primary element in this idea must
be placed the intellect, or rational nature of the soul in
man ; the power or capacity of mind, which enabled him
in discernment to rise above the impressions of sense, and
in action to follow the guidance of an intelligent aim or purpose, instead of obeying the blind promptings of appetite
or instinct.   Without such a faculty, there had been wanting the essential ground of moral obligation ; man could
not have been the subject either of praise or of blame ;
for he should have been incapable, as the inferior animals
universally are, of so distinguishing between the true
and the false, the right and the wrong, and so appreciating the reasons which ought to make the one rather than
the other the object of one's desire and choice, as to
render him morally responsible for his conduct.   In God,
we need scarcely say, this property exists in absolute
perfection ; He has command over all the treasures of
wisdom and knowledge—ever seeing things as they really
are, and with unerring precision selecting, out of numberless conceivable plans, that which is the best adapted to
accomplish His end.   And made as man was, in this
respect, after the image of God, we cannot conceive of him
otherwise than as endowed with an understanding to

know everything, either in the world around him or his own relation to it, which might be required to fit him for accomplishing, without failure or imperfection, the destination he had to fill, and secure the good which he was capable of attaining. How far, as subservient to this end, the discerning and reasoning faculty in un- fallen man might actually reach, we want the materials for enabling us to ascertain ; but in the few notices given of him we see the free exercise of that faculty in ways perfectly natural to him, and indicative of its sufficiency for his place and calling in creation. The Lord brought, it is said, the inferior creatures around him—those, no doubt, belonging to the paradisiacal region—' to see what he would call them ; and whatsoever Adam called every creature, that was the name of it.'[1] The name, we are to understand, according to the usual phraseology of Scripture, was expressive of the nature or distinctive properties of the subject ; so that to represent Adam as giving names to the different creatures was all one with saying, that he had intelligently scanned their respective natures, and knew how to discriminate, not merely between them and himself, but also between one creature and another. So, again, when a fitting partner had been formed out of his person and placed before him, he was able, by the same discerning faculty, to perceive her like- ness and adaptation to himself, to recognise also the kindredness of her nature to his own—as ' bone of his bones, and flesh of his flesh '—and to bestow on her a name that should fitly express this oneness of nature and closeness of relationship (*isha*, woman ; from *ish*, man). These, of course, are but specimens, yet enough to shew the existence of the faculty, and the manner of its exer- cise, as qualifying him—not, indeed, to search into all

---

[1] Gen. ii. 19.

mysteries, or bring him acquainted with the principles of universal truth (of which nothing is hinted)—but to know the relations and properties of things so far as he had personally to do with them, or as was required to guide him with wisdom and discretion amid the affairs of life. To this extent the natural intelligence of Adam bore the image of his Maker's.[1]

The rational or intellectual part of man's nature, however, though entitled to be placed first in the characteristics that constitute the image of God (for without this there could be no free, intelligent, or responsible action) does not of itself bring us into the sphere of the morally good, or involve the obligation to act according to the principles of eternal rectitude. For this there must be a will to choose, as well as a reason to understand—a will

---

[1] This view of man's original state in an intellectual respect, while it is utterly opposed to the so-called philosophic theory of the savage mode of life, with all its ignorance and barbarity, having been the original one for mankind, is at the same time free from the extravagance which has appeared in the description given by some divines of the intellectual attainments and scientific insight of Adam—as if all knowledge, even of a natural kind, had been necessary to his perfection, as the image of God ! Thomas Aquinas argues,* that if he knew the natures of all animals, he must by parity of reason have had the knowledge of all other things ; and that, as the perfect precedes the imperfect, and the first man being perfect must have had the ability to instruct his posterity in all that they should know, so he must have himself known ' whatever things men in a natural way can know.' Protestant writers have occasionally, though certainly not as a class, carried the matter as far. And, as if such innate apprehension of all natural knowledge, and proportionate skill in the application of it to the arts and usages of life, were necessarily involved in the Scriptural account of man's original state, geologists, in the interest of their own theories, have not failed to urge, that, with such 'inspired knowledge,'† the remains should be found of the finest works of art in the remotest ages, ' lines of buried railways, or electric telegraphs,' &c. It is enough to say, that no enlightened theologian would ever ascribe such a reach of knowledge to primeval man, and that what he did possess soon became clouded and disturbed by sin.

---

* Summa, P. I. Quaest. 94, art. 3.   † Sir G. Lyell, on 'The Antiquity of Man,' p. 378.

perfectly free in its movements, having the light of reason
to direct it to the good, but under no constraining force
to obey the direction; in other words, with the power to
choose aright conformably to the truth of things, the
power also of choosing amiss, in opposition to the truth.
This liberty of choice, necessary from the very nature of
things to constitute man a subject of moral government,
was distinctly recognised by God in the scope given to
Adam to exercise the gifts and use the privileges conferred on him, limited only by what was due to his place
and calling in creation.   It was more especially recognised
in the permission accorded to him to partake freely of
the productions of the garden, to partake even of the tree
of the knowledge of good and evil, though with a stern
prohibition and threatening to deter him from such a
misuse of his freedom.   But the will in its choice is just
the index of the nature; it is the expression of the prevailing bent of the soul; and coupled as it was in Adam
with a spiritual nature untainted with evil, the reflex of
His who is the supremely wise and good, there could not
but be associated with it an instinctive desire to exercise
it aright,—a profound, innate conviction that what was
perceived to be good should carry it, as by the force of
an imperative law, over whatever else might solicit his
regard; resembling herein the Divine Author of his
existence, whose very being 'is a kind of law to His
working, since the perfection which God is gives perfection to what He does.'[1]   Yet, while thus bearing a near
resemblance to God, there still was an essential difference.   For in man's case all was bounded by creaturely
limitations; and while God never can, from the infinite
perfection of His being, do otherwise than choose with
absolute and unerring rectitude, man with his finite

[1] Hooker, 'Eccl. Polity,' B. I. c. 2.

nature and his call to work amid circumstances and conditions imposed on him from without, could have no
natural security for such unfailing rectitude of will ; a
diversity might possibly arise between what *should have
been*, and what actually *was*, willed and done.

These, then, are the essential characteristics of the
image of God, in which man was made—first, the noble
faculty of reason as the lamp of the soul to search into
and know the truth of things ; then the will ready at the
call of reason, with the liberty and the power to choose
according to the light thus furnished ; and, finally, the
pure moral nature prompting and disposing the will so to
choose.   Blessedness and immortality have by some been
also included in the idea.   And undoubtedly they *are*
inseparable accompaniments of the Divine nature, but
rather as results flowing from the perpetual exercise of its
inherent powers and glorious perfections, than qualities
possessed apart—hence in man suspended on the rightful
employment of the gifts and prerogatives committed to
him.   Blessed and immortal life was to be his portion if
he continued to realize the true idea of his being, and
proved himself to be the living image of his Maker ; not
otherwise.   But that the spiritual features we have exhibited as the essential characteristics of this image are
those also which Scripture acknowledges to be such,
appears from this, that they are precisely the things
specified in connection with the restoration to the image
of God, in the case of those who partake in the new creation through the grace and Gospel of Christ.   It is said
of such[1] that they are created anew after God, or that
they put on the new man (*new* as contradistinguished
from the oldness of nature's corruptions), which is renewed
after the image of Him that created him.   And the

[1] Eph. iv. 24 : Col. iii. 10.

renewal is more especially described as consisting in knowledge, righteousness, and true holiness—knowledge, the product of the illuminated reason made cognizant of the truth of God ; righteousness, the rectitude of the mind's will and purpose in the use of that knowledge ; true holiness, the actual result of knowledge so applied in the habitual exercise of virtuous affections and just desires.   These attributes, therefore, of moral perfection must have constituted the main features of the Divine image in which Adam was created, since they are what the new creation in Christ purposely aims at restoring. And in nature as well as in grace, they were of a derivative character ; as component elements in the human constitution they took their being from God, and received their moral impress from the eternal type and pattern of all that is right and good in Him.   Man himself no more made and constituted them after his own liking, or can do so, than he did his capacity of thought or his bodily organization; and the power of will which it was given him to exercise in connection with the promptings of his moral nature, had to do merely with the practical effect of its decisions, not with the nature of the decisions themselves, which necessarily drew their character from the conscience that formed them.   If, therefore, this conscience in man, this governing power in his moral constitution, had in one respect the rightful place of authority over the other powers and faculties of his being, in another it stood itself under authority, and in its clearest utterances concerning right and wrong could only affirm that there was a Divine *must* in the matter—the law of its being rendered it impossible for it to think or judge otherwise.

In reasoning thus as to what man originally was, when coming fresh and pure from the hands of his Creator, we must, of course, proceed in a great degree on the ground

of what we still know him to be—sin, while it has sadly
vitiated his moral constitution, not having subverted its
nature or essentially changed its manner of working.
The argument, indeed, is plainly from the less to the
greater : if even in its ruin the actings of our moral
nature thus lead up to God, and compel us to feel ourselves under a rule or an authority established by Him,
how much more man in the unsullied greatness and beauty
of his creation-state, with everything in his condition
fitted to draw his soul heavenwards, standing as it were
face to face with God !   Even now, ' the felt presence of
a judge within the breast powerfully and immediately
suggests the notion of a supreme judge and sovereign,
who placed it there.   The mind does not stop at a mere
abstraction ; but, passing at once from the abstract to the
concrete, from the law of the heart it makes the rapid inference of a lawgiver.'[1]   Or, as put more fully by a
German Christian philosopher,[2] ' There is something
above the merely human and creaturely in what man is
sensible of in the operation of conscience, whether he may
himself recognise and acknowledge it as such or not.
The workings of his conscience do not, indeed, give
themselves to be known as properly divine, and in reality
are nothing more than the movements of the human soul ;
but they involve something which I, as soon as I reflect
upon it, cannot explain from the nature of spirit, if this
is contemplated merely as the ground in nature of my
individual personal life, which after a human manner has
been born in me.   I stand before myself as before a riddle,
the key of which can be given, not by human self-consciousness, but by the revelation of God in His word.   By
this word we are made acquainted with the origination of
the human soul, as having sprung from God, and by God

---

[1] Chalmers, ' Nat. Theology,' B. III. c. 2.   [2] Harless, ' Christ. Ethik.,' sec. 8.

settled in its creation-state.   This relationship as to origin
is an abiding one, because constituted by God, and, however much it may be obscured, incapable of being dissolved.
It is one also that precedes the development of men's
self-consciousness ; their soul does not place itself in
relation to God, but God stands in relation to their soul.
It is a bond co-extensive with life and being, by which,
through the fact of the creation of their spirit out of God,
it is for the whole course of its creaturely existence indis-
solubly joined to God ; and a bond not destroyed by the
instrumentality of human propagation, but only transmitted onwards.   On this account, what is the spirit of
life in man is at the same time called the light (lamp) of
God (Prov. xx. 27).'[1]

On these grounds, derived partly from the testimony
of Scripture, partly from the reflection on the nature and
constitution of the human soul, we are fully warranted to
conclude, that in man's creation-state there were implanted
the grounds of moral obligation—the elements of a law

[1] In substance, the same representations are given in all our sounder writers
on Christian ethics—for example, Butler, M'Cosh, Mansel.   'Why (asks the
last named writer) has one part of our constitution, merely as such, an imperative authority over the remainder ?   What right has one part of the human
consciousness to represent itself as *duty*, and another merely as *inclination ?*
There is but one answer possible.   The moral reason, or will, or conscience of
man can have no authority, save as implanted in him by some higher spiritual
Being, as a Law emanating from a Lawgiver.   Man can be a law unto himself,
only on the supposition that he reflects in himself the law of God.   If he is
absolutely a law unto himself, his duty and his pleasure are undistinguishable
from each other ; for he is subject to no one, and accountable to no one.
Duty in his case becomes only a higher kind of pleasure—a balance between
the present and the future, between the larger and the smaller gratification.
We are thus compelled by the consciousness of moral obligation to assume the
existence of a moral Deity, and to regard the absolute standard of right and
wrong as constituted by the nature of that Deity' ('Bampton Lecture,' p. 81,
Fifth Ed.).   For some partial errors in respect to conscience in man before the
fall, as compared with conscience subsequent to the fall, *see* Delitzsch, 'Bibl.
Psych.,' iii. sec. 4.

inwrought into the very framework of his being, which called him perpetually to aim at conformity to the will and character of God.   For what was the law, when it came, but the idea of the Divine image set forth after its different sides, and placed in formal contrast to sin and opposition to God?[1]   Strictly speaking, however, man at first stood *in* law, rather than *under* law—being formed to the spontaneous exercise of that pure and holy love, which is the expression of the Divine image, and hence also to the doing of what the law requires.   Not uncommonly his relation to law has had a more objective representation given to it, as if the law itself in some sort of categorical form had been directly communicated to our first parents. Thus Tertullian, reasoning against the Jews, who sought to magnify their nation, by claiming as their exclusive property the revelation of law, says,[2] that 'at the beginning of the world God gave a law to Adam and Eve'— he refers specifically to the command not to eat of the tree of the knowledge of good and evil; but he thus expounds concerning it, 'In this law given to Adam we recognise all the precepts as already established which afterwards budded forth as given by Moses. . . . . . For the primordial law was given to Adam and Eve in paradise as the kind of prolific source (quasi matrix) of all the precepts of God.'   In common with him Augustine often identifies the unwritten or natural law given originally to man, and in a measure retained generally, though imperfectly, in men's hearts, with the law afterwards introduced by Moses and written on the tables of stone (On Ps. cxviii., Sermo 25, § 4, 5; Liber de Spiritu et Lit., § 29, 30; Opus Imp., Lib. vi. § 15).   In later times, among the Protestant theologians, from the *Loci Theol.* of Melancthon downwards, the moral law was generally

---

[1] *See* Sartorius, 'Heilige Liebe,' p. 168.   [2] Adv. Judæos, c. 2.

regarded as in substance one with the Decalogue, or the
two great precepts of love to God and love to man, and
this again identified with the law of nature, which was in
its fulness and perfection impressed upon the hearts of
our first parents, and still has a certain place in the hearts
of their posterity ; hence such statements as these : 'The
moral law was written in Adam's heart,' 'The law was
Adam's lease when God made him tenant of Eden' (Lightfoot, Works, iv. 7, viii. 379) ; 'The law of the ten commandments, being the natural law, was written on Adam's
heart on his creation' (Boston, 'Notes to the Marrow,'
Introd.); or, as in the Westminster Confession, 'God gave
to Adam a law, as a covenant of works, by which He bound
him to personal, entire, exact, and perpetual obedience ;'
which law, after the fall, 'continued to be a perfect rule
of righteousness, and, as such, was delivered by God upon
Mount Sinai in ten commandments, and written in two
tables' (ch. xix.).   We should, however, mistake such
language did we suppose it to mean, that there was either
any formal promulgation of a moral law to Adam, or that
the Decalogue, as embodying this law, was in precise
form internally communicated by some special revelation
to him.   It was a brief and popular style of speech, inti-
mating that by the constitution of his spiritual nature,
taken in connection with the circumstances in which he
was placed, he was bound, and knew that he was bound,
to act according to the spirit and tenor of what was afterwards formally set forth in the ten commands.   And so
Lightfoot, for example, who is one of the most explicit
in this mode of representation, brings out his meaning,
'The law writ in Adam's heart was not particularly
every command of the two tables, written as they were
in two tables, line by line ; but this law in general,
of piety and love towards God, and of justice and love

toward our neighbour. And in these lay couched a law to all particulars that concerned either—to branch forth as occasion for the practice of them should arise : as in our natural corruption, brought in by sin, there is couched every sin whatsoever too ready to bud forth, when occasion is offered.'[1] In like manner, Delitzsch, who among Continental writers adheres to the same mode of expression, speaks of the conscience in man, pre-eminently of course in unfallen man, by what it indi-cates of moral duty, as 'the knowing about a Divine law, which every man carries in his heart,' or 'an actual con-sciousness of a Divine law engraven in the heart;' but explains himself by saying, that 'the powers of the spirit and of the soul themselves are as the decalogue of the Thora (Law) that was in creation imprinted upon us ;'[2] that is to say, those powers, when in their proper state, work under a sense of subjection to the will of God, and in conformity with the great lines of truth and duty un-folded in the Decalogue.[3]

Understood after this manner, the language in question

---

[1] Sermon on Exodus xx. 11, Works, IV. 379.

[2] 'Biblische Psychologie,' pp. 138, 140.

[3] Were it necessary, other explanations of a like kind might be given, espe-cially from our older writers. Thus, in the 'Marrow of Modern Divinity,' where the language is frequently used of the law of the two tables being written on man's heart, and forming the matter of the covenant of works,* this is again explained by the fact of man having been made in God's image or likeness, and more fully thus, ' God had furnished his soul with an understand-ing mind, whereby he might discern good from evil and right from wrong ; and not only so, but also in his will was most perfect uprightness (Eccl. vii. 29), and his instrumental parts (i.e., his executive faculties and powers) were in an orderly way framed to obedience.' Much to the same effect Turretine, ' Inst. Loc. Undecimus, Quæst. II.,' who represents the moral law as the same with that which in nature was impressed upon the heart, as to its substance, though not formally and expressly given as in the Decalogue, sec. III. 2. xvii. ; also Colquhoun, ' Treatise on the Law and the Gospel,' p. 7.

---

* P. I. c. 1.

is quite intelligible and proper, though certainly capable
of being misapplied (if too literally taken), and in form
slightly differing from the Scriptural representation ;[1] for
in the passage which most nearly resembles it, and on which
it evidently leans, the apostle does not say that the law
itself, but that the *work* of the law, was written on men's
hearts, in so far as they shewed a practical acquaintance
with the things enjoined in it, and a disposition to do
them.   Such in the completest sense was Adam, as made
in the Divine image, and replenished with light and
power from on high.   It was his very nature to think
and act in accordance with the principles of the Divine
character and government, but, at the same time also, his
imperative obligation ; for to know the good, and not to
choose and perform it, could not appear otherwise than
sin.   Higher, therefore, than if surrounded on every side
by the objective demands of law, which as yet were not
needed—would, indeed, have been out of place—Adam
had the spirit of the law impregnating his moral being ;
he had the mind of the Lawgiver Himself given to bear
rule within—hence, not so properly a revelation of law, in
the ordinary sense of the term, as an inspiration from the
Almighty, giving him understanding in regard to what,
as an intelligent and responsible being, it became him to
purpose and do in life.   But this, however good as an
internal constitution—chief, doubtless, among the things
pronounced at first very good by the Creator—required,
both for its development and its probation, certain ordinances of an outward kind, specific lines of action and
observance marked out for it by the hand of God, for the
purpose of providing a proper stimulus to the sense of
right and wrong in the bosom, and bringing its relative
strength or weakness into the light of day.   And we now

[1] Rom. ii. 14, 15.

therefore turn, with the knowledge we have gained of the fundamental elements of man's moral condition, to the formal calling and arrangements amid which he was placed, to note their fitness for evolving the powers of his moral nature and testing their character.

II. The first in order, and in its nature the most general, was the original charge, the word of direction and blessing, under which mankind, in the persons of the newly-created pair, were sent on their course of development—that, namely, which bade them be fruitful, multiply, and replenish the earth, and subdue it, and have dominion over its living creatures and its powers of production. This word was afterwards brought into closer adaptation to the circumstances of our first parents, in the appointment given them to dress and keep the blessed region, which was assigned them as their more immediate charge and proper domain. Taken by itself, it was a call to merely bodily exercise and industrious employment. But considered as the expression of the mind of God to those who were made in the Divine image, and had received their place of dignity and lordship upon earth, for the purpose of carrying out the Divine plan, everything assumes a higher character; the natural becomes inseparably linked to the moral. Realizing his proper calling and destiny, man could not look upon the world and the interests belonging to it, as if he occupied an independent position; he must bear himself as the representative and steward of God, to mark the operations of *His* hand, and fulfil His benevolent design. In such a case, how could he fail to see in the ordinances of nature, God's appointments? and in the laws of life and production, God's methods of working? Or if so regarding them, how could he do otherwise than place him-

self in loving accord with them, and pliant ministration?
Not, therefore, presuming to deem aught evil which bore
on it the Divine impress of good ; but, as a veritable
child of nature, content to watch and observe that he
might learn, to obey that he might govern ; and thus,
with ever growing insight into nature's capacities and
command over her resources, striving to multiply around
him the materials of well-being and enjoyment, and
render the world a continually expanding and brightening
mirror, in which to see reflected the manifold fulness and
glorious perfections of God.

Such, according to this primary charge, was to be
man's function in the world of nature—his function as
made in God's image—and as so made capable of understanding, of appropriating to himself, and acting out the
ideas which were embodied in the visible frame and order
of things. He was to trace, in the operations proceeding
around him, the workings of the Divine mind, and then
make them bear the impress of his own. Here, therefore, stands rebuked for all time the essential ungodliness of an indolent and selfish repose, since only to man's
habitual oversight and wakeful industry was the earth
to become what its Maker designed it, and paradise itself
to yield to him the attractive beauty and plenteousness
of a proper home. Here, too, stands yet more palpably
rebuked the monkish isolation and asceticism, which
would treat the common gifts of nature with disdain, and
turn with aversion from the ordinary employments and
relations of life : as if the plan of the Divine Architect
had in these missed the proper good for man, and a nobler
ideal were required to correct its faultiness, or supplement its deficiencies ! Here yet again was authority
given, the commission, we may say, issued, not merely for
the labour of the hand to help forward the processes of

nature, and render them productive of ever varying and beneficent results, but for the labour also of the intellect to explore the hidden springs and principles of things, to bring the scattered materials which the experience of every day was presenting to his eye and placing at his disposal under the dominion of order, that they might be made duly subservient to the interests of intellectual life and social progress ; for in proportion as such results might be won was man's destined ascendency over the world secured, and the mutual, far-reaching interconnections between the several provinces of nature brought to light, which so marvellously display the creative foresight and infinite goodness of God.

We may even carry the matter a step farther. For, constituted as man was, the intelligent head and responsible possessor of the earth's fulness, the calling also was his to develop the powers and capacities belonging to it for ornament and beauty, as well as for usefulness.   With elements of this description the Creator has richly impregnated the works of His hand, there being not an object in nature that is incapable of conveying ideas of beauty ;[1] and this beyond doubt that each after its kind might by man be appreciated, refined, and elevated. ' Man possessed,' so we may justly say with a recent writer,[2] 'a sense of beauty as an essential ground of his intelligence and fellowship with Heaven.   He was therefore to cultivate the feeling of the beautiful by cultivating the appropriate beauty inherent in everything that lives. Nature ever holds out to the hand of man means by which his reason, when rightly employed, may be enriched with true gold from Heaven's treasury.   And even now, in proportion to the restoration to heavenly enlighten-

[1] Ruskin's ' Modern Painters,' Vol. II. p. 27.
[2] Moore's ' First Man and his Place in Creation,' p. 299.

ment, we perceive that every kind of beauty and power is but an embodiment of truth, a form of love, revealing the relation of the Divine creative mind to loveliness, symmetry, and justness, as well as expressing tender thought towards the susceptibilities of all His sentient creatures, but especially for the instruction and happy occupation of man himself.' This too, then, is to be reckoned among the things included in man's destination to intelligent and fruitful labour—an end to be prosecuted in a measure for its own sake, though in great part realizing itself as the incidental result of what was otherwise required at his hand.

But labour demands, as its proper complement, rest : rest *in* God alternating with labour *for* God.   And here we come upon another part of man's original calling ; since in this respect also it became him, as made in God's image, to fall in with the Divine order and make it his own.   ' God rested,'[1] we are told, after having prosecuted, through six successive days of work, the preparation of the world for a fit habitation and field of employment for man. ' He rested on the seventh day from all His work which He had made ; and He blessed the seventh day and sanctified it, because that in it He had rested from all His work which he created and made '—a procedure in God that would have been inexplicable except as furnishing the ground for a like procedure on the part of man, as, in that case, the hallowing and benediction spoken of must have wanted both a proper subject and a definite aim. True, indeed, as we are often told, there was no formal enactment binding the observance of the day on man ; there is merely an announcement of what God did, not a setting forth to man of what man should do; it is not said, that the Sabbath was expressly enjoined upon man.   And

Gen. ii. 2, 3.

neither, we reply, should it have been; for, since man was made in the image of God, it was only, so long as this image remained pure, the general landmarks of moral and religious duty, which were required for his guidance, not specific and stringent regulations: he had the light of Heaven within him, and of his own accord should have taken the course, which his own circumstances, viewed in connection with the Divine procedure, indicated as dutiful and becoming. The real question is, did not the things recorded contain the *elements* of law? Was there not in them such a revelation of the mind of God, as bespoke an obligation to observe the day of weekly rest, for those whose calling was to embrace the order and do the works of God? Undoubtedly there was—if in the sacred record we have, what it purports to give, a plain historical narrative of things which actually occurred. In that case —the only supposition we are warranted to make—the primeval consecration of the seventh day has a moral, as well as religious significance. It set up, at the threshold of the world's history, a memorial and a witness, that as the Creator, when putting forth His active energies on the visible theatre of the universe, did not allow Himself to become absorbed in it, but withdrew again to the enjoyment of His own infinite fulness and sufficiency; so it behoved His rational creature man to take heed, lest, when doing the work of God, he should lose himself amid outward objects, and fail to carry out the higher ends and purposes of his being with reference to God and eternity. Is it I alone who say this? Hear a very able and acute German moralist: 'It is, indeed, a high thought (says Wuttke[1]) that in Sacred Scripture this creation-rest of God is taken as the original type and ground of the Sabbath solemnity. It is thereby indi-

---

[1] 'Handbuch der Christlichen Sittenlehre,' I. p. 469.

cated, that precisely the innermost part of what constitutes
the likeness of God is that which demands this solemnity
—the truly reasonable religious-moral nature of man, and
not the natural necessity of rest and enjoyment.   What
with God are but two sides of the eternal life itself, no
temporal falling asunder into active working, and then re-
treating into one's self, *that* with respect to the finite spirit
falls partially, at least, into separate portions—namely, into
work and Sabbath-rest.   God blessed the seventh day :
—there rests upon the sacred observance of this day a
special and a higher blessing, an imparting of eternal,
heavenly benefits, as the blessing associated with work is
primarily but the imparting of temporal benefits.   The
Sabbath has not a merely negative significance ; it is not
a simple cessation from work ; it has a most weighty, real
import, being the free action of the reasonable God-like
spirit rising above the merely individual and finite, the
reaching forth of the soul, which through work has been
drawn down to the transitory, toward the unchangeable
and Divine.'   Hence (as the same writer also remarks),
the ordinance of the Sabbath belongs to the moral sphere
considered by itself, not merely to the state of redemption struggling to escape from sin—though such a state
obviously furnishes fresh reasons for the line of duty contemplated in the ordinance.   But at no period could it
be meant to stand altogether alone.   Neither before the
fall nor after it, could such calm elevation of the soul to
God and spiritual rest in Him be shut up to the day
specially devoted to it ; each day, if rightly spent, must
also have its intervals of spiritual repose and blessing.

So far, then, all was good and blessed.   Man, as thus
constituted, thus called to work and rest in harmony and
fellowship with God, was in a state of relative perfection
—of perfection after its kind, though not such as pertains

to the regeneration in Christ. Scripture itself marks the difference, when it speaks of the natural or psychical (ψυχικόν) coming first, then that which is spiritual (πνευματικόν, 1 Cor. xv. 46). The first man was of the earth, earthy—in the frame and mould of his being simply a part of this mundane existence, though incomparably its noblest part, and allied, through his spirit, with the Divine; but the second man was the Lord from heaven. The creation of the one was welcomed by the silent homage and regard of the living creaturehood on earth; the advent of the other was celebrated by angelic hosts in anthems of joy from the heavenly places. In Adam there was an intelligence that could discriminate wisely between irrational natures and his own, as also between one kind of inferior natures and another; in Christ there was a spirit that knew what was in man himself, capable of penetrating into his inmost secrets, yea, even of most perfectly knowing and revealing the Father. Finally, high as man's original calling was to preside over and subdue the earth, to improve and multiply its resources, to render it in all respects subservient to the ends for which it was made; how mightily was this calling surpassed by the mission of Him, who came to grapple with the great controversy between sin and righteousness, to restore the fallen, to sanctify the unclean, and bring in a world of incorruptible glory and blessed life, with which God should be most intimately associated, and over which He should perpetually rejoice!

The superiority, however, of the things pertaining to the person and the work of Christ does not prevent those relating to man's original state from being fitly viewed as *relatively* perfect. But then there was no absolute guarantee for this being continued; there was a possibility of all being lost, since it hung on the steadfastness of a

merely created head; and hence, as regarded man himself,
there was a need for something of a more special and
definite kind to *test* his adherence to the perfect order and
rectitude incumbent on him.   There might, we can readily
conceive, have been defections from the right and good in
respect to his *general* calling and destination—failures
distinct enough, perhaps, in themselves, but perceptible
only to the eye of Him who can look on the desires and
intents of the heart.   Here, however, it was indispensable
that the materials for judgment should be patent to all.
For, in Adam humanity itself was on its trial—the whole
race having been potentially created in him, and destined
to stand or fall, to be blessed or cursed, with him.   The
question, therefore, as to its properly decisive issue, must
be made to turn on conformity to an ordinance, at once
reasonable in its nature and specific in its requirements—
an ordinance which the simplest could understand, and
respecting which no uncertainty could exist, whether it
had been kept or not.   Such in the highest degree was
the appointment respecting the tree of the knowledge of
good and evil, forbidding it to be eaten on the pain of
death—an appointment positive in its character, in a
certain sense arbitrary, yet, withal, perfectly natural, as
relating to a particular tree singled out for the purpose
from many others around it, imposing no vexatious
burden, requiring only the exercise of a measure of
personal restraint in deference to the authority, and
acknowledgment of the supreme right, of Him of whom
all was held—in short, one of the easiest, most natural,
most unexceptionable of probationary enactments.   It was
not exactly, as put by Tertullian, as if this command respecting the tree of knowledge formed the kind of quint-
essence or prolific source of all other moral commands;
for in itself, and apart from the Divine authority imposing

it, there was nothing about it strictly moral : not on this account therefore was it given, but as serving to erect a standard, every way proper and becoming, around which the elements of good and evil might meet, and the ascendency of the one or the other be made manifest.[1] And so the Sovereign Disposer of events by the very appointment undertook to order it. If the Divine image should anyhow begin to lose the perfection of its parts, if a spirit of disaffection should enter the bosoms of our first parents, it could not be left to their own choice or to merely adventitious circumstances, in what form or direction this should appear. It *must* assume an attitude of contrariety to this Divine ordinance, and discover itself in a disposition to eat of that tree of which God had said, They should not eat of it, lest they died. *There*, precisely, and not elsewhere—thus and not otherwise was it to be seen, if they *could* maintain their part in this covenant of life ; or, if not, then the obvious mastery of the evil over the good in their natures.

III. We are not called here to enter into any formal discussion of the temptation and the fall. Profound mysteries hang around the subject ; but the general result, and the overt steps that led to it, are known to all. Hearkening to the voice of the tempter, that they should be as God, knowing good and evil, our first parents *did* eat of the interdicted tree ; and, in doing so, broke through the law of their being, which bound them ever

---

[1] So, indeed, Tertullian, when he explains himself, virtually regarded it : ' Denique si dominum deum suum dilexissent' (viz., Adam and Eve), ' contra præceptum ejus non fecissent ; si proximum diligerent, id est semetipsos, persuasioni serpentis non credidissent,' etc. And the general conclusion he draws is, ' Denique, ante legem Moysi scriptam in tabulis lapideis, legem fuisse contendo non scriptam, quæ naturaliter intelligebatur et a patribus custodiebatur.' (Adv. Judæos, sec. 2).

to live and act in loving allegiance to the God who made them, and of whom they held whatever they possessed. Self now took the place of God ; they would be their own rule and their own end, and thereby gave way to the spirit of apostacy ; first entertaining doubts of God's goodness, as if the prohibition under which they had been placed laid an undue restraint on their freedom, limited too much their range of action and enjoyment ; then disbelieving God's testimony as to the inevitable result of disobedience ; finally, making the gratification of their own self-will and fleshly desire the paramount considera- tion which was to determine their course.   At every step a violation of the principle of love—of love in both its departments ; first, indeed, and most conspicuously, in reference to God, who was suspected, slighted, disobeyed ; but also in reference to one another, and their prospective offspring, whose interests were sacrificed at the shrine of selfishness.   The high probation, therefore, issued in a mournful failure ; humanity, in its most favoured condi- tions, proved unequal to the task of itself holding the place and using the talents committed to it, in loving subjection to the will of Heaven ; and the penalty of sin, not the guerdon of righteousness, became its deserved portion.   Shall not the penalty take effect ? Can the Righteous One do otherwise than shew Himself the enemy and avenger of sin, by resigning to corruption and death the nature which had allied itself to the evil ? Where, if He did, would have been the glory of His name ? Where the sanction and authority of His righteous government ?   It was for the purpose, above all, of insti- tuting such a government in the world, and unfolding by means of it the essential attributes of His character, that man had been brought on the stage of being as the proper climax of creation ; and if, for this end, it was necessary that righteousness should be rewarded, was it not equally necessary that sin should be punished ? So, death entered, where life only should have reigned ; it entered as the stern yet sublime proof, that in the Divine government of the world the moral must carry it over the natural ; that conformity to the principles of righteousness is the indispensable condition of blessing ; and that even if grace should interpose to rectify the evil that had emerged, and place the hopes of mankind on a better footing than that of nature, this grace must reign through righteousness, and overcome death by overcoming the sin which caused it.

To have these great principles written so indelibly and palpably on the foundations of the world's history was of incalculable moment for its future instruction and well-being ; for the solemn lessons and affecting memories of the fall entered as essential elements of men's views of God, and formed the basis of all true religion for a sinful world. They do so still. And, certainly, if it could be proved by the cultivators of natural science, that man, simply as such—man by the very constitution of his being—is mortal, it would strike at the root of our religious beliefs ; for it would imply, that death did not come as a judgment from God, and was the result of physical organization or inherent defectibility, not the wages of sin. This, however, is a point that lies beyond the range of natural science. It may be able to shew, that death is not only now, but ever has been, the law of merely sentient existence, and that individual forms of sentient life, having no proper personality—if perpetuated at all, must be perpetuated in the species. But man is on one side only, and that the lower side, related to sentient forms of being. In what constitute the more essential characteristics of his nature—intelligence, reason, will,

conscience—he stands in close affinity to God; he is
God's image and representative, and not a liability to
death, but the possession of endless life, must be regarded
as his normal state of being.   And to secure this for the
animal part of his frame, so long as spiritually he lived to
God, was, at least, one part of the design of the tree of
life (whatever higher purposes it might also have been
intended to serve as the pledge or symbol of life to his
soul) : it was the specific antidote of death.   A most inadequate provision, it may perhaps be alleged, for such
a purpose, suited only for a single pair, or for a comparative handful of people, but by no means for a numerous
race.   Let it be so : He who made the provision knew
well for how many, or how long, it might be required ;
and, in point of fact, from no misarrangement or defect
in this respect, the evil it was ordained to guard against
found an entrance into the world.   By man's disobedience, by that alone, came sin, and death by sin—
such is the teaching of Scripture alike in its earlier and
later revelations ; and the theology which would eliminate this doctrine from its fundamental beliefs must be
built on another foundation than the word of the living
God.

LECTURE III.

THE REVELATION OF LAW, STRICTLY SO CALLED, VIEWED IN RE-
SPECT TO THE TIME AND OCCASION OF ITS PROMULGATION.

A PRINCIPLE of progression pervades the Divine plan as unfolded in Scripture, which must be borne in mind by those who would arrive at a correct understanding, either of the plan as a whole, or of the characteristic features and specific arrangements which have distinguished it at one period, as compared with another. We can scarcely refer in proof of this to the original constitution of things, since it so speedily broke up—though, there can be no doubt, it also had interwoven with it a principle of progression. The charge given to man at the moment of creation, if it had been in any measure executed, would necessarily have involved a continuous rise in the outward theatre of his existence; and it may justly be inferred, that as this proceeded, his mental and bodily condition would have partaken of influences fitted indefinitely to ennoble and bless it. But the fatal blow given by the fall to that primeval state rendered the real starting-point of human history an essentially different one. The progression had now to proceed, not from a less to a more complete form of excellence, but from a state of sin and ruin to one of restored peace, life, and purity, culminating in the possession of all blessing and glory in the kingdom of the Father. And, in accordance with this plan of God for the recovery and perfecting of those who should be heirs of salvation, His revelation of spiritual and divine things assumes the form of a gradual development and progressive history—beginning as a small stream amid the wreck and desolation of the fall, just enough to cheer the heart of the fallen and brace it for the conflict with evil, but receiving additions from age to age, as the necessities of men and the purpose of God required, until, in the incarnation and work of Christ for the salvation of the world, it reached that fulness of light and hope, which prompted an apostle to say, ' The darkness is past, and the true light now shineth.'

It may seem strange to our view—there is undoubtedly in it something of the dark and mysterious—that the plan of God for the enlightenment and regeneration of the world should have been formed on such a principle of progression, and that, in consequence, so many ages should have elapsed before the realities on which light and blessing mainly depended were brought distinctly into view. Standing, as we ourselves do, on a point of time, and even still knowing but in part the things of God's kingdom, we must be content, for the present, to remain ignorant of the higher reasons which led to the adoption of this principle as a pervading characteristic of the Divine administration. But where we can do little to explain, we are able to exemplify ; for the ordinary scheme of providence presents us here with a far-reaching and varied analogy. On the same principle of progression is the life-plan of each individual constructed ; so that, on an average, a half, and in the case of multitudes greatly more than a half, of their earthly life is spent before the capacity for its proper employments has been attained. In the history, also, of nations and communities, of arts and sciences, we see the principle in constant operation, and have no difficulty in connecting with it much of the activity, enjoyment, and well-being of mankind. It is this very principle of progression which is the mainspring of life's buoyancy and hopefulness, and which links together, with a profound and varied interest, one stage of life with another. Reasons equally valid would doubtless be found in the higher line of things which relates to the dispensations of God toward men, could we search the depths of the Divine counsels, and see the whole as it presents itself to the eye of Him who perceives the end from the beginning.

It is the fact itself, however, which we here think it of importance to note; for, assuming the principle in question to have had a directive sway in the Divine dispensations, it warrants us to expect measures of light at one stage, and modes of administration, which shall bear the marks of relative imperfection as compared with others. This holds good of the revelation of law, which we now approach, when placed beside the manifestation of God in the Gospel; and even in regard to the law itself the principle of progression was allowed to work; for it might as well be said, that the law formed the proper complement and issue of what preceded it, as that it became the groundwork of future and grander revelations. To this, as a matter of some importance, our attention must first be given.

Considering the length of the period that elapsed from the fall of man to the giving of the law, the little that remains in the Divine records of explicit revelation as to moral and religious duty, appears striking, and cannot be regarded as free from difficulty when contemplated from a modern point of view. It may be so, however, chiefly from the scantiness of our materials, and our consequent inability to realize the circumstances of the time, or to take in all the elements of directive knowledge which were actually at work in society. This deficiency is certainly not to be supplied, after the fashion of Blunt, by combining together the scattered notices in the early history of the Bible, and looking upon them as so many hints or fragmentary indications of a regularly constituted patriarchal church, with its well furnished rubric as to functions, places, times, and forms of worship.[1] These are not the points on which the comparatively isolated and artless families of those early times might be expected to have received special and unrecorded communications from Heaven. It had been as much out of place for them as for the early Christian communities, while worshipping in upper chambers, hired school-rooms, and sequestered retreats, to have had furnished to their hand a ritual of service fit only for spacious cathedrals and a fully developed hierarchy. We are rather to assume, that brief as the outline which Scripture gives of the transactions of the period, it is still one that contains whatever is to be deemed essential to the matter as a history of Divine revelation; and that only by making proper account of the things which are recorded, not by imagining such as are not, can we frame to ourselves an adequate or well-grounded idea of the state of those earlier generations of mankind, as to the means of knowledge they possessed, or the claims of service that lay upon them, in respect to moral and religious duty. Let us endeavour to indi-

---

[1] Some of these, as might be expected, are obtained in a very arbitrary manner, and look almost like a caricature of the text of Scripture :—as when in Esau's 'goodly raiment,' furtively used by Jacob, is found the sacerdotal robes of the first-born,* and something similar also in Joseph's coat of many colours— as if this mere boy were already invested with priestly attire, and not only so, but in that attire went about the country, since he certainly wore it when he visited his brethren at Dothan. Can any parallel to this be found even in the complicated legislation of the Mosaic ritual? The priests who were ministering at the tabernacle or temple had to wear robes of office, but not when engaged in ordinary employments.

---

* 'Scripture Coincidences,' p. 12.

cate some of the leading points suggested by Scripture on the subject, without, however, dwelling upon them, and for the purpose more especially of apprehending the relation in which they stood to the coming legislation of Sinai.

1. At the foundation of all we must place the fact of man's knowledge of God—of a living, personal, righteous God—as the Creator of all things, and of man himself as His intelligent, responsible creature, made after His image, and subject to His authority. Whatever effect the fall might ultimately have on this knowledge, and on the conscious relationship of man to his Maker, his moral and religious history started with it—a knowledge still fresh and vivid when he was expelled from Eden, in some aspects of it even widened and enlarged by the circumstances that led to that expulsion. ' Heaven lies about us in our infancy:'—it did so pre-eminently, and in another sense than now, when the infancy was that of the human race itself; and not as by 'trailing clouds of glory' merely, but by the deep instincts of their moral being, and the facts of an experience not soon to be forgotten, its original heads knew that ' they came from God as their home.' Here, in a moral respect, lay their special vantage-ground for the future; for not the authority of conscience merely, but the relation of this to the higher authority of God, must have been among their clearest and most assured convictions. They knew that it had its eternal source and prototype in the Divine nature, and that in all its actings it stood under law to God. Goodness after the pattern of His goodness must have been what they felt called by this internal monitor to aim at; and in so far as they might fall beneath it, or deviate from it, they knew—they could not but know—that it was the voice of God they were virtually disobeying.

2. Then, as regards the manner in which this call

E

to imitate God's goodness and be conformed to His will was to be carried out, it would of course be understood that, whatever was fairly involved in the original destination of man to replenish and cultivate the earth, so as to make it productive of the good of which it was capable, and subservient to the ends of a wise and paternal government, this remained as much as ever his calling and duty.   Man's proper vocation, as the rational head of this lower world, was not abolished by the fall; it had still to be wrought out, only under altered circumstances, and amid discouragements which had been unknown, if sin had not been allowed to enter into his condition. And with this destination to work and rule for God on earth, the correlative appointment embodied in God's procedure at creation, to be ever and anon entering into His rest, must also be understood to have remained in force.   As the catastrophe of the fall had both enlarged the sphere and aggravated the toil of work, so the calm return of the soul to God, and the gathering up of its desires and affections into the fulness of His life and blessing, especially on the day peculiarly consecrated for the purpose, could not but increasingly appear to the thoughtful mind an act of homage to the Divine will, and an exercise of pious feeling eminently proper and reasonable.

3. Turning now, thirdly, to the sphere of family and domestic life, the foundation laid at the first, in the formation of one man, and out of this man one woman to be his bosom companion and wife, this also stood as before— and carried the same deep import.   The lesson originally drawn from the creative act, whether immediately drawn by Adam himself or not—' therefore shall a man leave his father and his mother, and shall cleave unto his wife, and they shall be one flesh '[1]—was a lesson for all time.   Our

[1] Gen. ii. 24.

Lord (who as the creative Word was the immediate agent
in the matter) when on earth set to His seal, at once to
the historical fact, and to the important practical deduction
flowing from it ; and He added, for the purpose of still
further exhibiting its moral bearing, 'So then they are
no more twain, but one flesh. What therefore God hath
joined together, let not man put asunder.'[1] Thus was impressed on the very beginnings of human history the
stamp of God's appointed order for families—the close
and endearing nature of the marriage-tie—the life-union
it was intended to form—the mutual sympathy and affection by which it should be sustained—and the common
interest it created, as well as the loving regard it naturally
tended to evoke, in behalf of the offspring that might
issue from it. All this, though not formally imposed by
definite rules and prescriptions, was yet by the moral
significance of that primeval fact laid upon the consciences
of men, and indicated the place which the family constitution and its relative duties were to hold in the organization
and progress of society.[2]

[1] Mark x. 8, 9.

[2] The objections that have been made to the sacred narrative respecting the
fact of Eve's formation out of a rib of Adam, as that it was unworthy of God ;
that his posterity are not deficient in that part of their bodily organization,
which they would have been if Adam had been actually deprived of a rib ;
that we have therefore in the story not a fact but a myth, teaching the com-
panionship of the woman to man—are entitled to no serious consideration. It
is the very foundations of things we have here to do with, in a social and moral
respect, and for this, not shadowy myths (the inventions, always, of a comparatively late age) but great outstanding facts were necessary to furnish the requisite
instruction. Since important moral ends were in view for all coming time, why
could not God have taken a portion of Adam's frame for the formation of his
partner in life, and afterwards repaired the loss ? or, if the defect continued
in him as an individual, prevented its transmission to posterity ? Somehow,
the formation of the first woman, as well as the first man, had to be brought
about by a direct operation of Deity ; and why not thus rather than otherwise,
if thus only it could be made the symbol of a great truth, the embodiment of
an imperishable moral lesson ? No reason can be shewn to the contrary.

4. Of devotion as consisting in specific acts of religious worship, the record of man's creation, it must be admitted, is altogether silent, nor does anything appear in the form of a command for ages to come. This cannot, however, be fairly regarded as a proof, either that nothing in the matter of worship was involved in the fundamental grounds of moral obligation, or that the sense of duty in that respect did not from the first find some fitting expression. The hallowing of a particular day of the week, and connecting with its observance a peculiar blessing, evidently implied the recognition of the religious sentiment in man's bosom, and formed an ever-recurring call to exercises of devotion. For what is devotion in its proper nature, and stript of its mere accessories ? It is just the Sabbath idea realized, or, in the simple but expressive language of Bishop Butler,[1] 'Devotion is retirement from the world God has made, to Him alone : it is to withdraw from the avocations of sense, to employ our attention wholly upon Him as upon an object actually present, to yield ourselves up to the influence of the Divine presence, and to give full scope to the affections of gratitude, love, reverence, trust, and dependence, of which infinite power, wisdom, and goodness is the natural and only adequate object.' The constitution of man's nature, and the circumstances in which he was originally placed, could not but lead him to cherish and exercise the feelings of such a spirit of devotion—though with what accompaniments of outward form we have no indication, nor is it of any practical moment, since they can only be understood to have been the natural and appropriate manifestations of what was felt within. With the fall, however, matters in this respect underwent a material change ; for the worship which became a sinner could not be the same

---

[1] Sermons, Ser. XIV.

with that which flowed spontaneously from the heart of
one who was conscious only of good, nor could it be left
entirely to men's own unaided conceptions; for if so left,
how could they be assured that it was accepted of their
Maker? how know it to be such as He would bless?
Somehow, therefore—apparently, indeed, in connection
with the clothing of the shame of our first parents by
means of the skins of slain victims—they were guided to
a worship by sacrifice as the one specially adapted to their
state as sinners, and one which probably from the very
first (by means of the supernatural agencies associated
with the entrance to Eden and its tree of life, viz., the
flaming sword and the cherubim), received upon it the
marks of Divine approval. At all events, in the history of
their earliest offspring, worship by the sacrifice of slain
victims becomes manifest as the regular and approved mode
of access to God in its more formal acts of homage. Here
then, again without any positive command, far less any
formally prescribed ritual, there still were in the Divine
procedure, taken in connection with men's moral convictions and feelings, the grounds of moral obligation and
specific duty—not law, indeed, in the formal sense of the
term, but the elements of law, or such indications of the
Divine will as were sufficient to guide truly humble and
God-fearing men in the earlier ages of the world to give
expression to their faith and hope in God by a mode of
worship suited to their condition and acceptable to Heaven.

5. Another thing also ought to be borne in mind in
respect to those varied materials of moral and religious
duty, which is this—that while they belonged to the
origination of things on earth, to things of which the first
heads of the human family were either the only witnesses,
or the direct and immediate subjects, they had the advantage of being associated with a living testimony, which

was capable of preserving it fresh and unimpaired for many generations. The longevity of .the first race of patriarchs had doubtless many important ends to serve ; but we cannot be wrong in mentioning this among the chief. He who had received his being direct and pure from the hand of God, to whom had been revealed the wonders of God's work in creation, who had himself walked with God in paradise, was present with his living voice to tell of all he had seen and heard, and by his example (as we can scarcely doubt) to confirm and commend his testimony, down even to the times of Lamech, the father of Noah. So that, if the materials of knowledge respecting God's will to men were comparatively few, and were in many respects linked to the facts of a primeval past, this continuous personal testimony served to render that past a kind of perpetual present, and so to connect, as by a living bond, the successive generations of men with the original grounds of faith and hope for the world. There were, also, as is clear from the case of Enoch and other incidental notices, closer communings occasionally maintained by God with believing men, and for special seasons more definite communications made of His will. Sparse, therefore, as the memorials are, in a religious respect, which belong to this period, as compared with its great length, God still did not leave Himself without a witness ; and men who were alive to the responsibilities of their position, and disposed to follow the impulses of their moral nature, could not, complain of being without any sure direction as to the great landmarks of truth and duty.

6. Yet, it is impossible to carry the matter further ; and to speak of law in the moral and religious sphere— law in some definite and imperative form, standing outside the conscience, and claiming authority to regulate

its decisions, as having a place in the earlier ages of mankind, is not warranted by any certain knowledge we possess of the remoter periods of God's dispensations. That 'all human laws are sustained by one that is divine' (a saying ascribed to Heraclitus), seems, as several others of a like kind that might be quoted, to point to a traditional belief in some primitive Divine legislation; and in a well-known noble passage of Cicero, which it is well to bring into remembrance in discussions of this nature, there is placed above all merely local and conventional enactments of men, a law essentially Divine, of eternal existence and permanent universal obligation,[1] *Est quidem vera lex*, etc. 'There is indeed a true law, right reason, conformable to nature, diffused among all, unchanging, eternal, which, by commanding, urges to duty; by prohibiting, deters from fraud; not in vain commanding or prohibiting the good, though by neither moving the wicked. This law cannot be abrogated, nor may anything be withdrawn from it; it is in the power of no senate or people to set us free from it; nor is there to be sought any extraneous teacher or interpreter of it. It shall not be one law at Rome, another at Athens; one now, another at some future time; but one law, alike eternal and unchangeable, shall bind all nations and through all time; and one shall be the common teacher, as it were, and governor of all—God, who is Himself the Author, the Administrator, and Enactor of this law.' Elsewhere, he expresses it as the opinion of the wisest men,[2] that 'this fundamental law and ultimate judgment was the mind of Deity either ordering or forbidding all things according to reason; whence that law which the gods have given to mankind is justly praised. For it fitly belongs to the reason and judgment of the wise to

---

[1] De Republica, III. 22.   [2] De Leg., II. 4.

enjoin one thing and prohibit another.' And in thus having its ground in right reason, which is the property of man as contradistinguished from beasts, and is the same in man as in God, he finds the reason of this law being so unchanging, universal, and perpetually binding. But the very description implies that no external legislation was meant coming somewhere into formal existence among men; it is but another name for the findings of that intelligent and moral nature, which is implanted in all men, though in some is more finely balanced and more faithfully exercised than in others. Under the designation of the supremacy of conscience, it appears again in the discourses of Bishop Butler, and is analysed and described as ' our natural guide, the guide assigned us by the Author of our nature,' that by virtue of which ' man in his make, constitution, or nature, is, in the strictest and most proper sense, a law to himself,' whereby ' he hath the rule of right within; what is wanting is only that it be honestly attended to.' But this has already been taken into account, and placed at the head of those moral elements in man's condition which belonged to him even as fallen, and which, though possessing little of the character of objective or formal law, yet carried with them such directive light and just authority as should have had the force of law to his mind, and rendered inexcusable those who turned aside to transgression.[1]

7. The result, however, proved that all was insufficient; a grievous defect lurked somewhere. The means of knowledge possessed, and the motives to obedience

[1] It is only in this sense, and as connected with the means of instruction provided by the course of God's providential dealings, that we can speak of the light possessed by men as sufficient for moral and religious duty. The light of conscience in fallen man by itself can never reach to the proper knowledge of the things which concern his relation to God and immortality.

with which they were accompanied, utterly failed with
the great majority of men to keep them in the path of
uprightness, or even to restrain the most shameful degeneracy and corruption. The principle of evil which
wrought so vehemently, and so early reached an over-
mastering height in Cain, grew and spread through a
continually widening circle, till the earth was filled with
violence, and the danger became imminent, unless averted
by some forcible interposition, of all going to perdition.
Where lay the radical defect? It lay, beyond doubt, in
the weakness of the moral nature, or in that fatal rent
which had been made by the entrance of sin into man's
spiritual being, dividing between his soul and God, dividing even between the higher and the lower propensities
of his soul, so that the lower, instead of being regulated
and controlled by the higher, practically acquired the
ascendency. Conscience, indeed, still had, as by the
constitution of nature it must ever have, the right to
command the other faculties of the soul, and prescribe
the rule to be obeyed ; but what was wanting was the
power to enforce this obedience, or, as Butler puts it, to
see that the rule be honestly attended to ; and the want
is one which human nature is of itself incompetent to
rectify. For the bent of nature being now on the side of
evil, the will, which is but the expression of the nature,
is ever ready to give effect to those aims and desires
which have for their object some present gratification,
and correspondingly tend to blunt the sensibilities and
overbear the promptings of conscience in respect to things
of higher moment. In the language of the apostle, the
flesh lusts against the spirit, yea, and brings it into bondage to the law of sin and death. And the evil, once
begun, is from its very nature a growing one, alike in the
individual and in the species. For when man, in either

respect, does violence to the better qualities of his nature, when he defaces the Divine image in which he was made, he instinctively turns away from any close examination of his proper likeness—withdraws himself also more and more from the thoughts and the companionships which tend to rebuke his ungodliness, and delights in those which foster his vanity and corruption. Hence, the melancholy picture drawn near the commencement of the epistle to the Romans, as an ever deepening and darkening progression in evil, realizes itself wherever fallen nature is allowed to operate unchecked. It did so in the primitive, as well as the subsequent stages of human history: *First*, men refused to employ the means of knowledge they possessed respecting God's nature and will, would not glorify Him as God (γνόντες τὸν Θεὸν οὐκ ἐδόξασαν); *then*, having thus separated themselves from the true light, they fell into the mazes of spiritual error and will-worship, became frivolous, full of empty conceits, mistaking the false for the true, the shadowy for the real; *finally*, not thinking it worth while to keep by the right knowledge of God (οὐκ ἐδοκίμασαν τὸν Θεὸν ἔχειν ἐν ἐπιγνώσει), treating it as comparatively a thing of nought, they were themselves made to appear worthless and vile—given up by God to a reprobate mind (ἀδόκιμον νοῦν), whereby they lost sight of their true dignity, and became the slaves of all manner of impure, hurtful, and pernicious lusts, which drove them headlong into courses equally offensive to God, and subversive of their own highest good.

8. This process of degeneracy, though sure to have taken place anyhow, had opportunities of development and license during the earlier periods of the world's history, which materially helped to make it more rapid and general. If there were not then such temptations to

flagrant evil as exist in more advanced states of society, there were also greatly fewer and less powerful restraints. Each man was to a larger extent than now the master of his own movements : social and political organizations were extremely imperfect ; the censorship of the press, the voice of an .enlightened public opinion in *any* systematic form, was wanting, and there was also wanting the wholesome discipline and good order of regularly constituted churches ; so that ample scope was found for those who were so inclined, to slight the monitions of their moral sense, and renounce the habits and observances which are the proper auxiliaries of a weak virtue, and necessary in the long run to the preservation of a healthful and robust piety in communities. The fermentation of evil, therefore, wrought on from one stage to another, till it reached a consummation of appalling breadth and magnitude. And yet not for many long ages —not till the centuries of antediluvian times had passed away, and centuries more after a new state of things had commenced its course—did God see meet to manifest Himself to the world in the formal character of Lawgiver, and confront men's waywardness and impiety with a code of objective commands and prohibitions, in the peremptory tone, Thou *shalt* do this, and Thou shalt *not* do that :— A proof, manifestly, of God's unwillingness to assume this more severe aspect. in respect to beings He had made in His own image, and press upon them, in the form of specific enactments, His just claims on their homage and obedience ! He would rather—unspeakably rather—that they should know Him in the riches of His fatherly goodness, and should be moved, not so much by fear, as by forbearance and tenderness, to act toward Him a faithful and becoming part ! Hence He delayed as long as possible the stringent and imperative revelation of law, which by the time alone of its appearance is virtually acknowledged to have been a kind of painful necessity, and in its very form is a ' reflection upon man's inconstancy of homage and love.'[1]

God did not, however, during the long periods referred to, leave Himself without witness, either as to His displeasure on account of men's sin, or the holiness in heart and conduct which He required at their hands. If His course of administration displayed little of the *formal aspect* of law, it still was throughout impregnated with the *principles* of law ; for it contained manifestations of the character and purposes of God which were both fitted and designed to draw the hearts of men toward Him in confiding love, and inspire them with His own supreme regard to the interests of righteousness. Of law, strictly so called, we find nothing applicable to the condition of mankind generally, from the period of the fall to the redemption from Egypt, except the law of blood for blood, introduced immediately after the Deluge, and the ordinance of circumcision, to seal the covenant with Abraham, and symbolize the moral purity which became those who entered into it. But even these, though legal in their form, partook in their import and bearing of the character of grace ; they came in as appendages to the fresh and fuller revelations which had been given of God's mercy and loving-kindness—the one in connection with Noah's covenant of blessing, and as a safeguard thrown around the sacredness of human life ; the other in connection with the still richer and more specific covenant of blessing established with Abraham. Indeed, during the whole of what is usually called the patriarchal period, the most prominent feature in the Divine administration consisted in the unfoldings of promise, or in the materials

[1] ' Ecce Deus,' p. 234.

it furnished to sinful men for the exercise of faith and hope. God again condescended to hold familiar intercourse with them. He gave them, not only His word of promise, but His oath confirming the word, that He might win from them a more assured and implicit confidence; and by very clear and impressive indications of His mind in providence, He made it to be understood how ready He was to welcome those who believed, and to enlarge, as their faith and love increased, their interest in the heritage of blessing. It is the history of grace in its earlier movements—grace delighting to pardon, and by much free and loving fellowship, by kind interpositions of providence and encouraging hopes, striving to bring the subjects of it into proper sympathy and accord with the purposes of Heaven.

Yet here also grace reigned through righteousness; and the righteousness at times ripened into judgment. There was the mighty catastrophe of the Deluge lying in the background—emphatically God's judgment on the world of the ungodly, and the sure presage of what might still be expected to befall the wicked. At a later period, and within the region of God's more peculiar operations in grace, there was the overthrow of the cities of the plain, which were made for their crying enormities to suffer 'the vengeance of eternal fire.' So still onwards, and in the circle itself of the chosen seed, or the races most nearly related to them, there were ever and anon occurring marks of Divine displeasure, rebukes in providence, which were designed to temper the exhibitions of mercy, and keep up salutary impressions of the righteous character of God. And it may justly be affirmed, that for those who were conversant with the events which make up the sacred history of the period, it was not left them to doubt that the face of God was towards the righteous, and is set against them that do wickedly.

9. Such, certainly, *should* have been the result ; such also it *would* have been, if they had wisely considered the matter, and marked the character and tendency of the Divine dispensations. But this, unfortunately, was too little done ; and so the desired result was most imperfectly reached. So much so, indeed, that at the close of the patriarchal period all seemed verging again to utter ruin. The heathen world, not excepting those portions of it which came most in contact with the members of God's covenant, had with one consent surrendered themselves to the corruptions of idolatry ; and the covenant seed themselves, after all the gracious treatment they had received, and the special moral training through which they had passed, were gradually sinking into the superstitious and degrading manners of Egypt—their knowledge of Jehovah as the God of their fathers became little better than a vague tradition, their faith in the promise of His covenant ready to die, and all ambition gone, except with the merest remnant, to care for more than a kind of tolerable existence in the land of Goshen.[1] A change, therefore, in the mode of the Divine administration was inevitable, if living piety and goodness were really to be preserved among men, and the cause of righteousness was not wholly to go down. This cause had come to be quite peculiarly identified with the people of Israel. God's covenant of blessing was with them ; they were the custodiers of His word of salvation for the world ; and to fulfil their calling they must be rescued from degradation, and placed in a position of freedom and enlargement. But even this was not enough. The history of the past had made it manifest that other

[1] Exodus, ii. 14 ; v. 21 ; xvi. 4. Ezekiel, xxiii. 25, 39.

securities against defection, more effectual guarantees
for righteousness than had yet been taken, would require
to be introduced. Somehow the bonds of moral obligation must be wound more closely around them, so as to
awaken and keep alive upon their conscience a more profound and steadfast regard to the interests of righteousness. And when, looking forward to what actually took
place, we find the most characteristic feature in the new
era that emerged to be the revelation of law, we are
warranted to infer that such was its primary and leading
object. It could not have been intended—the very time
and occasion of its introduction prove that it could not
have been intended—to occupy an independent place ; it
was of necessity but the sequel or complement of the
covenant of promise, with which were bound up the hopes
of the world's salvation, to help out in a more regular
and efficient manner the moral aims which were involved
in the covenant itself, and which were directly contemplated in the more special acts and dealings of God
toward His people. It formed a fresh stage, indeed, in
the history of the Divine dispensations ; but one in which
the same great objects were still aimed at, and both the
ground of a sinner's confidence towards God, and the
nature of the obligations growing out of it, remained
essentially as they were.

10. This becomes yet more clear and conclusively certain, when we look from the general connection which
the revelation of law had with preceding manifestations
of God, to the things which formed its more immediate
prelude and preparation. The great starting-point here
was the redemption from Egypt ; and the direct object
of this was to establish the covenant which God had
made with the heads of the Israelitish people. Hence,
when appearing for the purpose of charging Moses to

undertake the work of deliverance, the Lord revealed
Himself as at once the Jehovah, the one unchangeable
and eternal God, and the God of Abraham, of Isaac, and
of Jacob,[1] who was going at last to do for their posterity
what He had pledged His word to accomplish for them.
And as soon as the deliverance was achieved, and the
tribes of Israel lay at the foot of Sinai, ready to hear what
their redeeming God might have to say to them, the first
message that came to them was one that most strikingly
connected the past with the future, the redeeming grace
of a covenant God with the duty of service justly expected of a redeemed people: ' Thus shalt thou say to
the house of Jacob, and tell the children of Israel;[2] Ye
have seen what I did unto the Egyptians, and how I
bare you on eagles' wings, and brought you unto myself.
Now therefore, if ye will obey my voice indeed, and keep
my covenant, then ye shall be a peculiar treasure unto
me above all people: for all the earth is mine.   And ye
shall be unto me a kingdom of priests, and an holy
nation.   These are the words which thou shalt speak unto
the children of Israel.'   They were, indeed, words of
profound significance and pregnant import, comprising in
substance both the gospel and the law of the covenant.
Primarily, indeed, the gospel; for Jehovah announces
Himself at the outset as, in a quite peculiar sense, the
God of Israel, who had vindicated them to Himself by
singular displays of His power and glory—had raised
them to the position of a people, given them national
existence, for the very purpose of endowing them with
the richest tokens of His favour and loving-kindness.   It
drew a broad distinction between Israel as a nation, and
all merely worldly kingdoms, which spring into existence
by dint of human powers and earthly advantages, and

---

[1] Ex. iii. 6, 9, 13, 15-17.   [2] Ex. xix. 3-7.

can attain to nothing more than that kind of secondary glory and evanescent greatness, which such inferior means and resources may be able to secure. Israel, however, stands related from the first to a higher sphere ; it comes into being under special acts of Divine providence, and has both its place of peculiar honour assigned it, and the high prerogatives and powers needful for fulfilling aright its calling by reason of its living connection with Him who is the eternal source of all that is great and good. Considered, therefore, in its now ransomed and independent position among the nations, Israel is the creation of God's omnipotent goodness—the child, in a manner, which He has taken to His bosom, which He will endow with His proper inheritance,[1] and whose future safety and well-being must be secured by Divine faithfulness and power. But for this very reason that God identified Himself so closely with Israel, Israel in return must identify itself with God. Brought into near relationship and free intercommunion with the Source of holiness and truth, the people must be known as the holy nation ; they must even be as a kingdom of priests, receiving from His presence communications of His mind and will, and again giving forth suitable impressions of what they have received to the world around them. This, henceforth, was to be their peculiar calling ; and to instruct them how to fulfil it—to shew them distinctly what it was (as matters then stood) to be a kingdom of priests and an holy nation—the law came with its clear announcements of duty and its stern prohibitions against the ways of transgression. What, then, are the main characteristics of this law ? and how, in one part of its enactments, does it stand related to another ? This naturally becomes our next branch of inquiry.

---

[1] Lev. xxv. 23.

F

LECTURE IV.

THE LAW IN ITS FORM AND SUBSTANCE—ITS MORE ESSENTIAL
CHARACTERISTICS—AND THE RELATION OF ONE PART OF ITS
CONTENTS TO ANOTHER.

IN this particular part of our inquiry, there is much
that might be taken for granted as familiarly known
and generally admitted, were it not that much also is
often ignored, or grievously misrepresented ; and that, for
a correct view of the whole, not a little depends on a
proper understanding of the spirit as well as formal contents of the law, of its historical setting, and the right
adjustment of its several parts.   If, in these respects, we
can here present little more than an outline, it must
still be such as shall embrace the more distinctive features
of the subject, and clear the ground for future statements
and discussions.

   I. We naturally look first to the DECALOGUE—the *ten
words*, as they are usually termed in the Pentateuch,
which stand most prominently out in the Mosaic legislation, as being not only the first in order, and in themselves a regularly constructed whole, but the part which
is represented as having been spoken directly from
Heaven in the audience of all the people, amid the most
striking indications of the Divine presence and glory—
the part, moreover, which was engraven by God on
the mount, on two tablets of stone—the only part so
engraven—and, in this enduring form, the sole contents

of that sacred chest or ark which became the centre of the whole of the religious institutions of Judaism—the symbolical basis of God's throne in Israel. Such varied marks of distinction, there can be no reasonable doubt, were intended to secure for this portion of the Sinaitic revelation the place of pre-eminent importance, to render it emphatically THE LAW, to which subsequent enactments stood in a dependent or auxiliary relation.

1. And in considering it, there is first to be noted the aspect in which the great Lawgiver here presents Himself to His people : ' I am Jehovah thy God, who have brought thee out of the land of Egypt, out of the house of bondage.' The words are merely a resumption of what had been shortly before, and somewhat more fully, declared in the first message delivered from Sinai ; they give, in a compendious form, the Gospel of the covenant of promise. Jehovah, the unchangeable and eternal, the great I AM ; this alone, had it been all, was a lofty idea for men who had been so long enveloped in the murky atmosphere of idolatry; and if deeply impressed upon their hearts, and made a pervading element in their religion and polity, would have nobly elevated the seed of Israel above all the nations then existing on the earth. But there is more a great deal than this in the personal announcement which introduces the ten fundamental precepts ; it is that same glorious and unchangeable Being coming near to Israel in the character of their redeeming God, and by the very title, with the incontestable fact on which it rested, pledging His faithful love and sufficiency for all future time, to protect them from evil or bring them salvation.[1] So that, in coming forth in such a character to declare the law that was henceforth to bind their consciences and regulate their procedure

[1] Ex. xv. 26.

alike toward Himself and toward one another, there was embodied the all-important and salutary principle, that redemption carries in its bosom a conformity to the Divine order, and that only when the soul responds to the righteousness of Heaven is the work of deliverance complete.

The view now given received important confirmation in the course of the historical transactions which immediately ensued. The people who had heard with solemn awe the voice which spake to them from Sinai, and undertook to observe and do what was commanded, soon shewed how far they were from having imbibed the spirit of the revelation made to them, how far especially from having attained to right thoughts of God, by turning back in their hearts to Egypt, and during the temporary absence of Moses on the mount, prevailing upon Aaron to make a golden calf as the object of their worship. The sensual orgies of this false worship were suddenly arrested by the re-appearance of Moses upon the scene; while Moses himself, in the grief and indignation of the moment, cast from him the two tables of the law, and broke them at the foot of the mount[1]—an expressive emblem of that moral breach which the sin of the people had made between them and God. The breach, however, was again healed, and the covenant re-established; but before the fundamental words of the covenant were written afresh on tables of stone, the Lord gave to Moses, and through him to the people, a further revelation of His name, that the broken relationship might be renewed under clearer convictions of the gracious and loving nature of Him whose yoke of service it called them to bear. Even Moses betrayed his need of some additional insight in this respect, by requesting that God would

[1] Ex. xxxii. 19.

shew him His glory; though, as may seem from the response made to it, he appears to have had too much in his eye some external form of manifestation. Waiving, however, what may have been partial or defective in the request—at least, no farther meeting it than by presenting to the view of Moses what, perhaps, we may call a glimpse of the incarnation in a cleft of the rock—the Lord did reveal His more essential glory—revealed it by such a proclamation of His name as disclosed all His goodness.[1] ' The Lord,' it is said, ' passed by before Moses, and proclaimed, Jehovah, Jehovah God, merciful and gracious, long-suffering, and abundant in goodness and truth ; keeping mercy for thousands, forgiving iniquity, transgression, and sin, and that will by no means clear the guilty ; visiting the iniquity of the fathers upon the children, and upon the children's children, unto the third and to the fourth generation.' This emphatic proclamation of the Divine name, or description of the character in which God wished to be known by His people, is in principle the same with that which heads the ten words ; but it is of greater compass, and remarkable chiefly for the copious and prominent exhibition it gives of the gracious, tender, and benignant character of God, as the Redeemer of Israel, that they might know how thoroughly they could trust in His goodness, and what ample encouragement they had to serve Him. It intimates, indeed, that justice could not forego its claims, that obstinate transgressors should meet their desert, but gives this only the subordinate and secondary place, while grace occupies the foreground. Was this, we ask, to act like One, who was more anxious to inspire terror, than win affection from men ? Did it seem as if He would have His revelation of law associated

[1] Ex. xxxiii. 19 ; xxxiv. 6, 7.

in their minds with the demands of a rigid service, such
as only an imperious sense of duty, or a dread of consequences, might constrain them to render ? Assuredly
not ; and we know that the words of the memorial-name,
which He so closely linked with the restored tables of the
law, did take an abiding hold of the more earnest and
thoughtful spirits of the nation, and ever and anon, amid
the seasons of greatest darkness and despondency, came
up with a joyous and re-assuring effect into their hearts.[1]
So that, whatever of awful grandeur and majesty attended
the revelation of the law from Sinai, as uttered amid
thrilling sounds and sights that flashed amazement on
the eyes of the beholders, it still had its foundation in
love, and came from God expressly in the character of
their most gracious and faithful Redeemer, as well as
their righteous Lord.

2. Yet—and here is a second point to be noted—it
did not the less on that account assume—being a revelation of law in form as well as substance, it could not
but assume—a predominantly stringent and imperative
character. The humane and loving spirit in which it
opens, is not, indeed, absent from the body of its enactments, though, for the most part, formally disguised ;
but even in form it reappears more than once—especially
in the assurance of mercy to the thousands who should
love God and keep His commandments, and the promise
of long continuance on the land of rest and blessing,
associated respectively with the second and the fifth
precepts of the law. But these are only, as it were, the
relieving clauses of the code—reminiscences of the grace
and loving-kindness which had been pledged by the
Lawgiver, and might be surely counted on by those who
were willing to yield themselves to His service : the law

[1] Ps. lxxxvi. 5, 15 ; ciii. 8 ; cxlv. 8 ; Joel ii. 13 ; Jonah iv. 2 ; Neh. ix. 17.

itself, in every one of the obligations it imposes, takes (as we have said) the imperative form—'Thou shalt do this,' 'Thou shalt not do that ;' and this just because it *is* law, and must leave no doubt that the course it prescribes is the one that *ought* to be taken, and *must* be taken, by every one who is in a sound moral condition. This is the case equally whether the precepts run in the positive or the negative form. For, as justly stated by a moralist formerly quoted,[1] 'Since morality rests upon freedom of choice, and this again consists in the fact, that under several modes of action that are possible, a particular one is chosen through one's own independent exercise of will, every moral act is at the same time also a refraining from a contrary mode of action that might have been taken. The moral law is hence always double-sided ; it is at once command and prohibition ; nor can it make any essential difference, whether the law comes forth in the one or the other form ; and as the moral life of man is a continuous one, he must every moment be fulfilling a Divine law; a mere abstaining would be a disowning of the moral.' No peculiar learning or profound reach of thought is required to understand this ; it must commend itself to every intelligent and serious mind ; for if, in respect to those precepts which take the negative form of prohibitions, the mere omitting to do the thing forbidden were all that is enjoined, there would be nothing properly moral in the matter—the command might be fulfilled by the simple absence of moral action, by mere inactivity, which in the moral sphere is but another name for death. Hence it has ever been the maxim of all judicious and thoughtful commentators on the law of the two tables, that when evil is forbidden, the opposite good is to be understood as enjoined ; just

[1] Wuttke, 'Handbuch der Christlichen Sittenlehre,' I. p. 385.

as, on the other side, when a duty is commanded, everything contrary to it is virtually forbidden. Thus Calvin,
after substantially affirming the principle now stated,
referring to the commandment, 'Thou shalt not kill,'
repudiates the idea that it is to be regarded merely as
an injunction to abstain from all injury, or wish to inflict
it.[1] 'I hold (he says) that it means besides, that we are
to aid our neighbour's life by every means in our power.'
And he proves it thus : ' God forbids us to injure or hurt
a brother, because He would have his life to be dear and
precious to us ; and therefore when He so forbids, He at
the same time demands all the offices of charity which
can contribute to his preservation.' So also Luther, who,
under the same precept, considers all indeed forbidden
that might lead to murder, but holds this also to be
included, that ' we must help our neighbour and assist
him in all his bodily troubles.' Higher than both, our
Lord Himself brings out the principle strongly in His
exposition of that and of other precepts of the Decalogue
in His sermon on the mount ; as again also in reference
to the prohibition regarding work on the Sabbath, when
taken as an excuse for refusing to administer help to a
brother's necessities, by asking, ' Is it lawful on the
sabbath-days to do good, or to do evil? to save life, or
to destroy it?'[2]—which plainly involves the principle,
that mere negatives in matters of moral obligation have
the force of positives ; that to reject virtue is to choose
vice ; that not to do the good we can is to consent to
the evil we allow ; to let a life we might have saved
perish, is to be guilty of another's death.

On this ground, which has its justification in the very
nature of things, there can manifestly be no adequate
knowledge of this revelation of law, or proper exhibition

[1] 'Institutes,' B. II. c. 8, sec. 9.   [2] Luke vi. 9.

of its real nature and place in the Divine economy, without perceiving its relation, as well in those who received as in Him who gave it, to the great principle of love. Apart from this, it had been a body without a soul, a call to obedience without the slightest chance of a response ; for aiming, as the law did, at securing a conformity in moral purpose and character between a redeeming God and a redeemed people, not one of its precepts could reach the desired fulfilment, unless the love which had exhibited itself as the governing principle in the one should find in the other a corresponding love, which might be roused and guided into proper action.   Hence, as if to make this unmistakeably plain, no sooner had Moses given a rehearsal of the Decalogue in the book of Deuteronomy, than he proclaimed aloud the memorable words : 'Hear, O Israel, the Lord our God is one Lord ; and thou shalt love the Lord thy God with all thine heart, and with all thy soul, and with all thy might :'[1] —which our Lord declared to be the first and great commandment,[2] and He added another, which He pronounced the second and like to it, ' Thou shalt love thy neighbour as thyself'—the same also which centuries before had issued from the lips of Moses.[3] ' On these two commandments,' He further declared, ' hang all the law and the prophets.' The apostles also freely interchange the precept of love with the commands of the Decalogue, as mutually explanatory of each other.[4]   And thus, in part at least, may be explained the negative form of the ten commandments.   They assume throughout the known existence of a positive ; and that, primarily, in the moral nature of man, as the image (though marred) of the Divine—without which, latent but living in the bosom,

---

[1] Deut. vi. 4, 5.   [2] Matt. xxii. 40.
[3] Lev. xix. 18.   [4] Rom. xiii. 9, 10 ; Jas. ii. 8-11.

they had been incapable of awakening any response, or creating the slightest sense of obligation. Yet not in that alone does the law assume the existence of a positive, but also in the revealed character of God, as recognised and exhibited in the law itself. *There* Israel, as the redeemed of Jehovah, had ever before them the perfection of excellence, which they were bound to aim at, and for the sake of which—lest they should lose sight of it, or think little of the obligation—they had their path fenced and guarded by those prohibitions of law, on the right hand and the left. Still, the negative is doubtless in itself the lower form of command ; and when so largely employed as it is in the Decalogue, it must be regarded as contemplating and striving to meet the strong current of evil that runs in the human heart. This may not improperly be deemed the main reason—only not the exclusive one, since even in paradise a negative form was given to the command which served as the peculiar test of love.

3. Viewing the law thus, as essentially the law of love, which it seeks to guard and protect, as well as to evoke and direct, let us glance briefly at the details, that we may see how entirely these accord, alike in their nature and their orderly arrangement, with the general idea, and provide for its proper exemplification. As love has unspeakably its grandest object in God, so precedence is justly given to what directly concerns Him—implying also that religion is the basis of morality, that the right adjustment of men's relation to God tends to ensure the proper maintenance of their relations one to another. God, therefore, must hold the supreme place in their regard, must receive the homage of their love and obedience :—and this in regard to His *being*, His *worship*, His *name*, and His *day*. He is the one living God—therefore

no others must be set up in His presence ; He alone must have the place of Deity (the first). Spiritual in His own nature, His worship also must be spiritual—therefore no idol-forms are to appear in His service, for none such can adequately represent Him; they would but degrade men's notions concerning Him, virtually change His truth into a lie (second). His name is the expression of whatever is pure, holy, and good—therefore it must be lifted up to nothing that is vain, associated with nothing false, corrupt, wicked, or profane, but only with words and deeds which breathe its spirit and reflect its glory (third). The day, too, which He has specially consecrated for Himself, being the signature of His holiness on time and labour—the check He lays upon human activity as naturally tending to work only for self, His ever-recurring call in providence on men to work so as to be again perpetually entering into His rest—this day, therefore, must be kept apart from servile labour, withdrawn from the interests of the flesh, and hallowed to God (fourth).

The next command may also be taken in the same connection—a step further in the same line, since earthly parents are in a peculiar sense God's *representatives* among men, those whom He invests with a measure of His own authority, as standing for a time in His stead to those whom instrumentally they have brought into being, and whom they should train for His service and glory—these, therefore, must be honoured with all dutiful and ready obedience, that the hearts of the fathers may in turn become the hearts of the children. This, however, touches on the second division of moral duty, that which concerns men's relation to each other ; and according to the particular aspect in which it is contemplated, the fifth command may be assigned to the first or to the second table of the law. Scripture itself makes no formal division. Though it speaks frequently enough of two tables, it nowhere indicates where the one terminates and the other begins —purposely, perhaps, to teach us that the distinction is not to be very sharply drawn, and that the contents of the one gradually approximate and at last pass over into the other. Already, in the fourth commandment, distinct reference is made to persons in the humbler ranks of life, and a kind consideration is required to be had of them— though still the primary aim and aspect of the command bore upon interests in which all were alike concerned. In like manner with the fifth : what it directly enjoins is certainly such love and regard as is due from one human being to another ; and yet the relation involved is not that exactly of neighbour to neighbour, but rather of wards under persons bearing Heaven's delegated trust and authority ; so that in the honouring of these God Himself receives somewhat of the homage due to Him, and they who render it, as the apostle says, ' shew piety at home.'[1]   With the sixth command, however—the first of the second five—we are brought to what most distinctly relates to the human sphere, and to the exercise of that love, which may in the strictest sense be called love to one's neighbours.   These the law enjoins us not to injure, but to protect and cherish, in regard to their *life;* then, to what next to life should be dearest to them, the *chastity and honour* of wife or daughter, to their *property*, to their *character and position* in life.   In respect to one and all of these, the imperative obligation imposed is, that we do our neighbour no harm by the false testimony of our tongues, or the violence of our hands, or any course of procedure that is fitted to tell injuriously upon what he has and loves.   And, finally, to shew that neither tongue, nor hands, nor any other

---

[1] I. Tim. v. 4.

member of our body, or any means and opportunities at our command—that not these alone are laid under contribution to this principle of love, but the seat also and fountain of all desire, all purpose and action—the Decalogue closes with the precept which forbids us to lust after or covet wife, house, possessions, anything whatever that is our neighbour's—a precept which reaches to the inmost thoughts and intents of the heart, and requires that all even there should be under the control of a love which thinketh no evil, which abhors the very thought of adding to one's own heritage of good by wrongfully infringing on what is another's.

Viewed thus as enshrining the great principle of love, and in a series of commands chalking out the courses of righteous action it was to follow, of unrighteous action it was to shun, the law of the two tables may justly be pronounced unique—so compact in form, so orderly in arrangement, so comprehensive in range, so free from everything narrow and punctilious—altogether the fitting reflex of the character of the Supremely Pure and Good in His relation to the members of His earthly kingdom. It is emphatically a revelation of God—of God generally, indeed, as the moral Governor of the world, but more peculiarly as the Redeemer of Israel; and to lower it to the position of a kind of semi-political and religious code, were to deprive it of all that is most distinctive in its spirit and bearing, and render utterly inexplicable the singular prominence assigned it, not alone in the legislation of the old covenant, but in the Scriptures generally alike of the Old and the New.[1]

[1] Those who will calmly reflect on the statements advanced in the preceding pages will not, I think, be much moved by the extraordinary assertions in the following passage: 'What is termed the moral law is certainly in no way to be peculiarly identified with the Decalogue, as some have strangely imagined

II. Subordinate to this grand revelation of *moral* law, yet closely related to it, is what has usually been called the *judicial* law of the Theocracy—though this is too limited a term for what must be comprised under it. A more fitting designation would be, *Statutory directions and enactments for the practical ordering of affairs amid the complicated relations and often untoward events of life.*

[*some* indeed!] Though moral duties are specially enjoined in many places of the Law, yet the Decalogue most assuredly does not contain all moral duties, even by remote implication, and on the widest construction. It totally omits many such, as, *e.g.*, beneficence, truth, justice, temperance, control of temper, and others; and some moral precepts omitted here are introduced in other places. But many moral duties are hardly recognised, *e.g.*, it is difficult to find any positive prohibition of drunkenness in the Law. In one passage only an indirect censure seems to be implied (Deut. xxix. 19).'* As if God's grand summary of moral law might be expected to run in the style of an act of Parliament, and go into endless specifications of the precise kinds and forms of wickedness which would constitute breaches of its enactments! Such cumbrous details would have been unsuited to its design, and marred rather than aided its practical effect. What was needed was a brief but comprehensive series of precepts, which for thoughtful and considerate minds would be found to embrace the wide range of duty, and, if honestly complied with, would render acts of ungodliness and crime practically unknown. And this is what the Decalogue really contains. That any one who sincerely opens his heart to the reception of its great principles of truth and duty, and lives in the loving connection it implies with God and his fellow-men, should deem himself otherwise than bound to practise justice, temperance, beneficence, and truth, it is impossible to conceive. And the same substantially may be said of another alleged omission—the moral obligation of missions. For, how could any one entering into the spirit of the revelation of law, and believing the practical acknowledgment of its great principles of truth and righteousness to be the essential condition of all true peace and well-being, fail to recognise it as his duty to do what he could to bring others acquainted with them? The very position and calling of Israel partook of a missionary character: it had for its grand aim the communication of the peculiar blessing of the covenant to all nations; and the missionary spirit breathed in such passages as Ps. lxvii., lxxii., xcviii.; Isa. ii., xlix., lx., etc., is but an expression of the love, in its higher exercise, which, as members alike of the covenant of law and the covenant of promise, the people of God were bound, as they had opportunity, to manifest.—For some points of a formal kind connected with the Decalogue, *see* Supplementary Dissertation, No. I.

* Baden Powell's 'Christianity without Judaism,' p. 104.

The law, strictly so called, being the absolute expression of the Divine will toward a people redeemed for the Divine service and glory, was necessarily oblivious of difficulties and defects ; it peremptorily required conformity with its own perfect ideal of rectitude, and made no account of any deviation from this, except to warn against and condemn it.   But in the circumstances in which mankind generally, and the Israelites in particular, actually stood, such conformity could never be more than partially realized ; transactions, interests, would be sure to come up, which might render it doubtful even to sincere men how to apply, or how far to carry out, the precepts of the Decalogue ; and, what was likely to be of much more frequent occurrence, wayward and selfish men would take occasion to traverse the pure and comely order, which it was the design of those precepts to establish among the covenant people.   In the event of such things arising, how was the external polity to be regulated and maintained ?   What modes of procedure in definite circumstances should be held in accordance with its spirit ?   What, as between one member of the community and another, might be tolerated, though falling somewhat below the Divine code of requirements ?   What, again, calling for excision, as too flagrantly opposed to it to consist with the very being of the commonwealth ?

It was to provide some sort of answer to these questions that the statutory directions and enactments now under consideration were introduced.   They are called, in the first mention that is made of them, *the mishpatim*,[1] the statutes or judgments, because bearing that character in relation to the ten commandments going immediately before.   A series of particular cases is supposed—by way of example and illustration, of course, not as if exhausting

---

[1] Ex. xxi. 1.

the entire category of possible occurrences—and, in connection with them, instructions are given as to what may or should be done, so as to preserve the spirit of the constitution, and to restrain and regulate, without unduly cramping, the liberty of the people. Indeed, the range which is allowed through the whole class of provisions now in question, for the exercise of individual liberty in official and even social arrangements, is one of the most noticeable points connected with them. In civil and economical respects, the people were left in great measure to shape their domestic institutions, and model their administrative polity as they thought fit. There were to be judges to determine in matters of dispute between man and man, and to maintain the fundamental laws of the kingdom; but how these judges were to be appointed, or what their relative places and spheres of jurisdiction, nothing is prescribed. A regular gradation of officers was introduced by Moses shortly before the giving of the law;[1] but this was done at the suggestion of Jethro, as a merely prudential arrangement, and, for anything that appears, was in that specific form confined to the wilderness-sojourn. Neither the time, nor the mode of its introduction, brings it properly within the circle of legal appointments. Even when, at a later period, the supposition is made of the general government assuming a kingly form, it is spoken of as a thing to be left to the people's own choice, restricted only by such rules and limitations regarding the mode of election, and the future conduct of the king, as would render the appointment compatible with the Theocratic constitution.[2] And a similar reserve was maintained in respect to whatever did not come distinctly within the province of religion and morals; the people stood, in regard to it, much on

[1] Ex. xviii.   [2] Deut. xvii. 14-20.

the same platform as the other nations of the earth.
And these, we know, were still in a comparatively imperfect state of order and civilization : education and
learning in the modern sense were unknown, the arts and
conveniences of life in their infancy, the civil rights of
the different classes of society little understood, and
usages of various kinds prevailing which partook of the
rudeness of the times.   It was in such a state of things
that the kingdom of God, with its formal revelation of
law, was set up in Israel ; and while that revelation, in
so far as it met with due consideration and was honestly
applied, could not fail to operate with effect in elevating the
tone and habits of society even in the strictly temporal and
earthly sphere, yet, we must remember, it only indirectly
bore upon this, and had to make its way amid much that
was out of course, and that could only admit of a gradual
amelioration.   Here, too, unless violence were to be done
to the natural course of development, and a mechanical
order made to supersede the free action of mind, the
principle of progression must have had scope given it to
work, and consequently, in the actual administration of
the affairs of the kingdom, not always what was absolutely the best, but only the best practicable in the circumstances, was to be authoritatively enjoined.   If only
contemplated thus from a right point of view, the things
sometimes excepted against in this part of the Mosaic
legislation would be seen to admit of a just defence or
reasonable explanation.

1. But to take the points connected with it in order.
A considerable portion of the statutes and judgments are,
as we have said, a simple application of the great principles of the Decalogue to particular cases, intended at
once to explain and confirm them.   That in its general
spirit and tenor the Decalogue is an embodiment of love

—in its second part of brotherly love, extending through the entire circle of one's thoughts, words, and deeds— might be conceded. But must it be exercised in every case ? even toward one from whom injury has been received ? If we think he has acted to us unjustly, may not we in turn take our revenge ? No; the judicial reply is—a neighbour, though an enemy, in trouble, as when his ass or his ox strays, or his ass has fallen helplessly under a burden, ought to receive our help.[1] So that the action of love enjoined in the command must not be thought to depend on the mere accidents of one's position; and in the most untoward circumstances, in respect even to an enemy, must shew itself in the positive as well as the negative form. Revenge is strictly excluded, and love to every brother or neighbour enforced ;[2] nor in words merely, but also in giving to him in his time of need without usury, and imitating toward him the Divine beneficence.[3] Other statutes in the same line cut off the excuse, which some might be ready to offer, that the injury sustained by their neighbour had been done by a mere act of inadvertence or rashness on their part (as by kindling a fire, which spread into another's vineyard, or by keeping open a pit into which his ox fell) ;[4] done, per- haps, in a sudden outburst of passion,[5] or through the vicious propensities of their cattle ;[6] for such things also men were held responsible, because failing to do within their proper domain the kind and considerate part of love to those around them. But then it was possible some might be disposed occasionally to press the matter too far, and hold a man equally responsible for any violence done by him to the life or property of another, whether done from sheer carelessness, from heedless impetuosity,

[1] Ex. xxiii. 4, 5.   [2] Lev. xix. 18.   [3] Ex. xxii. 25-27.
[4] Ex. xxii. 5, xxi. 33.   [5] Ex. xxi. 22-27.   [6] Ex. xxi. 28-36.

or from deliberate malice. Here, again, the statutory enactments come in with their wise and discriminating judgments—distinguishing, for example, between death inflicted unwittingly, or in self-defence, or in the attempt to arrest a burglary, and murder perpetrated in cool blood.[1] Thus there is delivered to us, for a principle of interpretation and personal guidance, that the law under any particular head is violated or fulfilled, not by the bare act anyhow performed, but by the act taken in connection with the circumstances, especially the feeling and intent of the heart, under which it has been done. Once more, the question might be stirred by some in a perverse, by others in a partial or prejudiced spirit, whether the law should be understood as applying to all with absolute equality? whether an exemption more or less might not be allowed, at least to persons in what might be called the extremes of social position? Here, also, the decision is given with sufficient plainness, when it is ordained that the poor man was neither to have his judgment wrested, nor be unduly countenanced in his cause, from respect to his poverty; that even the friendless stranger was to be treated with kindness and equity; and that the rich and powerful were not to be allowed to use their resources for the purpose of gaining an advantage to which they were not entitled.[2]

2. It thus appears that the class of enactments referred to have an abiding value, as they serve materially to throw light on the import and bearing of the Decalogue, confirming the views already given of its spiritual and comprehensive character. Another class, which, like the preceding, involve no difficulty of interpretation, also reflect, in a somewhat different way, a measure of light on the Decalogue, viz., by the judicial treatment they

[1] Ex. xxi. 12-14, xxii. 2.   [2] Ex. xxiii. 2, 3, 6, 9 ; Deut. i. 17; xix. 7-19.

award to the more flagrant violation of its precepts. The deeds which were of this description had all the penalty of death attached to them—shewing that the precepts they violated were of a fundamental character, and entered as essential principles into the constitution of the Theocracy. Such was the doom suspended over the introduction of false gods, in violation of the *first* command,[1] to which also belong all the statutes about witchcraft, divination, and necromancing, which involved the paying of homage to another object of worship than Jehovah ; over the worshipping of God by idols, in violation of the *second* command ;[2] over the profanation of God's name, in violation of the *third* ;[3] over the deliberate profanation of the Sabbath, in violation of the *fourth* ;[4] over shameful dishonour and violence done to parents, in violation of the *fifth* ;[5] over murder, adultery, bestiality, men-stealing, and the more extreme cases of oppression, violence, and false witness-bearing, in violation of the successive commands of the second table.[6] Why the breaches of these great precepts of the Decalogue should have been met so uniformly with the severity of capital punishment, is to be accounted for by the nature of the kingdom set up in Israel, which was a theocracy, having God for its supreme Lawgiver and Head, and for its subjects a people bearing His name and occupying His land. How completely would the great end of such an institution have been frustrated, if the holiness to which the people were called had been outraged, and the sins which ran counter to it openly practised ? To act thus had been to traverse the fundamental laws of the kingdom, nay, to

---

[1] Ex. xxii. 20 ; Deut. xiii. 9, 10.   [2] Ex. xxxii. ; Deut. iv. 25-28.
[3] Ex. xx. 7 ; Lev. xxiv. 16.   [4] Ex. xxxi. 14, 15 ; Numb. xv. 35.
[5] Ex. xxi. 15-17.
[6] Ex. xxi. 12 ; Lev. xxiv. 17, xx. 10 ; Ex. xxii. 19, 22-24 ; Deut. xix. 21.

manifest an unmistakeable hatred to its Divine Head,
and could no more be tolerated there than overt treason
in an earthly government. The law, therefore, right-
eously laid the sin of deliberate transgression on the head
of the sinner as guilt, which could only be taken away
by the punishment of him who committed it.[1] If this
should be deemed excessive severity, it can only be
because the right is virtually denied on the part of God
to establish a Theocracy among men in conformity with
His own revealed character, and for the manifestation of
His name. That right, however, is assumed as the
ground on which the whole legislation of Sinai proceeds ;
and if the penal enactments of the Theocracy are to be
rightly interpreted, they must be placed in immediate
connection with the authority and honour of God. In
respect to all judicial action, when properly administered,
the judgment, though administered by man, was held to
be the Lord's.[2] To bring a matter up for judgment was
represented as bringing it to God (so the rendering
should be in Ex. xxii. 8, 9, not ' the judges,' as in the
English version) ; and persons standing before the priests
and the judges to have sentence pronounced upon them,
were said to stand before the Lord.[3] If the judges and
the judged realized this to be their position, would there
have been any just ground to complain of undue severity?
Would there not rather have been diffused throughout
the community a deep sense of the Divine righteousness, and an earnest striving to have its claims and
penalties enforced, as the indispensable pre-requisite of
peace and blessing ?[4]   Besides, it was not they alone who

---

[1] *See* Weber, ' Von Zorne Gottes,' p. 142.   [2] Deut. i. 17.   [3] Deut. xix. 17.
[4] Human theories of jurisprudence often entirely repudiate the relation here
implied of sin or crime to punishment. The maxim of Seneca (*nemo prudens
punit, quia peccatum est, sed ne peccetur; revocari enim praeterrita non possunt,
futura prohibentur*), which abjures the thought of inflicting punishment, except

were to be considered ; for in planting them in Canaan,
' in the midst of the nations,' and furnishing them with
such a polity, God's design was to use them as a great
teaching institute—a light placed aloft on the moral
heights of the world amid surrounding darkness. What
incalculable blessings might have accrued to ancient
heathendom had that high calling been fulfilled ! But
to this end the stern proscription of open ungodliness and
flagrant immoralities was indispensable.[1]

3. Another class of the statutes and judgments under
consideration is one which more directly bore on the imperfect state of order and civilization then everywhere
existing, and which has often been misunderstood and
objected to. The law of compensation — frequently,
though improperly, termed the law of retaliation—does
not strictly belong to the class, but may be included in it,
on account of the assaults to which it has been subjected.
It is, indeed, so far of the class in question, as it comes
first directly into view in connection with a very rude
and barbarous state of manners. The supposition is made

as a check or means of prevention against its future commission, has found not
a few defenders in recent times, though more in Germany than here. Yet
there also some of the profoundest thinkers have given it their decided opposition. Hegel, for instance, taught that ' punishment is certainly to be regarded
as the necessary abolition of crime which would otherwise predominate, and as
the re-establishment of right.' More fully and distinctly Stahl, ' To man is
given, along with the power, the authority also of performing a deed, but this
he can only have *with* God, not *against* Him. If, therefore, he acts amiss, he
comes to have a glory in the world antagonistic to God. Not, however, to
undo the deed itself, and its consequence, can be demanded by the Divine
righteousness, but only to destroy this glory of the deed ; and if this can be
destroyed, the antagonism is brought to an end.'—(*See* in Baumgarten's Comm.
on Pent., II. pp. 29, 30.) But the relation of capital punishment to moral transgressions of the first table, and to some extent also of the second, which was
proper to a Theocracy, cannot be justly transferred to an ordinary civil commonwealth ; and, in this respect, Christian states have often grievously erred
in assimilating their penal statutes too closely to those of the Mosaic legislation.

[1] *See* the remarks in my ' Commentary on Ezekiel,' pp. 68-70.

of two men striving together, and a woman with child
(whether by chance or from well-meant interference on her
part) happening to receive some corporeal injury in the
fray ; and it was ordained, that her husband was entitled
to claim compensation from the offender, according to the
extent of the injury ; proceeding further, the statute provides generally for all like cases, that there should be
' life for life, eye for eye, tooth for tooth, hand for hand,
foot for foot, burning for burning, wound for wound,
stripe for stripe.'[1] Stript of its concrete form, this is
simply a rule for the proper administration of justice
between man and man, requiring that when a particular
wrong was done to any one, and through him to society,
an adequate compensation should be rendered. So far
from being peculiar to the Mosaic code, no legislation
that is not capricious and arbitrary can dispense with
such a rule, nor could society exist in peace and comfort
without its faithful application. ' In fact,' to use the
words of Kalisch in his commentary on the passage, ' our
own Christian legislation could not dispense with similar
principles : life is punished with. life, and intentional
injuries are visited with more than equivalent penalties.
Not even the most sentimental and romantic legislator
has ever had the fancy to pardon all criminals out of
Christian love. For, in reality, every simple law in our
criminal code is based on the *jus talionis* (the law of compensation), with the limitation that bodily mutilation is
converted into an adequate pecuniary fine, or incarcera-
tion ; but the same modification (he adds) has been
universally adopted by traditional Judaism.' Such a
limitation was in perfect accordance with the general
spirit of the Mosaic code, and must have been from the
first intended. The literal application of the rule, as in

[1] Ex. xxi. 22-25.

the case of burning for burning, or wound for wound, would often have been impracticable, for who could have undertaken to make a second that should always be precisely equivalent to the first ? or unjust, for the severity of a bodily infliction may, in particular circumstances, be a widely different thing to one person from what it is to another. To insist on the exact counterpart of such corporeal injuries, even when it could have been secured, in preference to a reasonable compensation, would plainly have been to gratify a spirit of revenge ; and this, as already stated, was expressly disallowed. There was one thing, and only one, in regard to which compensation was formally interdicted : the life of a deliberate murderer must be given for the life of the murdered, without satisfaction, without pity ;[1] and the emphatic exclusion of compensation here, was justly regarded by the Jewish doctors as virtually sanctioning its admission in cases of a lighter kind, where no such exclusion was mentioned. The real bearing of this law, then, when rightly understood and applied as it was meant, in judicial decisions, was in perfect accordance with the principles of equity ; it was merely a practical embodiment of these ; and the reference made to it by our Lord in His sermon on the mount, where it forms a kind of contrast to the injunction laid on His followers not to resist evil, but when smitten on the one cheek to turn the other also, and so on,[2] can imply no disparagement of the old rule in its proper intention. In so far as it breathed a tone of censure, or assumed a position of antagonism, it was only in regard to those who, in their personal endeavours after the pure and good, had not known to rise above the level of a formal and rigid justice. Not questioning the claims of justice in the public administration of affairs, our Lord

---

[1] Numb. xxxv. 31 ; Deut. xix. 13.   [2] Mat. v. 38.

still made it to be known that He sought a people who would be ready to forego these, whenever by doing so they could promote the good of their fellow-men. But the law of brotherly love, when requiring the suppression of revenge, and the exercise of forbearance and kindness even to an enemy, in reality did the same, as was perfectly understood by the better spirits of the old covenant.[1] So that nothing properly different, but only a greater fulness and prominence in the exhibition or enforcement of such love, can be claimed for the Gospel dispensation.[2]

4. More distinctly than the statutes just noticed may some of those connected with the punishment of murder be ranked in the class now under consideration. In this branch of the Mosaic legislation there is generally apparent a spirit of humanity and moderation. First of all, murder in the proper sense is carefully discriminated from death brought about in some casual manner. In every case of real murder it was necessary to prove preceding malice or hatred, a lying in wait or taking deliberate measures to compass the death of its victim, and an assault with some violent weapon accomplishing the end in view.[3] But if, on the other hand, while a man had proved the cause of a neighbour's death, the act inflicting it was merely the throwing of a stone or other weight, which incidentally lighted upon some one, and took away his

[1] Ps. vii. 4 ; Prov. xxv. 21, 22 ; 1 Sam. xxiv., xxvi.

[2] The same view is given of the Mosaic statute by the leading authorities ; for example, by Michaelis, Salvador ' His. des Institutions de Moise ' (who says, ' The *jus talionis* is a principle rather than a law ; as a law it cannot, nor does it actually come in general to be executed') ; Saalschütz ' Des Mosaische Recht ;' Kalisch gives some specimens of the Rabbinical discussions on the subject, from Bab. Talmud ; and Maimonides. For the compensations by which the Arabs and Egyptians carry out the principle, see Kitto's ' Pictorial Bible,' on Ex. xxi., and Lane's ' Modern Egyptians,' ch. III.

[3] Deut. xix. 2.

life—or if by some sort of sudden thrust, in a freak or
fury, without aught of preconceived malice or deliberate
intent, a neighbour's life was sacrificed, the instrument
of doing it could not be arraigned for murder; but neither
could he be deemed altogether innocent.   There must
usually have been, in such cases, at least a culpable degree
of heedlessness, which would always call for careful investigation, and might justly subject the individual to a
limited amount of trouble, or even of punishment.   It
does so still in the civilized communities of modern times,
with their regulated forms of judicial procedure and vigilant police : the man-slayer, however unwittingly he may
have been the occasion of taking another's life, must lay
his account to the solemn inquest, often also the personal
arrest, and it may be, ultimately, the severe reprimand,
pecuniary fine, or temporary imprisonment, which may be
thought due as a correction to his improper heedlessness
or haste.   But at the period of Israel's settlement in
Canaan there were not the opportunities for calm inquiry,
and patient, satisfactory adjustment of such cases as exist
now ; and there were, besides, feelings deeply rooted in
Asiatic society, and usages growing out of them, which
tended very considerably to embarrass the matter, and yet
could not be arbitrarily set aside.   These arose out of the
relation of *Goel*, according to which the nearest of kin had
the wrongs, in particular circumstances, as well as the
rights of the deceased, devolved upon him ; especially the
obligation to avenge his blood in the event of its having
been unrighteously shed.   On this account the term *Goel*
is very commonly reckoned synonymous with 'avenger'
(*Goel haddam*, avenger of blood), and in the passages bearing on this subject they are invariably so rendered in our
English Bible.[1]   To the mere English reader, however,

[1] Numb. xxxv. 12 ; Deut. xix. 6, 12 ; Jos. xx. 5, 9, etc.

in modern times, this is apt to convey a somewhat wrong idea; for in its proper import *Goel* means not avenger, but redeemer (as in Job xix. 25, ' I know that my Redeemer liveth'), and *Goel haddam* is strictly ' redeemer of blood,' one to whom belonged the right and duty of recovering the blood of the murdered kinsman, of vindicating in the only way practicable its wronged cause, and obtaining for it justice. In him the blood of the dead, as it were, rose to life again and claimed its due. In other cases, it fell to the Goel to redeem the property of his relative, which had become alienated and lost by debt;[1] to redeem his person from bondage, if through poverty he had been necessitated to go into servitude;[2] even to redeem his family, when by dying childless it was like to become extinct in Israel, by marrying his widow and raising up a seed to him.[3] It thus appears that a humane and brotherly feeling lay at the root of this Goel-relationship; and in regard to the matter more immediately before us, it did not necessarily involve anything revengeful or capricious in its mode of operation. In ordinary cases, all its demands might have been satisfied by the Goel appearing before the judges as the prosecutor of the man-slayer, and calling upon them to examine the case and give judgment in behalf of the deceased. But there can be no doubt that it might also quite readily run to evil, that it might degenerate—if not very carefully guarded and checked—into what, from time immemorial, it has been among the Arab races—a kind of wild and vengeful spirit of justice, which would take the law into its own hands, and, in defiance alike of personal danger and of the forms of legal procedure, would pursue the shedder of blood till his blood in turn had been shed. This was the vicious extreme of the system; yet one, it

---

[1] Lev. xxv. 25.　　　[2] Lev. xxv. 48-50.　　　[3] Deut. xxv. 5-10.

ought to be remembered, which operated as a powerful check—perhaps, in the circumstances of the place and times, the only valid check that could be devised against another and still more pernicious extreme, for which peculiar facilities were afforded by the vast deserts of Arabia and the regions lying around Palestine. How easy might it have been for the daring and successful murderer, by making his escape into these, to get beyond the reach of the regular tribunals and officers of justice! Only the dread of being tracked out and having his own measure summarily meted back to him, by one on whom the charge to avenge the wrong lay as a primary and life-long obligation, might be sufficient to deter him from trusting in such a refuge from evil. We have it on the testimony of those who have been most thoroughly conversant with the regions in question, and the races inhabiting them, that nothing has contributed so much as this institution (even in its most objectionable Arab form) to prevent the warlike tribes of the East from exterminating one another.[1]

In these circumstances, Moses, legislating for a people already familiar with the Goel-relationship, and going to occupy a region which presented to the more lawless spirits of the community, tempting opportunities for escaping from judicial treatment of a more orderly kind, took the wise course of grounding his statutes in respect to manslaughter and murder on the hereditary rights and duties of the Goel. But he so restrained and regulated them, that, if faithfully carried out, the checks he introduced could scarcely fail to arrest the worst tendencies of the system, and indeed reduce the position of the Goel to that of the recognised and rightful prosecutor of the

---

[1] See in Layard's 'Nineveh and Babylon,' p. 305, for his own and Burckhardt's testimony.

shedder of blood. To prevent any sudden assault upon the latter, and afford time for the due investigation of his deed, a temporary asylum was provided for him in the cities of refuge, which were appointed for this purpose at convenient distances—three on the one side and three on the other of the Jordan.[1]   When actually appointed, the cities were most wisely distributed, and belonged also to the class of Levitical cities (Golan in Bashan, Ramoth in Gilead, and Bezer on the east side; Kadesh in Galilee, Shechem and Hebron on the west),[2] and as such were sure to contain persons skilled in the knowledge of the law and capable of giving intelligent judgment.   Arrived within the gates of one of these cities, the man-slayer was safe from the premature action of the Goel ; but only that the judges and elders of the place might take up the case and pronounce impartial judgment upon it.   If they found reason to acquit him of actual murder, then he remained under their protection, but was obliged to submit to a kind of partial imprisonment, because not allowed to go beyond the borders of the city till the death of the existing high-priest—after which, if he still lived, he was at liberty to return to his own possession.   Were not these conditions, however, somewhat arbitrary ?   If not really guilty of blood in the proper sense, why should he not have been placed at once under the protection of the law, and restored to his property and home ? And why should the period of his release have been made to hang on the uncertain and variable moment of the high-priest's death? Perhaps there may have been grounds for these limitations at the time they were imposed, which cannot now be ascertained ; but a little consideration is sufficient to shew that they could not be deemed unreasonable.   In the great majority of cases, the death of the person slain must

[1] Numb. xxxv.   [2] Jos. xx. 7, 8.

have been owing to the want of due circumspection, fore-
thought, or restraint on the part of him who had occasioned
it ; and it could not, to thoughtful minds, appear otherwise than a salutary discipline, that he should be adjudged
to a temporary abridgment of his liberty.   Arbitrarily to
break through this restraint after it had been judicially
imposed, would clearly have argued a self-willed, im-
petuous, and troublesome humour, which refused correction, and might readily enough repeat in the future the
rashness or misdeed of the past ; so that it was but dealing with him according to his folly to leave him in such a
case at the mercy of the Goel.[1]   Nor could the connection
of the period of release with the death of the existing
high-priest carry much of a strange or capricious aspect
to the members of the Theocracy.   For the high-priest
was, in everything pertaining to sin and forgiveness, the
most prominent person in the community; in such things,
he was the representative of the people, making perpetual
intercession for them before God ; and though there was
nothing expiatory in his death, yet being the death of
one in whom the expiatory ritual of the old covenant had
so long found its centre and culmination, it was natural—
more than natural, it was every way proper and becoming—that when he disappeared from among men, the
cause of the blood that had been incidentally shed in his
life-time, and from its nature could admit of no very
definite reckoning, should be held to have passed with
him into oblivion—its cry was to be no more heard.[2]

It was made very clear, however, by other statutes on

---

[1] Lev. xxv. 26, 27.

[2] This appears to me the natural explanation of the rule, and sufficient for
the purpose intended.   The older evangelical divines (some also still, as Keil)
think that in the death of the high-priest there was a shadow of the death of
Christ ; consequently something that might be regarded as having a sort of
atoning value for the sins of the people.   This I cannot but consider arbitrary

this subject, that when actual murder had been committed, no advantage was to accrue to the perpetrator from the cities of refuge ; though he might have fled thither, he was, on the proof of his guilt, to be delivered up to the Goel for summary execution.[1] Nor was the altar of God—a still more sacred place than the cities of refuge, and in ancient times almost universally regarded as an asylum for criminals—to be permitted in such cases to afford protection ; from this also the murderer was to be dragged to his deserved doom.[2] In short, deliberate murder was to admit of no compromise and no palliation : the original law, ' whoso sheddest man's blood by man shall his blood be shed,'[3] must be rigorously enforced ; and, doubtless, mainly also on the original ground, ' because in the image of God made He him.' To disregard the sanctity of human life, and tread it vilely in the dust, was like aiming a thrust at God Himself, disparaging His noblest work in creation, and the one that stood in peculiar relationship to His own spiritual being. Therefore, the violation of the sixth command by deliberate murder involved also a kind of secondary violation of the first ; and to suffer the blood of the innocent to lie unavenged, was, in the highest sense, to pollute the land ;[4] it was to render it unworthy of the name of God's inheritance. So great was the horror entertained of this unnatural crime, and so anxious was the Lawgiver to impress men with the feeling of its contrariety to the whole spirit and object of the law, that, even in the case of an

in interpretation, and involving a dangerous element in respect to the work of atonement. For if the death of a sinful man, because he was anointed with oil, the symbol of the Spirit's grace, had such a value then, why should not the death of martyrs and other saints, richly endowed with the Spirit, have something of the same now ?

[1] Deut. xix. 11-16.   [2] Ex. xxi. 14.
[3] Gen. ix. 6.   [4] Numb. xxxv. 34.

uncertain murder, there was a cry of blood which could
not be disregarded ; and when every effort had failed to
discover the author of the deed, the elders of the city
which lay nearest to the corpse were to regard themselves
as in a manner implicated ; they had to come publicly
forward, and not only protest their innocence of the crime,
and their ignorance of the manner in which it had been
committed, but also to go through a process of purification by blood and water, that the charge of blood-guilti-
ness might not rest upon them and their land.[1]

5. We pass on now to the statutes on slavery and the
treatment of those subject to it, which have in various respects been deemed inconsistent with the spirit of the
Decalogue, as embodying the law of brotherly love.
Here, again, it is especially necessary to bear in mind the
state of the world at the time the law was given, and the
relation in which it stood to manners and usages, which
bespoke a very imperfect development both of economical
science and of civil rights.   It was necessary that the
law should take things as it found them, and, while
setting before the covenant people the correct ideal of all
that was morally right and good, should still regulate
what pertained to the enforcement of discipline with a
due regard to circumstances more or less anomalous and
perplexing.   By constitutional right, all the members of
the covenant were free ; they were the Lord's redeemed
ones, whom He vindicated to Himself from the house of
bondage, that they might be in a condition to serve and
honour Him ;[2] they were not again to be sold as bondmen ;[3] and that they might remain in this freedom from
human servitude, every one had an inheritance assigned
sufficient for the maintenance of himself and his family.
The precautions, too, which were taken to secure the

[1] Deut. xxi. 1-9.   [2] Ex. xx. 2 ; Deut. xv. 15.   [3] Lev. xxv. 42.

perpetuity of these family possessions, were admirably devised ; if properly guarded and carried out, nothing had been wanting to provide, so far as external arrangements could effect it, the means of a comfortable livelihood and independence for the families of Israel. But much must still depend on the individual character of the people, and the current of events in their history. If, through adverse circumstances, desolation fell on any portion of the territory—or if, from slothful neglect, particular inheritances were not duly cultivated, or the resources they furnished were again improvidently squandered—above all, if the people in whole or in part should become involved in the reverses or triumphs of war—such inequalities might readily spring up as, in the existing state of civic life and political arrangements, would most naturally lead to the introduction of a certain kind of slavery. It is even possible that, as matters then stood, the humanest, if not the only practicable thing, that could be done by legislative enactment, was to bound and regulate, rather than absolutely interdict, some modified form of this in itself unhappy relationship. Such, at least, appears to have been the view countenanced by the Divine Head of the Theocracy ; for the statutes bearing on the subject of slavery are entirely of the kind just indicated, and, when temperately considered, will be found to involve a wise adaptation to the circumstances of the time. Even a brief outline may be enough to establish this.

(1.) The language alone is of importance here, as indicative of the spirit of the Hebrew Theocracy : it had no term to designate one class as slaves (in the stricter sense) and another who did hired service. The term for both alike is *Ebed* (עֶבֶד), properly, a *labourer* or *worker*, and hence very naturally one whose calling in life is emphati-

cally of this description, a *servant*. And, as justly noted
by Saalschütz,[1] 'among a people who were engaged in
agricultural employments, whose lawgiver Moses, and
whose kings Saul and David, were taken straight from the
flock and the plough to their high calling, there could not
seem to be anything degrading in a designation derived
from *work;* and the name of honour applied to Moses
and other righteous men was that of " servant of God." '
The only ground for concern could be, lest occasion might
be taken to render work galling and oppressive, or incidentally subversive of the great principles of the constitution.

(2.) As a check upon this, at the outset a brand was
set upon man-stealing ; he who should be found to have
kidnapped a soul (meaning thereby man or woman) of
the children of Israel, for the purpose of using or selling
that soul as a slave, incurred the penalty of death, as a
violator of the fundamental laws of the kingdom.[2]

(3.) But a man might, under the constraint of circumstances, to save himself and his family from the extre-
mities of want, become fain to part with his freedom, and
bind himself in servitude to another. In such cases, which
should never have been but of an exceptional kind, a
whole series of prescriptions were given to set bounds to
the evil, and secure, during its continuance, the essentials
of a brotherly relationship. The service required was in
no case to be that of an absolute bondman—or, as the
expression literally is, service of a servant (עֲבֹדַת עֶבֶד)—
rigorous service, such as might be expected of one into
whose condition no higher element entered.[3] His relation
to Jehovah as the Redeemer of Israel must not be allowed
to fall into abeyance. Hence, his general rights and

---

[1] 'Mosaische Recht,' c. 101, sec. 1.   [2] Lev. xxi. 17 ; Deut. xxiv. 7.
[3] Lev. xxv. 39-43.

privileges as a member of the covenant remained untouched : he could inherit property if it accrued to him, could be redeemed by a kinsman at a fair ransom, was entitled to the rest of the weekly Sabbaths, and to the joy and consolation of the stated festivals.[1] Besides, the period of service was limited ; it could not extend beyond six years, after which, in the seventh, came the year of release ; and even then the master was not to let him go empty, but was to furnish him with supplies to help him toward an independent position (Ex. xxi. 2 ; Deut. xv. 12-14).[2] So that the relation of a Hebrew bondman to his master did not materially differ from that of one now, who sells his labour to a particular person, or engages to work to him on definite terms, for a stated period. A certain exception, no doubt, has to be made in respect to the provision concerning his wife and children : if the wife belonged to him when he entered into the bond-service, then both wife and children went out with him ; but if the wife had been given him by the master, wife and children could be claimed by the master. In the latter case, of course, the servant

---

[1] Lev. xxv. 42-52.

[2] In respect to the period of release, there is an apparent discrepance in the passages relating to it ; in Ex. xxi. 2, also Deut. xv. 12, the seventh year is fixed definitely as the time of release ; while in Lev. xxv. 40, the year of Jubilee is named as the terminating point. In the latter passage, and throughout the chapter, the chief subject of discourse is the Jubilee, and it is only as connected with it that the other subject comes into consideration. The natural explanation, therefore, as given by many of our recent writers, is, that in ordinary circumstances the servitude terminated with the commencement of the seventh year, but when a Jubilee intervened, the bond of servitude, like all other bonds, ceased as a matter of course. This simple explanation renders quite unnecessary Ewald's resort to his theory of earlier and later documents. The seventh year, however, was not the Sabbatical year, but the seventh from the entrance of the servitude—the principle of the arrangement being, that, as after seven days' work there came the day of rest, and after seven years' husbandry a year of repose, so after seven years' servitude a return to freedom.

would be at perfect liberty to refuse what was offered;
and as it must have been a person of heathen birth that
in the case supposed was offered him for wife (for Hebrew
maid-servants were, equally with the men, entitled to
release in the seventh year),[1] the proper Israelite could
not have complied with it, unless the woman had ceased
in spirit to be a heathen, and he had himself made up his
mind to abide in perpetual servitude to his master. The
laws respecting marriage involved these two conditions,
as in a moral respect binding upon the individual in
question; for temporary marriages, and marriages with
unconverted heathens, were alike forbidden. A man
might, however, choose to remain in the position of a
bondman, rather than avail himself of his right to become
free; the supposition of such a case is distinctly made,
and it was ordered that he should go through what could
not but be regarded as a degrading ceremony. On declaring that he loved his master, his wife and children,
and that he would not go out free, his master was to
place him before the judges, and in their presence bore
his ear through with an awl into the door or door-post.[2]
The perforating of the ear and fixing it with the awl to
the door (as appears from the passage in Deuteronomy
to have been the full rite), was undoubtedly intended to
signify the servant's personal surrender of the freedom
proper to him as an Israelite, that he might attach himself to the authority and interest of the master. By the
door, therefore, is most naturally understood the door of
the master's house, in which the man and his family now
became a kind of fixtures; but whether the 'for ever'
connected with his obligation of servitude indicated a
strictly life-long continuance, or an unbroken service only
till the year of Jubilee, is differently understood, and can-

[1] Deut. xv. 12.   [2] Ex. xxi. 6; Deut. xv. 17.

not be quite definitely determined—though the natural impression is in favour of the former view. The whole object and bearing of the ceremony were obviously to fix a sort of stigma on any one who voluntarily assumed the condition of such prolonged servitude. His claim, however, to lenient treatment, and the usual Israelitish privileges, remained as before.

(4.) A still further supposition is made, that, namely, of the daughter of an Israelite—not going into ordinary servitude for the legal term of years, as in Deut. xv. 12, in which case the regulations laid down for male servants were in substance applicable here—but being sold (according to a prevailing custom in the East) with the double view of service and betrothal.[1] She was, in the circumstances, supposed to go as a maid-servant, namely, to engage actively in domestic work ; and, at the same time, she is represented as standing in a betrothed condition to her master. If he was satisfied with her, and either himself took her to wife, or gave her to his son in that capacity, then she, of course, became a member of the family and had the rights of a spouse ; but if the connexion, after being formed, was again broken off, then (besides all the moral blame that might be incurred in the matter, of which this branch of the law does not treat) the master was obliged to forfeit the money he had paid—the maid could not be re-sold, but was instantly to regain her liberty ; though it may be doubtful if she had the right to sue for a regular divorce. This part of the question, however, belongs rather to the subject of marriage than to that of servitude.

(5.) Servitude, in a stricter sense than that which the preceding regulations contemplate, might be exacted of foreigners. Of the heathen that were round about them,

---

[1] Ex. xxi. 7-11.

the Israelites might buy persons for bondmen and bond-maids, also of the strangers who might be sojourning among them.[1] Then, those who were taken captive in war, as a matter of course fell into the hands of the victors, and were reduced to the condition of bondmen.[2] The children also, if any should be born to either of the preceding classes, formed a third source of supply. But from the very constitution of the kingdom, which secured a general distribution of the land along with the rights of citizenship, and rendered next to impossible large accumulations of property, or fields of enterprise that would call for much servile labour, there was comparatively little scope or occasion for the growth of this kind of population. The circumstances of the covenant-people presented no temptation to it; beyond very moderate limits, the presence of such a population must have been a source of trouble and annoyance, rather than of comfort or strength; and hence, in the historical records, no indication exists of any regular commerce being carried on in this line, or even of any considerable numbers being held in the condition of bondmen. The Phœnician slave trade is noticed only in connection with what Israel suffered by it, not for anything they gained;[3] and so little sympathy were they to have with the slave system practised among the nations around them, that a slave flying to them for refuge from his heathen master was not to be delivered up, but to be allowed, under Israelitish protection, to fix his abode in whatever city he himself might choose.[4] The strangers or foreigners sometimes mentioned, and especially in the times of David and Solomon, as ready for the execution of servile work,[5] seem rather to have been a kind of serfs, than slaves in the ordinary

[1] Lev. xxv. 44, 45.   [2] Num. xxxi. 26-35; Deut. xx. 14, etc.   [3] Mic. i. 9; Ob. 20.
[4] Deut. xxiii. 15-17.   [5] 1 Kings ix. 20; 2 Chron. ii. 16; viii. 7.

sense—chiefly the descendants, in all probability, of the
heathen families that remained in the land. Of that
class certainly were the Gibeonites, only with a special
destination as to the form of service they were taken
bound to render.[1]

From the facts just stated, one is naturally led to infer,
that bond-service in the strict sense must have been of
very limited extent among the covenant people, and that,
in so far as it did exist, it must have ever tended to
work toward its own extinction. This also is the impression which the particular statutes on the subject are
fitted to convey. As a rule, the persons belonging to the
house as bondmen or bondmaids were to be treated as
members of the family ; they were to enjoy the Sabbath
rest, and partake of the sacrificial meals ;[2] even if the
priest should have any servants in that position, they
were to eat of the consecrated food which fell to the share
of the master.[3] When they submitted to the rite of circumcision—which, according to Rabbinical tradition, and,
indeed, to the obvious proprieties of things, required
their own deliberate consent—as they thereby entered
into the bond of the covenant, so they became entitled to
eat of the Passover, and, of course, to participate fully in
all the privileges of the covenant.[4] If the master should
smite any of his bondmen with a murderous weapon, so
as to cause his death, he was himself liable to the penalty
of murder—for smiting to death with intent to kill is,
without exception, in the case of the stranger as well as the
native Israelite, placed under one condemnation.[5] Smiting only to the effect of destroying a tooth or an eye, was
to be followed with the freedom of the slave.[6] But when

[1] Jos. ix. 23 ; 2 Sam. xxi.   [2] Deut. v. 14, xii. 12, xvi. 11.
[3] Lev. xxii. 11.   [4] Ex. xii. 44.
[5] Ex. xxi. 12 ; Numb. xxxv. 16-18 ; Lev. xxiv. 17-22.
[6] Ex. xxi. 26, 27.

smiting of that description—smiting, namely, with a rod in the way of chastisement, with no intent to kill—went so far as to produce death, it was to be met by deserved punishment—the atrocity was to be avenged—though it is not said by what particular infliction (Ex. xxi. 20.)[1] The penalty was apparently left to the discretion of the judges, and would doubtless vary according to the circumstances. But if death did not immediately follow, if the servant lingered a day or two, no additional penalty was to be imposed ; the delay was to be taken as proof that no fatal result was contemplated by the master, and, in a pecuniary respect, the death of the victim had itself inflicted a heavy mulct.[2] Not that, in a moral point of view, this was an adequate compensation for the undue severity he had practised, but that the temporal loss having equalled the recognised value of the subject, it was deemed inexpedient to go farther in that direction. For the higher bearing of his procedure, he had still to place himself in contact with the revelations respecting sin and atonement.

Taken as a whole, the statutes upon the subject of slavery, it is impossible to deny, are largely pervaded by a spirit of mildness and equity, tolerating rather than properly countenancing and approving of it, and giving to it a very different character, both as to extent and manner of working, from what belonged to it in the nations of heathen antiquity. If brought into comparison, indeed, with the arrangements of modern civilization, one

---

[1] I take here the view which seems the most probable, which is that also of Saalschütz, Kalisch, Œhler in ' Hertzog,' art. *Sklaverei*, and many others. The smiting to death, in the verse referred to, was only with a rod— not with a heavy or deadly weapon ; and the death, though immediate, was not intentional. The phrase, he shall be avenged or punished, must therefore refer to something less than capital punishment.

[2] Ex. xxi. 21.

can readily point to features in it which, considered by themselves, were not in accordance with the ideal of a well-ordered commonwealth. But such a comparison would be essentially unfair. For, however high the standard of moral rectitude set up in the Hebrew commonwealth, and in its entireness laid upon the consciences of the people, the commonwealth in its political administration could not move in total isolation from the state of things around it. At various points it necessarily took a certain impress from the age and time ; and from the universal prevalence of slavery among their heathen neighbours, it must often have been impracticable for the people, when seeking the service they needed, to obtain it otherwise than in the form of bond service. But as the persons acquired for the purpose must usually have been brought from heathen districts, they could not possibly be placed on a footing with the proper subjects of the Theocracy. Even, however, as strangers in a depressed condition, they were to be treated in a kind and considerate manner, as by those who, in their own persons or through their ancestors, had known the heart and experience of a stranger ;[1] and all proper facilities were besides afforded them, and reasonable encouragements held out, to their entering into the bond of the covenant, and merging their condition and prospects with those of the covenant people. If, after all, things were often not ordered as they should have been, who that calmly considers the actual position of affairs, would venture to affirm that it could have been made better by any statutory regulations given for authoritative enforcement ? These must limit themselves to the practically attainable —if they were not to produce other, and perhaps greater, evils than those they were intended to prevent.

[1] Ex. xxiii. 9.

6. The only remaining class of statutes and judgments calling for consideration here are those relating to the subject of marriage. The fundamental law on the subject merely declared, ' Thou shalt not commit adultery ;' but, as in all the other precepts of the Decalogue, so here, what should constitute a breach of the command was left to the moral instincts of mankind ; no specific description was given of adultery, nor was a right marriage relationship more nearly defined. But that marriage, according to its proper ideal, consisted of the life-union of one man and one woman, and that the violation of this union by sexual commerce with another party constituted adultery, was well enough understood in the earlier ages of the world, and especially among the covenant-people. ' The notion of matrimony has in the Old Testament, from the very commencement, been conceived in admirable purity and perfection. Already the wife of Adam is called " a help at his side," that is, a companion through life, with whom he coalesces into one being' (Gen. ii. 18–24).[1] And this being testified of man in his normal state, as he came pure and good from the hand of his Creator, clearly indicated for all coming time what in a family respect should be his normal condition—as is, indeed, formally stated in the inference drawn from the original fact : ' Therefore shall a man leave his father and his mother, and shall cleave to his wife (*his wife*, the one individual standing to him in that relation), and they shall be one flesh.' It was a great thing for the covenant-people to have had this view of the marriage relation placed so prominently forward in those sacred records which together formed their Thorah, or law. And we see it distinctly reflected, both in the dignity which is thrown around the wife in ancient Scripture, and in the prevalent

---

[1] Kalisch on Exod. xx. 13.

feeling in behalf of monogamy as the proper form of matrimonial life.   The two, indeed, hang inseparably together; for wherever polygamy exists, woman falls in the social scale.   But in the glimpses afforded us of family life in Israel, the women have much freedom and consideration accorded to them;[1] and those of them especially who are presented as the more peculiar types of their class, appear in an honourable light, as the fitting handmaids of their husbands, the rightful mistresses of the house.   Such, certainly, was Sarah in relation to Abraham, and Rebekah to Isaac; and similar examples, ever and anon throughout the history, rise into view of married women, who acted with becoming grace and dignity the part that properly belonged to them in the household— as the wife of Manoah, Hannah, Abigail the prudent and courteous spouse of Nabal, the Shunamite woman, who dealt so kindly with Elisha, and others of a like description. It was from no fancy musings, but from living exemplars such as these, that Solomon drew his noble portraiture, unequalled in any ancient writing, of the virtuous wife;[2] and pronounced such a wife to be a crown to her husband, and a gift bestowed on him from the Lord.[3]   So fully also did the lawgiver himself accord with these sentiments, that he allowed the new married man to remain at home for a year, free from military service and other public burdens, that he might gladden his wife;[4] and in the reverence and affection charged on children towards their parents, the mother ever has her place of honour beside the father.[5]

In perfect accordance with this regard for woman as the proper handmaid and spouse of man, there is evidence of a prevailing sense in men's minds in favour of mono-

---

[1] Ex. xv. 20 ; 1 Sam. xviii. 6, 7; Ps. lxviii. 25, etc.   [2] Prov. xxxi. 10-31.
[3] Prov. xii. 4; xix. 14.   [4] Deut. xxiv. 5.   [5] Ex. xx. 12; xxi. 17, etc.

gamy as the normal state of things, while polygamy
carried with it an aspect of disorder and trouble. It was
not by accident, but as an indication and omen of its real
character, that the latter first made its appearance in the
Cainite section of the human family, and has its memorial
in an address savouring of violence and blood.[1] How
strongly the mind of Abraham was set against any departure from the original order, is evident from his reluct-
ance to think of any one but Sarah as the mother of the
seed promised to him—only at last yielding to her advice
respecting Hagar, when no other way seemed open to him
for obtaining the seed he had been assured of—yet for
this also receiving palpable rebukes in providence to mark
the course that had been pursued as an improper violation
of the Divine order. We see this order beautifully kept
by Isaac, though his patience was long tried with the
apparently fruitless expectation of a promised seed ; no
thought of another spouse than Rebekah seems ever to
have been entertained by him ; nor did Jacob purpose
differently, till by deceit in the first instance, then by
artful cozening, he was drawn into connexions which
brought their recompenses of trouble after them. The
sons of Jacob, the patriarchal heads of the covenant-
people, are at least not known (with the exception, perhaps, of Simeon) to have possessed more at a time than
one wife ; such, more certainly, was the case with Moses,
as also with Aaron ; and in the rule laid down for the
priests, who might be regarded as the pattern-men for
Israel, it was ordained that each should take a virgin of
his own people for wife[2]—purposely contemplating but
one such connexion. In the later descriptions also of
rightly constituted and happy families, the wife is always
spoken of as the one spouse and mother of offspring ; and

---

[1] Gen. iv. 23, 24.   [2] Lev. xxiii. 14.

severe denunciations are occasionally uttered against unfair dealing toward her.[1]   So that, while there were
unquestionably notorious exceptions, especially among persons in high places, yet with the great mass of the covenant-people monogamy must have been the general rule,
and the one properly recognised order.

Holding this view of the marriage union, the greater
part of the statutes bearing on it in the books of Moses
present no difficulty ; their obvious design was to guard
its sanctity, and punish with unsparing rigour its deliberate violation.   Sexual commerce with another man's
wife rendered both parties liable to the penalty of
death;[2] and if the woman, instead of being actually married, was simply betrothed, the penalty remained the
same.[3]   A man who seduced a girl, and robbed her of
her chastity, was obliged to marry her, and pay fifty
shekels to her father;[4] on the other side, a married woman
who was only suspected of having improper intercourse
with another, was subjected to a severe and humiliating
test of her innocence;[5] and while suppositions are made of
men having sexual connexion with women, not betrothed
or married, and of entering into relationships not consistent
with strict monogamy, there is never any pronounced
sanction of their conduct, nor is the word concubine (*pile-
gesh*) once named in the Mosaic statutes as a kind of
recognised relation, separate from and superadditional to
that of wife.   The nearest thing to it, perhaps, is in
Ex. xxi. 8, where we have the case formerly referred to
of a man purchasing a maid-servant, under a pledge or
betrothal to take her to wife, or to give her in that capacity to his son.   As a maid-servant she was so far in his
power, that he could, if he so pleased, break his connexion

---

[1] Ps. xlv., cxxviii. ; Prov. xxxi. ; Mal. ii. 14.   [2] Lev. xx. 10 ; Deut. xxii. 22.
[3] Deut. xxii. 23.   [4] Deut. xxii. 28, 29.   [5] Num. v.

with her, and cease to keep her as a wife. Yet this is
spoken of as a moral wrong; it was 'dealing deceitfully
with her;' and, as already noticed under the statutes
about slavery, he lost his purchase-money — the maid
regained her freedom—a penalty so far being thus imposed
on such capricious behaviour. If, however, he should
retain the person so acquired for his wife, and at the same
time take another, the first was to be continued in her
rights—' her food, her raiment, and her duty of marriage'[1]
—as if still she alone properly stood in the relation of
spouse, and the other was superadded merely for show
or fleshly indulgence. But did not this also involve a
wrong, as well as the former mode of treatment? And
was it not an anomaly in legislation, that she should
have a certain compensation in the one case and none in
the other? Nay, that while the man was bound by the
nature of the marriage tie to be as one flesh with her, he
should become the same with another person?

Undoubtedly, a certain ground existed for such questions; and the spiritual guides of the community should
have made it clear, that men had no constitutional right
to act after such a fashion; that in doing so they violated
great moral principles; and that the guilt and the responsibility of such procedure were all their own—the judicial
statutes of the commonwealth only not interposing against
it by specific enactments and penalties. In its moral
bearings, the case was very nearly parallel with another,
which has been even more generally excepted against,
and by our Lord Himself was allowed to be justly liable
to exception; that, namely, of a divorce executed against
a wife for some cause less than actual infidelity.[2] This
was the point brought into consideration by the Pharisees;
but it is proper to notice—the rather so as the English

[1] Ex. xxi. 10.   [2] Deut. xxiv. 1-4.

Bible fails to give a quite correct translation of the original—that it was not the one which formed the direct or formal subject of the statute. Exactly rendered, the passage stands thus :—' When a man has taken a wife and married her, and it come to pass that she does not find favour in his sight, because he has found something of shame (or nakedness) in her, and he writes for her a bill of divorcement, and gives it into her hand, and sends her out of his house : and she has departed from his house, and gone and become another man's : and the latter husband hates her, and writes for her a bill of divorcement, and gives it into her hand, and sends her forth out of his house, or the latter husband has died that took her to wife :—The first husband that sent her away cannot return to take her for his wife after she has been defiled ; for that were abomination before Jehovah ; and thou shalt not pollute the land which Jehovah thy God gives thee as an inheritance.'

Thus read, it will be seen that the thing directly forbidden in the passage is simply the return of the divorced woman to be again the wife of the man who had first divorced her ; this would indicate a total looseness in regard to the marriage relationship, and was to be interdicted as an abomination which would utterly pollute the land. There is marked, indeed, a double or progressive defilement : the woman was defiled by her commerce with another man after being divorced from her first husband ; and to re-marry her, when so defiled, was to aggravate the pollution. All, however, that goes before this prohibitory part is simple narration : when a man marries a woman, and is displeased with her, and gives her a bill of divorce, and sends her from him, and another man does after the same manner—not as our translators, after Luther and some others, ' then let him write her a bill of divorce,' and so on. The words do not properly admit of this rendering; and on that very point may be said to turn the diversity of view exhibited in the Gospel narrative,[1] the one presented by the Pharisees, the other given by our Lord. They asked, ' Why did Moses *command* (ἐνετείλατο) to give a writing of divorcement, and to put away ?' The Lord replied, ' Moses, from respect (πρός) to the hardness of your hearts, *suffered* you (ἐπέτρεψεν ὑμῖν) to put away your wives :'—not a privilege to be enjoyed, or a duty to be discharged, but a permission or tolerance merely suffered to continue, because of Israel's participation in the evil of the times— their moral unfitness for a more stringent application of the proper rule. The permission in question, so far as the Mosaic legislation was concerned, went no further than not distinctly pronouncing upon the practice, or positively interdicting it. The practice, it is implied, was not unknown; in all probability it prevailed extensively among the corrupt nations among whom Israel was to dwell (since things greatly worse were of everyday occurrence among them); and in so far as any might adopt it, the judicial authorities were not empowered to prevent it—that is all; but whatever rashness, or contravention of the proper spirit and design of the marriage relation might be involved in it, this lay still with the conscience of the individual; he was answerable for it.

Viewed in respect to the grounds of his supposed procedure, there is a certain vagueness in the form of expression, which gave rise even in ancient times to very different modes of interpretation. The two chief words in the original (עֶרְוַת דָּבָר) certainly form a somewhat peculiar combination—strictly, *nakedness of a matter*, and as the term for nakedness is very commonly used for what is

---

[1] Matt. xix. 7, 8.

unbecoming or indecent, it may most naturally be regarded as indicating something distasteful or offensive in
that direction. The two great Jewish schools, those of
Hillel and Shammai, were divided in their opinions on
the subject; the school of Hillel included in the expression everything that might cause dissatisfaction in the
husband, even the bad cooking of his victuals,[1] while the
school of Shammai restricted it to uncleanness in the
conjugal sense—defilement of the marriage bed. That
something different, however, something less than this,
must have been intended, is evident alone from a comparison of other parts of the Mosaic legislation, which
ordained that a woman guilty of adultery should be, not
divorced, but put to death. It is also evident from the
explanation of our Lord, which ascribed this liberty of
divorce to the hardness of the people's hearts, and declared its inconsistence with the fundamental principle of
the marriage union, which admitted of a justifiable dissolution only by the death or the adulterous behaviour of
one of the parties. The truth appears to have lain between
the two extremes of the Jewish schools referred to; and
something short of actual impurity, yet tending in that
direction—something unbecoming, and fitted to create
dislike in the mind of the husband, or take off his affections from her—was understood to form, in the case supposed, an occasion .for dismissing a wife. It is also
supposed, that if such a step were taken, it would be
done in an orderly manner—not by a mere oral renounce-
ment, as among some Eastern nations, but by a formal
writing, which would usually require the employment of
a neutral person, and perhaps also the signature of
witnesses; that this writing should be deliberately put
into the woman's hand, and that she should thereafter

[1] See quotations in Lightfoot and Wetstein, on the passage in Matthew.

I

leave the house and go to another place of abode. These things, requiring some degree of deliberation and time, and so far tending to serve as a check on the hasty impulses of passion, are not directly enjoined (as already said), but presupposed as customary and indispensable parts of the process in question ; and the liberty thereby granted to the woman to ally herself to another man, coupled with the strict prohibition against a return to her first husband, were evidently intended as additional checks—reasons calling for very serious consideration before the consummation of an act which carried such consequences along with it.   Still, the act *could* be done ; no positive statute, capable of legal enforcement, was issued to prevent it ; and was not the licence thus granted, however arising, a sign of imperfection ?

Beyond doubt it was ; our Lord admits as much, when He accounts for it by the hardness of the people's hearts. But the person who should avail himself of the licence was not thereby justified—no more than in Christian times a wife, or a husband, who, by wilful abandonment or criminal behaviour, turns the marriage bond into a nullity. The apostle distinctly states, that a believing woman is not bound by the law of her husband, when he, remaining in unbelief and displeased with her procedure, has forced her into separation ;[1] he holds such a case not to be included in the general law of Christ respecting the perpetuity of marriage, except through death or fornication ; and, by parity of reason, the same must be held respecting parties, either of whom has become incapable of fulfilling matrimonial obligations, by being imprisoned or banished for life. There is here, at least, an approach to the Old Testament state of things, arising from the same cause, the hardness of the people's hearts ; and for

[1] 1 Cor. vii. 15.

the greater measure of licence, and consequently of practical imperfection adhering to the old, the question, in its moral bearings, resolves itself into a wider one—it touches the principle of progression in the Divine government; for if, in progress of time the light and privileges granted to men became much increased, should not the practical administration or discipline in God's house receive a corresponding elevation ? It stands to reason that it should; and hence certain things might be tolerated, in the sense of not being actively condemned, at an earlier stage of the Divine dispensations, which should no longer be borne with now; while still the standard of moral duty, absolutely considered, does not change, but is the same for men of every age.   There is the same relative difference, and the same essential agreement, between the church in its present and in its ultimate stage on earth—the period of millennial glory : things tolerated now, will not be then.

It is further to be borne in mind, that this, above all other points in the social system, was the one in respect to which Orientals stood at a relative disadvantage, and that feelings and practices were widely prevalent, which would render stringent regulations of a disciplinary kind worse than inoperative with a certain class of persons. There was comparatively little freedom of intercourse, prior to marriage, between the sexes, especially among those who were of age.   In many cases espousals were made *for* the young, rather than *by* them ; multitudes found themselves joined in wedlock who had scarcely ever seen each other—never, at least, mingled in familiar converse ; and often, too, they came from such different classes of society and spheres of life, especially when the wife was purchased as a bond-maid, or taken as a captive in war, that it would have been a marvel if estrangements, jealousies, tempers that repelled each other rather

than coalesced into a proper unity of heart and life, did
not at times appear as the result.   Still, doubtless, the
moral obligation remained, growing out of the essential
nature of the marriage relation, and no way invalidated
but enforced by the tenor of the Mosaic revelation, that
the parties should cleave one to another, and abstain
from all that might tarnish the sanctity of their union,
or mar the ends for which it was formed.   But in such a
state of things to exclude by positive and rigid enactment
any possibility of relief, even for such as did not in their
hearts realize that obligation, could only have tended to
produce a recoil in the opposite direction ; it would have
led them probably to resort to violent measures to rid
themselves of the hated object, or to employ such treatment as would have made death rather to be desired than
life.

The general regulations of the judicial code in respect
to marriage, as well as to other points of moment, thus
appear to admit of justification, when they are considered
with reference to the actual condition of the world.   But
when particular· cases are looked at, as they arose in the
subsequent history of the people, things are certainly
sometimes met with of which it is difficult to find any
adequate explanation :—the case, for example, of Elime-
lech, a Levite, and apparently a man of probity, not only
married to two wives without any specific reason assigned,
but one of these (Hannah) a person of distinguished piety,
and the subject of special direction and blessing from
Heaven ; much more the case of David, and that of his
highly gifted and honoured son Solomon, adding wife to
wife, and concubines to wives, without any apparent consciousness of wrong in the matter—yet all the while possessing the more peculiar endowments of God's Spirit; and
though receiving counsels, revelations, sometimes also re-

bukes from above, still never directly reproved for departing on this point from the right ways of the Lord. It is true, on the other hand, they had no proper warrant for what they did; they sinned against law—judicial as well as moral law; and it is also true, that painful results attended their course, such as might well be deemed practical reproofs.   Such considerations do help us a certain way to the solution—we can say no more; perplexing difficulties still hang around the subject, which cannot meanwhile be cleared satisfactorily away, only they are difficulties which relate to the practical administration of affairs, rather than to the Divine constitution of the kingdom.   There are certain things in other departments of which the same might be affirmed. But for all in the Old Economy that bears on it the explicit sanction of Heaven, though formally differing from what is now established, the principle so finely exhibited by Augustine in his contendings with the Manichees is perfectly applicable. Having compared the kingdom of God to a well-regulated house, in which for wise reasons certain things are permitted or enjoined at one time, which are prohibited at another, he adds: ' So is it with these persons who are indignant when they hear that something was allowed to good men in a former age, which is not allowed in this; and because God commanded one thing to the former, another thing to the latter, for reasons pertaining to the particular time, while each were alike obedient to the same righteousness :—And yet in a single man, and in a single day, and in a single dwelling, they may see one thing suiting one member, another a different one ; one thing permitted just now, and again after a time prohibited ; something allowed or ordered in a certain corner, which elsewhere is fitly forbidden or punished. Righteousness is not therefore various and mutable, is it ? But

the times over which it presides do not proceed in a
uniform manner, just because they *are* times. But men,
whose life on earth is short, because they are not able
intelligently to harmonize the causes of earlier times and
of other nations, of which they have not had cognizance,
with those wherewith they are familiar—though in one
body, or day, or house, they can easily see what would
suit a particular member, particular times, particular
offices or persons—take offence at the one, but fall in
with the other.'[1]

III. There yet remains to be noticed the third great
division of the Law—namely, *the rites and ceremonies
which more directly pertained to religion;* or, as it is
very commonly designated, *the Levitical code of worship
and observance.* In what are called the statutes and
judgments, which immediately succeeded the delivery of
the ten commandments, there is scarcely any reference
made to ordinances of this description. A few words
were spoken to the people respecting the kind of altar
they should erect,[2] implying that sacrifices were to form
an essential part of worship; also respecting the consecration of the first-born for special service to God, the
offering of the first-fruits, and the appearance of the
males annually at three stated feasts before the Lord;
but that was all. And it was only after the covenant
had been formally ratified and sealed with blood over

[1] Confes. L. III. c. 7. Sic sunt isti qui indignantur, cum audierint illo
sæculo licuisse justis aliquid, quod isto non licet justis; et quia illis aliud
præcipit Deus, istis aliud pro temporalibus causis, cum eidem justitiæ utrique
serviunt; cum in uno homine, et in uno die, et in unis ædibus videant aliud
alii membro congruere, et aliud jamdudum licuisse, post horam non licere;
quiddam in illo ungulo permitti aut juberi, quod in isto juste vetetur et vinde-
citur, etc.

[2] Ex. xx. 24-26.

' the ten words' from Sinai, with those supplementary statutes, that the ritual of the Levitical system, in its more distinctive form, came into existence. From its very place in the history, therefore, it is to be regarded, not as of primary, but only of secondary moment in the constitution of the Divine kingdom in Israel; not itself the foundation, but a building raised on the foundation, and designed, by a wise accommodation to the state of things then present, and by the skilful use of material elements and earthly relations, to secure the proper working of what really was fundamental, and render it more certainly productive of the wished for results. The general connexion is this : God had already redeemed Israel for His peculiar people, called them to occupy a near relation to Himself, and proclaimed to them the great principles of truth and duty which were to regulate their procedure, so that they might be the true witnesses of His glory, and the inheritors of His blessing. And for the purpose of enabling them more readily to apprehend the nature of this relation, and more distinctly realize the things belonging to it, the Lord instituted a visible bond of fellowship, by planting in the midst of their dwellings a dwelling for Himself, and ordering everything in the structure of the dwelling, the services to be performed at it, and the access of the people to its courts, after such a manner as to keep up right impressions in their mind of the character of their Divine Head, and of what became them as sojourners with Him in the land that was to be emphatically His own. In such a case, it was indispensable that all should be done under the express direction of God's hand ; for it was as truly a revelation of His will to the members of the covenant as the direct utterances of His mouth ; it must be made and ordered throughout according to the pattern of things presented

to the view of Moses ; while the people, on their part,
were to shew their disposition to fall in with the design,
by contributing the materials requisite for the purpose,
and fulfilling the offices assigned them.[1]

The connexion now indicated between the revelation of
law in the stricter sense, and the structure and use of the
sacred dwelling, comes out very strikingly in the description given of the tabernacle, which, after mentioning the
different kinds of material to be provided, begins first
with the ark of the covenant—the repository, as it might
equally be called, of the Decalogue, since it was merely a
chest for containing the tables of the law, and as such
was taken for the very seat or throne from which Jehovah
manifested His presence and glory.[2]   It was, therefore,
the most sacred piece of furniture belonging to the
Tabernacle—the centre from which all relating to men's
fellowship with God was to proceed, and to derive its
essential character.   To break this link of connexion
between the ceremonial and the moral, or to invert their
relative order as thus impressed from the first on the
very framework of the Tabernacle, had been virtually to
reject the plan of God, and frustrate the design contemplated in this part of His covenant arrangements.   For
those who practically ignored the revelation of truth and
duty in the Decalogue, there was properly no house of
God in Israel, no local throne, in connexion with which
they could hold communion with the living Head of the
Theocracy, and present acceptable worship before Him.
And for such as did acknowledge and own that revelation, there could be only this one.   The fundamental
truth, that Jehovah the God of Israel is one Lord, before
whom no other God can stand, nor even any form of
worship be allowed which might countenance the idea

[1] Ex. xxv. 2, 9, 40, etc.   [2] Ex. xxv. 21, 22.

of a diversity of nature or will in the supreme object of worship—this must have its expression in the absolute oneness of the place where Jehovah should put His name, and where, in the more peculiar acts of worship, He should be approached by the members of the covenant. The place itself might be different at one time from what it was at another; it was left, indeed, altogether undetermined at what particular point in the chosen territory, or even within what tribe, the sacred dwelling should have its location. This might change from one period to another; the dwelling itself also might, as the event proved, change its exterior form—pass from the humble tent to a gorgeous temple; but its unity must ever remain intact, so as to exclude the entrance of different theocratical centres, and thereby prevent what would, in those times, have been its inevitable sequence, the idea of a plurality of gods to be acknowledged and served.

When we proceed from the sacred dwelling itself to the institutions and services associated with it, we find only further proofs of the close connexion between the Levitical code and the Decalogue, and of the dependence of the one upon the other. ' The Levitical prescriptions,' says Weber excellently,'[1] follow the establishment of the covenant and its realization in the indwelling of Jehovah in Israel. They are not conditions, but consequences of the Sinaitic covenant. After Jehovah, in consequence of His covenant, had taken up His abode in Israel, and Israel must now dwell before Him, it was necessary to appoint the ordinances by which this intercourse should be carried on. Since Israel in itself is impure, and is constantly defiling itself, because its natural life stands under the power of sin, it cannot quite directly enter into fellowship with Jehovah; but what took place at Sinai

[1] ' Von Zorne Gottes,' p. 143.

must be ever repeating itself—it must first, in order to meet with Jehovah, undergo a purification.   Hence, one department of the ordinances of purification in the Levitical part of the Law.   But even when it has become pure, it still cannot approach Jehovah in any manner it may please, but only as He orders and appoints.   It will not, in spite of all purifications, be so pure, as that it could venture to approach immediately to the Lord.   The glory of the Lord enthroned above the cherubim would consume the impure.   Therefore must Israel come near to the Lord through priests whom He has Himself chosen ; and still not personally, but by means of the gifts which ascend in the fire and rise into Jehovah's presence, nor even so without the offerer having been first covered from the fiery glance of the Holy One through the blood of His victim.   This is the second part of the Levitical law.'[1]

It would be impossible here, and, besides, is not required for the purpose we have more immediately in view, to go into all the details which belong to a complete and

---

[1] In nothing is the imperfect and temporary nature of the Levitical economy more distinctly marked than in the appointment of a separate priesthood, which was rather necessitated by circumstances, and superinduced upon the original constitution of the Theocracy, than properly germane to its spirit. The priestly institution sprang out of the weaknesses and defections of the time (Ex. xix. 21-24, xxxii. ; Lev. xvi. ; Num. xvi., etc.), hence was destined to pass away when a higher spiritual elevation was reached by the people of God.   And this (as justly remarked by Ewald, Vol. II. p. 185) 'is the finest characteristic of the Old Testament, that even when its original elevated truths suffer through the violence of the times, it still always gives us to recognise the original necessary thought, just because in this community itself the consciousness of it could never be wholly lost.   At the last, there still stands prominently out, here and alone, the great gospel of Ex. xix. 5, which was there before any kind of hereditary priesthood, and continues after it, however firmly such a priesthood had for long ages rooted itself ; and even while it stood, the circumstance that this priesthood had always to tolerate by its side the freest prophetic function, prevented it from becoming altogether like an Egyptian or a Brahminical one.'

exhaustive treatment of the subject. It will be enough to indicate the leading points relating to it. There is, then, first of all, in the Levitical code, a *teaching element*, which leans upon and confirms that of the Decalogue. The grand lesson which it proclaimed through a multitude of rites and ordinances was, the pure, the good have access to God's fellowship and blessing ; the unholy, the wicked are excluded. But who constitute the one class, and who the other ? Here the Levitical code may be said to be silent—excepting in so far as certain natural and outward things were ingrafted into it as symbols of what, in the spiritual sphere, is good or evil. But for the things themselves which properly are such, it was necessary to look to the character of God, the Head of the Theocracy, and as such the type of all who belonged to it—to His character especially as revealed in that law of moral duty, which He took for the foundation of His throne and the centre of His government in Israel. *There* the great landmarks of right and wrong, of holy and unholy in God's sight, were set up ; and in the Levitical code they are presupposed, and men's attention called to them, by its manifold prescriptions concerning clean and unclean, defilement and purification. Thus, its divers washings and ever-recurring atonements by blood bespoke existing impurities, which were such because they were at variance with the law of righteousness imposed in the Decalogue. The Decalogue had pointed, by the predominantly negative form of its precepts, to the prevailing tendency in human nature to sin ; and in like manner the Levitical code, by making everything that directly bore on generation and birth a source of uncleanness, perpetually reiterated in men's ears the lesson, that corruption cleaved to them, that they were conceived in sin and brought forth in iniquity. The very institution of a separate order for immediate approach to God, and performing, in behalf of the community, the more sacred offices of religion, was, as already noticed, a visible sign of actual short-comings and transgressions among the people : it was a standing testimony, that they were not holy after the lofty pattern of holiness exhibited in the law of Jehovah's throne. The distinction, also, between clean and unclean in food, while it deprived them of nothing that was required either to gratify the taste or minister nourish-ment to the bodily life—granted them, indeed, what was best adapted for both—yet served as a daily monitor in respect to the spiritual dangers that encompassed them, and of the necessity of exercising themselves to a careful choosing between one class of things and another, re-minded them of a good that was to be followed, and of an evil to be shunned. And then there is a whole series of defilements springing from contact with what is emphatically the wages of sin—death, or death's livid image, the leprosy, which, wherever it alighted, struck a fatal blight into the organism of nature, and rendered it a certain prey to corruption :—things, the very sight and touch of which formed a call to humiliation, because carrying with them the mournful evidence, that, while sojourners with God, men still found themselves in the region of corruption and death, not in that brighter and purer region, where life, the life that is incorruptible and full of glory, for ever dwells.[1]

---

[1] The passages bearing on the particular subjects adverted to in the text are contained chiefly in Lev. x.-xv., Numb. xix. For detailed explanations respect-ing them, and the specific import of each as briefly indicated in the preceding remarks, *see* my ' Typology,' B. III. c. 8. Though some of the ordinances may now seem, in their didactic aspect, to be somewhat arbitrary, it would be quite otherwise for those who were accustomed to symbolical institutions ; if sincere and earnest, they would readily pass from the natural to the spiritual, and would find in them all the lesson expressed in regard to the class first mentioned (Lev. xi. 44), that they should be holy as God Himself was holy.

Viewed in this light, the law of fleshly ordinances was a great teaching institute—not by itself, but when taken (according to its true intent) as an auxiliary to the law of the two tables. Isolated from these, and placed in an independent position, as having an end of its own to reach, its teaching would have been at variance with the truth of things; for it would have led men to make account of mere outward distinctions, and rest in corporeal observances. In such a case it would have been the antithesis rather than the complement of the law from Sinai, which gave to the moral element the supreme place, alike in God's character, and in the homage and obedience He requires of His people. But, kept in its proper relation to that law, the Levitical code was for the members of the old covenant an important means of instruction; it plied them with warnings and admonitions respecting sin, as bringing defilement in the sight of God, and thereby excluding from His fellowship. That such, however, was the real design of this class of Levitical ordinances—that they had merely a subsidiary aim, and derived all their importance and value from the connexion in which they stood with the moral precepts of the Decalogue—is evident from other considerations than those furnished by their own nature and their place in the Mosaic legislation. It is evident, first, from this, that whenever the special judgments of Heaven were denounced against the covenant people, it never was for neglect of those ceremonial observances, but always for palpable breaches of the precepts of the Decalogue;[1] evident, again, from this, that whenever the indispensable conditions of access to God's house and abiding fellowship with His love are set forth, they are made to turn on

[1] Jer. vii. 22-31; Ezek. viii., xviii. 1-13; Hosea iv. 1-3; Amos ii. 4-9; Micah v., vi.

conformity to the moral precepts, not to the ceremonial observances ;[1] evident, yet again and finally, from this, that whenever the ceremonial observances were put in the foreground by the people, as things distinct from, and in lieu of, obedience to the moral precepts, the procedure was denounced as arbitrary, and the service rejected as a mockery.[2]

Beside the teaching element, however, which belonged to the Levitical institutions, there was another and still more important one, which we may call their *mediating design*. Here also they stood in a kind of supplementary relation to the law of the ten commandments, but a relation which implied something more than a simple re-echoing of their testimony respecting holiness and sin— something, indeed, essentially different. For that law, in revealing the righteous demands of God, from its very nature could make no allowance or provision for the sins and shortcomings by which those demands were dishonoured ; it could but threaten condemnation, and, with its cry of guilt under the throne of God, terrify from His presence those who might venture to approach. But the Levitical code, with its mediating priesthood, its rites of expiation, and ordinances of cleansing, had for its very object the effecting of a restored communion with God for those who through sin had forfeited their right to it. While it by no means ignored the reality or the guilt of sin—nay, assumed this as the very ground on which it rested, and so far coincided with the Decalogue—it, at the same time, secured for those who acknowledged their sin and humbled themselves on account of it, a way of reconciliation and peace with God. The more special means for effecting this was through sacrifice—the blood of slain

[1] Ps. xv., xxiv., l., etc.
[2] 1 Sam. xv. 22 ; Ps. xl. 7, li. ; Isa. i. 2 ; Micah vi. 8.

victims—the life-blood of an irrational creature, itself unconscious of sin, being accepted by God in His character of Redeemer for the life of the sinner. A mode of satisfaction no doubt in itself unsatisfactory, since there was no just correspondence between the merely sensuous life of an unthinking animal and the higher life of a rational and responsible being ; in the strict reckoning of justice the one could form no adequate compensation for the other. But in this respect it was not singular ; it was part of a scheme of things which bore throughout the marks of relative imperfection. The sanctuary itself, which was of narrow dimensions and composed of earthly and perishable materials, how poor a representation was it of the dwelling-place of Him who fills heaven and earth with His presence ! And the *occasional* access of a few ministering priests into the courts of that worldly sanctuary—an access into its *inmost* receptacle by one person only, and by him only once a year—how imperfect an image of the believer's freedom of intercourse with God, and habitual consciousness of His favour and blessing ! Such things might be said to lie upon the surface, and could not fail, as we shall see, to give a specific direction to the minds of the more thoughtful and spiritual worshippers. But there still was, in the structure of the tabernacle, and the regulated services of its worship, a provisional arrangement of Divine ordination by which transgressors, otherwise excluded, might obtain the forgiveness of their sins, and enjoy the blessings of communion with Heaven. Through this appointed channel God did in very deed dwell with men on earth ; and men, who would have been repelled with terror by His fiery law, could come nigh to His seat, and in spirit dwell as in the secret of His presence.[1]

---

[1] For the specific ordinances, I must again refer to my 'Typology,' Vol. II.

One can easily see, however, that the very imperfections attendant on this state of things required that its working be very carefully guarded. Definite checks and limits must be set to the possibility of obtaining the blessings of forgiveness. For, had an indefinite liberty been given to make propitiation for sin, and to wash away the stains of its defilement, how certainly would it have degenerated into a corrupt and dangerous license ! The Levitical code would have become the foster-mother of iniquity. The ready access it gave to the means of purification would have encouraged men to proceed on their evil courses, assured that if they should add sin to sin they might also bring victim after victim to expiate their guilt. Therefore, the right and privilege of expiation were limited to sins of infirmity, or such as spring from the weakness and imperfection of nature in a world abounding with temptation ; while sins committed with a high hand, that is, in open and deliberate violation of the great precepts of the Decalogue, were appointed only to judgment, as subversive of the very ends of the Theocracy.[1] So that here, again, the Levitical code of ordinances leant on the fundamental law of the Decalogue, and did obeisance to its supreme authority. Only they who devoutly recognised this law, and in their conscience strove to walk according to its precepts, had any title to an interest in the provisions sanctioned for the blotting out of transgression. Then, as now, ' to walk in darkness,' or persistently adhere to the practice of iniquity, was utterly incompatible with having fellowship with God.[2]

One thing further requires to be noted respecting the Levitical institutions, which is, that while under one aspect they constituted the rights and privileges of the

[1] Lev. iv. 2 ; Num. xv. 22-30.   [2] 1 John i. 6.

Israelite, under another they added to his obligations of duty. They took the form of law, as well as the Decalogue, and, wilful violators of its prescriptions, were not less amenable to justice than those who were guilty of gross immorality.[1] And the reason is obvious : for these Levitical ordinances of purification bore on them the authority of God as well as those which related to the strictly moral sphere, and to set them at nought was to dishonour God ; it was also to make light of the means He had appointed—the only available means—of having the guilt of transgression covered, which therefore remained unforgiven, yea aggravated, by the despite that was done to the riches of God's mercy. Yet, practically, the difficulty and the danger did not lie much in this particular direction. Though guilt was no doubt frequently incurred by neglecting the provisions and requirements of the Levitical code, yet this was sure to be preceded and accompanied by the far greater guilt of violating the fundamental precepts of the Decalogue. And, hence, it was always guilt of this latter description which drew down the heaviest judgments.

If anything, indeed, has more clearly discovered itself than another, from the whole of this investigation, it is the fundamental character of the Decalogue—its pre-eminent and singular place in the Revelation of Law. This was itself emphatically THE LAW ; and all, besides, which bore that name was but of secondary rank, and derived its proper value and significance from the relation in which it stood to the other. Hence, the prominent regard, as in due time will appear, which, in the use of the term *Law* by our Lord and His apostles, was had to the moral precepts of the Decalogue. Hence, also, the groundlessness of the statement, which has been often made by modern writers, that the distinction, with which

[1] Lev. vii. 20, xvii. 4, 14 ; Num. ix. 13.

K

we are so familiar, between moral and ceremonial, was not
so sharply drawn in the Books of Moses, and that precepts of both kinds are there often thrown together, as
if, in Jewish apprehension, no very material difference
existed between them.   It is easy to pick out a few
quotations which give a plausible support to such a view.
But a careful examination of the subject as a whole, and
of the relation in which one part stands to another, yields
a quite different result.   And Mr Maurice does not put
it too strongly when he says, ' The distinction between
these commandments and the mere statutes of the Jewish
people has strongly commended itself to the conscience of
modern nations, not because they have denied the latter
to have a divine origin, but because they have felt that
the same wisdom which adapted a certain class of commands to the peculiarities of one locality and age, must
intend a different one for another.   The ten commandments have no such limitation. . . .   All the subsequent legislation, though referred to the same authority,
is separated from these.   All the subsequent history was
a witness to the Jew, that in the setting up of any god
besides the Unseen Deliverer ; in the fancy that there
could be any likeness of Him in heaven above, or in the
earth beneath, or in the waters under the earth ; in the
loss of awe for His name ; in the loss of the distinction
between work and rest as the ground of man's life, and
as having its archetype in the Divine Being, and as
worked by Him into the tissue of the existence of His
own people ; in the loss of reverence for parents, for life,
for marriage, for property, for character ; and in the
covetous feeling which is at the root of these evils, lay
the sources of political disunion, and the loss of all personal dignity and manliness."[1]

[1] 'Moral and Metaphysical Philosophy,' p. 13.

LECTURE V.

THE POSITION AND CALLING OF ISRAEL AS PLACED UNDER THE
COVENANT OF LAW, WHAT PRECISELY INVOLVED IN IT—FALSE
VIEWS ON THE SUBJECT EXPOSED—THE MORAL RESULTS OF THE
ECONOMY, ACCORDING AS THE LAW WAS LEGITIMATELY USED
OR THE REVERSE.

HAVING now considered the nature of the Law as
revealed from Sinai, and the relation in which both
the judicial statutes and the Levitical ordinances stood
to it, our next line of investigation naturally turns on
Israel's position under it; in which respect such questions as these press themselves on our regard: How did
the being placed under the covenant of law of itself tend
to affect the real well-being of Israel as a people? or
their representative character as the seed of blessing, the
types of a redeemed church? How far did the proper
effects of the covenant realize themselves in their history,
or others not proper—the result of their own neglect and
waywardness—come in their stead? And did the covenant, in consequence of the things, whether of the one
sort or the other, which transpired during its continuance,
undergo any material alterations, or remain essentially
the same till the bringing in of the new covenant by the
mission and work of Christ?

1. In entering upon the line of thought to which such
questions point, we are struck at the outset with a somewhat remarkable diversity in the representations of Scrip-

ture itself respecting the natural tendency and bearing of the law on those who were subject to it. Coming expressly from Jehovah in the character of Israel's Redeemer, it cannot be contemplated otherwise than as carrying a benign aspect, and aiming at happy results. Moses extolled the condition of Israel as on this very account surpassing that of all other people : ' What nation is there so great, who hath God so nigh unto them, as the Lord our God is in all things that we call upon him for ?   And what nation is there so great, that hath statutes and judgments so righteous as all this law, which I set before you this day.'[1]   The very last recorded utterance of the legislator was a rapturous exclamation over Israel's now enviable condition and joyful prospects : ' Happy art thou, O Israel ; who is like unto thee, O people saved by the Lord !'[2]   And the sentiment is re-echoed under various forms in other parts of ancient Scripture, especially in the Psalms.   Among the great acts of mercy and loving-kindness for which the Lord is praised in Ps. ciii., is the fact that ' He made known His ways unto Moses, His acts unto the children of Israel ;' or, as it is put in another Psalm, ' He shewed His statutes and His judgments to Israel ; He hath not dealt so with any nation.'[3]   And then the law itself, and the blessedness arising from a just acquaintance with its precepts, are celebrated in the very strongest terms: ' The law of the Lord is perfect, converting (quickening) the soul : the testimony of the Lord is sure, making wise the simple : the statutes of the Lord are right, rejoicing the heart : the commandment of the Lord is pure, enlightening the eyes.'[4]   ' O how I love thy law ! it is my meditation all the day.'   ' I will never forget thy precepts, for

---

[1] Deut. iv. 7, 8,   [2] Deut. xxxiii. 29.
[3] Ps. cxlvii. 19, 20.   [4] Ps. xix. 7, 8.

with them thou hast quickened me ;' and, generally,
' Great peace have they who love thy law, and nothing
shall offend them.'[1]   But another set of passages appear
to point in the very opposite direction ; they represent
the law as a source of terror or trouble—a bondage from
which it is true liberty to escape : ' The law worketh
wrath ;' ' by the law is the knowledge of sin ;' ' the
strength of sin is the law ;' and referring distinctly to the
law in the stricter sense—as indeed these other passages
also do—the law engraven in stones—the apostle designates it ' the ministration of condemnation and of death.'[2]

It is clear, on a moment's reflection, that such diverse,
antagonistic representations could not have been given of
the law in the same respects, or with the same regard to
its direct and primary aim.   If both alike were true—as
we cannot doubt they were, being alike found in the
volume of inspiration—it must be from the law having
been contemplated in one of them from a different point
of view, or with regard to different uses and applications
of it from what it was in the other.   At present, as we
have to do with the place of the law in the Old Testament economy, it is more especially the happier class of
representations which come into consideration ; they may
fitly, at least, be viewed as occupying the foreground,
while the others may come into particular notice afterwards.

2. Now, the view which we have seen reason to take
of the nature of the law as revealed through Moses, will
render it unnecessary to do more than make a passing reference to such modes of explanation as would resolve everything in the covenant with Israel into merely outward
and carnal elements—would make the law, as delivered

[1] Ps. cxix. 93, 97, 165.
[2] Ro. iii. 20, iv. 15 ; 1 Cor. xv. 56 ; 2 Cor. iii. 7, 9 ; Gal. iv. 1-3, v. 1-3.

to them at Sinai, a comparatively easy and lightsome thing—satisfied if it could but secure outward worshippers of Jehovah, and respectable citizens of the commonwealth. The law, we are told by writers of this class, was one that dealt only 'in negative measures:' 'the precepts were negative that the obedience might be the more possible;' and he was 'the good man who could not be excused to have done what the law forbade, he who had done the fewest evils.' So Jeremy Taylor,[1] and at more length Spencer, in his learned work on the Laws of the Hebrews, who endeavoured to shew that the one great end of the Decalogue, as well as of the ceremonial law, was to extirpate idolatry, and the fruits that more immediately spring from it.[2] Warburton improved on it a little, by turning the negative respecting idolatry into a positive respecting God; but that was all. The primary end of the law (moral and ceremonial alike) according to him was, 'not to keep the Israelites from idolatry,' but 'to preserve the memory of the one God in an idolatrous world till the coming of Christ,'[3]—a distinction, one might almost say, without a difference, and of use only as a polemical weapon in the hands of its author. Michaelis followed in the same track, and could find nothing in the first part of the Decalogue but a provision for the acknowledgment and worship of one God, in opposition to the idolatries of heathenism, nor in the second—not even as condensed into the positive form of love to one's neighbour as one's-self—but a dry injunction to have respect to one another's civil rights.[4] And to mention no more (though many more might be noticed), we meet, in a comparatively late work, with such assertions as the following respecting the Old Covenant, which

---

[1] 'On Conscience,' B. II. c. 2, sec. 4; c. 3, sec. 2.   [2] L. I. c. 2.
[3] 'Leg. of Moses,' B. V. sec. 2.   [4] 'Laws of Moses,' secs. 34, 72.

had the law of the two tables for its basis, that 'it had nothing whatever to do with any, except with the nation of Israel, and nothing whatever with any mere individual in that nation ; that it was made with the nation collectively, and was entirely temporal ;' that its whole substance lay in this, God promised to give the land of Canaan to the nation of Israel, so long, but 'only so long, as the nation collectively acknowledged Jehovah as the one God.' Hence the holiness required was 'quite irrespective of individual righteousness ;' Israel was still the holy nation, whatever sins might be harboured in its bosom, so long as it did not cease from the formal recognition and worship of Jehovah.[1]

We appeal from all such representations to the plain reading of the law itself (as we have endeavoured to give it), looked at, as it should be, in its historical connection and its general bearings. The blinding influence of theory will obscure even the clearest light ; but it is scarcely possible that any unbiassed mind should apply itself earnestly to the subject, and take up with so partial and meagre a view of what, not in one place merely, but in all Scripture, is made known to us as distinctively God's revelation of law to men. The immediate circumstances that led to it—the special acts and announcements which might be said to form its historical introduction, are alone sufficient to compel a higher estimate of the revelation. The people had just been rescued, it was declared, from Egypt, had been borne by God on eagles' wings, and brought to Himself—for what ? Not simply that they might acknowledge His existence, or preserve His memory, in the face of surrounding idolatry, but that they might 'obey His voice and keep His covenant,' and so be to Him 'a kingdom of priests and an holy nation.'[2]

---

[1] Johnstone's 'Israel after the Flesh,' pp. 7, 87.   [2] Ex. xix. 4-6.

Peculiar nearness to God in position, and, as the proper
consequence and result of that, knowing and reflecting
His character, entering into His mind and will, striving
to be holy as He is holy—this was the end to which all
was directed—the purpose, also, for which they stood
before God as a separate people, and were gathered around
Sinai to hear the law from His mouth :—And if that law
had been aught else than a real disclosure of the mind of
God as to what he demands of His people toward Himself and toward each other in the vital interests of truth
and righteousness, it had been (we need not hesitate to
say it) beneath the occasion ; failing, as it should have
done, to present the proper ideal, which it was Israel's
calling to endeavour constantly to have realized.   The
formal acknowledgment, forsooth, of Jehovah as the
one true God, and paying due respect to one another's
civil rights !   And that, too, chiefly in the general,
without any distinct bond of obligation on the individual
conscience, quite irrespective of personal righteousness !
Was this a thing so important in itself, so well-pleasing
in the eyes of the pure and heart-searching Jehovah, that
the law requiring it should have been laid as the very
foundation of His throne in Israel, and that the period of
its promulgation should have formed a marked era in the
history of His dispensations among men ?   The thought
is not for a moment to be entertained.   The eternal God
could not so abnegate or demean Himself—no more for
any temporal purpose than for one directly bearing on
the interests of eternity ; for in such a matter nothing is
determined by the mere element of duration.   He could
not, in consistence with His own unchangeable character,
either ask or accept what should be other than a fit
expression of the homage that is supremely due to Him,
and the love that willingly yields itself to His require-

ments.[1] This, also, is what a fair examination of the law itself has impressed upon our minds.

Were it necessary to say more, we might add, that there is a conclusive historical reason against the view of the law, and the polity founded on it, to which we have been adverting. According to it, the religion of the Old Covenant had been nothing more than a kind of bald theism, adapted to the circumstances of the time—a sort of natural religion, enshrined amid a cumbrous framework of ordinances and political regulations, which partly humoured the semi-heathenish state of the people, and partly kept them off from the more flagrant pagan corruptions. Had that, however, been all, the Jews of our Lord's time should have been presented to our view as the best exemplars and most satisfactory results of the Sinaitic covenant. For in what age of its continuance was the doctrine of the unity more strictly adhered to ? or when were the institutions connected with it more generally and punctually observed ? It will not do to say, by way of explanation, that in rejecting Jesus they set themselves against the very Head of the Theocracy, and so ran counter to its primary design ; for it was not in that character that He formally appeared and claimed the homage of men, but rather as Himself the living embodiment of its great principles, the culmination of its spiritual aims. It was the *practical* oversight of these which constituted the fatal error of those later Jews ; and

---

[1] 'To know and to serve God, that is religion, whether it be with a view to the present life or to the next, and whatever inducements or encouragements He may choose to supply. The greatest rewards of endless felicity sought, or expected, in any other service than His, cannot consecrate that service, nor make it a part of essential religion. In every original right of moral authority, the essence of the obligation, and the virtue of compliance with it, are independent of the kind, or the degree, of the retribution annexed.'—*Davison* ' *On Prophecy*,' Dis. IV.

the *theoretical* oversight of the same, in any view that may be taken of the covenant of law under which they were placed, must be equally fatal to its acceptance.

2. Belonging almost to the opposite pole of theological sentiment, writers of the Cocceian school have sometimes gone to a different extreme, and have given, if not a false, yet an artificial and perplexing, rather than a plain and Scriptural view of Israel's position under the law. They were themselves embarrassed by the habit of ranging everything pertaining to covenant engagements under one of two heads—the covenant of works, and the covenant of grace. They differ, however, to some extent in their mode of representation—all, indeed, holding that the ten commandments, in which the covenant of law more peculiarly stood, was for substance the same with the covenant of works; in other words, embodied that perfect rule of rectitude, on conformity to which hung man's original possession of life and blessing; but differing as to the precise form or aspect under which they supposed this rule of rectitude to have been presented to Israel in the Sinaitic covenant. Cocceius himself, in his mode of representation, did not differ materially from the view of Calvin, and that generally of the Reformed theologians. He held that the Decalogue was not formally proposed to the Israelites as the covenant of works; that it proceeded from Jehovah as the God and Redeemer of Israel, implying that He had entered with them into a covenant of grace; that the covenant of law was given to subserve that covenant of grace, pointing out and enjoining what was necessary to be done, in order that the children of the covenant might see how they should live, if they were to enjoy its blessings—precisely as the evangelical precepts and exhortations in the New Testament do in subservience to the Gospel. Its language, he thinks,

was not, I demand that you do these precepts, and so live (this had been to mock men with impossibilities); but, I have called you to life, and now, laying aside fear, come and hear my voice.[1]   Indeed, one might say Cocceius leant rather too much to the assimilation of the law to the form of things in the New Testament Scriptures. Witsius, the more systematic expounder of the Cocceian theology, discriminates more exactly; he finds in the precepts of the Decalogue the moral elements of the covenant of works, and in the terror and majesty with which they were delivered, a sort of reduplication (*ingeminationem*) of the covenant of works; but still they were not proposed in the character of that covenant, as if through obedience to its precepts the people were to attain to life; they only assumed somewhat of the appearance of the covenant of works to convince the people of their sinfulness, and drive them out of themselves to look for the hope of salvation in Christ.   But with all this it in reality assumed and was founded upon the covenant of grace already made with Israel—Israel, as partakers in such a covenant of grace, promising to God a sincere observance of the precepts imposed, and God in turn promising to accept and bless such observance, though in itself imperfect.[2]   A different view, however, came to

[1] Animad. de Vet. Test. Quaest. 33; also De Foed., chap. xi. 49-58.

[2] De Œcon. Foederum, Lib. IV. chap. iv. secs. 47-54.   It is astonishing how Mr Johnstone, if he really had the entire work of Witsius in his hands, could have so grossly misrepresented his views on this subject.   He says, p. 3, 'It is the usual, but an utterly unfounded conception of the old covenant, that "it points out the way in which, by means of works, salvation is obtained;" that "the form of this covenant is, The man which doeth these things shall live by them, and that in it there is a promise of eternal life, consisting in the immediate fruition of God."   I do not hesitate to say, that there is not the shadow of an authority for this all but universal view of the old covenant.'   The authority referred to, and briefly quoted, for this sweeping declaration, is Witsius, De Œcon. Foederum, Lib. I. chap. i. sec. 15.   But there Witsius is treating, not of the old covenant properly so called, but of the covenants

prevail pretty generally among the English Puritans, who
generally belonged to the Cocceian school, and found its
expression in a book which attained to great popularity,
and became the occasion of a prolonged controversy—
Fisher's 'Marrow of Modern Divinity.' Here it is broadly
asserted, and at some length maintained, that the ten
commandments were formally delivered on Mount Sinai
as the covenant of works, or as a renewal of the Adamic
covenant—not, however, as if the Israelites were expected
to fulfil it, and justify themselves by deeds of law—but
for this, and no other end, 'that man being thereby convinced of his weakness, might flee to Christ. So that it
was renewed only to help forward and introduce another
and a better covenant.'[1] And various authors are referred
to as having previously adopted the same style of representation (in particular Preston, Pemble, Walker). Boston,
who was a more correct theologian, and a more discriminating writer, than the author of the 'Marrow,' in his
notes to that work admits that the view in question was
held by 'some late learned writers,' but gave it only a
qualified approval. He conceives that *both* covenants
were delivered on Mount Sinai to the Israelites : ' *First*,
the covenant of grace made with Abraham, contained in
the preface, repeated and promulgated there to Israel, to
be believed and embraced by faith, that they might be
saved; to which were annexed the ten commandments,
given by the Mediator Christ, the head of the covenant,
as a rule of life to His covenant people. *Secondly*, the

abstractly—namely, of works and grace. It is at a much later part of his
treatise that he comes to discuss the old covenant, or covenant of law, and
which, as we have said, he holds to have been neither formally a covenant of
works nor a covenant of grace. As for the assertion that the view ascribed to
Witsius is nearly universal, we can only designate it as for present times a
great exaggeration.

[1] Part I. chap. ii.

covenant of works made with Adam, contained in the same ten commands, delivered with thunderings and lightnings, the meaning of which was afterwards cleared by Moses describing the righteousness of the law and the sanction thereof, as the original perfect rule of righteousness to be obeyed ; and yet they were no more bound thereby to seek righteousness by the law than the young man was by our Saviour's saying to him, If thou wilt enter into life, keep the commandments.' Thus, he adds, ' there is no confounding of the two covenants of grace and works.'[1]

I fear, in saying this, the good man forgot at what period it was in the Divine dispensations that the law was given from Sinai. It was still the comparatively dim twilight of revelation, when the plan of God could be seen only in a few broken lines and provisional arrangements, which tended to veil, even while they disclosed the truth. The men of that age could not so easily distinguish between the two aspects of law here presented, even if they had got some hint of the diversity ; but, as matters actually stood, it could scarcely be said, that the two were ever distinctly before them. No one can read

---

[1] Substantially the same representation is given by Colquhoun, ' Law and Grace,' chap. I. sec. 2 ; Beart's 'Eternal Law and Everlasting Gospel ;' and, to name no more, in the work of the late Dr R. Gordon, ' Christ in the Old Testament,' Vol. I. p. 385, seq. It is there said, ' The giving of the law was thus a new exhibition of the covenant of works—a declaration of what was necessarily incumbent on men, if they expected to secure for themselves the favour and fellowship of God ;' while, shortly after, it is denied that ' the law was prescribed to Israel as the covenant of works, so as that their acceptance with God absolutely depended on their fulfilling the condition of that covenant.' This ground of acceptance is referred to the previous exhibition of grace and mercy. What we except to in such a statement is, that it is fitted to create confusion, to embarrass and perplex people's minds. It was adopted by the writers in question very much from the view they took of the passages, Rom. x. 5, Gal. iii. 12, where the righteousness of works is described in language derived from the writings of Moses. But see the exposition on Rom. x. 5, in Supplement.

the history of the transaction without being convinced, that in whatever character the law was declared to the Israelites and established with them as a covenant, it carried with it the bond of a sacred obligation which they were to strive to make good ; and of any other meaning or design, either on God's part in imposing, or on their part in accepting the obligation, the narrative is entirely silent.

3. But a class—one can scarcely say of theologians (for the name would be misapplied to persons who in most things make so complete a travesty of Scripture)—a class, however, of very dogmatic writers (the Plymouthists) have recently pushed to its full extreme the view of the law just stated as the covenant of works—not, like the later Cocceians, as a kind of side view or secondary aspect which might also be taken of it, but as its direct, formal, and only proper character. ' Law,' we are told by one of them, ' was a distinct and definite dispensation of God, according to which life was promised consequent on obedience, and had its whole nature from this, a righteousness characterized by this principle : obedience first, then life therein, righteousness.'[1] This is given as the import of ' the reasoning of the apostles' on the subject ; and another of the party, in his ' Notes on Exodus,' interprets the narrative respecting the giving of the law so as to make it tell in support of the same view. When God, in the nineteenth chapter of Exodus, delivered to Moses on the mount the tender and touching address, in which He related what He had done for the people, what He now called them to be in honour and blessing, and how, in order to maintain and enjoy this, they must be ready to obey His voice and keep His covenant ; and when Moses, after hearing the words, went at God's bidding and

---

[1] Darby ' On the Law,' p. 22.

reported them to the people, and received for answer, 'All that the Lord hath spoken we will do'—this, we are told, was a virtual renunciation, on the part of Israel, of their blessed position : 'instead of rejoicing in God's holy promise, they undertook the most presumptuous vow that mortal lips could utter. Nor was this the language of a few vain, self-confident spirits, who presumed to single themselves out from the whole congregation. No, "All the people answered together, and said, All that the Lord hath spoken we will do." '[1] And then we are informed, that because of this proud and presumptuous spirit, the Lord immediately gave 'a total alteration to the aspect of things :' He wrapt Himself up in the cloud of thick darkness, assumed an appearance of terrible majesty, and issued that fiery law, the object of which was to shew them how incompetent they were to fulfil what they had undertaken, to reveal what on their own assumption they ought to be, and place them under the curse for not being it.

If this were the correct reading of the matter, why, we naturally ask, should God Himself have taken the initiative in this so-called abandonment of the covenant of promise ? for it was He who sent Moses to the people with the words, which manifestly sought to evoke an affirmative reply. Why, after such a reply was returned, did it call forth no formal rebuke, if so be it displayed an intolerable arrogancy and presumption ? and the reason, the only reason, assigned for the Lord's declared intention to appear presently in a thick cloud, why should this have been simply that the people might hear His voice, and believe Moses for ever ?[2] Why, also, at the rehearsal of the transactions in the book of Deuteronomy, did God say, ' The people had well said all they had spoken,' and

[1] 'Notes on Exodus,' by A. M., p. 232.   [2] Ex. xix. 9.

only further breathed the wish, ' O that there were such
an heart in them, that they would fear me, and keep all
my commandments always, that it might be well with
them and with their children for ever?'[1]   Why, above all, if
the case were as now represented, should the formalities of
a covenant transaction have been gone through in the name
of God over the words uttered by Him and responded
to by the people—based, as it must in that case have
been, on what were known on the one side to be impossible conditions, and on the other palpable delusions and
lies ?   And why, after all, should Israel not the less, but
the more rather, have been pronounced most exalted in
privilege, peculiarly destined to honour and blessing ?[2]
Nothing, surely, can be more fitted to shake our confidence in the transparent simplicity and faithfulness of
God's recorded dealings with men, than to be taught, as
by a look from behind the scenes, that what wears the
aspect of a solemn transaction, was in reality but a formal
display or an empty mockery.   And such, beyond all
reasonable doubt, would be the effect with the great
majority of minds, if the mode of representation before
us should come to be accepted as valid.

4. But it rests upon no solid ground, and has more the
character of an interpolation thrust into the sacred record
than a fair and natural interpretation of its contents.
The revelation of law from Sinai did not come forth in
independence, as if it were to lay the foundation of something altogether new in men's experience ; nor did it
proceed from God in His character as the God of nature,
exercising His right to impose commands of service on the
consciences of His creatures, which with no other helps
and endowments than those of nature, they were required
with unfailing rectitude to fulfil ;—not, therefore, when

----

[1] Deut. v. 28, 29.   [2] Ex. xxiii. 27-29 ; Deut. vi. xxxiii.

when made to take the form of a covenant, was it with
the view of exacting what must be given as the prior and
indispensable conditions of life and joy?   No, the history
of Israel knows nothing of law except in connection with
promise and blessing.[1]   It was as the Redeemer of Israel
that God spake the words—as in a special sense Israel's
God ('I am Jehovah thy God')—a relation which, we
have our Lord's explicit testimony for asserting, carries
in its bosom the dowry of life eternal;[2] so that grace
here also took precedence of law, life of righteousness;
and the covenant of law, assuming and rooting itself in
the prior covenant of grace, only came to shut the heirs
of promise up to that course of dutiful obedience toward
God, and brotherly kindness toward each other, by which
alone they could accomplish the higher ends of their calling.   In *form* merely was there anything new in this, not
in *principle*.   For what else was involved in the command
given to Abraham, at the establishment of the covenant of
promise, to have it sealed with the ordinance of circumcision—the symbol of a sanctified nature and a holy life?
Nay, even before that, the same thing in effect was done,
when the Lord appeared to Abraham and said, 'I am the
Almighty God, walk before me and be thou perfect,'[3]—a
word which (as Cocceius justly observes)[4] was comprehensive of all true service and righteous behaviour.   But an
advance *was* made by the entrance of the law over such
preceding calls and appointments, and it was this—the
obligation to rectitude of life resting upon the heirs of
promise was now thrown into a categorical and imperative
form, embracing the entire round of moral and religious
duty; yet, not that they might by the observance of this
work themselves into a blissful relation to God, but that,

[1] Harless, 'Ethik.,' sec. 13.   [2] Luke xx. 37, 38.
[3] Gen. xvii. 1.   [4] De Foed., c. xi. sec. 338.

L

as already standing in such a relation, they might walk worthy of it, and become filled with the fruits of righteousness, which alone could either prove the reality of their interest in God, or fulfil the calling they had received from Him.

5. It is true, the people who entered into the bond of the covenant, as thus proposed, could not of themselves keep the precepts of the law ; and the shameful backsliding which took place so shortly after they had formally undertaken to do all that was commanded, but too plainly shewed how little they yet understood either the height of their obligations, or the degree of moral strength that would be required to meet them. It was but gradually, and through a succession of painful and trying experiences, that the truth in this respect could work itself into their minds. The law undoubtedly was exceeding broad. In its matter, that is, in the reach and compass of its requirements, it did (as the writers formerly referred to maintained) comprise the sum of moral excellence—the full measure of goodness that man as man is bound to yield to God and his fellow-men. It was impossible that God, in His formal revelation of law to His people, could propound less as the aim of their spiritual endeavours ; for conformity to His mind and will, to be made holy or good after the type of that which He Himself is, was the ultimate design contemplated in His covenant arrangements. But in these arrangements He stood also pledged to His people as the author of life and blessing ; and that mercy and loving-kindness which prompted Him so to interpose in their behalf, and which (as if to prevent misapprehension) He embodied even in His revelation of law, could not possibly be wanting, if earnestly sought for the ministration of such help as might be needed to enable them to give, though not a

faultless, yet a hearty and steadfast obedience.   Was not the whole tabernacle service, springing from the covenant of Sinai as its centre, and ever circling around it, a standing and palpable proof of this ?   Through the rites and ordinances of that service, access continually lay open for them to God, as their ever-present guardian and strength; *there* the incense of prayer was perpetually ascending to draw down supplies of help on the needy : and when consciousness of sin clouded their interest in God, and troubled them with apprehensions of deserved wrath, there was the blood of atonement ready to blot out their guilt, and quicken them, under a fresh sense of forgiveness, to run the way of God's commandments.   Thus viewed, every thing is in its proper place ; and the covenant of law, instead of coming to supersede the earlier covenant of promise, was introduced merely as an handmaid to minister to its design, and help forward the moral aims it sought to promote.

6. If now we turn to the writings of the Old Covenant, we shall find the evidence they furnish in perfect accordance with the view just given ; only, we must take it under two divisions—the one as connected with the sincere members of the covenant, who made an honest, a *legitimate* use of the things belonging to it ; the other with such as made an *illegitimate* use of them, whose hearts were not right with God, and who only incidentally, and as it were by contraries, became witnesses to the truth.   We shall look successively at both, considering each under a threefold aspect—with reference to God, to sin and holiness, and to salvation.

7. We look, then, in the first instance, to those who may be regarded as the more proper representatives of the Old Covenant ; and to these, primarily, in respect to what concerns their relation to God — His being and

character.   It was certainly not, as we have had occasion already to state, the sole design of the moral law, or even of the first table of the law, to preserve the belief in one personal God, as opposed to the polytheism of the ancient world ; but this was, unquestionably, a very prominent and fundamental part of the design.   The tendency in those remote times was all in the opposite direction. Polytheism, the offspring of guilt and terror, leading to the deification and worship of the powers of nature under the different aspects in which they present themselves to the natural mind, set in like a mighty flood, and swept over the earth with an all-subduing force.   The very name of religion came to be identified, in the different countries of the world, with the adoration of these false gods ; and as civilization and refinement advanced, it became associated with all that was imposing in architecture, beautiful in art, joyous and attractive in public life. There was just one region of the earth, one little territory, within which for many an age this wide-wasting moral pestilence was withstood—not even there without sharp contendings and struggles, maintained sometimes against fearful odds ; yet the truth held its place, the moral barrier raised in defence of it by the Decalogue preserved the better portion of the covenant-people from the dangers which in this respect beset them—preserved them in the knowledge and belief of one God, as the sovereign Lord and moral Governor of the world.   So deeply did this great truth, from the prominence given to it in the Old Covenant, and the awful sanctions there thrown around it, strike its roots into the hearts and consciences of the people, that it was not only handed down through successive ages in the face of every adverse influence, but made itself practically known as a principle of commanding power and ennobling influence.   Of this

the writings of the Old Testament are a varied and prolonged witness. These writings were indited by men of
very different grades of intellect and feeling, composed in
circumstances, too, and at periods, widely remote from
each other; yet they are all pervaded by one spirit; they
exhibit a profound belief in the existence of one God, as
the moral Governor of the world, and in His right—His
sole and indefeasible right—to the homage and obedience
of men. It is the religious view of the world, of the events
of life and the interests of mankind,—the relation in which
these severally stand to the one living God—which is continually presented in them, and stamps them with a quite
peculiar character and a permanent value. What has
antiquity transmitted to us that in this respect may be
compared to them? We have, doubtless, much to learn
from the literature of Greece and Rome, as regards the
history of kingdoms, the development and portraiture of
character, the arts and refinements of the natural life;
but it is to the writings which enshrined the principles
and breathed the spirit of the Divine law, that the nations
of the world are indebted for that knowledge of God,
which is the foundation at once of true religion and of
sound morality.[1]

Look at the matter for a moment in its concrete form.
See the mighty difference which appears between Hebrew
monotheism and the polytheism of heathendom, even in
its better phases, on that memorable occasion, in the
closing period of the old economy, when the extremes of
both might be said to meet—the one as represented by
the polished senators of Athens, the other by Paul of
Tarsus. There cannot well be conceived a bolder, and,
morally, a more sublime attitude, than was presented by
this man of God when, addressing the supreme council

[1] See Luthardt's 'Fundamental Truths of Christianity,' Lecture VIII.

of the city on Mars' hill, he assailed the idolatry of Greece
in the very metropolis of its dominion, and in the presence
of its most wonderful creations.   On that elevated platform of religion and art, he had immediately in front of
him the Acropolis, adorned with an entire series of statues
and temples:—among others, the Propylaea, one of the
most expensive and beautiful works of Athenian architecture, with its temple and bronze statue of Minerva,
under the name of Niké Apteros (wingless victory); the
Erectheium, the most revered of all the sanctuaries of
Athens, containing, as it did, the most ancient statue of
their patron goddess, which was supposed to have fallen
down from heaven, and the sacred olive tree which she
was believed to have called forth from the earth in her
contest with Neptune for the guardianship of the city;
and, towering above all, the Parthenon, the most perfect
structure of ancient heathendom, with its gold and ivory
statue of Minerva, the masterpiece of Phidias; and sculp-
tures besides of such exquisite workmanship, that the
mutilated remains of them have been the admiration of
the world, and, when made accessible in recent times to
the studious of other lands, served to give a fresh impulse
and higher style to the cultivation of modern art :—
Think of all this, and then think of Paul of Tarsus, an
unknown and solitary stranger, a barbarian, a Jew,
standing there, and telling his Athenian audience, in the
midst of these consecrated glories, that the Godhead
could not be likened to objects graven by art or man's
device, nor dwell in temples made with hands ; and that
out of the whole amphitheatre of their shrines and temples
he had been able to discover only one thing which proclaimed a truth, and *that* remarkable for the ignorance it
confessed, rather than the knowledge it revealed—an
altar to the Unknown God; adding, as from his own

higher vantage-ground, 'Whom therefore ye ignorantly worship, Him declare I unto you.'

8. Here, then, was a great result accomplished in the case of those who in a becoming spirit submitted themselves to the bond of the Sinaitic covenant ; in the most fundamental point of religion they became the lights of the world, the chosen witnesses of Heaven.   And such also they were in a closely related point: their convictions in regard to holiness and sin.   The polytheism of the heathen world wrought with disastrous effect here ; for losing sight of the one great source and pattern of moral excellence, and making to themselves gods after their own likeness, men's notions of holiness became sadly deranged, and their convictions of sin were consequently irregular and superficial.   Even the more thoughtful class of minds—those who sought to work themselves free from popular delusions, and to be guided only by the dictates of wisdom—never attained, even in conception, to the proper measure : the want of right views of sin cleaves as a fundamental defect to all ancient philosophy.   But Israel's knowledge of the character and law of God, as it placed them in a different position spiritually, so it produced different results in experience.   How was God Himself commonly present to their apprehensions ? Pre-eminently as the Holy One of Israel, loving righteousness, and hating iniquity.[1]   Or, how did their writers of devotion portray the true worshipper of Jehovah, the man who had a right to draw near and abide with Him, as a dweller in His house ?   It was the man who had entered into the spirit of the Decalogue—the man of clean hands and a pure heart, who had not lifted up his soul to vanity, nor sworn deceitfully—the man who had been wont to walk uprightly, work righteousness, speak

[1] Deut. xxxiii. 8; Ps. v. 4, xlv. 7; Isa. i. 4; Heb. i. 12, 13, etc.

the truth in his heart, exercise himself, in short, to all
suitable manifestations of love to God and man—he alone
was the person to ascend the hill of God, and worship and
serve before Him.[1]   But, then, who had actually done so ?
In whom was the ideal properly realized ?   Such questions could not but arise in thoughtful bosoms, and lead
to both profound convictions of sin and a trembling awe
on the spirit when venturing into the presence of God.
Hence the language of penitence, the cry of guilt with
which we are so familiar in Old Testament Scripture :
iniquity is felt cleaving to men as a girdle, yea, entering
as a virulent poison into their natures, breaking out continually into unhallowed tempers, marring the perfection
of things that were outwardly correct, and taking away
all hope of justification or acceptance with God, on the
ground of personal conformity to His requirements.[2]
Alive to the fact of an infinitely perfect God, Israel was
also, and on that very account, alive to painful misgiv-
ings and fears of guilt ; the humiliating truth comes
forcibly out in its history, that by the law is the knowledge of sin ; and, unlike all other nations of antiquity,
its one most solemn service throughout the year was that
of the day of atonement—the day for bringing to remembrance all its transgressions and all its sins, that they
might be blotted out.

9. Had there been nothing more than law in the Old
Covenant, there had also been nothing further in Israel's

[1] Ps. iv. 3, xv., xxiv. 3-6, xxvi., etc.   It cannot be said of these, and many
similar passages in the Psalms, that they indicate an advanced state of things,
higher views of goodness and acceptable worship, than those sanctioned at the
institution of the tabernacle service.   For it belonged to Moses, as the mediator
of the Old Covenant, to settle all that pertained to its worship ; no one, during
its continuance, had any warrant to prescribe new conditions to the worshipper ;
nor indeed was this done in the passages quoted, for they evidently lean on the
terms of the Decalogue.

[2] Ps. xix. 12, 13, xxxii. 5, li. 5, cxliii. 2 ; Isa. lxiv. 6 ; Job xv. 16, etc.

experience, except the penalties that were the just desert of sin. But with the true members of the covenant another thing invariably appears—a fleeing to God as the Redeemer from sin, the Healer of Israel—or a falling back from the covenant of law on the covenant of grace and promise out of which it sprung. Take as an example the rich and varied record of a believer's experience contained in the 119th Psalm. The theme of discourse there, from beginning to end, is the law of God —its excellence, its breadth and fulness, its suitableness to men's condition, the blessedness of being conformed to its requirements, and the earnest longings of the pious heart after all that properly belongs to it :—but things of this sort perpetually alternate with confessions of backslidings and sins, fervent cries for pardoning mercy and restoring grace, and fresh resolutions formed in dependence on Divine aid to resist the evil, and strive after higher attainments in the righteousness it enjoins. And so elsewhere ; the consciousness of sin and moral weakness ever drove the soul to God for deliverance and help ; and especially to the use of that gracious provision made through the rite of sacrifice for expiating the guilt of sin and restoring peace to the troubled conscience. But then this *present* deliverance bore on it such marks of imperfection as might well seem to call for another and more perfect arrangement ; since both the means of reconciliation were inferior (the blood of bulls and goats), and the measure of it also, even as things then stood, was incomplete ; for the reconciled were still not permitted to have direct and personal access into the *presence-chamber* of Jehovah—they were permitted only to frequent the *courts* of His house. The law, therefore, awakening a sense of guilt and alienation which could not then be perfectly removed, creating wants and desires it but partially satisfied, while it could not fail to be productive of fear, was also well fitted to raise expectations in the bosom of the worshipper of some better things to come, and dispose him to listen to the intimations concerning them which it was the part of prophecy to utter. And in proportion as men of humble and earnest faith acted on the hints thus given, they would, in answer to believing prayer and pious meditation, understand that, however the existing provisions of mercy were to be appreciated, there was a sense also in which they might be disparaged ;[1] that they were indeed ' God's treasure-house of mysteries,' wonderful in themselves, but wonderful and precious most of all for the hidden reference they bore to realities which were not yet disclosed, and into which the eye of faith naturally desired to look.[2]

[1] As in the following passages : Ps. xl. 6, l. 7-14, li. 16 ; Hos. vi. 6.

[2] *See* Davison 'On Prophecy,' p. 143, who, after referring to the obvious imperfections in the religion of the Old Covenant, says, ' The action of the moral and ceremonial law combined, I conclude to have been such as would produce, in reasonable and serious minds, that temper which is itself eminently Christian in its principle, viz., a sense of demerit in transgression ; a willingness to accept a better atonement adequate to the needs of the conscience, if God should provide it, and a desire after inward purity which bodily lustration might represent but could not supply ; in short, that temper which David has confessed and described when he rejects his reliance upon the legal rites : For thou desirest not sacrifice, else would I give it thee, etc. (Ps. li.).' At the same time, considering the provision actually made under the law for sin, and the expectations raised concerning something better to come, it is clear that the fear spoken of in connection with it could not be, with the true members of the covenant, properly *slavish* fear ; for in their case the native effect of the law was always checked by the prayer and hope which grew out of the covenant of promise. It was only that in a more intense degree, which in a certain degree is still experienced in serious and thoughtful minds under the Gospel. And in so far as the law then, or at any time, might be found to work wrath and despair, this, as justly remarked by Harless ('Ethik,' p. 161), ' is the guilt of men who do not rightly understand, or who misuse the law. For, if the law were understood, or rather the God who gave the law, then it would be known that the same God, who in the law threatens death, does not wish the death of the sinner.'

Such, briefly, is the evidence furnished by one portion of the covenant-people, those who constituted the true Israel, and who used the covenant of law, as it was intended, in due subservience to the prior covenant of grace. Even with the imperfections cleaving to the Divine plan, as one of a merely provisional nature, and corresponding imperfections in the spiritual results produced by it, we may yet ask if there was not, as regards that portion of the people, fruit that might well be deemed worthy of God? Where, in those ancient times, did life exhibit so many of the purer graces and more solid virtues? Or where, on the side of truth and righteousness, were such perils braved, and such heroic deeds performed? *There* alone were the claims of truth and righteousness even known in such a manner as to reach the depths of conscience, and bring into proper play the nobler feelings, desires, and aspirations of the heart. It is to Israel alone, of all the nations of antiquity, that we must turn alike for the more meek and lovely, and for the more stirring examples of moral excellence. Sanctified homes, which possessed the light, and were shone upon by the favour of Heaven; lives of patient endurance and suffering, or of strong wrestling for the rights of conscience, and the privilege of yielding to the behests of duty; manifestations of zeal and love in behalf of the higher interests of mankind, such as could scorn all inferior considerations of flesh and blood, and even rise at times in 'the elected saints' to such a noble elevation, that they 'have wished themselves razed out of the book of life, in an ecstasy of charity, and feeling of infinite communion' (Bacon): for refreshing sights and inspiring exhibitions like these, we must repair to the annals of that chosen seed, who were trained to the knowledge of God, and moulded by the laws and institutions of His kingdom. Must we not, in consideration of them, re-echo the saying of Moses, 'O Israel, what people was like unto thee !—a people saved by the Lord !'[1]

10. But, unfortunately, there is a darker side to the picture. There was another, and, for the most part, a larger and more influential portion of the covenant-people, who acted very differently, who either openly resiled from the yoke of the law, or perverted it to a wrong purpose, and in whom also, though after another fashion, the truth found a remarkable verification. In this class, the most prominent thing—that which was always the first to discover itself, was a restive and reluctant spirit, fretting against the demands of the law, often even against that fundamental part of them, which might be said to involve all the rest—the devout acknowledgment and pure worship of Jehovah. With this class, the prevailing tendency to idolatry in the ancient world had attractions which they were unable to resist. Like so many around them, in part also among them, they wished a less exacting, a more sensuous and more easily accessible mode of worship, than that which was enjoined in the law and connected with the tabernacle ; and so idolatrous sanctuaries in various localities, with their accompanying rites of will-worship, were formed : these generally first, and then, as a natural consequence, altogether false deities, local or foreign, came to take the place of Jehovah. There was a strong tide from without bearing in this direction ; it was the spirit of the age, which human nature is ever ready to fall in with ; but the real ground of the defection, and that which rendered the apostatizing disposition a kind of chronic disease in Israel, lay in the affinity between those corrupt idolatries and the natural inclinations of the heart. Living in

[1] See 'Typology,' Vol. II. p. 491.

Gospel times, *we* are wont to speak of the carnal and ritual-istic nature of the Old Testament worship; but underneath it all there was a spiritual element, which was distasteful to the merely natural mind, and the reverse of which was found in the showy and corrupt rites of heathenism. These fostered and gratified the sinful desires of the heart, while the worship of Jehovah repressed and con-demned them : this was the real secret of that inveterate drawing in the one direction, and strong antipathy in the other, which were perpetually breaking forth in the his-tory of Israel, and turned it, we may say, into a great battle-ground for the very existence of true religion.   In its essence, it was the conflict of human corruption with the will, the authority, and the actual being of God ; and, therefore, it never failed to draw down those rebukes in providence, by which God vindicated the honour of His name, and made the backslidings of His people to reprove them.   Viewed in this light, the history of Israel, how-ever melancholy in one respect, is instructive and even consolatory in another : it shewed how every thing for Israel, in evil or in good, turned on the relation in which they stood to the living God, as the object of faith and worship—how inexcusable, as well as foolish, they were in hardening their hearts against His ways, and preferring the transitory pleasures of sin to the abiding recompenses of His service—and how, in spite of all manifestations of folly, and combinations of human power and wisdom against the truth of God, that truth still prevailed, and they who stood by it, the godly seed, though comparatively few, proved the real strength or substance of the nation.[1]

11. There was, however, another form of evil which manifested itself in this portion of the covenant-people, which latterly became a very prevalent form, and which so

[1] Isa. vi. 13.

far differed from the other, that it could consist with an outward adherence to the worship of Jehovah, nay, with apparent zeal for that worship, while the great ends of the covenant were trampled under foot. The failure here lay in false views respecting holiness and sin, necessarily leading also to an utterly false position in regard to salvation. Instead of viewing the institutions and services connected with the tabernacle—the ceremonial part of the law—as the complement merely of the Sinaitic tables, intended to help out their design and provide the means of escape from their just condemnation of sin, the persons in question exalted it to the first place, and, however they might stand related to 'the weightier matters of the law, judgment, mercy and faith,' thought all in a manner accomplished, if they kept the ordinances and presented the appointed offerings. Many sharp reproofs and severe denunciations are pronounced against this mode of procedure, and those who pursued it, in the writings of the Old Testament, especially the prophets. Asaph asks such persons in his day, asks them indignantly in the name of God, what *they* had to do with declaring God's statutes, or going about the things of His covenant, since they were full of backbiting and deceit, taking part with thieves and adulterers ?[1]   Isaiah is still more severe in his language ; he finds such characters, after a period of much backsliding and rebuke, professing great concern for the interests of religion, diligently frequenting the courts of God's house, heaping sacrifices upon the altar, and stretching out their hands in prayer, while oppression and iniquity were in their dwellings, and their hands were even stained with blood. In such a case—so flagrantly at variance with the fundamental precepts and obligations of the covenant—what right, the prophet

[1] Psalm l.

demands, had *they* to tread the courts of God's house or take part in its services ? Who required it ? There was no sincerity, he tells them, in what they did ; their altar-gifts were but lying offerings ;[1] and their whole service an abomination in the sight of the Holy One.[2] Jeremiah, in like manner, points out the inexpressible hardihood and folly of men trusting to the temple and its services for a blessing, who by their ungodly and wicked lives had turned it into a resort of evil-doers, a den even of robbers (vii.) ; so also Ezekiel (xviii., xxxiii.), and some of the other prophets. By and by, however, a phase of things entered, although not till after the return from Babylon, and of which we have no very exact portraiture in Old Testament times ; we see the beginnings of it merely in the writings of Malachi. The fires of Divine judgment had now at last purged out from among the people the more heinous and abominable forms of transgression ; monotheism had come to be rigidly maintained ; and from being neglecters of the law, they passed, many of them, in a formal respect into the opposite extreme—the extreme, namely, of making the law, in a manner, every thing for life and blessing—more than it was ever intended to be, or in reality could be, consistently with the moral character of God and the actual condition of men. So the feeling continued and grew, and meets us in full efflorescence among the more prominent religionists of the Gospel era. And there is not, perhaps, a more remarkable example to be found in history than their case affords of that form of deceitfulness of the human heart, by which it can pass from the extreme of dislike to the law and service of God, to the extreme of outward regard and

---

[1] So the expression should be rendered in Isa. i. 13, not merely ' vain oblations.'

[2] See also ch. xxix. 13, lviii., lix.

honour ; and yet retain, in the one extreme as well as the other, the ungodly frame of mind, which is opposed to their essential character and aim.

It is this latter form of the evil that has most of interest for us, as it comes prominently into view in New Testament Scripture. Its fundamental error, as I have said, lay in isolating the covenant of law, taking it apart from the prior covenant of promise, as if it was alone sufficient for men—and not only so, but failing to distinguish between what was of prime, and what of only secondary moment in the law, throwing the ceremonial into precisely the same category with the moral. From this grievous mistake (which some would still most unaccountably confound with proper Judaism) three fatal results of a practical kind inevitably followed. *First*, they shut their eyes upon the depth and spirituality of the law's requirements. They were *obliged* to do so ; for had they perceived these, the idea must of necessity have vanished from their minds, that they could attain to righteousness on a merely legal footing; they could never have imagined that 'touching the righteousness which is in the law they were blameless.' [1] Thoughts of this description could only enter when the law was stript of its proper import as the revelation and sum of moral duty, and reduced to an outward discipline of specific rules of conduct. When so reduced, it was quite possible for any one to feel that the law's requirements lay within the compass of the practi-

---

[1] Phil. iii. 6. That Paul speaks thus of his earlier life from a Pharisaic point of view, is evident from the connection ; as he is avowedly recounting the things which had reference to the flesh (v. 4), and which gave him a merely external ground of glorying. It is further evident, from what he says of his relation to the law elsewhere, when he came to a proper understanding of its real import (Rom. vii.) ; and also from the utter want of satisfaction, which even here he expresses, of his former life after the light of truth dawned upon his mind (v. 7, 8).

cable; the task-work of services might with laudable regularity be gone through; and the feeling of self-righteousness, so far from being repressed, would only be the more fostered and sustained by the number and variety of the materials it had to work upon. A *second* result was the servile spirit in which all in such a case came to be done. The covenant of Sinai—taken by itself, simply as the revelation of law—'genders unto bondage;'[1] if it begets children, they will inevitably be children of a carnal and slavish, not of a free, loving, and devoted spirit. It cannot be otherwise. When any one submits to a yoke of service for which he has no natural inclination, for the sake merely of certain benefits he expects to reap from it, the heart cannot but be conscious of a burden; it does what is exacted, not from any high motives or generous impulses, but simply because necessary to the end in view—it must earn its wages. I need hardly say, that it was much in this spirit the Scribes and Pharisees of our Lord's time acted—they were hirelings, and not sons. And the explanation of their case was what we have just indicated —they put the law out of its proper place, and applied themselves to get through a formal obedience to its requirements, what it was altogether incapable of giving —what, if got at all by sinful men, must come through the channel of Divine grace and loving-kindness. It is the covenant of promise alone, not the covenant of law, that is the true mother of children in the kingdom of God. *Finally,* as a still further result, the persons who thus erred concerning the law's place and spirit, could neither rightly look for the Messiah, nor, when He came, be at all prepared to receive Him. They fancied they had already of themselves attained to righteousness, and were little disposed to think they must be indebted for it to Christ.

[1] Gal. iv. 24.

M

They naturally regarded it as foul scorn to be put virtually
on a level with those who had been without law, and
clung to the law as the ground of all their distinctions,
the very charter of their privileges and hopes.   So completely, by misapprehending the proper nature and
relations of things, did the major part of the later Jews
frustrate the object of the law, and turn it from being a
schoolmaster to lead them to Christ, into the jealous and
lordly rival that would keep them at the remotest distance from Him.   And the mournful result for themselves
was, that the rock in which they trusted, itself rose
against them ; the law which could condemn but not
expiate their sin, cried for vengeance with a voice that
must be heard, and wrath from heaven fell upon them to
the uttermost.

A marvellous history, on whichever side contemplated !
—whether in the evil or the good connected with it—and
fraught with important lessons, not for those alone who
were its immediate subjects, but for all nations and for
all time.   God constituted the seed of Israel the direct
bearers of a Divine revelation, made them subjects alike
of law and promise, and shaped their history so that in
it men might see reflected as in a mirror the essential
character of His kingdom, the blessings that flow from a
hearty submission to His will, and the judgments that
not less certainly come, sooner or later, in the train of
wilful perversion and incorrigible disobedience.   In a
sense altogether peculiar, they were called to be God's
witnesses to the world ;[1] and by the word of God, which
has embodied itself in their experience and history, they
still remain such—a light in its better aspect to guide
and comfort, in its worse a beacon to admonish and warn.
Like every revelation of God, this word also liveth and

[1] Isa. xliii. 10.

abideth for ever ; and among other lessons to be learned from it, this, which is common to all dispensations, embodied in a pregnant utterance of Augustine, should never be forgotten, *Lex data est ut gratia quaereretur ; gratia data est ut lex impleretur*[1]—the law was given that grace might be sought; grace was given that the law might be fulfilled.

[1] De Sp. and Lit., sec. xix.

LECTURE VI.

THE ECONOMICAL ASPECT OF THE LAW—THE DEFECTS ADHERING
TO IT AS SUCH—THE RELATION OF THE PSALMS AND PROPHETS
TO IT—MISTAKEN VIEWS OF THIS RELATION—THE GREAT PRO-
BLEM WITH WHICH THE OLD TESTAMENT CLOSED, AND THE
VIEWS OF DIFFERENT PARTIES RESPECTING ITS SOLUTION.

IN the preceding lecture we have seen what advantages
accrued to Israel, and through them to the world,
from the revelation of law at Sinai, in so far as that
revelation was rightly understood, and was kept in its
proper place.   But as yet we have only looked at a part
of the considerations which require to be taken into account, in order to get a comprehensive view of the work
which the law had to do in Israel, and of much that is
written concerning it in Scripture.   There can be no
doubt that the law, taken in its entirety, and as forming
the most prominent feature in the economy brought in by
Moses, however wisely adapted to the time then present,
was still inlaid with certain inherent defects, which discovered themselves in the working of the system, and
paved the way for its ultimate removal.   As an economy,
it belonged to an immature stage of the Divine dispensations, and as such was constituted after a relatively
imperfect form.   The institutions and ordinances, also,
which were associated with it, and became an integral
part of its machinery, were in many respects suited to a
comparatively limited territory, and even within the
bounds of that involved not a little that must often have
proved irksome and inconvenient—what an apostle said

to his brethren, neither they nor their fathers were able
to bear.[1] It is plain, therefore, that matters existed then
only in a provisional state, and that a change must somehow be introduced into the Divine economy, to adapt it
to the general wants and circumstances of mankind. It
becomes, therefore, an interesting and important question,
wherein precisely lay the inherent defects of an economy
modelled so much after the legal form. Also, how these
defects practically discovered themselves ; and what other
elements or agencies came into play, to compensate
for the defects in question, and to prepare the way for
the entrance of another and higher state of things. To
such points we shall now endeavour to address ourselves.

I. Whatever may be the contents of law—even if
comprising what is of universal import and obligation—
simply as law, written on perishable materials, and
imposed in so many formal enactments, it has a merely
outward and objective character. And this is what first
falls to be noted here ; for the main element of weakness
in the Sinaitic law, viewed in its economical bearings, stood
in its having so much of the outward and objective. It
was engraved on tables of stone, and stood there before
men as a preceptor to instruct them, or a master to
demand their implicit submission, but without any direct
influence or control over the secret springs and motives of
obedience. And the same, of course, holds with respect
to the ordinances of service, which were appended to it
as supplementary means to subserve its design—more so,
indeed ; for they not only possessed the same formally
written character, though not on tables of stone, but bore
throughout on men's relation to a material fabric, and
their submission to bodily restraints or exercises. The

---

[1] Acts xv. 10.

whole, therefore, taken by itself, formed a kind of legal institute, and in its working naturally tended to the mechanical and formal. It is of the nature of law, whether Divine or human, when imposed as a bond of order and discipline, to work from without inwards— acting as an external pressure or constraint on the vital energies, and seeking to bind them into an orderly and becoming course. ' Laws politic,' says Hooker,[1] ' ordained for external order and regiment amongst men, are never framed as they should be, unless presuming the will of man to be inwardly obstinate, rebellious, and averse from all obedience unto the sacred laws of his nature; in a word, unless presuming man to be, in regard to his depraved nature, little better than a wild beast, they do accordingly provide, notwithstanding, so to frame his outward actions, that they be no hindrance to the common good, for which societies are instituted.' It is the same thing substantially which was uttered long before by the apostle, when, with reference more immediately to the Divine law, he said, ' The law is not made for a righteous man, but for the lawless and disobedient, for the ungodly, and for sinners :'[2] it is such alone who need the stringent rules and prohibitions of an outward code of enactments ; those who are firmly rooted in the principles of rectitude, and animated by a genuine spirit of love, will be a law to themselves. Essentially the sum, as well as spirit, of the law is love. But then the law does not of itself elicit love ; its object rather is to supplement the deficiency of love, and by means of an external discipline form the inner nature to the habit and direction which would have been instinctively taken by the spirit of love. Still, this spirit could not be altogether wanting in those for whom the

---

[1] ' Eccl. Polity,' I. sec. 10.   [2] 1 Tim. i. 9.

discipline availed anything, otherwise the result would have been at most but a well-drilled and heartless formalism.   It was with them, as in the case of children who, through the yoke of parental discipline, are trained to goodness and virtue : the elements of the good are all there though existing in comparative feebleness, and by means of the discipline are stimulated to a readiness and constancy of exercise, which they would otherwise have failed to put forth.   And as a natural consequence, both of the feebleness of love and of the magisterial presence and power of law, the principle of fear must have had relatively greater sway than would belong to it in a more perfect state of things.   The dread of incurring the wrath of an offended God, and suffering the penalties which guarded on every side the majesty of His law, would often deter from sin when no other consideration might prevail, and quicken the soul to exertions in duty which it would not have otherwise put forth.

These were, undoubtedly, marks of imperfection impressed on the very nature of the old economy; it wrought, as the apostle tells us, to a large extent by weak and beggarly elements; and it did so because it was the comparative nonage of the church, and the materials of a more spiritual economy did not yet exist. 'The atonement was yet but prospective; the Holy Spirit did not operate as He does under the Gospel; and God's gracious designs, as regards the redemption of our race, lay embedded and concealed in the obscure intimation, that the seed of the woman should bruise the serpent's head, and in the promises to Abraham.   Nor were these defects perfectly remedied throughout the whole course of the dispensation.   To the last the Jew walked in comparative darkness; to the last the powerful motives which affect the Christian, derived from the infinite love

of God as exhibited in the completed work of redemption, and from the authoritative announcement of a
future resurrection to life or death eternal, could not be
brought to bear on the ancient believer; to the last,
therefore, he needed stimulants to his piety drawn from
inferior sources.'[1]

The practical result in some measure corresponded.
It might, indeed, have been greatly better than it
actually was, and would have been, if the proper use
had been generally made of the grace offered in the
covenant of promise; the people would then have had
the law of God in their hearts.[2]   But this proved to be
the case only with a portion.   In many the pulse of life
beat too feebly and irregularly for the requirements of
the law being felt otherwise than a difficult, if not
oppressive yoke.   Too often, also, those who should have
been the most exemplary in performing what was enjoined, and from their position in the commonwealth
should have checked the practice of evil in others, were
themselves the most forward in promoting it.   Hence,
the theory of the constitution as to the strict connection
between transgression and punishment gave way : souls
that *should* have been cut off from the number of their
people, as deliberate covenant-breakers, and in God's
judgment *were* cut off, continued to retain their place
in the community, and to exercise its rights.[3]   By degrees, also, the faulty administration of the covenant by

---

[1] Litton's 'Bampton Lecture,' p. 50.   [2] Ps. xxxvii. 31.

[3] The expression, 'that soul shall be cut off,' refers primarily to God's act,
and is sometimes used where, from the nature of things, human authority could
not interfere—viz., where the violation of law was quite secret, as in Lev.
xvii. 10, xviii. 29, xxii. 3.   Hence the words sometimes run, 'I will cut off
that soul,' or 'I will cut him off from my presence.'   But when the act was
open, and the guilt manifest, God's decision should have been carried out by
the community, as at Num. xv. 30; Josh. vii. 24-26.

human authority re-acted on the state of heart out of which it sprung, and strengthened yet more the tendency to fall away. And there being but a partial and defective exhibition of holiness on the part of the people, there necessarily ensued on God's part a proportionate withdrawal of the promised blessing. So that the aspect of things in Canaan never presented more than a broken and irregular impression of that righteousness and prosperity which, like twin sisters, should have accompanied the people through the whole course of their history. But did not the Mediator of the covenant Himself apprehend this, and at the outset proclaim it, when on the plains of Moab He so distinctly portrayed the future backslidings of the people, and foretold the desolations which should in consequence overtake them ?[1] Coincident with the birth of the covenant there were thus given intimations of its imperfect character and temporary purpose ; and it was made clear that, not through the provisions and agencies therewith connected could the ultimate good for mankind, or even for Israel itself, be secured.[2]

II. The comparative failure in this respect, while in itself an evil, was overruled to bring out very distinctly, among the covenant-people, the spiritual element which was in the law ; and this we note as the second point which here calls for consideration. By spiritual element I mean the great moral truths embodied in the law in their relation to the individual heart and conscience. This could not, of course, be said in any proper sense to be dependent on the defective observance and faulty administration of the covenant, but it would, we can easily understand, be aided by them. The law bore so

[1] Deut. xxviii., xxxii.   [2] *See* Davison ' On Prophecy,' p. 165.

much of an external character, that it was quite possible
for persons to maintain a conduct free from all just exceptions of a public kind, while still it wanted much to bring
it into accordance with the real spirit and design of the
law ; for the outward was of value only as expressive of
the desires and principles of the heart.   Even in any circumstances, the thoughtful meditation of the law must
have had the effect of leading the soul apart, instead of
losing itself amid the decent formalities of a generally
approved behaviour, of bringing it into close personal
dealing with God regarding sin and righteousness.   It
could scarcely fail to force itself on the convictions of
those who were thus spiritually exercised, that their
relation to the law, and to Him whose glory was identified
with its proper observance, must materially differ, according as it might be the outward man merely that was
drilled into the keeping of the law's requirements, or along
with this, and under this, the outgoing also of reverent
feelings, holy desires, and pure affections.   The members
of the covenant, it would thus come to be felt, were not
alike children of the covenant, even though they might
present much the same appearance of outward conformity
to its handwriting of ordinances.   An Israel would be
known as developing itself within Israel—a more special
and select class, who individually came nearer to God than
others, and who might reasonably expect to find God
coming nearer to them, and bestowing on them the more
peculiar tokens of His goodness.

But, plainly, a conviction of this sort, which was
almost unavoidable anyhow, would gather strength in
proportion as differences appeared among the members of
the covenant ; and some were seen making conscience of
keeping the statutes of the Lord, while others resigned
themselves to selfish indifference or courses of sin.   Re-

flecting and serious minds would feel assured, that the one class held a relation to the God of truth and rectitude, which could not belong to the other ; and though all might still be called the seed of Israel, and might alike enjoy the common privileges of the covenant, yet those who alone properly answered to the description, and had any just right to look for the favour and protection of God, must have appeared to be such as, like Abraham, were observed to keep the commandments of the Lord and obey His voice.[1]   We judge this to have been the case from the very nature of things.   The law recognised important relations, general and particular, human and Divine, and, in connection with them, established great moral obligations, which not only called for a certain appropriate demeanour, but demanded also a suitable state of feeling and affection.   These, of necessity, formed elements of spiritual thought and comparative judgment with the better class of Israelites, and must have done so the more, the more they found themselves surrounded by persons of another spirit than themselves—mere formal observers of the law, or open transgressors of its precepts.   And that such actually was the case, we have conclusive evidence in those writings of the Old Covenant, which give expression to the personal feelings and reflective judgments of godly men on the state of things around them.

Take, for example, the Book of Proverbs, immensely the richest storehouse of thoughtful utterance and practical wisdom that any nation, not to say single individual, has given to the world, does not its leading characteristic, as a writing, stand in the skill and discrimination with which it draws moral distinctions — distinctions between one principle of action and one line of conduct

[1] Gen. xviii. 19.

and another ? It proceeds throughout on the profound conviction that there are such distinctions—a right and a wrong unalterably fixed by the law of God and the essential nature of things ; and, corresponding to this, a good and an evil in experience, a blessing and a curse. The Book is the record of a most careful and extensive observation, gathered, no doubt, in part from the general field of the world's history, but chiefly and most especially from the land of the covenant—the territory which lay in the light of God's truth and in the bond of His law. The comparison is never formally made between Israel as a nation and the idolatrous nations around it ; no, but rather between class and class, individual and individual in Israel. There are the fearers of Jehovah on the one side—those who sincerely listen to the voice of Divine wisdom, and apply themselves in earnest to all the works of a pious, upright, and beneficent life ; and, on the other, the vain and foolish, the corrupt and profligate, the envious, the niggardly, the unjust, the scornful, and the wicked. With both classes, and with manifold shades and diversities in each, the writer's experience had manifestly made him familiar ; and, according to their respective moral condition—in other words, their relation to the law and service of God—such also is the portion of good or evil he associates with their history.

In various portions of the Book of Psalms, the spiritual element comes out, if possible, still more strongly, and the moral distinctions are drawn with a yet keener edge ; because for the most part drawn from a personal point of view, and with reference to a contrast or an antagonism which was pressing on the faith and interests of the writer. In such a psalm as the 37th, the contrast assumes its milder form, and approaches to the style of the Proverbs ; yet still there is perceptible the feeling of one who knew himself to be in a struggling minority, and who needed to encourage his own heart, and the hearts of those he represented, with considerations drawn from the eternal principles of God's law, and the recompenses of good and evil therewith connected.   But more commonly the theme of the Psalms in question turns on the trials of the Lord's servant in his contendings for truth and righteousness against those who, though formally members of the covenant, ranged themselves in opposition to its real interests.   It was the representative of Heaven's cause, the true wrestler for righteousness, on the one side, and those, on the other, who had not the fear of God before their eyes, and sought ,to strengthen themselves by their wickedness.   It was the former alone, the Psalmist with manifold frequency proclaims, the godly ones, whom the Lord had chosen ; the others were objects of His displeasure, aliens, heathen at heart, who should be made to perish from the land, or become entangled in their own arts of destruction.   Thus it appears that the principle, ' not all Israel who are of Israel'—in other words, an election within the election, a spiritual seed from among the visible community of the covenant-people—though not recognised in the Theocratic constitution, yet came practically into distinct and palpable operation.   It was present as a fact to the minds of the faithful in almost every age of its history ; and so gave promise of a time when the really distinctive and fundamental things in men's relation to God should rise to their proper place.   It follows, therefore, that the law, considered as a national covenant, did not, in its actual working, tend to perpetuate, but rather to antiquate itself ; it led to a state of things, which was the prelude and virtual commencement of an era in which primary regard should be had, not to men's natural descent or hereditary position, but to their personal relation to the redeeming grace of God, and their heartfelt sympathy with the interests of His kingdom.[1]

III. The sacred writings just referred to, more especially the Psalms, besides incidentally testifying to the existence of a spiritual along with a carnal seed in Israel, had another and more direct end to serve in respect to the question now under consideration : by their didactic and devotional character they made a fresh advance in the Divine administration toward men, and so far tended to modify the operation of law. They formed the introduction of an agency, perfectly harmonious, indeed, with the outward prescriptions and observances of the law, but in its own nature higher, and as such tending to pre-

---

[1] There was unavoidably connected with the state of things now described certain anomalies of a moral kind, which exercised the patience, sometimes even for a time staggered the faith, of God's people—cases in which, contrary to the general tenor of the covenant, wrong appeared to triumph, and the righteous cause or person was put to the worse. We have specimens of the painful reflections they gave rise to in such Psalms as xlix., lxxiii.; also in the Book of Ecclesiastes, and various passages in the prophets. They are to be explained, so far as an explanation was possible, from the broken and disordered state of things brought in by the wide-spread unfaithfulness of the people to the covenant, which necessarily rendered the administration of temporal rewards and punishments also broken and irregular—although still of such a kind, that thoughtful observers had enough to satisfy them that there was a righteous God who judged in the earth. This is surely a better and more Scriptural mode of viewing such cases, than the rough and sceptical sort of treatment they receive in ' Ecce Homo'—where, in reference to acts of moral delinquency not punished by the judge, it is said, ' What did Jehovah do ? Did He suffer the guilty man to escape, or had He other ministers of justice beside the judge and the king ? It was *supposed* that in such cases He called in the powers of nature against the transgressor, destroyed his vines with hailstones, etc. But this theory was found to be unsatisfactory. Life is a short term, and prosperous villany was seen going to an honoured grave. Another *conjecture was hazarded:* it was said the bad man prospers sometimes, but he has no children, or at least his house soon dies out,' etc. (p. 38). All mere human thought and vain speculation about the matter!

pare the way for yet further advances in the same direction.

The service rendered by this kind of agency was various ; but, in whichever way considered, the effect must have been in the line now indicated. It undoubtedly bore respect, and may be said, perhaps, to have more immediately owed its origin, to the form of worship associated with the covenant of law. Partaking as this did so much of the outward and ceremonial, it was, as a matter of course, largely identified with particular times and places, which for the great body of the people necessarily circumscribed very much the opportunities of public worship. Long intervals elapsed between the solemnities which drew them around the one altar of burnt-offering, and the place where Jehovah, in a more peculiar sense, put His name. Not only so, but when the people held their holy convocations in their several localities (such as the law itself contemplated,[1] and which ought to have been of frequent occurrence) no special legislation was made in respect to the mode of conducting them ; the worshippers were left to their own discretion and resources, doubtless on the supposition that the lack would be supplied by the more gifted members of the community. And in the circumstances of the time, when written helps were as yet so scanty, one of the readiest, and one also of the most effectual modes of supplying it, was by means of the lofty and stirring notes of sacred song, accompanied by simple but appropriate melodies. How near this lay to the thoughts of the better class of the people, is evident from the frequency which, even in the earlier periods of their national existence, remarkable incidents and memorable occasions gave rise to such spirited effusions, as appears from the

---

[1] Lev. xxiii. 3, 24, 27 ; Num. xxix. 1, 7.

songs intermingled with the records of their history.[1] These songs were manifestly composed for use in religious meetings, and were sure to be increasingly employed, and also to grow in number, in proportion as a spirit of earnest piety diffused itself among the people. Accordingly, in the period of revival which was originated by Samuel, this appears as one of the more distinguishing features of the time. The schools of the prophets, as they were called—that is, companies of the more select and godly members of the community, gathered together into a kind of spiritual brotherhood, under the presidency of a prophet, made such abundant use of sacred lyrics that they had for their distinctive badges musical instruments —the psaltery, the tabret, the pipe, and the harp.[2] David himself, in his earlier years, was no stranger to these institutions, and not improbably, by what he witnessed and felt in them, had his heart first moved to stir up the gift that was in him to add to their materials of devotion. But what he received he repaid with increase. The fine poetical genius with which he was endowed, ennobled as it was and hallowed by the special gifts of God's Spirit, singularly fitted him for giving expression to the spiritual thoughts and feelings of the people, and even for imparting to these an elevation and a fervour beyond what should otherwise have belonged to them. And to him, in his vocation as the sweet Psalmist of Israel, it was not a little owing that such associations became, not only means of spiritual culture, but centres of religious awakening.

Nearly akin to this was another service, which the Psalmodic literature, and the writings that were some-

---

[1] Ex. xv.; Num. xxi. 17-27; Deut. xxxii.; Judges v.; also Balaam's prophecies, and the Psalm of Moses.

[2] 1 Sam. x. 5.

what allied to it, rendered to the religion of the Old
Covenant—one more immediately connected with their
didactic character. That religion was predominantly of
a symbolical nature. The very writing of the Decalogue
on tables of stone possessed this character; and every
act of lustration, every ordinance of service at the temple
or away from it, had couched under it a spiritual meaning.
It had this, however, practically not for all, but only for
those who possessed discernment to look through the
shell into the kernel. The native tendency of the soul
was to rest in the outward; and, instead of searching
into the hidden treasures which lay enclosed in the
external forms of worship, to turn the mere ritualism of
these into a kind of sacred pantomime, which, for all
higher purposes, left the worshipper much where it found
him. The proneness of ancient Israel to give way to this
unthinking, fleshly disposition, comes out with mournful
frequency through the whole of their history. And for
the purpose of correcting it—for the purpose, we may
also say, of providing in this behalf a needed complement
to the institutions and services of the Old Covenant, it
became the calling of the more gifted members of the
community to extract from them their spiritual essence—
to detach the great truths and principles they enshrined,
and, by linking them to the varied experiences and prospects as well of individual as of national life, to invest
them with a significance and a power that might be level
to every understanding, and touch a chord of sympathy
in every reflecting bosom. This was pre-eminently the
calling of David, and of those who succeeded him in the
line of reforming agency he initiated. It was to pour
new life and vigour into the old religion, not merely by
rectifying the partial disorders that had crept into its
administration, and promoting the due observance of its

solemnities with the lively accompaniment of song and
music—not merely this, but also, and much more, by
popularizing its lessons in compositions adapted to general
use, and providing appropriate forms of utterance for
the devout feelings and desires which the ordinances
of God and the events of life were fitted to call forth.
The thought of God as the Creator and moral Governor
of the world—the Redeemer, the Shepherd, the King of
Israel—of His glorious perfections and wonderful works
—the deliverances He had wrought for His people, the
careful guardianship He exercises over them, the spirituality of His holy law, as requiring truth in the inward
parts not less than integrity and kindness in the outward
life, His mercy to the penitent, His special nearness to
the humble, to the needy, to the souls struggling with convictions of sin or sharp conflicts in the cause of righteousness, yea, His readiness to keep them as in the secret of
His tabernacle, and compass them about with His presence
as with a shield :—these and such-like thoughts, which
were all interwoven with the facts of sacred history and
with the structure and services of the Tabernacle, were
in these inspired productions plainly set forth, clothed in
the forms of an attractive and striking imagery, and
enkindled with the glow of human sympathies and devout
emotions.   It is impossible not to see what an approach
was here made to the directness and simplicity both of
instruction and worship, which are the characteristics of
a spiritual dispensation.   In proportion as the members
of the covenant became conversant with and used these
helps to faith and devotion, they must have felt at once
more capable of profiting by the worship of the sanctuary,
and less tied to its formal routine ; in spirit they could
now realize what was transacted there, and bring it home
to the sanctuary of their bosoms.   Jehovah Himself,

though His dwelling-place was in Zion, was through these utterances of His Spirit brought near to every one of them ; and alike in their private communings and in their holy convocations, they possessed the choicest materials for holding sweet and hallowed converse with Heaven.   And therefore must these Psalms have been pre-eminently to the Jewish believer what they have been said to be also in a measure to the Christian—even well-nigh ' what the love of parents and the sweet affections of home, and the clinging memory of infant scenes, and the generous love of country, are to men of every rank and order and employment, of every kindred, and tongue, and nation.'[1]

IV. The tendency in this direction, however, was greatly increased by the operation of another element— the prophetical agency and writings, which attained only to their greatest fulness and power when the affairs of the Old Covenant approached their lowest depression.   The raising up of persons from time to time, who should come with special messages from God to the people, suited to the ever varying states and exigences of life, was from the first contemplated in the Theocratic government;[2] and certain directions were given both for trying the pretensions of those who claimed to have such messages from God, and for treating with becoming reverence and regard such as had them.   This was, certainly, a very singular arrangement—as justly noticed by G. Baur :—

---

[1] Irving. An incidental proof of this is found in the touching notices in Ps. cxxxvii., where the Jewish captives are represented as hanging their harps on the willows, and incapable, when requested by their conquerors, of singing one of the songs of Zion. It shews how deep a hold the psalmody had taken of the better minds of the community, and what a powerful influence it exercised over them.

[2] Num. xii. 6 ; Deut. xviii. 17-22.

'That the holy will of the one true God should have been set up before the Israelites in the definite prescriptions of a law, and that, in order to carry this Divine law into effect, and prepare for its proper fulfilment, prophets must appear on the scene,—this is what distinguishes the religion of Israel, not only from all other pre-Christian religions, but also from Christianity itself. For, the legal and prophetical elements of the Old Testament religion are precisely those through which it stood in marked contrast to the other religions, and made an approach to Christianity, while at the same time it thereby bore the character of a religion which could not of itself present the most perfect religious state of things, but could only prepare for it, and hand over the completion to another.'[1]

The close relation of prophecy to the law is not too strongly stated here, and must be kept steadily in view. In its earlier stages the aim of the prophetic agency was almost exclusively directed to the one object of diffusing a better knowledge of the law, and promoting a more dutiful observance of its institutions and precepts. It was essentially a spirit of revival, called forth by the grievous disorders and wide-spread degeneracy that prevailed. Such, as has been already stated, was the leading character and aim of the religious associations which have received the name of the 'schools of the prophets.' They were composed of earnest and devoted men, who, under the direction of one or more persons of really supernatural gifts (such as Samuel at first, afterwards of Elijah and Elisha), set their faces boldly against the corruptions which prevailed, and endeavoured, by religious meetings in various places, with the powerful excitation of sacred

[1] 'Geschichte der Alttestamentlichen Weissagung,' by Dr Gustav Baur, p. 9.

song, to stir up the languid zeal of the people, and engage them to a hearty surrender to the Divine service.   It was a kind of action which, though apparently somewhat irregular and spasmodic in its movements, was in nature not unlike to the evangelistic operations often carried on in modern times, and reached its end in proportion as people were brought to consider aright and discharge their duty as placed under the economy set up by the hand of Moses.   The labours of David, and those gifted men, chiefly of Levitical families, who succeeded him in the work of sacred song, so far coincided with the class of agencies instituted by Samuel, that they also had in view the proper understanding and due appreciation of what pertained to the old economy, but employed more of literary effort, especially of lyrical compositions, for the purpose, and in these sometimes gave delineations of the kingdom of God as it should exist in the future, and of the King who should preside over its affairs and destinies, which could scarcely be conceived capable of realization, except by some mighty change in the form of the constitution and the powers brought to bear on its administration. But by and by a state of things entered, which proved the comparative failure of those reforming agencies, and called for prophetic work of a different kind.   Back-sliding and corruption perpetually returned, after seasons of revival, and with ever-deepening inveteracy.   The royal house itself, which should have ruled only for Jehovah, became infected with worldly pride, luxury, idolatry with its host of attendant vices.   Judgment after judgment had been sent to correct the evil, but all without permanent effect ; and not the realization of splendid hopes, but the sinking of all into prostration and ruin, was the fate that seemed more immediately impending.   It was when matters were verging toward

this deplorable condition, that the prophets, distinctively
so called, came upon the field, and fulfilled, one after
another, their appointed mission.   The circumstances
were very materially changed in which they had to act,
from those which belonged to the times of Samuel and
David; but they still stood in substantially the same
relation to the law, differing only in the application
which was made of it to the state and prospects of the
people.

The prophets without exception took up their position
on the basis of law : they appeared as the vindicators of
its authority, the expounders of its meaning, and in a
sense also the avengers of its injured rights ; for they
never fail to charge upon the people's culpable neglect
of its obligations, and persistent adherence to the practices
it condemns, all the visitations of evil which in the course
of God's providence had befallen them, or the yet greater
calamities that were in prospect.   Nor in pointing to the
possibility of escaping the worst, when there was the
utmost reason to apprehend its approach, do they ever
indicate another course than that of a return to the bond
of the covenant, by ceasing from all the acts and indul-
gences against which it was directed : this one path presented to the people a door of hope.   But in this
particular line the prophets abstain from going farther ;
they never attempt to improve upon the principles of the
Theocracy, or inculcate a morality that transcends the
ideal of the Decalogue.   A claim has sometimes been
made in honour of the prophets, as if their teaching did
transcend, and, in a manner, remodel what had been
previously given—though the quarter from which it
comes may justly beget doubts of its validity.   ' The
remark,' says Mr Stuart Mill,[1] ' of a distinguished

[1] ' On Representative Government,' p. 42.

Hebrew, that the prophets were, in Church and State, the equivalent of the modern liberty of the press, gives a just but not an adequate conception of the part fulfilled in national and universal history by this great element of Jewish life ; by means of which, the canon of inspiration never being complete, the persons most eminent in genius and moral feeling could not only denounce and reprobate, with the direct authority of the Almighty, whatever appeared to them deserving of such treatment, but could give forth better and higher interpretations of the national religion, which thenceforth became part of the religion.   Accordingly, whoever can divest himself of the habit of reading the Bible as if it was one book, sees with admiration the vast interval between the morality and religion of the Pentateuch, or even of the historical books, and the morality and religion of the prophecies— a distance as wide as between these last and the Gospels. Conditions more favourable to progress could not easily exist ; accordingly, the Jews, instead of being stationary, like other Asiatics, were, next to the Greeks, the most progressive people of antiquity, and, jointly with them, have been the starting-point.and main propelling agency of modern cultivation.'

There is just enough in the actual history of the case to give a plausible colour to this representation, and a measure of truth which may save it from utter repudiation.   The recognised place given to the function of prophecy in the Theocratic constitution, was unquestionably a valuable safeguard against arbitrary power ; it secured a right and warrant for freedom of speech on all that most essentially concerned the interests of the kingdom ; and as the function was actually exercised, it did unquestionably serve, in a very high degree, the purpose of reproving abuses, and of unfolding principles of truth and

duty, which needed only to be believingly apprehended
to fill the mind with a generous aspiration after everything
pure and good.   But the language quoted goes a great
deal beyond this.   It implies, that we have in the Bible
a specimen, not simply of growing light and progressive
development, but of diverse exhibitions of truth and
duty ; that the beginnings of the Hebrew commonwealth
were in this respect extremely crude and defective, but
that in process of time, as men of higher intellect and
finer moral sensibilities (the prophets, to wit) applied
themselves to the task of instruction, everything took a
nobler elevation, and a religion and morality were brought
forth which stood at a wide remove from those of the
Pentateuch.   This we altogether deny, and regret the
countenance it has met with from Dean Stanley (as
indeed from many other writers of the day).   He quotes
the passage from Mill without the slightest qualification,
and proceeds to support it by specifying the more leading
features in which the prophetic teaching constituted an
advance on what preceded.   The particular points are,
first, the unity of God ; then the spirituality of God
(meaning thereby His moral character, His justice, love,
and goodness) ; and lastly, as the necessary result of
this, the exaltation of the moral above the ceremonial
in religion ('not sacrifice, not fasting, not ablutions,' etc.,
but 'judgment, mercy, and truth').[1]   Beyond all doubt,
these *were* among the leading characteristics of the prophetical teaching ; and in that teaching they are set forth
with a clearness, a prominence, and a fervour, which may
justly be termed peculiar, and for which the church of
all ages has reason to be thankful.   The circumstances of
the times were such as to call, in a very special manner,
for the bold and explicit announcement of the vital

[1] 'Lectures on Jewish Church,' end of Lec. XIX. and beginning of Lec. XX.

truths and principles in question; only, it must be remembered, they were not given for the purpose of initiating a higher form of morality and religion, but rather of staying a perilous degeneracy, and recovering a position that had been lost.   For the truths and principles were in no respect new; they were interwoven with the writings and legislation of Moses; and only in the *mode and fulness* of the revelation, but not in the *things revealed*, does the teaching of the prophets differ from the handwriting of Moses.   So far from aiming at the introduction of anything properly new, either in the religion or the morality of the Old Covenant, it was the object of their most earnest strivings to turn back the hearts of the children to the fathers, the disobedient to the wisdom of the just;[1] and the very last in the long line of prophetic agency, while pointing to nobler messengers and grander revelations in the coming future, charges his countrymen, as with his parting breath, to 'remember the law of Moses which God commanded him in Horeb for all Israel, with the statutes and judgments.'[2]   It was virtually to say, This was meanwhile the best thing for them; the word of prophecy did not seek to carry them above the dispensation under which they lived; and not a higher position, in respect either to God or to one another, was to be gained by disregarding it, but a fall into vanity, corruption, and ruin.

But as regards the particular points mentioned by Stanley, which of them, we should like to know, is wanting in the books of Moses, or is denied its just place in the religious polity he brought in?   The grand truth of the Divine unity is assuredly not wanting; it stands in the very front of the Decalogue, and from the first chapter in Genesis to the last in Deuteronomy, it is the truth

---

[1] 1 Kings xviii. 37; Luke i. 17.   [2] Mal. iv. 4.

which above all others is prominent—so prominent, that (as we have seen) to guard and preserve this doctrine some would even take as the almost exclusive end of the Mosaic legislation. Nor is it much otherwise with the spirituality of God — understanding thereby not only His incorporeal nature, but also and more peculiarly His moral character ; for this, too, is a pervading element both in the history and the legislation. It is the key which opens out to us, so far as it can be opened, the mystery of paradise and the fall, and the principle which runs through the entire series of providential dealings, of blessings bestowed upon some, and judgments inflicted upon others, which make up so large a portion of patri- archal history. But the grand testimony for it is in the law of the ten commandments, given as the revelation of God's character, yea, laid as the very foundation of His throne in Israel—the most sublime exaltation of the moral above all merely physical notions of Deity, and of the spiritual over the outward and material in the forms of worship, to be found in the records of ancient times. The prophets could but unfold and vindicate the truth so presented ; they could add nothing to its relative signifi- cance. And if, in the law itself, there were many enact- ments of a ceremonial kind—and if the Jewish people, especially in later times, shewed an inclination to give these the foremost place, to make more account of sacri- fice, fasting, ablutions, than of judgment, mercy, and truth—it was in palpable violation (as we have already shewn) of the evident tendency and bearing of the law itself. It was only as testifying against an abuse, a culpable misreading of their religious institutions, that the prophets sometimes drew so sharply the distinction between the ceremonial and the moral in religion. At other times, they again shewed how they could appreciate the symbolical institutions of the law, and enforce their observance.[1]   There was, then, no proper diversity, much less any antagonism, between the teaching of the prophets and the instruction embodied in the commands and ordinances of the law.   And we must hold, with Harless, that there is no ground for regarding ' the law of God in Israel as the product of a development-process among the people of Israel, who gradually arrived at the consciousness of what is good and right in the relation of man to man, and in the relation of man to God.   On the contrary, God appears, in opposition to the prevailing spirit of the people, giving testimony to His will in a progressive revelation.   The law did not sink down into the people of God as a spiritual principle, the development of which was by God surrendered to the people ; but the entire compass of life's environments was among this people placed, through the variety of the law's enactments, under the prescription of the Divine commanding will.   Instead of being abandoned to the vacillations and gropings of human knowledge, it stands there (what can be said neither of conscience nor of any human law) as beyond doubt the ' holy law,' and its command as the ' holy and righteous and good command !'[2]

But with this fixed character as to the substance of the

---

[1] Ps. li. 19, cxviii. 27 ; Isa. xliii. 23, 24, lx. 6, 13 ; Mal. i. 11, iii. 9, 10.

[2] 'Christliche Ethik,' sec. 16.   If due consideration is given to what has been stated, one will know what to think of the loose and offensive statements often made by persons, however able, who give forth their 'short studies on grave subjects'—such as the following in Froude, ' The religion of the prophets was not the religion which was adapted to the hardness of heart of the Israelites of the Exodus.   The Gospel set aside the law,' etc.   A certain glimmering of truth, to give colour to an essentially wrong meaning !   It is also somewhat striking, in this connection, that the exercise of feelings of revenge, so often charged against the morality of the law, has more appearance of justification in the Psalms and Prophets than in the prescriptions of the law.   But even in these the countenance given to it is more apparent than real.   See Supplementary Dissertation on the subject.

law, there is undoubtedly in the prophetical writings an advance made in the mode, and along therewith in the perspicuity, the fulness, and motive power of the instruction. What in the one lay written in naked prescriptions, or wrapt in the drapery of symbol, is in the other copiously unfolded, explained, and reasoned upon, accompanied also with many touching appeals and forcible illustrations. Specific points, too, as occasion required, are brought out with a breadth and prominence which it was impossible for them to possess in the original revelation. And then in those prophetical writings of later times, as the falling down of the tabernacle of David was clearly announced, and the dissolution of the Theocracy in its original form distinctly contemplated, it was through those writings that the minds of believing men got such insight as they could obtain into the nature of that new and better form of things, through which the blessing (so long deferred) of the covenant of promise was to be realized, and practical results achieved far surpassing what had been found in the past. It is impossible to go here into any detail on this part of the prophetical writings ; but one thing ought to be noted concerning them, which may also be said to be common to them all, that while they speak plainly enough of the old being destined somehow to pass away, they not less plainly declare that all its moral elements should remain and come into more effective and general operation. When Isaiah, for example, makes promise of a king who should spring as a tender scion from the root of David, and not only retrieve the fortunes of His kingdom, but carry everything belonging to it to a state of highest perfection and glory, he represents him as bringing the very mind and will of God to bear on it, taking righteousness for the girdle of his loins, and establishing all with judgment and justice.[1] To magnify the law and make it honourable, is, in a later part of his prophecies, presented as the aim with which the Lord was going to manifest His name in the future, otherwise than He had done in the past; and, as the final result of the manifestation, there was to arise a kingdom of perfect order, a people all righteous, and because righteous full of peace, and blessing, and joyfulness.[2]   Jeremiah is even more explicit; he says expressly, that the Lord was going to make a new covenant with His people, different from that which He had made after the deliverance from Egypt; yet different rather in respect to form and efficient administration, than in what might be called the essential matter of the covenant; for this is the explanation given, ' After those days, saith the Lord, I will put my law in their inward parts, and write it in their hearts; and will be their God, and they shall be my people'[3]—the same law in substance still, only transferred from the outward to the inward sphere—from the tables of stone to the fleshy tables of the heart; and this so as to secure, what had in a great measure failed under the old form of the covenant, a people with whom God could hold the most intimate and endearing fellowship.   Then, following in the same line, there are such prophecies as those of Ezekiel, in which, with a glorious rise in the Divine kingdom from seeming ruin to the possession of universal dominion, there is announced a hitherto unknown work of the Spirit of God, changing hearts of stone into hearts of flesh, and imparting the disposition and the power to keep God's statutes and judgments;[4] the similar prophecy of Joel, according to which the Spirit was to be poured out in such measure, that spiritual gifts hitherto

[1] Isa. ix. 7, xi.   [2] Isa. xlii. 21, lx., lxv. 17, 18.
[3] Jer. xxxi. 33.   [4] Ezek. xvii. 23, 24, xxxvi. 25-27.

confined to a few should become, in a manner, the common property of believers ;[1] the prophecy of Micah, that the mountain of the Lord's house, the seat of the Divine kingdom, should be morally exalted by such a manifestation of the Divine presence, and such a going forth of the law of the Lord, as would reach all hearts and carry it with decisive sway over the most distant lands ;[2] and, to mention no more, the brief but clear and striking announcements of Malachi, telling of a sudden coming of the Lord to His temple, with such demonstrations of righteousness and means of effective working, as would burn like a refiner's fire, and bring forth a living community of pure and earnest worshippers.[3] From the general strain of these and many similar revelations in the prophetic Scriptures, it was evidently in the mind and purpose of God to give a manifestation of Himself among men for the higher ends and interests of His covenant, far surpassing anything that had been known in the history of the past ; and that, while the demands of law should thus be for ever established, the law itself should be made to take another place than it had been wont to do in economical arrangements, and should be so associated with the peculiar gifts and graces of the Spirit, as to bring out into quite singular prominence the spiritual elements of the covenant, and secure for these far and wide a commanding influence in the world. So that the volume of Old Testament prophecy might be said to close with the presentation of this great problem to the consideration of thoughtful and believing men—how the promised blessing for Israel and the world could be wrought out, so as to maintain in all its integrity the law of the Divine righteousness, and, at the same time, provide for powers and agencies coming into play, which

---

[1] Joel ii. 28-32.   [2] Micah iv. 1-5.   [3] Mal. iii. 1-6.

should necessarily change the law's place from a higher to a lower, from a greater to a less prominent position in the administration of the Divine kingdom !

V. There can be no doubt that, for generations before the Christian era, the minds of the better part of the Jewish people were more or less occupied with thoughts concerning this problem; and though from its very nature it was one of Divine, not of human solution, yet as the period approached for its passing into the sphere of history, expectation took very determinate forms of belief as to the manner in which it behoved to be done. These differed widely from each other, but were all so wide of the true mark, that the very conception of the plan by which the Divine purpose was to receive its accomplishment, proved the Divine insight of Him through whom it was at last carried into effect.   With two of those forms of thought and belief we are perfectly familiar, they come out so prominently in the Gospel history —represented, respectively, by the two great divisions of later Judaism in Palestine—those of the Pharisees and the Sadducees.   Neither party, perhaps, embraced more than a section of the Jewish people resident in Palestine, but together they undoubtedly included its more influential portions—the men who guided the sentiments and ruled the destinies of their country.   The Pharisees, as is well known, were by much the more numerous and influential party ; and taking their name from a Hebrew word (*parash*), which means to separate or place apart, it denoted them as *the men* by way of eminence, the more select and elevated portion of the community, those who stood 'at the summit of legal Judaism' (Neander).   In them the state of feeling described toward the close of last lecture found its more peculiar development.   The

law was in a manner everything with them; and to preserve it on all sides from dishonour and infringement,
they gradually accumulated an infinite number of rules
and precepts, which tended greatly more to mar than to
further its design.   For it led them to fix their regards
almost exclusively on the outward relations of things, to
turn both religion and morality into a rigid formalism;
and, as a matter of course, the form was substituted for
the power of godliness—weightier matters gave way in
practice to comparative trifles—and the law was in great
part made void by what was done to protect and magnify it.
Thus the Pharisees, as a class of religionists, proved themselves to be blind in regard to the great problem which was
then waiting its solution; and the more they multiplied
their legal enactments, they but wove a thicker veil for
their own understandings, and became the more incapable
of looking to the end of those things which the law aimed
at establishing.   A perpetuation and extension of *their*
system would have been a bondage and not a deliverance,
a misfortune and not a blessing; since it would have
served to case the world up in a hard, inflexible religious
coat of mail, fitted to repel rather than attract—the very
antithesis of a free, loving, devoted piety.

It had been no better, but in various respects worse, on
the principle of Sadduceeism; for here the deeper elements
of the Old Covenant were not merely overshadowed, or
relatively depreciated, as in Pharisaism, but absolutely
ignored.   The spiritual world was to it little more than a
blank; it had an eye only for the visible and earthly
sphere of things; therefore knew nothing of the spiritual
significance of the law, and the depth of meaning which
lay underneath its symbols of worship.   For men of this
stamp, the religion of the Old Covenant was the ground
merely of their national polity and of their hopes as a

people—which consequently had a claim on their respectful observance, but not such as was connected with painful convictions of sin, or earnest longings after a holier and better state of things. All that apparently entered into their dream of prospective glory would have been realized, if, without any material change in the religious aspect of things, they should be able, under the leadership of some second David, to rectify the political disorders of the time, relieve themselves of the shame and oppression of a foreign yoke, and rise to the ascendency of power and influence in the world, which the antecedents of their history gave them reason to expect. The more fundamental elements of the great problem could scarcely be said to come within their range of vision.

There was much more of an earnest and thoughtful spirit in a class of religionists who belonged to Judea, and had their chief settlements about the shores of the Dead Sea, but who, from their reserved and secluded habits, are never mentioned in the Gospel history. I refer to the Essenes, whose religion appears to have been a strange and somewhat arbitrary compound of ritualistic and theosophic elements—of Judaism (in the Pharisaic sense) and asceticism. They are reported to have sent offerings to the temple, but they did not themselves personally frequent its courts, deeming it a kind of pollution to mingle in the throng of such a miscellaneous company of worshippers; so that many of the most distinctly commanded observances in the religion of the Old Covenant must have been unscrupulously set aside by them. But while thus in one direction scorning the restraints of ceremonialism, and in their general abstinence from marriage, and their communism of goods, chalking freely out a path for themselves, in other respects the Essenes were ceremonialists of the straitest sect: they would not

kindle a fire or remove a vessel on the Sabbath, refused
to use victuals that had been prepared by persons out
of their own hallowed circle, resorted ever and anon to
corporeal ablutions, in particular after having been touched
by an uncircumcised person, or even one of an inferior grade
among themselves.[1] Their system was evidently a sincere
but ill-adjusted and abortive attempt at reform; on the
one side, a reaction from the mechanical, selfish, and
worldly spirit of Pharisaism; on the other, an adhesion
to specific forms and ascetic practices, as the choicest
means for reaching the higher degrees of perfection. At
how great a remove did the followers of such a system
stand from the spiritual elevation of the prophets! And
in themselves how obviously incapable of bursting the
shell of Judaism, and understanding how a religion might
be evolved from it of blessed peace, expansive benevolence, and son-like freedom! It was clear that no more
with them than with the others, was found the secret
of the problem which now lay before the people of God:
they could contribute nothing to its solution.

And the same, yet again, has to be said of another
class of reforming Jews, who brought higher powers to
the task than the narrow-minded Essenes, and who gave
to Judaism whatever light could be derived from the
most spiritual philosophy of Greece. I speak now not of
the Jews in Palestine, but of the Alexandrian Jews, more
especially as represented by the thoughtful and contemplative Philo. He shrunk from the extremes that some
of his countrymen, in their passion for philosophy, appear
to have run into—'trampling (as he says of them) upon
the laws in which they were born and bred, upturning
those customs of their country which are liable to no just
censure.' He, along with the great body even of the

---

[1] Josephus, 'Ant.' xviii. 1, sec. 4; 'Wars,' ii. 8, secs. 3-13.

philosophizing Jews, still held by the traditions and religious customs of his fathers, but threw over these a
kind of foreign costume, read them in a Hellenic light,
and thereby sought to obtain from them a more profound
and varied instruction than they were otherwise capable
of yielding.   Philo and his coadjutors were so far right,
that they conceived a letter and a spirit to belong to the
Old Testament ; but they entirely erred in trying to find
a key to the spirit in the sublimated physics of a Gentile
philosophy—in seeing, for example, in the starry hosts
choirs of the highest and purest angels, in the tabernacle
a pattern of the universe, in the twelve loaves of shew-
bread the twelve months of the year, in the two rows of
them the vernal and autumnal equinox, in the seven-
branched candlestick the seven planets, and so on.   This
was truly to seek the living among the dead.   It is the
moral, as we have had occasion frequently to repeat,
which is the essential element in the religion of the Old
Testament, underlying all its symbols, interwoven with
all its histories ; the spirit which pervades them throughout is the spirit of the ten commandments.   And in
trying to find in them the cover of philosophic ideas, or
the reflex of material nature, everything was turned into
a wrong direction ; it became merely the handmaid of an
intellectual refinement or a mystic lore, but in the same
proportion ceased to be of real value in the kingdom of
God.

On every side we see only misapprehension and failure.
Not one of the various sections, into which the covenant-
people latterly fell, sufficiently grasped the completed
revelation of the Old Testament, so as even to perceive
how its destined end was to be reached—how its great
problem was to be solved.   From the simply ritualistic
and patriotic spirit, as represented by the divergent

schools of the Pharisees and the Sadducees, it lay hid;
it lay hid also from the theosophic and ascetic spirit, as
represented by the earnest, but exclusive and somewhat
forbidding sect of the Essenes. And when philosophy,
with its intellectual culture and lofty aspirations, came to
the task, it fared no better; the real spirit of the old
economy was not evoked, nor any discovery made of the
way by which its apparent contradictories might be reconciled, and an influence of charmed power brought to
bear on the hearts and consciences of men. For anything
that such schools and parties could effect, or even knew
distinctly to propose, the world had slumbered on in its
ancient darkness and corruption—its moral degeneracy
unchecked, its disquieting terrors unallayed, its debasing
superstitions and foul idolatries continuing to hold captive
the souls of men. And if the real reform—the salvation-
work, and the better spirit growing out of it, which like
a vivifying pulse of life was to make itself felt through
society, to cause humanity itself to spring aloft into a
higher sphere, and commence a new career of fruitfulness
in intellectual and moral action—if this should have
found its realization in One who, humanly speaking, was
the least likely to be furnished for the undertaking—One
who not only belonged to the same people, but was
reared in one of their obscurest villages, and under the
roof of one of its humblest cottages—whence, we naturally
ask, could it have been found in Him, but from His
altogether peculiar connection with the Highest? A
failure in every quarter but the one which was most
palpably deficient in human equipment and worldly resources, manifestly bespeaks for that One the preter-
natural insight and all-sufficient help of God. Jesus of
Nazareth did what all others were unable not only to
accomplish, but even adequately to conceive, because He

was Immanuel, God with us; and so, in spite of the lack of human advantages, and the fierce opposition of powerful foes, He fulfilled the task with which expectation had been so long travailing in birth, and left the mysterious problem concerning the future of the Divine kingdom among men written out in the facts of His marvellous history, and the rich dowry of grace and blessing He brought in for His redeemed.

LECTURE VII.

THE RELATION OF THE LAW TO THE MISSION AND WORK OF
CHRIST—THE SYMBOLICAL AND RITUAL FINDING IN HIM ITS
TERMINATION, AND THE MORAL ITS FORMAL APPROPRIATION
AND PERFECT FULFILMENT.

AS the appearance of the Lord Jesus Christ for the
work of our redemption was unspeakably the greatest era in the history of God's dispensations toward men,
we cannot doubt that every thing respecting it was
arranged with infinite wisdom. It took place, as the
apostle tells us, ' in the fulness of the time' (Gal. iv. 4).
Many circumstances, both in the church and in the world,
conspired to render it such ; and among these may
undoubtedly be placed the fact, that there was not only
a general expectation throughout the world of some one
going to arise in Judea, who should greatly change and
renovate the state of things, but in Judea itself the more
certain hope and longing desire of a select few, who,
taught by the word of prophecy, were anxiously waiting
' for the consolation of Israel.' Yet even with them, as
may be reasonably inferred from what afterwards transpired in Gospel history, the expectation, however sincere
and earnest, was greatly wanting in discernment : it
might justly be said ' to see through a glass, darkly.'
The great problem which, according to Old Testament
Scripture, had to find its solution in the brighter future of
God's kingdom, was not distinctly apprehended by any

known section of the covenant-people; and in all the more prominent and active members of the community there were strong currents of opinion and deeply cherished convictions, which were utterly incompatible with the proper realization of the Divine plan. This condition of affairs immensely aggravated the difficulty of the undertaking for Him, who came in this peculiar work to do the Father's will; but it served, at the same time, more clearly to shew how entirely all was of God—both the insight to understand what was needed to be done, and the wisdom, the resolution, the power to carry it into execution.

If, however, from the position of matters now noticed, it was necessary that our Lord should move in perfect independence as regards the religious parties of the time, it was not less necessary that He should exercise a close dependence on the religion which they professed in common to maintain. Coming as the Messiah promised to the Fathers, He entered, as a matter of course, into the heritage of all preceding revelations, and therefore could introduce nothing absolutely new—could only exhibit the proper growth and development of the old. And so, while isolating Himself from the Judaism of the Scribes and Pharisees, Jesus lovingly embraced the Judaism of the law and the prophets; and, founding upon what had been already established, took it for His especial calling to unfold the germs of holy principle which were contained in the past revelations of God, and by word and deed ripen them into a system of truth and duty adapted to the mature stage which had now been reached of the Divine dispensations. It was only in part, indeed, that this could be done during the personal ministry of our Lord; for, as the light He was to introduce depended to a large extent on the work He had to accomplish for men, there were many things respecting it which could not be fully disclosed till the events of His marvellous history had run their course. It was the redeeming work of Christ which more than all besides was to give its tone and impress to the new dispensation ; and much of the teaching on men's relations to God, on their present calling and their future prospects as believers in Christ, had in consequence to be deferred till the work itself was finished. This our Lord Himself plainly intimated to His disciples near the close of His career, when pointing to certain things of which they could not even then bear the disclosure, but which the Spirit of truth would reveal to them after His departure, and qualify them for communicating to others.[1] Yet not only were the materials for all provided by Christ in His earthly ministry, but the way also was begun to be opened for their proper application and use ; and what was afterwards done in this respect by the hands of the apostles was merely the continuation and further unfolding of the line of instruction already commenced by their Divine Master.

I. Now, of one thing our Lord's ministry left no room to doubt—and it is the more noticeable, as in this He differed from all around Him—He made a marked distinction between the symbolical or ritual things of the Old Covenant, and its strictly moral precepts. He regarded the former, as the legal economy itself did, in the light merely of appendages to the moral—temporary expedients, or provisional substitutes for better things to come, which had no inherent value in themselves, and were to give way before the great realities they fore-

---

[1] John xvi. 12-15. See the point admirably exhibited in Bernard's Bampton Lecture, on 'The Progress of Doctrine in the New Testament.'

shadowed. Hence the reserve He manifested in regard to external rites and ceremonies. We read of no act of bodily lustration in His public history. He expressly repudiated the idea of washing having in itself any power to cleanse from spiritual defilement, or of true purification at all depending on the kind of food that might be partaken of.[1] He was the true, the ideal Nazarite, yet undertook no Nazarene vow. Though combining in Himself all the functions of prophet, priest, and king, yet He entered on them by no outward anointing : He had the real consecrating of the Holy Spirit, visibly descending and abiding with Him.[2] And though He did not abstain from the stated feasts of the Temple, when it was safe and practicable for Him to be present, yet we hear of no special offerings for Himself or His disciples on such occasions. Even as regards the ordinary services and offerings of the Temple, He claimed a rightful exemption, on the ground of His essentially Divine standing, from the tribute-money, the half-shekel contribution, by which they were maintained.[3] He was Himself, as the Son of the Highest, the Lord of that Temple ; it was the material symbol of what He is in His relation to His people ; and on the occasion of His first public visit to its courts, He vindicated His right to order its affairs, by casting out the buyers and sellers ; yea, and, identifying Himself with it, He declared that when *He* fell, as the Redeemer of the world, *it* too should virtually fall—the Great Inhabitant should be gone—and henceforth, no more in one place than another, but in every place where the children of faith might meet together, *there* should true worship and acceptable service be presented to God.[4] Utterances like these plainly rung the

[1] Matt. xv. 1-20. [2] John i. 32-34; Luke iii. 22, iv. 18.
[3] Matt. xvii. 24-27. [4] John ii. 13-22, iv. 21-24.

knell of the old ceremonialism. They bespoke a speedy
removing of the external fabric of Judaism, yet such a
removing as would leave greatly more than it took—
instead of the imperfect and temporary shadow, the
eternal substance. And if one might still speak, in the
hallowed language of the sanctuary, of a temple, and a
sacrifice, and a daily ministration, of a sanctity to be
preserved and a pollution to be shunned, it must be as
bound to no specific localities, or stereotyped forms, but as
connected with the proper freedom and enlargement of
God's true children.[1]

---

[1] The nature of this part of our Lord's work, and the substance of His teaching respecting it, was strikingly embodied in the first formal manifestation of
His supernatural agency—the σημεῖον, which He performed as an appropriate
and fitting commencement to the whole cycle of His miraculous working—
namely, the turning of water into wine at the marriage feast in Cana (John
ii. 1-10). Considered as such a beginning, it certainly has, at first sight, a
somewhat strange appearance ; but, on closer examination, this aspect of
strangeness gives way, and the Divine wisdom of the procedure discovers
itself. The transaction, like the period to which it belonged, found a point
of contact between the new and the old in God's kingdom—it was indicative
of the transition which was on the eve of taking place from the law to
the Gospel. The water-vessels used for the occasion were those ordinarily
employed for purposes of purification according to the law ; they stood there
as the representatives of the old economy—the remembrancers of sin and
pollution even in the midst of festive mirth ; and had they been associated
merely with water, they could not have been made the bearer of any higher
instruction. But when, after being filled with this, the water was turned into
wine—wine of the finest quality—such as drew forth the spontaneous testimony,
not that the old, but that the new was the better, they became the emblem of
the now opening dispensation of grace, which, with its vivifying and refreshing influences, was soon to take the place of the legal purifications. Yet, in
that supplanting of the one by the other, there was not the production of
something absolutely new, but rather the old transformed, elevated, as in the
transmutation of the simple and comparatively feeble element of water into
the naturally powerful and active principle of wine. In the very act of changing the old into the new, our Lord, so far from ignoring or disparaging the old,
served Himself of it ; and it was, we may say, within the shell and framework
of what had been, that the new and better power was made to come forth and
develop itself in the world. Such, in its main features and leading import,
was the sign here wrought by Jesus at the commencement of His public career.

II. Turning now to the moral part of the Old Testament legislation—to the law strictly so called—we find our Lord acting in a quite different manner—shewing the utmost solicitude to preserve intact the revelation at Sinai, and to have it made, through His teaching, both better understood, and with fresh sanctions enforced as the essential rule of righteousness in God's kingdom— nay, Himself submitting to bow down to it as the yoke which, in His great work of obedience, He was to bear, and, by bearing, to glorify God and redeem man. Let us look at it first in more immediate connection with the *teaching* of Christ.

There was undoubtedly a difference—a difference of a quite perceptible kind, and one that will not be overlooked by those who would deal wisely with the records of God's dispensations, in respect to the place occupied by law in the economies headed respectively by Moses and Christ. It was in His memorable Sermon on the Mount that our Lord made the chief formal promulgation of the fundamental principles of His Kingdom, which, therefore, stood to the coming dispensation in somewhat of the

The occasion, too, on which it was done, fitly accorded with its character; for, just as in the Old Testament arrangements the feasts were linked to appropriate seasons in nature, so was it here with the initiatory work of Christ: like the economical change which the miracle symbolized, the time was one of hope and gladness. It was the commencing era of a new life to the persons more immediately concerned, and one that, not only in its natural aspect, had the sanction and countenance of Christ, but also, from the higher turn given to it by His miraculous working, made promise of the joy and blessing which was to result from His great undertaking. Nay, by entering into the bridegroom's part, and ministering to the guests the materials of gladness, He foreshadowed how, as the Regenerator of the world, He should make Himself known as the kind and gracious Bridegroom of His church. And it seems as if the Baptist had but caught up the meaning couched under this significant action of our Lord, when, not long afterwards, he spoke of Jesus as the Bridegroom, whose voice he, as the Bridegroom's friend, delighted to hear, and whose appearance should have been welcomed by all as the harbinger of life and blessing.

same relation that the imposing promulgation of law from Sinai did to the ancient Theocracy ; and, as if on purpose to link the two more distinctly and closely together, He makes to that earlier revelation very frequent and pointed reference in His discourse. But how strikingly different in mode and circumstance the one revelation from the other ! The two dispensations have their distinctive characteristics imaged in the two historical occasions, exhibiting even to the outward eye the contrast expressed by the Evangelist John, when he said, ' The law was given by Moses, grace and truth came by Jesus Christ.'

What a difference in the external scenery alone, in the two mounts ! Sinai is less properly a mountain, in the ordinary sense of the term, than a lofty and precipitous rock, in the midst of a wilderness of rocks of similar aspect and formation — combining, in a degree rarely equalled, the two features of grandeur and desolation; ' The Alps unclothed,' as they have been significantly called—the Alps stript of all verdure and vegetation, and cleft on every side into such deep hollows, or rising into such rugged eminences, as render them alike of sullen mien and of difficult access. *There*, amid the sterner scenery of nature, intensified by the supernatural elements brought into play for the occasion, the Lord descended as in a chariot of fire, and proclaimed with a voice of thunder those ten words which were to form the basis of Israel's religion and polity. It was amid quite other scenes and aspects of nature, that the incarnate Redeemer met the assembled multitudes of Galilee, when He proceeded to disclose in their hearing the fundamental principles of the new and higher constitution He came to introduce. The exact locality in this case cannot, indeed, be determined with infallible certainty—though there is no reason to doubt its connection with the elevated table-land, rising prominently into view a few miles to the south of Capernaum, and jutting up into two little points called the ' Horns of Hattin,' to which tradition has assigned the name of ' The mount of the Beatitudes.' This elevated plain, we are informed, ' is easily accessible from the Galilean lake, and from that plain to the summit [or points just mentioned] is but a few minutes' walk. Its situation also is central both to the peasants of the Galilean hills, and the fishermen of the lake, between which it stands ; and would, therefore, be a natural resort to Jesus and His disciples, when they retired for solitude from the shores of the sea.'[1] The prospect from the summit is described even now as pleasing, though rank weeds are growing around, and only occasional patches of corn meet the eye ;[2] but how much more must it have been so then, when Galilee was a well-cultivated and fertile region, and the rich fields which slope downwards to the lake were seen waving with their summer produce ! It was on such an eminence, embosomed in so fair and pleasing an amphitheatre, and, as the multitudes assembled on the occasion seemed to betoken, under a bright sky and a serene atmosphere, that the blessed Redeemer chose to give forth this fresh utterance of Heaven's mind and will ; and Himself the while, not wrapt in thick darkness, not even assuming an attitude of imposing grandeur, but fresh from the benign work of healing, and seated in humble guise, as a man among his fellow-men, at the most as a teacher in the midst of His listening disciples. So did the Son of Man open His mouth and make known the things which concern His kingdom. What striking

[1] Stanley's 'Sinai and Palestine,' p. 368.
[2] Robertson's 'Researches,' III. p. 239.

and appropriate indications of Divine grace and conde-
scension ! How well fitted to inspire confidence and
hope ! As compared with the scenes and transactions
associated with the giving of the law from Sinai, it
bespoke such an advance in the march of God's dispensations, as is seen in the field of nature when it can be
said, ' The winter is past, the rain is over and gone, the
flowers appear on the earth, the time of the singing of
birds is come, and the voice of the turtle is heard in our
land.'

The discourse which our Lord delivered on the occasion entirely corresponds with the new era which it
marked in the history of God's dispensations. The
revelation from Sinai, though grafted on a covenant of
grace, and uttered by God as the Redeemer of Israel,
was emphatically a promulgation of law. Its direct and
formal object was to raise aloft the claims of the Divine
righteousness, and meet, with repressive and determined
energy, the corrupt tendencies of human nature. The
Sermon on the Mount, on the other hand, begins with
blessing. It opens with a whole series of beatitudes,
blessing after blessing pouring itself forth as from a full
spring of beneficence, and seeking, with its varied and
copious manifestations of goodness, to leave nothing un-
provided for in the deep wants and longing desires of
men. Yet here also, as in other things, the difference
between the New and the Old is relative only, not
absolute. There are the same fundamental elements in
both, but these differently adjusted, so as fitly to adapt
them to the ends they had to serve, and the times to
which they respectively belonged. In the revelation of
law there was a *substratum* of grace, recognised in the
words which prefaced the ten commandments, and *promises* of grace and blessing also intermingling with the

stern prohibitions and injunctions of which they consist. And so, inversely, in the Sermon on the Mount, while it gives grace the priority and the prominence, it is far from excluding the severer aspect of God's character and government. No sooner, indeed, has grace poured itself forth in a succession of beatitudes, than there appear the stern demands of righteousness and law—the very law proclaimed from Sinai—and that law so explained and enforced as to bring fully under its sway the intents of the heart, as well as the actions of the life, and by men's relation to it determining their place and destinies in the Messiah's kingdom.

Here, then, we have our Lord's own testimony regarding His relation to the law of God. His first and most comprehensive declaration upon the subject—the one which may be said to rule all the others—is the utterance on the mount, ' Think not that I came to destroy the law or the prophets, I came not to destroy (καταλῦσαι, to dissolve, abrogate, make void), but to fulfil (πληρῶσαι).'[1] This latter expression must be taken in its plain and natural sense ; therefore, not as some would understand it, to confirm or ratify—which is not the import of the word, and also what the law and the prophets did not require. God's word needs no ratification. Nor, as others, to fill up and complete their teaching—for this were no proper contrast to the destroying or making void. No ; it means simply to substantiate, by doing what they required, or making good what they announced. To fulfil a law (πληροῦν νόμον), was a quite common expression, in profane as well as sacred writings, and only in the sense now given.[2] So we find Augustine confidently urging

---

[1] Mat. v. 17.

[2] Luke xxiv. 44 ; Acts iii. 18 ; Rom. xiii. 8 ; Gal. v. 14.   *See,* for example, Meyer and Fritzsche on the words.   Alford points to what he

it against the Manichæan perverters of the truth in his day : ' The law (says he) is fulfilled when the things are done which are commanded. . . . Christ came not to destroy the law but to fulfil it : not that things might be added to the law which were wanting, but that the things written in it might be done—which His own words confirm; for He does not say, " One jot or one tittle shall not pass from the law" till the things wanting are added to it, but " till all be done." '[1]   And uttered as the declaration was when men's minds were fermenting with all manner of opinions respecting the intentions of Jesus, it was plainly meant to assure them that He stood in a friendly relation to the law and the prophets, and could no more, in His teaching than in His working, do what would be subversive of their design. They must find in Him only their fulfilment.   To render His meaning still more explicit, our Lord gives it the advantage of two specific illustrations, one hypothetical, the other actual.   ' Should any one, therefore (He says, in ver. 19), annul (not *break*, as in the English version, but put away, abrogate, annul, λύσῃ) one of these commandments—the least of them—and teach men so, he shall be called least in the kingdom of heaven ;' such is the exact rendering, and it very expressly asserts the validity of what was found in preceding revelations, down even to their least commands, in the kingdom presently to be set up.   There was to be no antagonism

calls parallel instances for another meaning ; but they are not parallel; for the question is not what πληροῦν by itself, but what πληροῦν νόμον signifies. The expression has but one ascertained meaning.

[1] Contra Faustum. L. xvii. sec. 6.   I have given only what he says on the expression of our Lord ; his mode of explaining the fulfilment, though not incorrect, is somewhat partial and incomplete :—Ipsa lex cum impleta est, gratia et veritas facta est.   Gratia pertinet ad charitatis plenitudinem, veritas ad prophetiarum impletionem.

between the new and the old ; so far from it, that any one
who had failed to discern and appreciate the righteousness embodied in the smaller things of the law, and on
that account would have them set aside—for so plainly
must the words be understood—he should exhibit such
a want of accordance with the spirit of the new economy,
he should so imperfectly understand and sympathize with
its claims of righteousness, that he might lay his account
to be all but excluded from a place in the kingdom. But
it was quite conceivable, that one might in a certain
sense not except even to the least, and yet be so defective
in the qualities of true righteousness, as to stand in an
altogether false position toward the greater and more
important. There were well-known parties in such a
position at that particular time ; and by a reference to
what actually existed among them, our Lord furnishes
another, and to His audience, doubtless, a more startling,
illustration. ' For I say unto you,' He adds, ' that except
your righteousness should exceed (περισσεύση, go beyond,
overpass) that of the Scribes and Pharisees, ye shall in no
wise enter into the kingdom of heaven.' The question is
now one of total unfitness and consequent exclusion. In
the preceding and hypothetical statement, our Lord had
declared how even a comparatively small antagonism to
the righteousness of the law should inevitably lower one's
position in respect to the kingdom ; and now, vindicating
this stringency, as well as exemplifying and confirming it,
He points to the mistaken and defective standard prevalent among the more conspicuous religionists of the time
as utterly incompatible with any place whatever in the
kingdom. The Scribes are joined with the Pharisees in
upholding the righteousness in question—the one as
representatives of its defective teaching, the other as
examples of its inadequate doing. The Scribes under-

P

stood and taught superficially, adhering to the mere letter of requirement, and hence unduly magnifying the little, relatively undervaluing or neglecting the great. The Pharisees, in like manner, practised superficially, intent mainly on the proprieties of outward observance, doing the works of law only in so far as they seemed to be expressly enjoined, and doing them without love, without life—hence leaving its greater things in reality undone. A righteousness of this description fell altogether below what Jesus, as the Head of the new dispensation, would require of His followers, below also, it is implied, what was taught in the law and the prophets ; for while He could place Himself in perfect accord with the one, He entirely repudiated any connection with the other : the kingdom, as to the righteousness recognised and expected in it, was to rise on the foundation of the law and the prophets ; but for any one to stand on the platform of the Scribes and Pharisees, was to belong to an essentially different sphere.

Now two conclusions seem plainly to flow from this part of our Lord's teaching. One is, that He must have had chiefly in view the moral elements of the old economy, or the righteousness expressed in its enactments :—I do not say simply the ten commandments ; for though these always occupied the foremost place in discourses on the law, did so also here (as appears from the examples presently referred to by our Lord), yet one can scarcely think of *them* when a ' least' is spoken of, as they one and all belonged to the fundamental statutes of the kingdom. Yet, as it is of the law, in connection with and subservient to righteousness, that our Lord speaks, primary respect must be had to the Decalogue, and, in so far as matters of a ceremonial and judicial nature were included, to these only as designed to inculcate and enforce the principles of holy living ; that is, not as mere outward forms or civil regulations, but as the means and the measure of practical goodness. For, otherwise, our Lord's teaching here would be at variance with what He taught elsewhere, and with the truth of things. What He said, for example, on the subject of defilement, that this does not depend upon corporeal conditions and questions of food, but simply on the state of the heart and the issues which proceed from it, formally considered, was undoubtedly an infringing upon the lesser things of the law ; but not so really, for it was merely a penetrating through the shell into the kernel, and in direct terms pressing upon the conscience the lessons intended to be conveyed by the law's carnal ordinances. If the letter fell away, it was only that the spirit might become more clear and prominent. And so in regard to all the ritual observances and factitious distinctions associated with the religion of the Old Covenant—while an entire change was hinted at by our Lord, and in His name was afterwards introduced—the commands imposing them were by no means dishonoured, since the righteousness, for the sake of which these commands were given, was still cared for, and even more thoroughly secured than it could be by them. Rightly viewed, the change was more properly a fulfilling than an abrogating ; an abrogating, indeed, formally, yet a fulfilling or establishing in reality.

Another conclusion which evidently flows from the statements made by our Lord respecting His own relation and that of His kingdom to the law and the prophets, is that the distinctions which He proceeds to draw, in the Sermon on the Mount, between what had been said in earlier times on several points of moral and religious duty, and what He now said, must have respect, not to

the teaching, strictly speaking, of the law and the prophets, but to the views currently entertained of that
teaching, or the false maxims founded on it.   After so
solemnly asserting His entire harmony with the law and
the prophets, and His dependence on them, it would
manifestly have been to lay Himself open to the charge
of inconsistence, and actually to shift the ground which
He professedly occupied in regard to them, if now He
should go on to declare, that, in respect to the great
landmarks of moral and religious duty, they said one
thing, and He said another.   This is utterly incredible ;
and we must assume, that in every instance where a
precept of the law is quoted among the things said in
former times, even though no improper addition is
coupled with it (as at vers. 27 and 33), there still was an
unwarrantable or quite inadequate view commonly taken
of them, against which our Lord directs His authoritative
deliverance, that He might point the way to the proper
height of spiritual attainment.   This view, which the
very nature of the case may be said to demand, is also
confirmed by the formula with which the sayings in
question are introduced : ' Ye have heard that it was
said to them of old time ' (τοῖς ἀρχαίοις, to the ancients).[1]

---

[1] Commentators are still divided on the construction here, whether the
expression should be taken in the dative or the ablative sense—*to* the ancients,
or *by* them.   The general tendency of opinion, however, is decidedly in favour
of the former ; and though the sense does not materially differ whichever construction is adopted, yet various philological considerations determine for the
dative.   (1.) The verb (obsol. ῥέω) is used with great frequency in Matthew's
Gospel in the passive, but always (unless the cases in chap. v. be exceptions)
with a preposition, ὑπό or διά, when the parties by whom the things spoken are
mentioned—they were spoken *by* or *through* such an one.   (2.) In the other
passages of Scripture, in which precisely ἐρρέθη is used, followed as here by
words in the dative without a preposition (Rom. ix. 12, 26 ; Gal. iii. 16 ;
Rev. vi. 11 ; ix. 4), it is beyond doubt the dative import that must be retained.   (3.) If it were to be read *by* the ancients, then a special emphasis must
rest upon the ancients; this will stand in formal contrast to the 'I' of our Lord.

It is a very general mode of expression, not such as we should have expected, if only the deliverances of Scripture were referred to, or the persons who at first hand received them from the messengers of Heaven. These were the honoured fathers of the covenant-people, not the ancients merely, who at some indefinite period in the past had heard and thought after some particular manner. Hence, while they all turn on certain precepts of the law, these, in two or three of the cases, are expressly coupled with later additions, indicative of the superficial view that was taken of them ;[1] and, throughout all the cases adduced, it is evident from our Lord's mode of handling them, that it is not the law *per se* that is under consideration, but the law as understood and expounded according so the frigid style of Rabbinical interpretation —by persons who looked no further than its form of sound words, who thought that to kill had to do with nothing but actual murder, and that a neighbour could be only one dwelling in good fellowship beside us ; who, in short, turned the law of God's righteousness, which, like its Divine Author, must be pervasively spiritual,

---

The collocation of the words, however, would in that case have been different ; it would have been ὅτι τοῖς ἀρχαίοις ἐῤῥέθη, not ὅτι ἐῤῥέθη τοῖς ἀρχαίοις. Not only so, but in most of the repetitions of the formula, in v. 27, according to what seems the best reading, and in v. 31, 38, 43, according to the received text, the τοῖς ἀρχαίοις is wholly omitted—shewing that it was on the saying of the things, not on the persons who said them, that the contrast mainly turns. (4.) It may certainly be regarded as a confirmation of this being, at least, the most natural and obvious construction (which itself is, in such a matter, of some moment), that it is the one adopted by all the leading Greek commentators—Chrysostom, Theophylact, Euthymius. It is that also of the Syriac and Vulgate. Beza was the first, I believe, who formally proposed the rendering *by* them of old time, taking the simple τοῖς ἀρχαίοις as equivalent to ὑπὸ τοῖς ἀρχ.

[1] These are, v. 21, after 'Thou shalt not kill,' 'And whosoever shall kill shall be liable to the judgment ;' and v. 33-36, in regard to several kinds of oaths ; and v. 43, after 'Thou shalt love thy neighbour,' 'Thou shalt hate thine enemy.'

into a mere political code or ecclesiastical rubric.   It is
of the law, as thus unduly curtailed, evacuated of its
proper meaning, treated by the Scribes or letter-men
(γραμματεῖς) as itself but a letter (γράμμα), that Christ
speaks, and, setting His profound and far-reaching view
in opposition to theirs, proclaims, ' But I say unto you.'
Never on any occasion did Jesus place Himself in such
antagonism to Moses ; and least of all could He do so
here, immediately after having so emphatically repudiated
the notion, that He had come to nullify the law and the
prophets, or to cancel men's obligation to any part of
the righteousness they inculcated.   It is to free this
righteousness from the restrictive bonds that had been
laid upon it, and bring it out in its proper breadth and
fulness, that our Lord's expositions are directed.   And
as if to guard against any wrong impressions being produced by what He now said—to shew that His views of
righteousness were in strict agreement with what is
written in the law and the prophets, and that the germ
of all was already there, He distinctly connected with
them, at a subsequent part of His discourse, His own
enunciation of the law of brotherly love, in what has been
called its finest form, ' Whatsoever ye would that men
should do to you, do ye even so to them ; *for this is the
law and the prophets'* (Matt. vii. 12).[1]

---

[1] I am convinced the connection of our Lord's discourse—the relation of
the specific illustrations, given in v. 21-48, to the fundamental positions which
they were brought to illustrate, v. 17-20—will admit of no other construction
than the one now given.   From early times, others have been adopted—by the
Manichæans, who sought to found on the illustrative expositions an absolute
contrariety between Christ and Moses ; and by the great body of the Greek
and Romish theologians, followed in later times by the Socinian, Arminian,
and rationalistic expositors, who understand them of a relative antagonism—
namely, that the law as given by Moses was good as far as it went, but was
carnal and imperfect, and so needed supplementing and enlarging by Christ.
Christ, consequently, according to this view, placed His sayings in contrast with

At the same time, there is nothing in all this to prevent us from believing, as, indeed, it is next to impossible for any one to avoid feeling, that an advance was made by our Lord in His own wonderful exposition of the law —if only that advance is confined to the clearer light which is thrown on the meaning of its precepts, and the higher form which is given to their expression. The Decalogue itself, and the legislation growing out of it, were in their form adapted to a provisional state of

the law itself, as well as with the external legalisms of the Scribes and Pharisees ; these, in fact, are regarded as in the main the true exponents of the Sinaitic law—contrary to the whole tenor of our Lord's representations of them, and the position He took up with reference to them. The other, and what I take to be the correct view, began to be distinctly unfolded and firmly maintained by Augustine, in his contendings with the Manichæans. This is the sense expressed in the passage already quoted from his writings, at p. 224 ; and in the treatise there referred to, L. xix. 27, he brings out the same meaning at still greater length, illustrating as well as stating this to have been Christ's object, either to give the explanation of the law that was needed, or to secure its better observance—omnia ex Hebraeorum lege commemoravit, ut quiquid ex persona sua insuper loqueretur vel ad expositionem requirendam valeret, si quid illa obscure posuisset, vel ad tutius conservandum quod illa voluisset. The Protestant church, generally, in its sounder representatives, took the same view,—Luther, Calvin, Chemnitz (who speaks of the whole passage being corrupted by those who think, Christum hanc suam explicationem opponere ipsi legi divinae), latterly, Stier, Meyer, Fritzsche, Olshausen, even De Wette, Bleek, Ewald, and others of a like stamp ; so also Tholuck, who gives a lengthened review of opinions on the subject, and expresses his own view, and that of many other of the best expositors thus :—' The object of the Saviour is twofold ; on the one hand, He seeks to exhibit the Mosaic law in its deeper import as the moral norm of the righteousness of His kingdom ; on the other hand, He aims at an exposure of the laxer Pharisaic righteousness of His contemporaries, shewing how inadequate it was to attain the high end in view.' Neander, Hofmann, and several others of note, have espoused the other view. In our own country, Mr Liddon (Bampton Lecture for 1866, p. 252) presents it with rhetorical confidence; while Mr Plumptre ('Christ and Christendom,' 1866, p. 235), substantially concurs with the old Protestant interpretation, looking on our Lord's discourse ' as a protest against the popular ethics of the Scribes and Pharisees, professing to be based upon the law, but representing it most imperfectly.' Alford would take a. middle course, but fails to make his meaning quite intelligible. The contrast, he thinks, is ' not between the law misunderstood, and the law rightly understood, but between the law and its

things ; they had to serve the end of a disciplinary institution, and as such had to assume more both of an
external and a negative character, than could be regarded
as ideally or absolutely the best. And it was only what
might have been expected in the progress of things—
when that which is perfect was come—that while the
law in its great principles of moral obligation and its
binding power upon the conscience remained, these
should have had an exhibition given to them somewhat
corresponding to the noon-day period of the church's

ancient exposition, which in their letter, and as given, were vain, and the same
as spiritualized by Christ ;' but the Divine law, when taken in its letter (that
is, we presume, as a mere outward regimen), is *mis*understood, for it never
was meant to be so taken ; psalmists and prophets, as well as Christ, protested
against that view of it ; and then the more spiritual a law is, if left simply as
law, the more certain is it to be vain as to any saving results.

The parts in our Lord's sermon which have most the appearance of contrariety to the old law, are what is said about swearing (v. 33-36), about the law of
recompense (v. 38-42) ; also, in a future discourse, what is said on the law of
divorce (Matt. xix. 1-9). In regard to the first, however, the specific oaths of
the Jews referred to by Christ, taken in connection with His later reference to
them in Matt. xxiii. 16-22, shew clearly enough that it is a prevailing abuse
and corruption of the law that was in view. And, as Harless remarks, 'What
the Lord, the Giver of the law, had commanded in the Old Covenant, namely,
that one should swear in His name (Deut. vi. 13, 18, 20 ; Ex. xxii. 11), that
could not be forbidden in the new by the Lord, the Fulfiller of the law, without
destroying instead of fulfilling it. Rather in this precisely consists the fulfilment, that what the law commanded without being able properly to secure the
fulfilment, that has now come in the Gospel, and, in consequecce, the precept
respecting swearing has also reached its fulfilment. It is just what Jeremiah
intimated, when he predicted that Israel, after being converted, would swear in
a true and holy manner (iv. 1,· 2). What is prohibited in the Gospel of
Matthew are light and frivolous forms of swearing, without any religious feeling' (Ethik, sec. 39). As to the law of recompense (not revenge), as meant by
Moses, it is substantially in force still, and must be so in all well-regulated
communities. (*See* in Lect. IV.) What our Lord taught in connection with it
was, that men in their private relations, and as exponents of love, should not
regard that judicial law as exhausting their duty : to do so was to misapply it.
They should consider how, by forbearance and well-doing, they might benefit a
brother, instead of always exacting of him their due. The case of divorce has
certain difficulties connected with it, yet rather from what in the Old Testament
was not enacted, permitted merely, than what was. But see in Lect. IV.

history, and the son-like freedom of her spiritual standing. Accordingly, our Lord does, in the Sermon on the Mount, and in other parts of His teaching, bring out in a manner never heretofore done, the spirituality of the law of God—shews how, just from being the revelation of His will who is Himself a Spirit, and, as such, necessarily has a predominant respect to spiritual states and acts, it reaches in all its precepts to the thoughts and intents of the heart, and only meets with the obedience it demands, when a pure, generous, self-sacrificing love regulates men's desires and feelings, as well as their words and actions. Hence, things pertaining to the inner man have here relatively a larger place than of old ; and, as a natural sequel, there is more of the positive, less of the negative in form ; the mind is turned considerably more upon the good that should be done, and less upon the evil to be shunned. It is still but a difference in degree, and is often grossly exaggerated by those who have a particular theory of the life of Christ to make out—as by the author of ' Ecce Homo,' who represents the morality enjoined in the Pentateuch as adapted only to half-savage tribes of the desert, the morality even of Isaiah and the prophets as ' narrow, antiquated, and insufficient for the needs' of men in the Gospel age, while, in the teaching of Christ, all becomes changed ' from a restraint to a motive. Those who listened to it passed from a region of passive into a region of active morality. The old legal formula began, " Thou shalt not ;" the new begins with " Thou shalt," ' etc.[1] That this style of representation, in its comparative estimate of the new and the old, goes to excess, it would not be difficult to shew ; but the mere circumstance that Mr J. S. Mill charges the expounders of Christian morality

---

[1] ' Ecce Homo,' ch. xvi.

with presenting an ideal essentially defective, because ' negative rather than positive, passive rather than active, innocence rather than nobleness, abstinence from evil rather than energetic pursuit of good,' is itself a proof that elements of this description cannot be wanting in the Christian system.[1]   In truth, in the New Testament as well as in the Old, the prohibitory is perpetually alternating with the hortatory, the *shall not* with the *shall ;* even in the Sermon on the Mount the one is nearly of as frequent occurrence as the other, and must be so in every revelation of spiritual obligation and moral duty that is suited to men with corrupt natures, and compassed about with manifold temptations.   It must lay a restraint upon their inclinations to evil, as well as direct and stimulate their efforts to what is good.   And the difference between the discourses of Christ and the earlier Scriptures on this and the other point now under consideration, cannot be justly exhibited as more than a relative one — adapted to a more advanced period of the Divine dispensations.   It is such, however, that no discerning mind can fail to perceive it ; and when taken in connection with the altogether peculiar illustrations given of it in the facts of Gospel history, places the Christian on a much higher elevation than that possessed by ancient Israel as to a clear and

---

[1] ' Essay on Liberty,' p. 89. It is due, however, to Mr Mill to state that, while his language in the passage referred to is not free from objection, he yet distinguishes between the teaching of Christ in this respect, and what he designates ' the so-called Christian morality' of later times.   The writer of ' Ecce Deus,' in his attack on Mill (p. 261), has not sufficiently attended to this distinction.   In another treatise, Mr Mill appears to find, in the fundamental principles of the Gospel, all that he himself teaches in morals.   ' In the golden rule of Jesus of Nazareth we read the complete spirit of the ethics of utility. To do as one would be done by, and to love one's neighbour as one's-self, constitute the ideal perfection of utilitarian morality.'—' *On Utilitarianism,*' p. 24.

comprehensive acquaintance with the obligations of moral duty.[1]

In perfect accordance with the views respecting the moral law exhibited in the Sermon on the Mount, and widely different from what He said of the ceremonial institutions, was the action of our Lord in regard to the Sabbatism enjoined in the fourth command of the Decalogue. He gives no hint whatever of its coming abolition, but, on the contrary, recognised its Divine ordination, and merely sought to establish a more wholesome and rational observance of it than was dreamt of or admitted by the slaves of the letter. On a variety of occasions He wrought cures on the Sabbath-day—so often, indeed, that the action must have been taken on purpose to convey what He deemed salutary and needful instruction for the time; and on one occasion He allowed His disciples to satisfy their hunger by plucking the ears of corn as they passed through a field.[2] His watchful

---

[1] The view now given is not, I think, materially different from that of Wuttke, who conceives something more to have been intended by Christ in His exposition of the law, than a mere repudiation of the false interpretations of the Pharisees, namely, such an elucidation and deepening of the import, as to constitute a further development, or spiritual enlargement (' Christliche Sittenlehre,' sec. 208). He still does not mean that anything absolutely new was introduced, or a sense put upon the law which was not contained in the Decalogue; for he had just declared the ' law of the Old Covenant to be simply the moral law, valid for all men and times,' comprehensive of all righteousness, so that he who should keep it in spirit and in truth would be altogether righteous before God (sec. 204). But in Christ's discourse it got a clearer, profounder exposition, and was thrown also into a higher form. It is much the same also, apparently, that is meant by Müller when he speaks of the Decalogue expressing the eternal principles of true morality, and, therefore, always fitted to bring about the knowledge of sin and repentance; while still a far more developed and deeper knowledge of the moral law is given to the Christian Church through the efficacy of the holy prototype of Christ and the Holy Spirit, than could have been communicated by Moses to the children of Israel (On ' Sin,' B. I. P. I. c. 1). For this includes, besides law strictly so called, all supplementary means and privileges.

[2] Matt. xii. 1-14; Mark i. 23, 24, iii. 1-5; Luke vi. 1-10, xiii. 10-16; John v., ix.

adversaries were not slow in marking this procedure, and charged our Lord with profaning the sacred rest of the Sabbath. How does He meet their reproaches? Not by quarrelling with the Divine command, or seeking to relax its obligation; but by explaining its true purport and design, as never meant to interfere with such actions as He performed or sanctioned. In proof of this He chiefly appeals to precedents and practices which His adversaries themselves could not but allow, if their minds had been open to conviction—such as David being permitted in a time of extremity to eat the shew-bread, or themselves rescuing a sheep when it had fallen into a pit on the Sabbath—things necessary to the preservation and support of life; or things, again, of a sacred nature, such as circumcising children on the legal day, though it might happen to be a Sabbath, doing the work at the Temple connected with the appointed service, which in some respects was greater on the seventh than the other days of the week, yea, at times involved all the labour connected with the slaying and roasting of the Paschal lamb for tens of thousands of people. With such things the parties in question were quite familiar; and they should have understood from them, that the prescribed rest of the Sabbath was to be taken, not in an absolute, but in a relative sense—not as simply and in every case cessation from work, irrespective of the ends for which it might be done, but cessation from ordinary or servile work, in order that things of higher moment, things touching on the most important interests of men, might be cared for. Its sacred repose, therefore, must give way to the necessary demands of life, even of irrational life, and to whatever is required to bring relief from actual distress and trouble. It must give way also to that kind of work which is more peculiarly con-

nected with the service of God and with men's restored
fellowship with the life and blessedness of Heaven; for
to promote this was the more special design of the Sabbatical appointment. So, plainly, existing facts shewed
even in Old Testament times, though the Pharisees,
in their zeal for an abstract and imperious legalism
missed the proper reading of them. Jesus grasped,
as usual, the real spirit of the institution; for, we are
to remember, He is explaining the law of the Sabbath
as it then stood, not superseding it by another. He
would have them to understand that, as it is not the
simple abstraction of a man's property (which may in
certain circumstances be done lawfully, and for his own
temporal good), that constitutes a violation of the eighth
commandment, but a selfish and covetous appropriation of
it by fraud or violence; so, in regard to the fourth, the
prohibition of work had respect only to what was at
variance with its holy and beneficent designs. 'The
Sabbath was made for man'—with a wise and gracious
adaptation to the requirements of his complex nature,
as apt to be wearied with the toils, and in his spirit
dragged downward by the cares of life; 'not man for
the Sabbath,' as if it were an absolute and independent
authority, that must hold its own, however hardly in
doing so it might bear on the wants and interests of
those placed under its control. It has an aim, a high
moral aim, for the real wellbeing of mankind; and by a
conscientious regard to this must everything, in regard
to its outward observance, be ruled.

Such is the view given by our Lord on the law of the
Sabbath, speaking as from the ground of law, and doing
the part merely of a correct expounder of its meaning;
but a thought is introduced and variously expressed, as
from His own higher elevation, in harmony with the

spiritual aspect of the subject He had presented, and
pointing to still further developments of it. The Temple,
He had said, has claims of service, which it was no proper
desecration of the Sabbath, but the reverse, to satisfy;
and 'a greater than the Temple was there.' 'The Temple
yields to Christ, the Sabbath yields to the Temple, therefore the Sabbath yields to Christ'—so the sentiment is
syllogistically expressed by Bengel; but yields, it must
be observed, in both cases alike, only for the performance
of works not antagonistic, but homogeneous, to its nature.
Or, as it is again put, 'The Son of Man is Lord of the
Sabbath.' Made, as the Sabbath was, for man, there
necessarily belongs to man, within certain limits, a regulating power in respect to its observance, so as to
render it more effectually subservient to its proper ends.
But this power is supremely resident in Him, who is the
Son of Man, in whom Humanity attains to its true ideal
of goodness, whose will is in all things coincident with the
will of God, and who, like the Father, works even while
He rests.[1] He is Lord of the Sabbath, and, as such, has
a right to order everything concerning it, so as to make
it, in the fullest sense, a day of blessing for man—a
right, therefore, if He should see fit, to transfer its
observance from the last day of the week to the first,
that it might be associated with the consummation of
His redemptive work, and to make it, in accordance with
the impulsive life and energy thereby brought in, more
than in the past, a day of active and hallowed employment for the good of men. So much was certainly
implied in the claim of our Lord in reference to the
Sabbath; but as regards the existence of such a day, its
stated place in the ever-recurring weekly cycle, which in
its origin was coeval with the beginning of the world,

[1] John v. 17.

which as a law was inscribed among the fundamental precepts of the Decalogue, which renders it on the one side a memorial of the paradise that has been lost, and on the other a pledge of the paradise to be restored—in this respect nothing of a reactionary nature fell from our Lord, nor was any principle advanced which can justly be said to point in such a direction.[1]

The same spirit substantially discovers itself in the other occasional references made by our Lord to the moral law of the Old Covenant, as in those already noticed; that is, there appears in them the same profound regard to the authoritative teaching of the law, coupled with an insight into its depth and spirituality of meaning, which was little apprehended by the superficial teachers and formalists of the time. Such, for example, was the character of our Lord's reference to the fifth command of the Decalogue, when, replying to the charge of the Pharisees against His disciples for disregarding the tradition of the elders about washing before meat, He retorted on them the greatly more serious charge of making void the law of God by their traditions—teaching that it was a higher duty for a son to devote his substance as an offering to God, than to apply it to the support of his parents—thereby virtually dishonouring those whom God had commanded him, as a primary duty,

---

[1] It needs scarcely to be said what an interval separates the sayings of our Lord in the Gospels respecting the Sabbath, from the story reported by Clement of Alexandria about Christ having seen a man working on the Sabbath, and saying to him, ' If thou knowest what thou dost, then art thou blessed ; but if thou knowest not, then art thou accursed.' It was a story quite in accordance with the spirit of the school to which Clement belonged ; but to call it, as Mr Plumptre does ('Christ and Christendom,' p. 237), a credible tradition of Christ's ministry, would certainly require some other test of credibility than accordance with what is written in the Gospels ; for nothing recorded there gives such a licence to the individual will for disregarding the Sabbath.

to honour.[1] The love and reverence due to parents was thus declared to be more than burnt-offering, and to have been so determined in the teaching of the law itself. The right principle of obedience was also brought out, but with a more general application, and the absolute perfection of the law announced, as given in one of its summaries in the Old Testament, when, near the close of His ministry, and in answer to a question by one of the better Scribes, Jesus said, ' The first of all the commandments is, Hear, O Israel, The Lord our God is one Lord; and thou shalt love the Lord thy God with all thy heart, and with all thy soul, and with all thy mind, and with all thy strength: this is the first commandment. And the second is like, namely this, Thou shalt love thy neighbour as thyself.' Not only did our Lord affirm, that ' on these two commandments hang all the law and the prophets,' but that ' there is none other commandment greater than these'[2]—evidently meaning that in them was comprised all moral obligation. And when the Scribe assented to what was said, and added, that to exercise such love was more than all whole burnt-offerings and sacrifices, Christ expressed His concurrence, and even pronounced the person who had attained to such knowledge not far from the kingdom of God. So, too, on another and earlier occasion, when the rich young ruler came running to Him with the question, ' What good thing he should do, that he might inherit eternal life ?'[3] And on still another, when a certain lawyer stood up and asked, ' What shall I do to inherit eternal life ?'[4] On both occasions alike, as the question was respecting things to be done, or righteousness to be attained, with the view of grounding a title thereon to eternal life,

[1] Matt. xv. 3-6.   [2] Matt. xxii. 40 ; Mark xii. 31.
[3] Matt. xix. 16.   [4] Luke x. 25.

Christ pointed the inquirers to the written law of God—
in the one case more particularly to the precepts of the
Decalogue, in the other to the two great comprehensive
precepts of supreme love to God and brotherly love to
man ; and, in connection with each, affirmed that, if the
commands were fulfilled, life in the highest sense, eternal
life, would certainly be inherited.   In other words, by
fulfilling those commands, there would be that conformity
to the pattern of Divine goodness, on which from the
first all right to the possession of life in God's kingdom
has been suspended.   At the same time, our Lord took
occasion to shew, in both the cases, how far His inquirers
were themselves from having reached this ideal excellence,
or even from distinctly apprehending what was actually
included in the attainment.

This surely is enough ; for, touching as these declarations do on the great essentials of religion and morality,
they must be understood in their plainest import ; and
anything like subtle ingenuity in dealing with them, or
specious theorizings, would be entirely out of place.
Manifestly, the revelation of law in the Old Testament
was, in our Lord's view, comprehensive of all righteousness—while still, in respect to *form*, it partook of the
imperfection of the times, and of the provisional economy,
with which it was more immediately connected ; and for
bringing clearly out the measure and extent of the obligations involved in it, we owe much—who can say how
much ?—to the Divine insight of Christ, and the truly
celestial light reflected on it by His matchless teaching
and spotless example.   In that respect our Lord might
with fullest propriety say, ' A new commandment I give
unto you, that ye may love one another ; as I have loved
you, that ye may so also love one another :'[1]—new, how-

[1] John xiii. 34.

Q

ever, not in regard to the command of love taken by itself, nor in regard to the degree of love, as if one were required now to love others, not merely as one's-self, but above one's-self—no, but new simply with reference to the peerless manifestation of love given in His own person, and the motive thence arising—altogether peculiar in its force and efficacy—for His people to strive after conformity to His example. This, indeed, is the highest glory that can here be claimed for Jesus ; and to contend with some, under the plea of glorifying His Messiahship, that He must have signalized His appearance on earth by the introduction of an essentially new and higher morality, were in effect to dishonour Him ; for it would break at a vital point the continuity of the Divine dispensations, and stamp the revelation of law which, at an earlier period of His own mediatorial agency, had in reality come forth from Himself, as in its very nature faulty—wanting something which it should have had as a reflection of the character of God, and a rule of life for those who, as members of His kingdom, were called to love and honour Him.

II. We turn now from what Christ *taught* to what He *did*. And here, still more than in regard to His prophetical agency, He had a mission peculiarly His own to fulfil for the good of men, yet not the less one which was defined beforehand, and in a manner ruled, by the prescriptions of law. For the work of Christ as the Redeemer neither was, nor could be, anything else than the triumph of righteousness for man over man's sin. And, accordingly, in the intimations that had gone before concerning Him, this characteristic (as formerly noticed) was made peculiarly prominent : He was to be girt about with righteousness, was to be known as the Lord's righteous servant, His elect one, in whom His soul should delight; so that He might be called 'The Lord our Righteousness,' as well as 'The Lord our Salvation,' since in Him all that believed should be justified, or made righteous, and should glory.[1] There have been those who questioned whether the reality corresponded with these predictions, or with the claims actually put forth in behalf of Jesus of Nazareth; but nothing has ever been alleged in support of such insinuations, except what has been found in mistaken ideas of His mission, or wrong interpretations put on certain actions of His life. Certainly, His enemies in the days of His flesh, who sought most diligently for grounds of moral accusation against Him, failed to discover them : He Himself boldly threw out before them the challenge, 'Which of you convinceth me of sin ?'[2] 'The prince of this world,' He again said—the great patron and representative of sin—' cometh, and hath nothing in me.'[3] Higher still, He said to the Father, 'I have glorified thee on earth; I have finished the work which thou gavest me to do'[4]—no indication whatever of the slightest failure or shortcoming ;—and this assertion of faultless excellence was re-echoed on the Father's side, in the word once and again heard from Heaven, 'This is my beloved Son, in whom I am well pleased.'[5]

It was an altogether strange phenomenon in the world's history. 'What an impression,' Dorner justly asks,[6] 'must have been made upon the disciples by Jesus, whose spirit was full of peace and of an undisturbed serenity, who never shewed the slightest trace of having worked Himself into this peaceful state through hard

---

[1] Isa. xi. 5, xlii. 1, liii. 11; Jer. xxiii. 6.   [2] John viii. 46.
[3] John xiv. 30.   [4] John xvii. 4.   [5] Matt. iii. 17, xvii. 5.
[6] ' Ueber Jesu Sündlose Vollkommenheit,' p. 34.

effort and conflict with sin. *There* was a man in whom
appeared no sign of repentance or of disquietude in regard
to Himself; a man without solicitude for His soul's salvation, for He is already possessed of eternal life ; He lives
as in heaven. No prayer is heard from Him for sin of
His own, nor is any aversion shewn to enter into the
company of publicans and sinners; in the most trying
moments of His life, it becomes manifest that He is without consciousness of sin. This is an unquestionable fact
of history, whatever explanation may be given of it. For
that He set before Him as His life-purpose the deliverance and reconciliation of the world, that for the execution
of this purpose He knew Himself to be committed to
suffer, even to the cross, and that He actually expired in
the consciousness of having at once executed the purpose
and maintained undisturbed His fellowship with God—
this no more admits of denial than that it would have
been an utterly foolish and absurd idea to have thought
of bringing in redemption for others, if He had been
Himself conscious of needing redemption. . . . . Jesus
was conscious of no sin, just because He was no sinner.
He was, though complete man, like God in sinless perfection; and though not, like God, incapable of being
tempted, nor perfected from His birth, and so not in that
sense holy, yet holy in the sense of preserving an innate
purity and incorruptness, and through a quite normal
development, in which the idea of a pure humanity comes
at length to realization, and prevents the design of the
world from remaining unaccomplished. The impression
made by Him is that of the free, the true Son of Man—
needing no new birth, but by nature the new-born man,
and no remedial applications, but Himself consciously
possessing the power fitted to render Him the physician
of diseased humanity.'

Could such an One really be subject to the law? Was He not rather above it? So some have been disposed to maintain, with the avowed design of magnifying the name of Jesus: it has seemed to them as if they were claiming for Him a higher honour, when they represented Him as *living* above law, precisely as others have sought to do with respect to His *teaching* above law. But it is a kind of honour incompatible with the actual position and calling of Jesus. To have so lived would have been to place Himself beyond the sphere which properly belongs to humanity. He could no longer have been the representative of the morality which *we* are bound to cultivate; His standing in relation to spiritual excellence had been something exceptional, arbitrary; and wherever this enters, it is not a higher elevation that is reached, but rather a descent that is made—the sentimental or expedient then takes the place of the absolutely righteous and good. To be the Lord of the law, and yet in all things subject to the law's demands—moving within the bounds of law, yet finding them to be no restraint; consenting to everything the law required as in itself altogether right, and of a free and ready mind doing it as a Son in the Father's house, so that it might as well be said the law lived in Him, as that He lived in the law:—this is the highest glory which could be won in righteousness by the man Christ Jesus, and it is *the* glory which is ascribed to Him in Scripture. Never do we find Him there asserting for Himself as a right, or claiming as a privilege, a release from ordinary obligations; never was that which is dutiful and good for others viewed as otherwise for Him, or as bearing less directly on His responsibilities; and in so far as the work He had to do was peculiar, so much the more remarkable was the spirit of surrender with which He yielded Himself to the authority that lay upon Him.

Of Himself He declared that He was loved of the Father, because He kept the Father's commandments ;[1] and it is said of Him, in a word which covers the whole of His earthly career, ' He was made of a woman, made under the law,'[2] therefore bound to a life-long subjection to its requirements ; bearing throughout the form of a servant, but bearing it with the heart of a Son.   It was, consequently, not His burden, but ' His meat to do the will of His Father, and to finish His work ;'[3] and the spirit in which He entered on and ever prosecuted His vicarious service was that expressed in the language long before prepared for Him, ' Lo I come : in the volume of the book it is written of me ; I delight to do thy will, O my God; yea, thy law is within my heart ;'[4] and if at other times, so especially when His work of obedience was reaching its culmination, and He was ready to perfect Himself through the sacrifice of the cross.   The necessity of this great act, and the place it was to hold in His mediatorial agency, had been from the first foreseen by Him : He knew (so He declared near the commencement of His ministry) that He *must* be lifted up for the salvation of the world.[5] When the awful crisis approached, though He had power either to retain or to lay down His life, the things which had been written concerning it (He said) *must* be accomplished, that He should be numbered with the transgressors ;[6] and the humble, earnest entreaty, ' Father, if it be possible, let this cup pass from me ; nevertheless, not my will but thine be done,' only shewed how nature recoiled from the terribleness, yet meekly bowed to the necessity, of the doom.   For here especially lay the ground of all that He was to secure of good for His people.   Here the work of reconciliation between sinful

---

[1] John x. 17, 18, xv. 11.   [2] Gal. iv. 4.   [3] John iv. 34.
[4] Ps. xl. 7, 8; Heb. x. 7.   [5] John iii. 14.   [6] Luke xxii. 37.

men and their offended God must be once for all accomplished ;—and it *was* accomplished, by His ' being made sin for them who knew no sin, that they might be made the righteousness of God in Him'—or, as it is again put, by ' redeeming them from the curse of the law, by being Himself made a curse for them.'[1]

It is impossible here to do more than very briefly glance at this all-important subject ; and the less needful, as it was so fully treated by the esteemed friend who immediately preceded me in this Lectureship.[2] But, surely, if there be any thing in the record of our Lord's work upon earth, in which more than another the language employed concerning it should be taken in its simplest meaning, it must be in what is said of the very heart of His undertaking—that on which every thing might be said to turn for the fulfilment of promise, and the exhibition of Divine faithfulness and truth. And there can be no doubt, that the representations just noticed, and others of a like description, concerning the death of Christ, do in their natural sense carry a legal aspect ; they bear respect to the demands of law, or the justice of which law is the expression. They declare that, to meet those demands in behalf of sinners, Christ bore a judicial death—a death which, while all-undeserved on the part of Him who suffered, must be regarded as the merited judgment of Heaven on human guilt. To be made a curse, that He might redeem men from the curse of the law, can have no other meaning than to endure the penalty, which as transgressors of law they had incurred, in order that they might escape ; nor can the exchange indicated in the words, ' He was made sin for us, that we might be made the righteousness of God

---

[1] 2 Cor. v. 21; Gal. iii. 13; Rom. v. 8-10.
[2] Rev. Dr J. Buchanan. *See* his Lecture on ' Justification.'

in Him,' be justly understood to import less than that
He, the righteous One, took the place of sinners in suffering, that they might take His place in favour and
blessing.   And the stern necessity for the transaction—a
necessity which even the resources of infinite wisdom, at
the earnest cry of Jesus, found it impossible to evade[1]—
on what could it rest but the bosom of law, whose
violated claims called for satisfaction ?   Not that God
delights in blood, but that the paramount interests of
truth and righteousness must be upheld, even though
blood unspeakably precious may have to be shed in their
vindication.

There are many who cannot brook the idea of these
legal claims and awful securities for the establishment of
law and right in the government of God ; the sacrifice on
the cross has no attraction for them when viewed in such
an aspect ; and the utmost ingenuity has been plied, in
recent times more particularly, to accept the language of
Scripture regarding it, and yet eliminate the element
which alone gives it value or consistence.   Thus, with
one class, the idea of sacrifice in this connection is identified with self-denial, with ' the entire surrender of the
whole spirit and body to God,' bearing with meek and
uncomplaining patience the impious rage of men, because
it was the will of the Father He should do so ; when otherwise He might have met it with counter-violence, or used
His supernatural power to save Himself from the humiliating ordeal.[2]   What, however, is gained by such a
mode of representation ?   It gets rid, indeed, of what is
called a religion of blood, but only to substitute for it a
morality of blood—and a morality of blood grounded

---

[1] Matt. xxvi. 39.
[2] So, for example, Maurice in ' Theological Essays ;' and ' Ecce Homo' (p.
48), with some artistic delineations.

(for aught that we can see) upon no imperative necessity, nor in its own nature differing from what has been exhibited by some of Christ's more illustrious disciples. Such a view has not even a formal resemblance to the truth as presented in Scripture ; it does not come within sight of the idea of vicarious sin-bearing or atonement, in any intelligible sense of the terms. Nor is the matter much improved by laying stress, with some, on the greatness of the opposition which the existing state of the world rendered it needful for Him to encounter—as when it is said, ' He came into collision with the world's evil, and bore the penalty of that daring. . . . He bore suffering to free us from what is worse than suffering, sin : temporal death to save us from death everlasting' (Robertson). Nor again, with others, by viewing it in a merely subjective light, and finding the work to consist in a kind of sympathetic assumption of our guilt, entering in spirit into the Father's judgment upon it, and feeling and confessing for it the sorrow and repentance it is fitted to awaken in a perfectly holy soul (Campbell) ; or as others prefer putting it, by the manifestation of a burdened love, of the moral suffering of God for men's sins and miseries, a Divine self-sacrificing love, to overmaster sin and conquer the human heart (Bushnell, Young, etc.).

In all such representations, which are substantially one, though somewhat different in form, there is merely an accommodation of Scripture language to a type of doctrine that is essentially at variance with it. For when expressed in unambiguous terms, what does it amount to but this : That Christ in His views of sin and righteousness, in the virtue of His life, and the sacrifice of His death, is the beau-ideal of humanity—our great pattern and example, the purest reflection of the Father's love and goodness ? But that is all. If we catch the spirit of

His antipathy to sin and devotion to righteousness, we
share with Him in His glory; we link ourselves to the
Divine humanity which has manifested itself in Him;
' God views us favourably as partaking of that holy, perfect, and Divine thing, which was once exhibited on
earth ; but there is no judicial procedure, no legal
penalty borne by the Saviour, and for His sake remitted
to the guilty ; no direct acceptance for them through the
blood of the atonement. And what comfort were such a
Gospel to the conscience-stricken sinner ? It is but a
disguised legalism ; for such a perfect exhibition of goodness in Christ, feeling, doing, suffering, with perfect conformity to the mind of God—what is it, considered by
itself, but the law in a concrete and embodied form ?
therefore the sinner's virtual condemnation ; the clear
mirror in which the more steadfastly he looks, the more
he must see how far he has gone from the righteousness
and life of God ; and if not imputed to him, till he is
conscious of having imbibed its spirit, where shall be his
security against the agitations of fear, or even the agonies
of despair ?

In the great conflict of life, in the grand struggle
which is proceeding, in our own bosoms and the world
around us, between sin and righteousness, the consciousness of guilt and the desire of salvation, it is not in such
a mystified, impalpable Gospel, as those fine-spun theories
present to us, that any effective aid is to be found.
We must have a solid foundation for our feet to stand
on, a sure and living ground for our confidence before
God. And this we can find only in the old church view
of the sufferings and death of Christ as a satisfaction to
God's justice for the offence done by our sin to His
violated law. *Satisfaction*, I say emphatically, *to God's
justice*—which some, even evangelical writers, seem dis-

posed to stumble at ; they would say, satisfaction to God's honour, indeed, but by no means to God's justice.[1] What, then, I would ask, is God's honour apart from God's justice ? His honour can be nothing but the reflex action or display of His moral attributes ; and in the exercise of these attributes, the fundamental and controlling element is justice. Every one of them is conditioned ; love itself is conditioned by the demands of justice ; and to provide scope for the operation of love in justifying the ungodly consistently with those demands, is the very ground and reason of the atonement—its ground and reason primarily in the mind of God, and because there, then also in its living image, the human conscience, which instinctively regards punishment as ' the recoil of the eternal law of right against the transgressor,' and cannot attain to solid peace but through a medium of valid expiation. So much so, indeed, that wherever the true expiation is unknown, or but partially understood, it ever goes about to provide expiations of its own.

---

[1] The language referred to occurs in Swainson's ' Hulsean Lecture,' p. 234. But by implication it is also adopted by those who sharply distinguish between vicarious suffering and vicarious punishment, accepting the former, but rejecting the latter, and treating the transference of guilt on which it rests as an enormity against which common sense revolts. So, no doubt, it is, as represented, for example, by Mr Jelletlet, in his ' Moral Difficulties of the Old Testament,' pp. 50-99, who holds the idea of guilt and punishment as inseparable from the moral qualities of the individual sinner, consequently inalienable. But Scripture does not so contemplate them, in the passages referred to in the text, or in Isa. liii. 56 ; 1 Pet. ii. 24, etc. And the church doctrine of the atonement undoubtedly is, and has always been, as stated by the younger Hodge, ' that the legal responsibilities of His people were by covenant transferred to Christ, and that He, as Mediator, was regarded and treated accordingly. The sinful act and the sinful nature are inalienable. The guilt, or just liability to punishment, is alienable, otherwise no sinner can be saved.'— ' The Atonement,' chap. xx. Hence the sufferings are penal in their character, in moral value equivalent and greatly more to the guilt of the redeemed, though not in all respects identically the same, which they could not possibly be.

Thus has the law been established[1]—most signally
established by that very feature of the Gospel, which
specially distinguished it from the law—its display of
the redeeming love of God in Christ. ‘ Just law indeed,’
to use the words of Milton—

> ‘ Just law indeed, but more exceeding love !
> For we by rightful doom remediless,
> Were lost in death, till He that dwelt alone,
> High throned in secret bliss, for us frail dust
> Emptied His glory, even to nakedness ;
> And that great covenant, which we still transgress,
> Entirely satisfied ;
> And the full wrath beside
> Of vengeful justice bore for our excess.’[2]

Yes ; hold fast by this broadly marked distinction, yet
mutual interconnection, between the law and the Gospel;
contemplate the law, or the justice which it reveals and
demands, as finding satisfaction in the atoning work of
Christ ; and this work again, by reason of that very satisfaction, securing an eternal reign of peace and blessing in
the kingdom of God ; and then, perhaps, you will not be
indisposed to say of law, as thus magnified and in turn
magnifying and blessing, with one of the profoundest of
our old divines, that ‘ her seat is the bosom of God, her
voice the harmony of the world : all things in heaven and
earth do her homage—the very least as feeling her care,
and the greatest as not exempted from her power ; both
angels and men and creatures, of what condition soever,
though each in different sort and manner, yet all with
uniform consent, admiring her as the mother of peace
and joy.’[3]

[1] Rom. iii. 31.   [2] Milton, Poem on the ‘Crucifixion.’
[3] Hooker, ‘ Eccl. Polity.’

LECTURE VIII.

THE RELATION OF THE LAW TO THE CONSTITUTION, THE PRIVILEGES, AND THE CALLING OF THE CHRISTIAN CHURCH.

HOW Christ, in His mediatorial work, stood related to the law, and how He bore Himself in respect to it, we have already seen ; and we have now a similar inquiry to prosecute in connection with the Christian church. This line of inquiry, in its more essential features, can be nothing more than the continuation of the one already pursued.   For whatever distinctively belongs to the Christian church—whether as regards her light, her privileges, her obligations, or her prospects—it springs from Christ as its living ground ; it is entirely the result of what He Himself is and accomplished on earth ; and whatever room there might be, when He left the earth, for more explicit statements or fuller illustrations of the truth regarding it, in principle all was already there, and only required, through apostolic agency, to be fitly expounded and applied, in relation to the souls of men and the circumstances of the newly constituted society.   But situated as matters then were, with prejudices and opinions of an adverse nature so deeply rooted in the minds of men, and long hallowed associations and practices that had to be broken up, it was no easy task to get the truth in its completeness wrought into men's convictions ; and only gradually, and through repeated struggles with error and opposition did the apostles of our Lord succeed

in gaining for the principles of the Gospel a just appreciation and a firm establishment.

Keeping to the general outline observed in the preceding discussion, we shall, in this fresh line of inquiry,
consider, first, how the Christian scheme of doctrine and
duty was adjusted, under the hand of the apostles, with
reference to things of a ceremonial nature—to *a law of
ordinances?* and, secondly, what relation it bore to the
great revelation of *moral law?*

I. As regards the former of these relations, the way
had been made, so far at least, comparatively plain by
Christ Himself: the law of ordinances, as connected with
the old covenant, now ceased to have any binding authority. The hour had come when the Temple-worship, with
every ceremonial institution depending on it, should pass
away, having reached their destined end in the death and
resurrection of Christ. Not immediately, however, did
this truth find its way into the minds even of the apostles,
nor could it obtain a footing in the church without express and stringent legislation. From the first, the disciples of our Lord preached in His name the free and full
remission of sins to the penitent and believing, but still
only to such as stood within the bond of the Sinaitic
covenant—the Gospel being viewed, not as properly superseding the ancient law of ordinances, but rather as giving
due effect to it—supplying what it was incompetent to
provide. Of what use, then, any more such a law?
Why still continue to observe it? This question, evidently, did not for a time present itself for consideration
to the apostles—their immediate work lying among their
own countrymen in Judea. But it could not be long
kept in abeyance; and such a direction was soon given
to affairs by their Divine head as left them no alternative

in the matter. The new wine of the kingdom began here to burst the old bottles first in Stephen and those who suffered in his persecution—although as to the mode, perhaps, somewhat prematurely, and with too much vehemence to reach a settled result. But shortly afterwards there came the remarkable success of the Gospel in Samaria, with gifts from the Holy Ghost attesting and sealing the work; and following upon that, the supernatural vision granted to Peter of the sheet let down from heaven with all manner of beasts, unclean and clean alike, immediately explained and exemplified, under the special guidance of the Spirit, by the reception into the Christian church of the heathen family of Cornelius. These things forced on a crisis in spite of earlier predictions; and by conclusive facts of Divine ordination shewed, that now Jew and Gentile were on a footing as regards the blessings of Christ's salvation; that, as a matter of course, the observances of the ancient ritual had ceased in God's sight to be of any practical avail. The discovery fell as a shock on the minds of Jewish believers. They did not hesitate to charge Peter with irregularity or unfaithfulness for the part he had acted in it; and though the objectors were for the time silenced by the decisive proofs he was able to adduce of Divine warrant and approval, yet the legal spirit still lived and again broke forth, especially when it was seen how the Gentile converts increased in number, and the church at Antioch, chiefly composed of such converts, was becoming a kind of second centre of Christian influence, and of itself sending forth mission-agencies to plant and organize churches in other regions of heathendom.[1] It hence became necessary to give forth a formal decision on the matter; and a council of the apostles and elders was held for the

---

[1] Acts xiii., xiv.

explicit purpose of determining whether, along with faith
in Christ, it was necessary in order to salvation that men
should be circumcised and keep the law of Moses.¹   It is
not needful here to go into the details of this council ; but
the judgment of the assembly as to the main point at
issue was clear and peremptory—namely, that the legal
observances were no longer binding, and that Gentile believers should only be enjoined so far to respect the feelings and usages of their Jewish brethren, as to abstain,
not merely from the open licentiousness which custom
had made allowable in heathendom, but also from liberties
in food which those trained under the law could not regard otherwise than as dangerous or improper.   Notwithstanding this decision, however, so tenaciously did the
old leaven cleave to the Jewish mind, that the ancient
observances retained their place in Jerusalem till the city
and temple were laid in ruins ; and the Judaizing spirit
even insinuated itself into some of the Gentile churches,
those especially of Galatia.   But it only led to a more
vigorous exposure and firm denunciation of the error
through the apostle to the Gentiles—who affirmed, that
now neither circumcision nor uncircumcision availed any
thing for salvation, but faith, or the regeneration which
comes through faith ; that if men betook to circumcision
and the Jewish yoke to secure their spiritual good, Christ
should profit them nothing ; that the teaching which led
to the imposition of such a yoke was really another gospel,
not to be encouraged, but anathematized by all who
knew the mind of Christ.²   And the cycle of Christian
instruction on the subject was completed by the explanation given in the epistle to the Hebrews of the general
nature and design of the Old Testament ritual, as at once
fulfilled and abolished in Christ.   So that there was here

¹ Acts xv.   ² Gal. i. 6, 9, ii. 14, etc.

on the negative side, a very full revelation and authoritative deliverance of the will of God.[1]

This result, however, not unnaturally gives rise to another question. If the new state and spiritual life of Christians was thus expressly dissociated from the old law of ordinances, was it not directly linked to another taking its place? The answer to this may be variously given, according to the sense in which it is understood. We have no law of ordinances in the New Testament writings at all corresponding to that which is contained in the Old. There was a fulness and precision formerly in the ceremonials of worship, because these belonged to a provisional and typical economy, and required to be adjusted with Divine skill to the coming realities for which they were intended to prepare. But the realities themselves having come, there is no longer any need for

[1] The considerations adduced in the text plainly shew that the apostles, in the later period of their agency, were of one mind as to the cessation of the ceremonial law in its binding form even upon Jewish Christians ; while still they continued, especially when resident in Jerusalem, to observe its provisions and take part in its more peculiar services. They did so, of course, from no feeling of necessity, but partly from custom, and partly also, apparently indeed still more, from regard to the strong prejudices of their less enlightened brethren. Of these there were multitudes, as James intimated to Paul (Acts xxi. 20), who were zealous of the law, and actuated by strong jealousy toward Paul himself because of the freedom maintained alike in his teaching and his example from the legal observances. They were in the position of those described by our Lord in Luke v. 39—like persons who, having been accustomed to old wine, did not straightway desire new, although in this case the new was really better. But the apostles felt that it was necessary to deal tenderly with them, lest, by a too sudden wrench from their old associations, their faith in the Gospel might sustain too great a shock. They therefore pursued a conciliatory policy, doubtless waiting and looking for the time when the Lord Himself would interpose, and, by the prostration of the Temple and the scattering of the Jewish nation, would formally take the Old Covenant institutions out of the way, and render their observance in great measure impossible. The history of the early church but too clearly proves how necessary this solemn dispensation was for the Christian church itself, and how dangerous an element even the partial observance of the old law to some sections of the Jewish believers after the destruction of the Temple, became to the purity of their faith in Christ.

such carefully adjusted observances. Hence, neither by
our Lord Himself, nor by His apostles, have any definite
appointments been made to things which were of great
importance under the law—to the kind of place, for
example, in which the members of the Christian community
were to meet for worship—or the form of service they
were to observe when they met—or the officials who were
to conduct it, and whether any particular mode of consecration were required to fit them for doing so. Even in
those ordinances of the new dispensation, which in character approached most nearly to the old—the Sacraments
of Baptism and the Lord's Supper—while no doubt is left
as to the permanent place they were to occupy in the
Christian church, how widely different is the manner of
their appointment from that of the somewhat corresponding ordinances of Circumcision and the Passover? In
Circumcision, the precise thing to be done is prescribed,
and the precise day also on which it must be done ; and
in the Passover, the kind of sacrifice to be provided, the
time when, and the place where it was to be killed, the
modes of using the blood and of preparing the food, the
manner also in which the feast was to be partaken, and
even the disposal that was to be made of the fragments.
In the Christian sacraments, on the other hand, the substance alone is brought into view—the kind of elements
to be employed, and the general purport and design with
which they are to be given and received ; all, besides, as
to the time, the place, the subordinate acts, the ministerial
agency, is left entirely unnoticed, as but of secondary
moment, or capable of being readily inferred from the
nature of the ordinances. The converts on the day of
Pentecost were baptized—so the inspired record distinctly
testifies ; but where, how, or by whom, is not indicated.
The Ethiopian eunuch was both converted and baptized

by Philip, one of the seven, who, so far as ordination was concerned, were ordained merely to 'serve tables;' and the person who baptized Paul is simply designated 'a certain disciple at Damascus.' When the Spirit had manifestly descended on Cornelius and his household, Peter 'commanded them to be baptized in the name of the Lord;' but the statement implies that the brethren accompanying Peter, rather than Peter himself, administered the rite. Paul, even when claiming to have founded the church at Corinth, expressly *dis*claims the administration of baptism to more than a very few—this being not what he had specially received his apostolic mission to perform: 'Christ sent him not to baptize, but to preach the Gospel.'[1] He even thanks God he had baptized but a few; could he possibly have done so, if, in his view, baptizing had been all one with regenerating? When he speaks of those whom he was the means of regenerating, he says they were 'begotten through the Gospel.'[2] And in the pastoral instructions given by him through Timothy and Titus to the bishops or presbyters of the apostolic church, we read only of what they should be as men of Christian piety and worth, and how they should minister and apply the word; but not so much as a hint is dropt as to their exclusive right to dispense and give validity to the Christian sacraments. All shewing, as clearly as could well be done by the facts of history, that nothing absolutely essential in this respect depends upon circumstances of person, and mode, and time; and that whatever restrictions might then be observed, or afterwards introduced, it could only be for the sake of order and general edification, not to give validity or impart saving efficacy to what were otherwise but empty symbols or unauthorised ceremonies.

[1] 1 Cor. i. 17.   [2] 1 Cor. iv. 15.

Nor does it appear to have been materially otherwise with the ordinance of the Supper.   The original institution merely represents our Lord, at the close of the paschal feast, as taking bread and wine, and, after giving thanks, presenting them to the disciples, the one to be eaten the other to be drunk in the character of His body and blood, and in remembrance of Him.   This is all; and when the church fairly entered on its new career, the record of its proceedings merely states, with reference to this part of its observances, that the disciples 'continued steadfastly in the apostles' doctrine and fellowship, and in breaking of bread;' that 'they continued in breaking bread from house to house,' and were wont to 'come together on the first day of the week to break bread.'[1]   St Paul, too, while rebuking certain flagrant abuses which had crept into the church at Corinth in the celebration of the ordinance, and rehearsing what he says he had received from the Lord concerning it, maintains a profound silence as to every thing of a ritualistic description: he mentions only a Lord's table with its bread and cup, and the action of giving and receiving, after the offering of thanks, in commemoration of Christ; but says nothing of the particular kinds of bread and wine, of the status, dress, or actions of the administrator, or the proper terms of celebration, or the attitude of the people when partaking, whether sitting, reclining, or kneeling.   These, plainly, in the apostle's account, were the non-essentials, the mere circumstantial adjuncts, which it was left to the church to regulate—not arbitrarily indeed, and assuredly not so as to change a simply commemorative and sealing ordinance into a propitiatory sacrifice and a stupendous mystery, but with a suitable adaptation to the nature of the feast and the circumstances of place and time.   This reserve, too, was the

[1] Acts ii. 42, 46, xx. 7, 11.

more remarkable, since the apostle did occasionally speak of Christian gifts and services in sacrificial language ; only never in connection with the ordinance of the Supper. He spake of the sacrifice of praise, but explains Himself by calling it the fruit of the lips,[1] and a sacrifice to be offered, not by a priest on earth, but by the one High Priest, Christ. Charitable contributions to the poor, or to the service of the Gospel, are in like manner designated sacrifices well-pleasing to God; also the presentations of the persons of believers to God's service, and His own presentation of converted heathen before the heavenly throne ;[2] but not in one passage is the commemoration of our Lord's death in the Supper so represented, or any expression employed which might seem to point in that direction.[3]

---

[1] Heb. xiii. 15.   [2] Heb. xiii. 16 ; Phil. iv. 18 ; Rom. xii. 1, xv. 16.

[3] Desperate efforts have been made by Roman Catholic writers to give another version to the whole matter, and even to find in the words of institution direct sacrificial language. Professedly Protestant writers are now treading to the full in their footsteps, and applying (we may say, perverting) the simple words of the original to a sense altogether foreign to them. They call the address of Christ, ' Do this in remembrance of me,' a sacrificial word ; and one paraphrases the words after the sense which he says the words ($τοῦτο ποιεῖτε$) ' bear in the Septuagint, Offer this as my memorial' (' The Church and the World,' pp. 499, 564). It is enough to give the substance of the comment made on these extraordinary statements by the learned editor of the *Contemporary Review*, No. 21, who says, ' The words which our Lord employed nowhere bear a sacrificial sense in the Septuagint. In not one place does such an expression as $ποιεῖν τοῦτο$ occur in a sacrificial sense ; it would have been absurd, and even impossible, that it should, unless $τοῦτο$ referred to some concrete thing then and there represented and designated—as, for example, Lev. ix. 10—$προσήνεγκε τὸ ὁλοκαύτωμα, καὶ ἐποίησεν αὐτὸ ὡς καθήκει$. To this, perhaps, the superficial ritualist will reply, that such a concrete object is present in the bread, of which it had just been said by our Lord, This is my body. If he committed himself so far, we should have to take him back to his school-days, and to remind him that the demonstrative pronoun, when applied to a concrete object, designates that and that alone, as distinguished from all others : so that if $τοῦτο ποιεῖτε$ signified, " Offer this," then, in order to obey it, that very bread must have been reserved to have been offered continually. We are driven, then, to the abstract reference, "this which I am doing ;" and this will rule the meaning of the verb to be " do," and not " offer." Such, indeed, is the only

This, however, is a conclusion which many refuse to acquiesce in. They think that the indeterminateness spoken of must somehow have been supplied ; and that if the needed materials are not furnished by Scripture, they must be sought in some collateral source adequate to meet the deficiency. Hence the Romish theory of unwritten traditions, eking out and often superseding the teaching of Scripture ; the theory of development, claiming for the church the inherent right and power to supplement and authoritatively impose what was originally defective in her ordinances ; and the theory of the apostolic succession and the impressed character. It were out of place here, where we have to do merely with the revelation of law in God's kingdom, to go into an examination of such theories, as none of them, except by an abuse of terms, can be brought within that description. The things for which those theories are intended to account, have no distinct place in the expressed mind of our Lord and His apostles ; and so, even if allowable, cannot be

sense of the phrase τοῦτο ποιεῖν wherever it occurs (*see* Gen. iii. 13, 14, xii. 18, xx. 5, etc.; Luke vii. 8, x. 28, xii. 18; Acts xvi. 18, etc.; Rom. vii. 15, 16, 20, xii. 20; 1 Cor. ix. 23). Is it conceivable that two authors (Luke and Paul), accustomed to the use of the phrase in its simple everyday meaning, should use it once only, and that once, on its most solemn occurrence, in a sense altogether unprecedented, and therefore certain not to be apprehended by their readers?' The reviewer goes on further to state that the historical evidence is also wholly against it : the church has, as a rule, understood the 'Do this' to mean doing, as he did, namely, taking the bread, breaking, and distributing it ; and adds, ' Can anything be plainer than that, but for the requirements of the sacrificial theory of the Eucharist, such an interpretation would never have been heard of? And even with all the warping which men's philology gets from their peculiar opinions, can, even now, a single Greek or Hellenistic scholar be found who would, as a scholar, venture to uphold it?' It is not too much to say, that the whole that is written respecting the original observance of the sacraments, the whole also that St Paul says respecting his own peculiar calling as an ambassador of Christ, and what he wrote for the instruction of others on the pastoral office, is a virtual protest against the priestly character of the ministry of the New Testament ; and the one must be ignored before the other can be accepted by sound believers.

deemed of essential moment. If it is asked—as Dodwell, for example, asked (Paraenesis, 34),—' Cannot God justly oblige men, in order to obtain the benefits which it is His good pleasure to bestow, to employ the means which His good pleasure has instituted?' We reply, if He had seen reason to institute them in such a sense as to render them in any way essential to salvation, the same reason which led Him to provide salvation would doubtless also have led Him to make His pleasure in this respect known— nay, to have inscribed it, in the most conspicuous manner on the foundations of the Christian faith; which assuredly has not been done. Undoubtedly, the form and mode (as has been further alleged) *may be*, and sometimes *have been*, of indispensable moment : ' God was not pleased to cleanse Naaman the Syrian from his leprosy by the water of any other river than the Jordan ; so that, had Naaman used the rivers of Syria for this purpose, he would have had no title to expect a cure.' Certainly ; but on this very account God made His meaning perfectly explicit : He hung the cure of the Syrian leper on the condition, not of a sevenfold dipping in water merely, but of such a dipping in the waters of the Jordan ; these particular waters entered as an essential element into the method of recovery. And so, doubtless, would have been the points referred to in connection with the Christian sacra- ments, if the same relative place had belonged to them ; they would have been noted and prescribed, in a manner not to be mistaken, in the fundamental records of the Christian faith ; and since they are awanting there, to introduce and press them in the character of essentials to salvation, is virtually to disparage those records, and to do so in a way that runs counter to the whole genius of Christianity, which exalts the spiritual in comparison with the outward and formal—retains, we may say, the mini-

mum of symbolism because it exhibits the maximum of
reality.

But while we thus contend against any law of ordinances in the Christian church of the circumstantial and
specific kind which existed under the old economy, the
two sacraments undoubtedly have the place of ordinances ; their observance has been prescribed with legislative sanction and authority ; and there can be no
question as to the duty of observing them among the
genuine disciples of Christ ; the only, or at least, the
main question is, in what relation do they stand to their
possession of the Spirit and of the life that is in Christ
Jesus ? Do they aim at originating, or rather at establishing and nourishing, the Divine life in the soul ? That
it is this latter in the case of the Lord's Supper admits
of no doubt ; the very name implies that the participants
are contemplated as having Spirit and life, since no one
thinks of presenting a feast to the dead. The same also
is implied in the formal design of its appointment, to
keep alive the remembrance of Jesus, and of His great
redemptive act in the minds of those who own Him as
their Lord and Saviour—presupposing, therefore, the
existence of a living bond between their souls and Him.
Hence, the one essential pre-requisite to a right and
profitable participation in the ordinance indicated by the
apostle is the possession and exercise of the life of faith :
' Let a man examine himself (viz., as to his state and
interest in Christ), and so let him eat of that bread and
drink of that cup.'[1] Not, then, to convert or quicken,
but to nourish and strengthen the life already implanted
in the soul, by bringing it into fresh contact and communion with the one source of all life and blessing to
sinful men, is the direct good to be sought in the ordi-

[1] 1 Cor. xi. 28.

nance of the Supper. And though the other sacrament, Baptism, has to do with the *commencement* of a Christian state, not its progressive advancement, and is hence termed *initiatory*, it is so, according to the representations of Scripture, only in a qualified sense ; that is, not as being absolutely originative, or of itself conditioning and producing the first rise of life in the soul, but associated with this early stage, and bringing it forth into distinct and formal connection with the service and kingdom of Christ. Such, certainly, is the relation in which the two stand to each other in the command of Christ, and the ministry of His immediate representatives—' Go and teach all nations, baptizing them,' etc. ; ' He that believeth and is baptized shall be saved.' Not, therefore, baptized in order to believing, but believing in order to be baptized ; so that, ideally or doctrinally considered, baptism presupposes faith, and sets the Divine seal on its blessings and prospects. And so we never find the evangelists and apostles thrusting baptismal services into the foreground, as if through such ministrations they expected the vital change to be produced, but first preaching the Gospel, and then, when this had come with power into the heart, recognising and confirming the result by the administration of the ordinance. So did Peter, for example, on the day of Pentecost ; he made proclamation of the truth concerning Christ and His salvation ; and only when this appeared to have wrought with convincing power and energy on the people, he pressed the matter home by urging them to ' repent and be baptized every one in the name of Jesus Christ for the remission of sins, and they should receive the gift of the Holy Ghost.' It was a call to see that they had every thing involved in a sound conversion ; for the kind of repentance spoken of is the *metanoia*, the change of mind which has its root in faith, and implies a spiritual acquaintance with Christ and the things of His salvation. At a later period, Peter justifies himself for receiving, through baptism, the household of Cornelius, on the ground that they had 'heard of the Gospel and believed,' or, as he again puts it, that 'God purified their hearts by faith.'[1]   Such was the process also with the Ethiopian eunuch, with Lydia, with the jailer at Philippi; so that baptism was administered by the apostles, not for the purpose of *creating* a relation between the individual and Christ, but of *accrediting and completing* a relation already formed.   And if baptism also is said to save, and is specially associated with the work of regeneration—as it undoubtedly is[2]—it can only be because baptism is viewed, in the case of the adult believer, as the proper consummation and embodiment of faith's actings in the reception of Christ.   For, constituting in such a case the solemn response of a believing soul and a purged conscience to the Gospel call, it fitly represents the whole process, marks by a significant action the passing of the boundary-line between nature and grace, and a formal entrance on the state and privileges of the redeemed.   But apart from this spiritual change presupposed and implied, nothing is effected by the outward administration; and to be regenerated in the language of Scripture and the estimation of the apostles, is not to find admission merely into the Christian church; it is to become a new creature, and enjoy that witness of the Spirit which is the pledge and foretaste of eternal life. What is said of regeneration, is equally said of faith in Christ (John iii. 18-36; 2 Cor. v. 17, etc.).[3]

---

[1] Acts xv. 7-9.   [2] Rom. vi. 4, 5; Titus iii. 5; 1 Peter iii. 21.
[3] *See* Litton on 'The Church of Christ,' p. 291, *seq.*, where this subject is fully handled.

A certain accommodation, it will be understood, requires to be made in applying this Scriptural view to the baptism of infants—much as in the Old Testament rite of circumcision, which took its beginning with Abraham in advanced life, and, as so begun, had its proper significance and bearing determined for all time,[1] though appointed also to embrace the children of the patriarch. Our object is merely to indicate the general purport and place of baptism, as also of the Lord's Supper, in relation to the spiritual life of the believer in Christ; and to shew that, in this respect, their place is not primary, but secondary, seeing that they presuppose a relation of the individual to Christ, a spiritual life already begun through faith in the word of Christ, which it is their design to confirm and build up. They themselves rest upon that word, and derive from it their meaning and use. Apart from the Gospel of Christ and an intelligent belief in its contents, they become, no matter by whom administered or with what punctuality received, but formal observances, without life and power. So that the grand ordinance, if we may so use the term, which has to do with the formation of Christ in the soul, or the actual participation of the life that is in Him, is this word of the kingdom—the Gospel, as the apostle calls it, of Christ's glory[2]—by the faith of which, through the Spirit, we are begotten as of incorruptible seed, are justified from sin, and have Christ Himself dwelling in us.[3] To abide in the doctrine of Christ and keep His word, is to have Him revealed in our experience for fellowship with that undying life which is hid with Him in God; it is to have both the Father and the Son; as, on the other hand, to be without His word abiding in the soul, is to be in a state of estrange-

---

[1] Rom. iv. 10-12.   [2] 2 Cor. iv. 4.
[3] James i. 18; 1 Peter i. 23; Rom. v. 1; Eph. iii. 17.

ment from Him, spiritually dead.[1] The position, therefore, which we are called to maintain toward Christ, rests
more immediately upon the presentation of His person and
work through the word ; it has its most decisive touch-
stone in the relation in which, as to spirit and behaviour,
we stand to this word.   And as the word comes into the
heart, and abides in the heart through faith, so, of
necessity, faith is the peculiar organ of spiritual life, since
it is that whereby we humbly receive and appropriate
what is freely given us in Christ—' whereby we trust in
Him, instead of trusting in *ourselves*—whereby, when
sinking under the consciousness of our blindness and
helplessness, the effect of our habitual sins, we take God's
word for our rule, God's strength for our trust, God's
mercy and grace for the sole ground of peace and comfort
and hope.'[2]

It is of incalculable moment for the interests of vital
Christianity, that these things should be well understood
and borne in mind ; for with the position now assigned to
the word, as connected with the life of Christ, and the
apprehension of that word by a reliant faith, is bound up
the doctrine of a salvation by grace, as contradistinguished
from that of salvation by works ; or, as we may otherwise
put it, the attainment of a state of peace and blessing by
fallen man, in a way that is practicable, as contrasted
with a striving after one which is utterly impracticable.
For whatever does not spring freshly and livingly from
faith, can neither be well-pleasing in the eyes of God, nor
can it secure that imperishable boon of eternal life in
God's kingdom, which comes to sinners only as His free
and sovereign gift.   And precisely as this is lost sight of,
whether in the case of individuals, or in the church at

---

[1] John viii. 31, 37, 51, xv. 7; Col. iii. 3; 2 John 9.
[2] Hare's ' Victory of Faith,' p. 78.

large, is there sure to discover itself, if not a total carelessness and insensibility about spiritual things, then the
resuscitation of a law of ordinances, an excessive regard
to outward forms and ceremonial observances, as if these
were the things of paramount importance, and there could
be no salvation without them ; for these are things which
the natural man *can* do, and, by taking pains to do them,
may readily fancy himself to be something before God.

It is true that, in a certain aspect, this relation of the
believer to the word, the salvation, and the life of Christ,
may be regarded as coming within the domain of law ; for
in every thing that concerns it—both the provision of
grace and blessing in Christ, and the way in which this
comes to be realized in the experience of men—there is a
revelation of the will of God, which necessarily carries
with it an obligation to obedience—has the essence and
the force of law. Men *ought* to receive the Gospel of
Christ, and enter into the fellowship of His death and
resurrection : they are commanded to do so, and in doing
it they are said to be obedient to the Gospel, or to the
truth therein exhibited.[1] It is even set forth as pre-
eminently the work which God calls or enjoins us in our
fallen condition to do, to believe on Him whom He hath
sent, and the refusing to do this work, and thereby rejecting the grace of God provided and offered in Christ, is
the crowning sin of those to whom the Gospel comes in
vain.[2] The more special and distinctive acts, also, of the
new life which is given to those who yield themselves to
the calls of the Gospel, are occasionally pressed on them
as duties to be discharged—such as seeking from the
Lord the gifts of grace, being converted to His love and
service, or transformed into the image of Christ, by

[1] John iii. 23; Acts xvi. 31; Rom. x. 16; 1 Pet. i. 14.
[2] John vi. 29, xv. 22, xvi. 9; Luke xix. 27.

putting off the old man and putting on the new.[1] And so, speaking from this point of view, the Apostle Paul does not hesitate, even while striving to exclude the idea of merit, or of salvation as attainable by obedience to any law of works, to represent the whole as proceeding in conformity to law—'the law of faith;' and the individuals themselves are described as, in consequence of their believing reception of the Gospel, 'children of obedience,' or such as have become obedient to the faith.[2] Undoubtedly the matter admits of being so represented. It is a mode of representation grounded in the essential nature of things, since by the very constitution of their being, men are bound to render account of the light they enjoy and the advantages placed within their reach; are responsible to God for what with His help they can attain of good, as well as for what they are expressly commanded to do. It is, too, a mode of representation which may justly be pressed when the object is to arouse men's dormant energies, and bring them to consider what solemn issues depend on the treatment they personally give to the claims and Gospel of Christ. But it still were a grievous mistake to suppose, that this is either the only or the principal light, in which our relation to the grace and truth of the Gospel ought to be contemplated. It is not that in which the Gospel formally presents itself, or is fitted to produce its happiest results ; and on the ground of such a mode of representation, only incidentally, and for purposes of moral suasion introduced, to do what Luther had too much reason for saying many great and excellent men had done—that they not only 'knew not how to preach Moses rightly, but sought to make a Moses out of Christ, out of the Gospel a law-book, out of the word works,'—is

---

[1] Mat. vii. 7; Acts iii. 19; Rom. xii. 2; Eph. iv. 22-24.
[2] Rom. i. 5, iii. 27; 1 Pet. i. 14; Acts vi. 17.

the most effectual method to render Gospel and law alike of no avail for salvation. The direct and immediate aspect under which Christ is made known to us in the Gospel is unquestionably that of a bestower of blessing, not a master of laws and services; a gracious and merciful Redeemer, who has at infinite cost wrought out the plan of our salvation, and laid freely open to our acceptance the whole treasury of its unsearchable riches. It is, therefore, with invitation and promise, rather than with any thing bearing the aspect of law, that the genuine disciple of Jesus will ever find that he has immediately to do : his part is to receive, in the use of Gospel privileges and the exercise of a living faith, the gifts so freely tendered to him; and endeavour increasingly to apprehend that for which he is apprehended of Christ, so as to grow up unto a close and living fellowship with his Divine Head in all that is His.

II. But leaving now this branch of the subject, we turn to the other—to consider the relation in which, as exhibited in the apostolic writings, the church of the New Testament stands to the *moral* law—the law as summarily comprised in the precepts of the Decalogue, or in the two great commandments of love to God and man.

Here, we must not forget, the prime requisite for a right perception of the truth is a proper personal relation to the truth. We must start from the position just described—that, namely, of a believing appropriation of the word of Christ, and the consequent possession of the Spirit of life which flows from Christ to the members of His spiritual body. It is from this elevated point of view that the matter is contemplated in the doctrinal portions of New Testament Scripture ; and hence statements are sometimes made concerning it, which, while entirely consonant with the experience of those who have received with some degree of fulness the powers of that higher life, cannot be more than imperfectly understood, and may even be regarded as inconsistent, by such as either stand altogether without the spiritual sphere, or have but partially imbibed its spirit. It was so in a measure under the law, the statements regarding which, in the recorded experience of Old Testament believers—as to its excellence, its depth and spirituality of meaning, their delight in its precepts yet tremblings of soul under its searching and condemning power, their desire to be conformed to its teaching yet perpetual declining from the way of its commandments—could not appear otherwise than strange and enigmatical to persons who, not having come practically under the dominion of the law, necessarily possessed but a superficial knowledge of it. And the same may justly be expected in a still higher degree now, amid the complicated and delicate relations as between Moses and Christ, law and grace, through which the experience of believers may be said to lie. There is here very peculiarly needed the spiritual discernment which belongs only to those who are living in the Spirit; and if it may be affirmed of such that, having a mind to do the will of God, they shall know of the doctrine that it is of God,[1] with equal confidence may it be affirmed of others not thus spiritually minded, that they cannot adequately know it, because wanting the proper frame and temper of soul for justly appreciating it.

The most distinguishing characteristic of the Gospel dispensation undoubtedly is its prominent exhibition of grace, as connected with the mediatorial work of Christ. The great salvation has come; and, in consequence, sins are not merely pretermitted to believers, as in former times,

---

[1] John vii. 17.

through the forbearance of God, but fully pardoned through the blood of the Lamb,[1] freedom of access is gained for them into the presence of God, and the gift of the Spirit to abide with them, and work in them much more copiously than had been done before. But there is a gradation only, not a contrast; and as under the Old Covenant the law-giving, was also the loving God, so under the New, the loving God is also the law-giving.[2] We have seen how much it was so, as represented in the personal ministry and work of Christ—how completely He appropriated for Himself and His followers the perfect law of God, and how also He continually issued precepts for their observance, in conformity with its tenor, though in form bearing the impress of His own mind and mission. The apostles, after the descent of the Holy Spirit, and the formal entrance of the new economy, pursued substantially the same course. Thus James, whose style of thought and expression approaches nearest to those of Old Testament Scripture, designates the law of brotherly love the *royal* law—as that which, in a manner, governs and controls every other in the sphere of common life—and tells the Christians that they would do well if they fulfilled it.[3] St Peter, though he specifies no particular precept of the law, yet points to an injunction in the book of the law, which is comprehensive of all its righteousness, 'Be ye holy in all manner of conversation; for it is written, Be ye holy, for I am holy.'[4] St John also speaks freely in his epistles of the Lord's commandments, and of the necessity of keeping them, especially of the great commandment of love; he speaks of the law as of the well-known definite rule of righteousness, and of sin as the transgression of the law, to live in which is to

---

[1] Rom. iii. 25, where the πάρεσις of the past stands in a kind of contrast to the ἄφεσις of the present. [2] *See* Wuttke, 'Handbuch der Sitt.,' chap. ii. sec. 208. [3] James ii. 8. [4] 1 Peter i. 16.

abide in death.[1] And St Paul, who in a very peculiar
manner was the representative and herald of the grace
that is in Christ, is, if possible, still more express : ' Ye
have been called to liberty,' says he to the Galatians,
' only use not liberty for an occasion to the flesh, but by
love serve one another ; for all the law is fulfilled in one
word—in this, Thou shalt love thy neighbour as thyself,'[2]
—plainly identifying the love binding upon Christians
with the love enjoined in the law. The same use is made
by him of the fifth commandment of the Decalogue, in
the Epistle to the Ephesians,[3] when urging the duty of
obedience to parents. And in the Epistle to the Romans,
when the course of thought has brought him to the enforcement of vital godliness and the duties of a Christian
life, the reference made to the perfection and abiding
authority of the written law is even more full and explicit;
for he gives it as the characteristic of the spiritual
mind, that it assents to the law as ' holy and just and
good,' and ' serves it;'[4] while of the carnal mind he says,
' it is not subject to the law of God, neither indeed can
be.'[5] And when speaking of Christian obligation in its
varied manifestations of kindness between man and man,
he sums up the whole, first in the specific precepts of the
Decalogue, and then in the all-embracing precept of loving
one's neighbour as one's-self.[6]

I should reckon it next to impossible for any one of
unbiassed mind—with no peculiar theory to support—
with no desire of any kind, but that of giving a fair and
natural interpretation to the teaching of Scripture—to
weigh calmly the series of statements now adduced, and
to derive from them any other impression than this—that

[1] 1 John ii. 7, 8, iii. 7, 8, 23, 24, v. 2, 3; 2 John 5, 6.
[2] Gal. v. 13, 14.   [3] Eph. vi. 1-3.   [4] Rom. vii. 12, 25.
[5] Rom. viii. 7.   [6] Rom. xiii. 8-10.

the moral law, as revealed in the Old Testament, had with the apostles of our Lord a recognised place in the Christian church, and was plainly set forth by them as the grand test of excellence, and the authoritative rule of life. They recognised and appealed to it thus simply as it stood in the written revelation of God, and *because so written ;*—knowing nothing, apparently, of the refined explanations of modern thought, which would hold the morality of the law, indeed, to be binding on Christians, but not as commanded in the law—that while the substance or principles of the law may be said to be still living, in its outward and commanding form it is dead—or that, as formally expressed law, it is no longer obligatory, whether with reference to justification, or as a rule of life.[1] And yet, unquestionably, there is something in the apostolic mode of contemplating the law which gives a certain colour to these representations. A marked distinction is made in various places between the position which Israel occupied toward the law, and that now occupied by believers in Christ ; such, that there is a sense in which Israel was placed under it, and in which Christians are not ; that it had a purpose to serve till the fulfilment of the covenant of promise in Christ, for which it is no longer specifically required ;[2] that somehow it is done away or abolished,[3] or, as it is again put, that we are done away from it, that is, set free, in regard to its right to lord it over us ;[4] that we are even dead to it, or are no longer under it ;[5] and that the scope or end for which the law was given is accomplished, and alone can be accomplished, in Christ for those who are spiritually united to Him.[6]

---

[1] *See* the references in Lec. I.
[2] Gal. iii. 19-25, iv. 1-6.
[3] 2 Cor. iii. 11 ; Eph. ii. 15 ; Col. ii. 14.
[4] Rom. vii. 6.
[5] Rom. vi. 14, vii. 4.
[6] Rom. viii. 3, 4, x. 4.

These are certainly very strong, at first sight even startling statements, and if looked at superficially, or taken up and pressed in an isolated manner, might easily be made to teach a doctrine which would conflict with the passages previously quoted, or with the use of the law actually made in them with reference to the Christian life. That there must be a mode of harmonizing them, we may rest perfectly assured—though it can only be satisfactorily made out by a careful examination of the particular passages, viewed in their proper connection, and with due regard to the feelings and practices of the time. For the present, a general outline is all that can be given; the detailed exegesis on which it leans must be reserved for another place. Very commonly, indeed, a comparatively brief method of explanation has been adopted by divines, according to which Christians are held to be, not under the law as a covenant, but under it as a rule of life. Doctrinally, this gives the substance of the matter, but with a twofold disadvantage : it leaves one point regarding it unexplained, and in form also it is theological rather than Scriptural. In respect to form, Scripture no doubt represents the covenant of law, the old covenant, as in some sense done away, or abolished; but then not exactly in the sense understood by the expression in the theological statement just noticed. That covenant of law, as actually proposed and settled by God, did not stand opposed to grace, but in subordination to grace, as revealed in a prior covenant, whose spiritual ends it was designed to promote; therefore, though made to take the form of a covenant, its object still was not to *give*, but to *guide* life;[1] in other words, to shew distinctly to the people, and take them bound to consider, how it behoved them to act toward God, and toward each other as an elect genera-

[1] Gal. iii. 21.

tion, God's seed of blessing in the earth. But this, in the language of theology, does not materially differ from the use of the law as a rule of life ; whereas to be under the law as a covenant, means in theology to be bound by it as a covenant of works, to make good, through obedience to its precepts, a *title* to life. In such a sense the Israelites were not placed under it any more than ourselves ; and hence Witsius was disposed to regard it as not possessing for them the form of a covenant properly so called, but as presenting merely the rule of duty. [1] That, however, were only to abandon a Scriptural for a theological mode of expression, for undoubtedly it is called a covenant in Scripture. But apart from the question of form, the manner of statement under consideration is, in one point of view, defective ; for it does not indicate any difference between the relation of Israel and the relation of Christians to the law, while still it is clear, from several of the passages referred to, that there is some considerable difference : the law had a function to perform for Israel, and through them for the world, which is not needed in the same manner or to the same extent now. Wherein does this difference lie ? There is here evidently room for more careful and discriminating explanations. And, in endeavouring to make them, we must distinguish between what was common to Israel with the people of God generally, and what was peculiar to them as belonging to a particular stage in the Divine plan, living under a still imperfectly developed form of the Divine dispensations.

Viewed in the former of these aspects, the Israelites were strictly a representative people ; they were chosen from among mankind, as in the name of mankind, to hear that law of God, which revealed His righteous-

[2] De Œcon. Foed., L. iv. chap. 4. sec. 56.

ness for their direction and obedience; and though this
came in connection with another revelation, a covenant
of promise through which life and blessing were to be
obtained, yet, considered by itself, it brought out before
them, and charged upon their consciences, the sum of
all moral obligation—whatever is due from men as men,
as moral and responsible beings, to God Himself, and
to their fellow-men.   In this the law demanded only
what was right and good—what therefore should have
been willingly rendered by all to whom it came—what,
the more it was considered, men could not but the
more feel *must* be rendered, if matters were to be put
on a solid footing between them and God, and they
were to have a free access to His presence and glory.
But the law could only demand the right, could not
secure the performance of it; it could condemn sin, but not
prevent its commission, which, by reason of the weakness
of flesh, and the heart's innate tendency to alienation
from God, continued still to proceed in the face of the
commands and threatenings of law :—so that the law, in
its practical working, necessarily came to stand over
against men as a righteous creditor with claims of justice
which had not been satisfied, and deserved retributions
of judgment which were ready to be executed.   In this
respect, it had to be taken out of the way, got rid of or
abolished, in a manner consistent with the moral government of God—its curse for committed sin borne—and its
right to lord it over men to condemnation and death
brought to an end.   It is this great question—a question
which only primarily concerned the Jews, as having been
the direct recipients of the revelation of law, but in which
all men as sinners were alike really interested—that the
apostle chiefly treats in the larger proportion of the
passages recently referred to.   It is of the law in this

point of view, that he speaks of it as a minister of death
—of believers being no longer married to it or under it—
yea, of their being dead to it, dead through the law itself
to the law—and of the law being consequently removed
as a barrier between them and the favour and blessing of
God. And he was led to do so the rather because of the
deep-rooted and prevailing tendency of the time to look
at the law by itself—apart from the covenant of promise
—and to find in obedience to its commands a title to life
and blessing. This, the apostle argues, is utterly to mistake its meaning and pervert its design. Taken so, the
law works wrath, not peace ; instead of delivering from
sin, it is itself the very sting of sin ; hence brings not
blessing, but a curse ; not life, but condemnation ; and
never till men renounce confidence in their deeds of law,
and lay hold of the hope set before them in Him who for
sinners has satisfied its just demands, and made reconciliation for iniquity, can they obtain deliverance from fear
and guilt, and enter into life. Thus Christ becomes ' the
end of the law for righteousness to every one that
believeth:' [1] in Him alone it reaches its proper aim as
regards the interests of righteousness, for He has perfectly fulfilled its commands, in death as well as life has
honoured its claims : and this not for Himself properly,
but for those who through faith join themselves to Him,
and become partakers, both in the work of righteousness
He has accomplished, and the spirit of righteousness He
puts into their hearts.

Such, briefly, is the import of that class of statements
in St Paul's writings ; and in this sense only do they
warrant us to speak of the moral law being done away,
or of our having been set free from it—a sense which
really enhances the importance of the law, most strik-

[1] Rom. x. 4.

ingly exhibits its eternal validity, because shewing us to
be delivered from it, only that we may be brought into
conformity to its spirit and requirements. And, in this
respect, as we have said, there is no difference between
the believer under the old covenant, and the believer
under the new—except that what was little more than
hope before is realization now, what was then but dimly
apprehended, and received only as by way of provisional
forestalments, is now disclosed in all its fulness, and
made the common heritage of believers in Christ. But
there was another respect in which the position of Israel
is to be considered, one in which it was peculiar, since,
according to it, they occupied a particular, and that a
comparatively early, place in the history of the Divine
dispensations. In this respect, the revelation of law had
a prominence given to it which was also peculiar, which
was adapted only to the immature stage to which it belonged, and was destined to undergo a change when the
more perfect state of things had come. Considered in
this point of view, the law must be taken in its entire
compass, with the Decalogue, indeed, as its basis, yet
with this not in its naked elements and standing alone,
but, for the sake of greater prominence and stringency,
made the terms of a covenant ; and not only so, but, even
while linked to a prior covenant of grace, associated with
pains and penalties which, in the case of deliberate transgression, admitted of no suspension or repeal—associated,
moreover, with a complicated system of rites and ordinances
which were partly designed to teach and enforce upon
men's minds its great principles and obligations of moral
duty, and partly to provide the means of escape from the
guilt incurred by their imperfect fulfilment or their occasional violation. It was in this complex form that the
law was imposed upon Israel, and interwoven with the

economical arrangements under which, as a people, they were placed. It is in that form that it was appointed to serve the design of an educational or pedagogical institute, preparatory to the introduction of Gospel times; and in the same form only that St Paul, in various places —especially in the Epistle to the Galatians, also in Eph. ii. 14-17 ; Col. ii. 14-23—contended for its having been displaced or taken out of the way by the work of Christ. In all the passages the moral law is certainly included in the system of enactment spoken of, but still always in the connection now mentioned—as part and parcel of a disciplinary yoke, a pedagogy suited only to the season of comparative childhood, therefore falling into abeyance with the arrival of a manhood condition. And the necessity of this change, it will be observed, he presses with special reference, not to the strictly moral part of the law, but to the subsidiary rules and observances with which it was associated—the value of which, as to their original design, ceased with the introduction of the Gospel. His view was, not that men were disposed to make more of the Decalogue, or of the two great commandments of love, than he thought altogether proper—precisely the reverse : it was, because they were allowing the mere temporary adjuncts, and ritualistic accompaniments of these fundamental requirements, to overshadow their importance, and pave the way for substituting a formal and fictitious pietism for true godliness and virtue. And hence to prevent, as far as possible, any misunderstanding of his meaning, he does not close the epistles in question without pointing in the most explicit terms to the simply moral demands of the law as now, not less than formerly, binding on the consciences of men.[1]

In short, the question handled by the apostle in this

---

[1] Gal. v. 13-22 ; Eph. vi. 1-9 ; Col. iii. 14, *seq.*

part of his writings upon the law, was not whether the
holiness and love it enjoined were to be practised, but how
the practice was to be secured. The utterance of the
law's precepts in the most peremptory and solemn form
could not do it. The converting of those precepts into
the terms of a covenant, and taking men bound under the
weightiest penalties to observe them, could not do it.
Nor could it be done by a regulated machinery of means
of instruction and ordinances of service, intended to minister subsidiary help and encouragement to such as were
willing to follow the course of obedience. All these had
been tried, but never with more than partial success—not
because the holiness required was defective, but because
the moral power was wanting to have it realized. And
now there came the more excellent way of the Gospel—the
revelation of that love which is the fulfilling of the law,
in the person of the New Head of humanity, the Lord
from heaven—the revelation of it in full-orbed completeness, even rising to the highest point of sacrifice, and
making provision for as many as would in faith receive it,
that the spirit of this noble, pure, self-sacrificing love
should dwell as a new life, an absorbing and controlling
power, also in *their* bosom. So that, ' what the law could
not do in that, it was weak through the flesh, God sending His own Son in the likeness of sinful flesh, and for sin
condemned sin in the flesh, that the righteousness of the
law might be fulfilled in us who walk not after the flesh,
but after the spirit.' He who is replenished with this
spirit of life and love, no longer has the law standing over
him, but, as with Christ in His work on earth, it lives in
him, and he lives in it ; the work of the law is written on
his heart, and its spirit is transfused into his life. ' The
man (it has been justly said) who is truly possessor of
" the spirit of life in Christ Jesus," *cannot* have any other

gods but his Father in heaven ; *cannot* commit adultery ; *cannot* bear false witness ; *cannot* kill ; *cannot* steal. Such a man comes down upon all the exercises and avocations of life from a high altitude of wise and loving homage to the Son of God, and expounds practically the saying of the apostle, " Whosoever is born of God sinneth not, but he that is begotten of God keepeth himself, and that wicked one toucheth him not." . . . . Christ's cross, then, delivers Christians from what may be termed moral drudgery ; they are not oppressed and pined serfs, but freemen and fellow-heirs, serving the Lord Christ with all gladness of heart. It magnifies the law and makes it honourable, yet delivers those who accept Jesus Christ as their Saviour from the bondage of the letter. Instead of throwing the commandments into contempt, it gave them a higher moral status, and even Sinai itself becomes shorn of its greatest terrors when viewed from the elevation of the cross. Love was really the reason of the law, though the law looked like an expression of anger. We see this, now that we love more ; love is the best interpreter of God, for God is love.' [1]

Thus it is that the Gospel secures liberty, and, at the same time, guards against licentiousness. To look only, or even principally, to the demands of law, constituted as human nature now is, cramps and deadens the energies of the soul, generates a spirit of bondage, which, ever vacillating between the fear of doing too little, and the desire of not doing more than is strictly required, can know nothing of the higher walks of excellence and worth. On the other hand, to look to the grace and liberty of the Gospel away from the law of eternal rectitude, with which they stand inseparably connected, is to give a perilous licence to the desires and emotions of the heart, nurses a

---

[1] 'Ecce Deus,' chap. xvi.

spirit of individualism, which, spurning the restraints of
authority, is apt to become the victim of its own caprice,
or the pliant slave of vanity and lust ; for true liberty, in
the spiritual as well as in the civil sphere, is a *regulated*
freedom ; it moves within the bonds of law, in a spirit of
rational obedience ; and the moment these are set aside,
self-will rises to the ascendant, bringing with it the
witchery and dominion of sin.[1]   It is only, therefore, the
combined operation of the two which can secure the proper
result ; and with whom is that to be found except with
those who have received the Spirit of life in Christ Jesus ?
To be replenished with this Spirit, is to be brought within
the sphere of Divine love, which, so far from recoiling
from the law's demands, can give expression even to its
noblest enthusiasm in a cordial response to the obligations
they impose, and a faithful obedience to the course of
action they prescribe.[2]

[1] Rom. vi. 16.

[2] So in the most emphatic moments of our Lord's life, as at Matt. xi. 26,
xxvi. 39 ; Jo. x. 18.   Nor is a certain correspondence wanting in the finer ex-
emplifications of the good in civil life—as in Lord Nelson with his famous
watchword, 'England expects every man to do his duty'—patriotism at its
highest stretch being deemed capable of no loftier aspiration or more glorious
service than to give honourable satisfaction to the calls of duty.   Statements
are often made by religious writers respecting service done with a special regard
to such calls. which is not strictly correct; as when it is said, 'Duty is the
very lowest conception of our relation to God—privilege is a higher—honour a
higher—happiness and delight a higher still' (Irving's Works, Vol. I. p. 23).
Doubtless, in certain states of mind it is so ; and he who does a service merely
because he deems it a duty, feeling himself dragged to it as by a chain, will
be universally regarded as in a low moral condition.   But this is by no means
necessary.   A sense of the dutiful may be felt, may even be most intensely
realized, when it is associated with the purest feelings and emotions ; and in
the higher spheres of spiritual light and excellence—with the elect angels in
heaven, or even the more advanced saints on earth, in their seasons of deepest
moral earnestness—a supreme regard to the dutiful, to the will of God as the
absolutely right and good, we may not hesitate to say, is the profoundest sentiment in the bosom.   All else, with such nobler spirits, is lost sight of in the
completeness of their surrender to the mind and will of the Eternal.

Besides, by thus calling into play the higher elements of a Divine life, there is necessarily set to work a spring or principle of goodness in the heart, which in aim is one with the law, but which in its modes of operation no law can exactly define. Experience shews, that in the complicated affairs of human life, it is impossible to prescribe a set measure to the exercise of any of the Christian graces, not even to justice, which in its own nature is the most determinate of them all. Numberless instances will arise in which, after all our attempts at precision, principle alone will need to guide our course, and not any definite landmarks previously set up on the right hand or the left. But especially is this the case with love, which of all the graces is the most free and elastic in its movements, and, if strong and fervent, adapts itself with a kind of sacred instinct to existing wants and opportunities. There still is, in every variety of state and circumstances, a right and a wrong—a bad course to be shunned, a good course to be followed, and possibly a better course still, a higher and nobler development of love, which it might be practicable to adopt, were there but grace and strength adequate to the occasion. But the proper path cannot be marked out beforehand by formulated rules and legal precedents. Love must in many respects be a law to itself, though still under law to God; and the more its flame has been kindled at the altar of Heaven, and it has caught the spirit of that Divine philanthropy, which, with the greatness of its gifts and sacrifices, triumphs over human enmity and corruption, the more always will it be disposed to do and sacrifice in return.

In this sense it may be said of Christianity, that it is more characterized by spirit than by law; that it does 'not prescribe any system of rules,' as was connected with the Old Covenant, that 'instead of precise rules it

rather furnishes sublime principles of conduct.'[1] But
such general statements have their limitations ; and if
understood in an absolute sense, with reference either to
the past or the present, they will only serve to mislead.
It *was* characteristic of the Old Covenant that it had a
system of rules, dealt in exact and definite prescriptions ;
but these, it ought to be remembered, were far from de-
fining every thing in the wide field of duty : a very large
proportion of them related merely to the sacrificial worship
of the Temple, and to particular conditions and circumstances of life ; while in a great variety of things besides,
things pertaining to the weekly service of God and the
procedure of ordinary life, men were to a large extent
thrown upon principle for their guidance, and if this failed,
then they had no specific rule to fall back upon. They
were commanded, for example, to honour the Lord with
their substance—to be kind to the stranger sojourning
amongst them—to treat with compassion and generosity
their poor—to love a brother, and in love rebuke him, if
sin were found to be upon him :—but for carrying out
such commands in all supposable cases, no precise rules
either were or could be given. Some leading instances
only are specified by way of example, but in the great
majority of cases the exact mode of behaviour was necessarily left to the individual. Look, for example, to the
poor widow who cast in her two mites into the treasury—
her whole living—who bade her do so ? What legal
enactment prescribed it ? Or that other woman, who
with her penitent and grateful tears washed the feet of
our Lord, and wiped them with the hair of her head—
what explicit word had so required it at her hands ? In
both cases alike, we may say, love was their only law,
prompting them to do what breathed, indeed, the inmost

1 Whately, ' Essay on Abol. of Law.'

spirit of the law, but what no express enactment of law either did or properly could demand. Yet such things belonged rather to the Old than to the New dispensation ; they occurred while the New was still only in the forming ; and things similar in kind should much more be expected now, since the great redemption has come, elevating the whole sphere of the Divine kingdom, and giving the Spirit to its real members as an abiding monitor and guide. This Spirit, in his directive influence, is himself a living law (*Spiritus Sanctus est viva lex*), and renders unnecessary a detailed system of rules and prescriptions concerning all that should be done, and how exactly to do it.[1] But as regards the grand outlines of moral obligation set forth in the law's requirements, these not the less

---

[1] Hence, the apostle Paul, when exhorting to the support of a Christian ministry, and liberality to the poor, specifies no definite proportion, such as the tenth, but calls upon believers to give according to their ability and as the Lord had prospered them (1 Cor. xvi. 2 ; 2 Cor. viii. ix. ; Gal. vi. 6.). In like manner, when dealing with Philemon respecting Onesimus, he refrains from prescribing any stringent rule, but plies him with great principles and moving considerations. But we are not thence warranted to speak of a morality in the Gospel which ' exceeds duty and outstrips requirement' (' Ecce Homo,' p. 145) ; or, which is but another form of the same thing, prompts us to deeds of supererogation. There can be no such deeds now, any more than in former times ; no one can do more than is required of him in the law of God ; for that law is the expression of God's will, and man's will cannot be better than God's. To love the Lord with all one's heart, soul, and strength, and one's neighbour as one's self, is the perfection of moral excellence : and what is beyond or beside this, is not a higher attainment, but a vicious excess or partial development. There may well enough, indeed, be particular acts of love, or sacrifices of self-interest, which are not specifically demanded in any formal requirement ; for, as already stated, it never was meant to traverse the whole field of moral action with such special demands, and the thing is practically impossible. But those higher moral deeds still come within the sphere of the law's general requirement of love; and not properly as to the degree of love to be manifested, but only as to the particular form or direction which may be given to the manifestation, can the course of duty ever be said to lie at the option of the individual. For a safe statement and application of the distinction between principles and rules, so far as it can be said to exist in Christianity, *see* the admirable sermon of Augustus W. Hare, entitled ' Principles above Rules.'

remain in force ; and that love which is the peculiar fruit
and evidence of the indwelling Spirit, can only be recognised as in any proper sense a law to itself, so long as it
runs in the channel of those requirements, and is controlled
by a sense of duty.   When turning into other directions,
it met once and again, even in the case of the chiefest
apostles, with our Lord's prompt and stern rebuke.[1]   And
St John—the most spiritual of all the apostles, if we may
distinguish among them—has in this respect most distinctly expressed the very heart and substance of the
whole matter, when he says, ' This is the love of God that
we keep His commandments ;'[2]—or, as it should rather be,
' This is the love of God, in order that we may keep His
commandments,"—ἵνα τὰς ἐντολὰς αὐτοῦ τηρῶμεν—not that we
do it as a fact, but that we may and should do it as a
scope or aim.   It is as if the love of God were implanted
in the bosom for no other end than to dispose and enable
us to keep His commandments; for only in so far as these
are kept, does the love of God in us reach its proper destination.   And, therefore, the sense of duty, or the felt
obligation to keep God's commandments, has with good
reason been called the very backbone of a religious character.[3]   It is that which more especially gives strength
and consistency to the soul's movements, and saves love
itself from degenerating into a dreamy sentimentalism,
from yielding to improper solicitations, or running into
foolish and fanciful extremes.   ' He that saith I know
Him, and keepeth not His commandments, is a liar, and
the truth is not in him.   But whoso keepeth His word,
in him verily is the love of God perfected : hereby know
we that we are in Him.'[4]

It was but a special application of this truth, when Mr

---

[1] Matt. xvi. 23 ; Luke ix. 55.   [2] 1 John v. 3.
[3] Temple's ' Sermons at Rugby,' p. 36.   [4] 1 John ii. 4, 5.

Maurice, in a recent production, along with a gentle rebuke to a Scotch friend, expressed his belief that ' the reverence for an unchangeable law and a living lawgiver, has given to the Scottish character its strength and solidity;'[1] and if so, surely an element of healthful vigour, which the friends of enlightenment and progress, instead of trying to weaken where it exists, would do well rather to encourage and strengthen where it is comparatively wanting. It was an utterance, too, in the same line, but with a more general reference and in a higher tone, when Ewald, who is often as true in his moral perceptions as loose and arbitrary in his theological positions, thus wrote, ' There exists among men no free and effective guidance but when the individual human spirit submits to be directed and governed by the eternal, all-ruling Spirit, because it has recognised that to resist His truths and demands is to oppose its own good. But whatever else may result from the many kinds of direction and government of men by men, this can only then prove just and beneficial when it does not run counter to this supreme law.'[2]

Enough, however, of human testimonies, and also of the general argument. We merely sum up in a few closing sentences what the church is entitled to hold respecting the still abiding use of the law. (1.) Though not by any means the sole, it yet is the formal, authoritative teacher of the eternal distinctions between right and wrong in conduct; the special instrument, therefore, for keeping alive in men's souls a sense of duty. Nothing has yet occurred in the history of mankind which can with any show of reason be said to supersede this use of

[1] Preface to ' Sermons on the Ten Commandments.'
[2] Geschichte, II. p. 165.

T

the moral law.   The theorists of human progression, who conceive such landmarks to be no longer needed, who fancy the world has outgrown them, are never long in meeting with what is well fitted to rebuke their groundless satisfaction :—in the disputes, for example, among themselves as to what oftentimes should be deemed virtuous conduct—in the spread of those philosophic systems, of the materialistic or pantheistic school, which would sap the very foundations of piety, and unsettle the distinctions between good and evil—or, after a coarser fashion, in the atrocities which are ever and anon bursting forth in society, and even finding their unscrupulous apologisers.   There is, we know, a condition of righteousness for which the law is not ordained ; [1] but it is clear as day, that not only not the world at large, but not even the most Christian nation in the world, has as yet approached such a condition.   (2.) The law, as the measure of moral excellence and commanded duty, provides what is needed to work conviction of shortcomings and sins—by looking steadfastly into which, men may come to be sensible of the deep corruption of their natures, their personal inability to rectify the evil, their guilt and danger, so that they may betake for refuge to where alone it can be found— in the blood and Spirit of Christ.   The experience of the apostle must be ever repeating itself anew, 'I had not known sin but by the law ;' 'Through the law I am dead to the law, that I might live unto God.'   Thus we come to the practical knowledge of our case ; and 'to know ourselves diseased is half our cure.'   (3.) Finally, the imperfections too commonly cleaving to the work of grace in the redeemed, call for a certain coercive influence of law even for them.   If it has not the function to discharge for such which it once had, it still has a function, there

[1] 1 Tim. i. 9.

being so little of that perfect love which casteth out fear, and fear being needed to awe where love has failed to inspire and animate. So, even St Paul, replenished as he was with the life-giving Spirit, found it necessary at times to place the severer alternative before him : 'If I preach the gospel willingly, I have a reward : but if against my will, a dispensation of the gospel is committed to me ; yea, woe is unto me, if I preach not the gospel.'[1] He even delighted to think of himself as in a peculiar sense the servant, the bondman, of God or Christ.[2] And for believers generally the two are thus mingled together, 'Let us have grace, whereby we may serve God acceptably, with reverence and godly fear : for our God is a consuming fire.'[3]

---

[1] 1 Cor. ix. 16, 17.   [2] Rom. i. ; Gal. i. 10 ; Tit. i. 1.   [3] Heb. xii. 29.

LECTURE IX.

THE RE-INTRODUCTION OF LAW INTO THE CHURCH OF THE NEW
TESTAMENT, IN THE SENSE IN WHICH LAW WAS ABOLISHED BY
CHRIST AND HIS APOSTLES.

THE history of the law, considered as a revelation of
God, reaches its close in the personal work of Christ
and the formal institution of His kingdom among men ;
every thing pertaining to it had then, as on God's part,
assumed its final norm.   But there is an instructive,
though at the same time a mournful sequel to that history,
which it will be proper briefly to trace before we take
leave of the subject.   It is the history of man's additions to
God's testimony—claiming, however, equally with this, the
sanction of Divine authority, and, by gradual and successive innovations, re-imposing upon the church a legalism,
precisely similar in kind to that which had been done
away in Christ, but greatly more pervasive and exacting
in its demands, and in its practical operation fundamentally at variance with the true spirit of the Gospel.

The rise of this false direction in the Christian church
is the more remarkable, that it not only had the clear
revelations of the Gospel against it, but even ran counter
to what may be called the later development of practical
Judaism itself.   The tendency of things under the Old
Covenant, especially from the time that the Theocracy
began outwardly to decay, we formerly saw, was to give
increasing prominence to the *spiritual* element in the
legal economy, and to make relatively less account of the

merely *outward* and *ceremonial.* This tendency was considerably strengthened by the prolonged dispersion of the Jewish people, and what everywhere accompanied it, the synagogal institution, which, to a large extent, took the place of the priestly ministrations and sacrificial worship of the Temple. The synagogue, in its constitution and services, was founded upon what was general, rather than upon what was distinctive and peculiar, in Judaism ; it made account only of the common priesthood of believers, and the essential elements of truth and righteousness embodied in the records and institutions of the Old Covenant ; and, consequently, the worship to which it accustomed the people at their stated meetings was entirely of a spiritual kind—prayer, the reading of inspired Scripture, and occasionally the word of brotherly counsel or admonition from some one disposed and qualified to impart it. Priests, as such, had no peculiar place either in its organization or its services ; and the rulers who presided over every thing connected with it were nominated by the people on the ground simply of personal gifts and reputed character. There still remained, of course, the observance of such things as the rite of circumcision, of the distinction of meats, and of days sacredly set apart from a common to a religious use, which depended upon nothing local or individual—might be practised anywhere and by any member of the community. It was this kind of legalism which first sought to press into the Christian church—the only kind that could press into it from the synagogue ; but which, though hallowed by ancient usage, and, besides, possessing nothing of a sacerdotal or ascetic nature, was yet firmly repressed by the apostles, and ejected from the bosom of the churches which had begun to follow it. No taint of evil, therefore, was allowed to insinuate itself from this quarter—not even at first, when not a few from the synagogue passed over into the membership of the church ; and much less afterwards, when the synagogue everywhere arrayed itself in fierce antagonism to the church :—while, on the other hand, in the simple polity of the synagogue and its spiritual, non-ritualistic, if somewhat imperfect worship, the church found a starting-point fashioned out of those elements in the Old Covenant, which had at once their correspondence and their more complete exhibition in the New.

Yet, with all this, one can easily understand, if due regard be had to the circumstances of the early church, how a disposition might arise and grow—if not very carefully guarded against—to assimilate the state of things in it to that of the preceding dispensation, and effect a virtual return to the oldness of the letter. There was the general relation between the two economies to begin with. Christianity sprang out of Judaism, and stood related to it as the substance to the shadow. More than that, a principal part of the Christian, as of the Jewish synagogal worship, consisted in the reading of the Scriptures of the Old Testament—proportionally a much larger part than in later times ; for the function of preaching was at first but imperfectly exercised, and the Scriptures of the New Testament were only by and by gathered into a volume, and made to share with those of the Old in the services of the sanctuary. Hence, the minds of the Christian people were kept habitually conversant with the religion, as well as the other affairs of the Old Covenant, with the Temple and its priesthood, its rites of purification and ever-recurring oblations ; and what might, perhaps, be still more apt to bias their views, they heard in the prophetical Scriptures delineations of Gospel times couched in legal phraseology—intimations, for example, of the Lord coming to His temple, that He might purify the sons of Levi, and receive from them an offering of righteousness; of incense and a pure offering being presented to the Lord from the rising to the setting sun; or of kings and far-off heathen bringing gifts to His temple. Inversely, also, in New Testament Scripture, spiritual things are sometimes described in the language of the Old—as when believers are said by St John to have an anointing from the Holy One; or when, in the Epistle to the Hebrews, they are represented as having an altar, which those who served the tabernacle had no right to partake of, and are exhorted to have their bodies washed with pure water. Such passages, if superficially considered, and interpreted otherwise than in accordance with the true spirit of the Gospel, might readily beget a disposition, might create even a kind of pious desire, to have the things of the New dispensation fashioned in some sort after the pattern of the Old, and so to give to the descriptions a concrete and sensible form, similar to what they had in the past.

There was, also, it must be added, a class of services and requirements occupying from the first an important place in the activities of the Christian church, in which the New necessarily came into a formal approximation to the Old. I refer to the pious and charitable contributions which the members of the Christian community brought for the relief of the poor, the support of the ministry, and the celebration of Divine ordinances. These contributions were essentially the same in kind with the tithes and free-will offerings of the elder economy; and the apostle, when treating of them in his first Epistle to the Corinthians, brought the one into express comparison with the other; and on the ground that they who were wont to minister about holy things lived of the Temple-offerings, he argued that they also who preached the Gospel should

live of the Gospel.[1]   In such a case the transition might
seem natural from an essential to a formal agreement.
Why, it might be asked, not give the New somewhat of
the same sacrificial character as the Old, and invest it with
the same sort of ritual accompaniments ?   Such thoughts
might the more readily occur, if there were influences at
work to dispose the early believers to forsake the channels
of Christian simplicity for the more sensuous attractions
of ritualistic observance.

Now, there *were* influences of this description not only
existing in all the centres of Christian agency, but also
very actively at work.   There was a current of opinion and
feeling perpetually bearing in from the scenes and intercourse of every-day life, in behalf of temples, altars,
sacrifices, priestly ministrations and dedicatory offerings,
as so essential to Divine worship that the one could hardly
be conceived of without the other ; the absence of such
outward materials and instruments of devotion seemed
incompatible with the very existence of the religious
element.   Hence, the reproach which was not infrequently
thrown out against the Christians as being *godless—ἄθεοι*
—because they refused to approach the altars, and take
part in the sacrificial rites of heathenism, without appearing to have any of their own as a substitute for them.[2]
The proper way to meet this prevailing sentiment was to
point to the one great High-Priest, the minister of a
higher than any earthly temple, and to the one perfect
sacrifice, by which, once for all, He accomplished what
never could be done by sacrifices of an inferior kind, and
which, by its infinite worth and ever-prevailing efficacy,
imparts to those interested in it a position so high, and a
character so sacred, that their services of faith and love
become in the sight of God sacrifices of real value.   This

---

[1] 1 Cor. ix. 12-14.   [2] Justin, ' Apol.,' chap. 6 ; ' Athenagoras,' chap. 4.

is the light in which the matter is presented in New Testament Scripture, where Christ is the one and all of a believer's confidence, and the whole company of the faithful have the character assigned them of the royal priesthood, to whom belongs the privilege of offering up in Him spiritual sacrifices, which for His sake are accepted and blessed—the sacrifices, namely, of thanksgivings, alms-deeds, works of beneficence and well-doing, which, when springing from genuine faith and love in Christ, are regarded as offerings of sweet-smelling savour to God.[1] But the church had not proceeded far on her course when she lost to some extent this clear discernment of the truth, and correct apprehension of the things relating to her proper calling and work in Christ; and continually as men who had been educated in heathenism pressed into the ranks of the visible church, the number increased of those within her pale whose preparation for the kingdom of God had been imperfect, and who had been too long accustomed to identify religion with the outward and the visible to be able to grasp sufficiently the spiritual realities of the Gospel.   There consequently arose a temptation to accommodate the form of Christianity to the taste of a lower class of persons, and by means of its external services work upon their natures, as by a new law of observance and discipline.   They might thus hope, without foregoing the realities of the faith, to retain the allegiance of the less informed, and accomplish by symbolical and ritual appliances what seemed less likely to be reached by means of a more elevated and spiritual kind.

In these circumstances, it devolved upon the church as a primary duty to take order for having proper counteracting checks and agencies brought into play; especially to see to it that those who were chosen to direct her

---

[1] 1 Pet. ii. 5 ; Phil. iv. 8 ; Heb. xiii. 15, 16.

counsels and preside over her assemblies, had become
soundly instructed, not only in the principles of the Christian faith, but also in the organic connection between
the Christian and Jewish dispensations, their respective
differences as well as agreements, and the points wherein
it was necessary to guard Christianity against any undue
approach either to Judaic or heathen observance. But this
was precisely what the early church failed to do—perhaps,
we may say, the greatest failure into which she fell, the
one fraught with the longest train of disastrous results.
For centuries there was no specific theological training
generally adopted for such as aspired to become her guides
in spiritual things, or actually attained to this position.
By much the larger portion even of those who contributed
in the most especial manner to mould her character and
government (Justin, Tertullian, Cyprian, Ambrose, Augustine, Jerome, etc.), were in their early days total or comparative strangers to the exact knowledge of Scripture ;
their period of culture and training was spent under
heathen guides, with a view to civic or military life ; and
when they passed, after a brief process of trial and
instruction, into the ecclesiastical sphere, it could scarcely
be otherwise than with many of the influences of the age
still cleaving to them. Coming to know Christianity
before they knew much of what preceded it, they wanted
what they yet very peculiarly needed—the discipline of a
gradual and successive study of the plan of God's dispensations, and the directive light of a well-digested scheme
of Scriptural theology. They knew the Bible in portions,
rather than as an organic and progressive whole ; and
even for that knowledge, especially in its earlier parts,
they were but poorly furnished with grammatical helps or
with judicious expositions. Should it surprise us if, in
such circumstances, they should often have caught but im-

perfectly the meaning of Old Testament Scripture—if they should even sometimes have shewn themselves to be insufficiently acquainted with its contents—and, in regard to the institutions and history of former times, should occasionally leave us at a loss to say whether the true or the false predominated—spiritualizing the most arbitrary going hand in hand with the crudest literalisms, profound thoughts intermingling with puerile conceits, and the most palpable Judaistic tendencies discovering themselves while evangelical principles were alone professedly maintained?   Such are the actual results ; and if there be one point more than another on which the spiritual discernment of those early Fathers was obviously defective, and their authority is least to be regarded, it is in respect to the connection between the New and the Old in the Divine economy.   In this particular department, so far from having any special lights to guide them, they laboured under peculiar disadvantages ; and their proper place in regard to it is that, not of the venerable doctors of the Christian church, but of its junior students.

Now let us mark the effect of the unfortunate combination of circumstances we have indicated, and see how, by gradual, yet by sure and successive steps, the tendency in the wrong direction, which was scarcely discernible at the outset, wrought till it became an evil of gigantic magnitude, and reduced the church to a worse than Judaic bondage.   In the earlier writings—such as have come down to us with probable marks of authenticity and genuineness—we notice nothing in the respect now under consideration, except a somewhat too close and formal application of the ritualistic language of the Old Testament to Christian times, coupled with certain puerile and mistaken interpretations of its meaning, in the line of extravagant literalisms.   Thus, to begin with the Epistle

of Clement, which in point of character as well as time is
entitled to the first place, when exhorting the Corinthians to lay aside their self-will and conform to the settled
and becoming order of God's house, he refers to the prescriptions given under the old economy respecting services and offerings, which were to be done at the appointed
times and according to God's good pleasure, nor anywhere men might please, but at the one altar and temple
in Jerusalem. This Clement assigns as a reason why
believers now should perform their offerings (προσφοράς) and
services (λειτουργίας) at their appointed seasons, and that each
should give thanks to God in his own order, and not
going beyond the rule of the ministry prescribed to him
(c. 40, 41). The passage cannot, as Romish controversialists
and some others have alleged, point otherwise than by
way of example to the legal sacrifices and services ; for it
would then, against the whole spirit and many express
statements in the epistle, absolutely merge the functions
and services of the Christian church in those of the
Jewish. On the contrary, in the Christian church he
recognises only two orders, those of bishops or presbyters
and deacons, and these standing related not to any Jewish
functionaries, as to the reason of their appointment, but
to a passage in the prophecies of Isaiah.[1] The only exception that can justly be taken to the statement of
Clement is, that, in referring to legal prescriptions, he did
not mark with sufficient distinctness the diversity existing between Old and New Testament times ; and, in describing the work proper to Christian pastors, characterized it in ritual language as consisting ' in a holy and
blameless manner of offering the gifts (προσενεγκόντας τὰ δῶρα).'
It is undoubtedly a departure from the style of New
Testament Scripture, and shews how readily, from the

---

[1] Isaiah lx. 17.

predominant use of the Scriptures of the Old Testament, their language was transferred to Christian acts and objects.   In this respect it formed a commencement which was but too generally followed, though not quite immediately.   For in the epistle of Polycarp, which in its approach to apostolic simplicity stands next to Clement's, there is not even such a slight departure from the mode of representation current in New Testament Scripture as we have marked in Clement; the epistle is throughout practical in its tone and bearing; the presbyters, deacons, and common believers are each exhorted to be faithful in their respective duties; and for the proper discharge of these, and for security against the spiritual dangers of the times, mention is made only of prayer, fasting, and a steadfast adherence to the teaching of the pure word of God.   Nor is it materially otherwise in the epistles of Ignatius, if with Cureton we take the Syriac form of the three preserved in that language as the only genuine ones, for in these there is nothing whatever of rites and ceremonies, priesthood and sacrifice, but only exhortations to prayer, watchfulness, steadfastness, and unity, with somewhat of an excessive deference to the bishop in respect especially to the formation of marriages.   Even in the seven epistles, in their shorter Greek form (which is as much as almost any one not hopelessly blinded by theory is now disposed to accept), omitting a few extravagant statements respecting the bishop, such as that 'nothing connected with the church should be done without him,' that 'it is not lawful without him either to baptize or to celebrate a love-feast,'[1] the style of exhortation and address, though often passionate and hyperbolical, can scarcely be deemed unscriptural: believers are spoken of as the temple or building of God, they break one and the

<hr>
[1] 'Smyr.,' chap. 8.

same bread, are related to one and the same altar (spiritually understood of course, for it is the entire body of the
faithful that is the subject of discourse), and have many
practical admonitions addressed to them.[1]

From the uncertainty, however, which hangs around
the epistles of Ignatius, both as to their authorship and
the time of their appearance, it is impossible to assign
them any definite place in the chain of evidences of which
we speak. The epistle to Diognetus, being entirely spiritual and evangelical in its spirit, going even to a kind of
extreme in its depreciation of the Jewish religion, does
not come within the scope of our argument. But the
so-called epistle of Barnabas, though in all probability a
production not earlier than the middle of the second century, while quite evangelical in its sentiments, knowing
no proper sacrifice but the one offering of Christ, no temple
but the regenerated souls of believers, is very arbitrary
in the use it makes generally of Old Testament Scripture,
and especially in the many outward, superficial agreements
and prefigurations of Gospel realities—as if the past had
in its very form and outline been intended for an image
of the future.[2] Passing on to Justin, he, too, designates
no select class, but the entire company of believers, 'the
true priestly race of God, who have now the right to offer
sacrifices to Him;'[3] and the sacrifices themselves are with
him, sometimes prayers and thanksgivings, sometimes
again the bread and the wine of the Supper, but these
simply as gratefully offered by the Christian people out of
their earthly abundance.[4] Sacrifices of blood and libations
of incense, he again says, are no longer required ; the only
perfect sacrifices are prayer and thanksgiving, and such

[1] Eph. ix., xvi., xxi. ; Phil. iv., etc.
[2] *See*, in particular, the fancied prefigurations of regeneration, baptism,
Christ and the cross, in chap. 7-12.
[3] 'Tryp.,' chap. 116, 117.   [4] 'Tryp.,' chap. 117 ; 'Apol.,' chap. 65-67.

things as can be distributed to the poor;[1] nor does he
know of any functionary who has to do with one or other
of these distinctive offerings but a presiding brother, or
the deacons of the church.   In Justin, the Eucharist, or,
as he also puts it, the Eucharistic bread and the Eucharistic cup, being especially connected with prayers and
thanksgivings for the great mercies of God, come into
view merely as a peculiar embodiment or representation
of these, and as such are classed with sacrifices and offerings—marking a certain departure from the language of
our Lord and the apostles, and that in the Old Testament
direction—though he also speaks of the celebration as
done in remembrance of Christ's suffering unto death for
men.[2]   But Irenaeus makes a further advance in the
same line by representing the Eucharist not merely as
having, like other spiritual acts, somewhat of a sacrificial
character, but as being emphatically the Christian oblation.
'The Lord gave instruction to His disciples to offer unto
God the first-fruits of His own creatures, not as if He
needed them, but, that they themselves might be neither
unfruitful nor ungrateful, He took that which by its
created nature was bread, and gave thanks, saying, This
is my body.   In like manner, also, the cup, which is of
that creation whereto we belong, He confessed to be
His own blood; and taught the new oblation of the New
Testament, which the church, receiving from the apostles,
offers throughout the whole world to God, to Him who
gives us the means of support—the first-fruits of His
gifts in the New Testament.'[3]   It can scarcely be doubted,
that the close connection which in early times subsisted
between the love-feast, in which the poor of the congregation partook of the charitable donations of their richer

[1] 'Apol.,' chap. 13 ; 'Tryp.' chap. 117.   [2] 'Tryp.,' chap. 41.
[3] Irenaeus, iv. chap. 17, sec. 5.

brethren, and the celebration of the Lord's Supper, materially contributed to the formation and entertainment of this view. But in the view itself, at least when so prominently exhibited, we cannot but perceive an evident approach to the symbolism of the Old Covenant, and a corresponding departure from the mode of representation in New Testament Scripture.[1] For, though in Irenaeus we find nothing of a priestly caste within the Christian church, and no altar or temple but such as are in Heaven,[2] yet once distinctly connect the communion elements (as he did) with the idea of an oblation—the oblation by way of eminence—an oblation, moreover, involving some mysterious change in the thing offered, and the thought was natural that a priest, a priest in the strictly official sense, must be required to offer it. So that we might presently expect to hear that the presiding brother of Justin, the episcopus or presbyter of Irenaeus, had risen to the dignity of a pontifex. And this is precisely the fresh advance that meets us in the next writer of eminence.[3]

[1] *See*, in preceding Lecture, p. 258.   [2] Irenaeus, iv. chap. 18, sec. 6.

[3] It is quite true, that the ordinance of the Supper may, without the least violation of its Scriptural character, be spoken of as the Eucharist, or the distinctively thanksgiving service. For, calling to remembrance, as it does, the great gift of God, and even pressing home on each individual a palpable representation and offer of that gift, it should call forth in a very peculiar manner the fervent and united thanksgivings of the church. Hence, from the first it was accompanied with the special offering of thanks to God and singing of hymns of praise ; and the service might not unjustly be regarded as the culmination of the church's adoring gratitude, poured forth over the crowning act of God's goodness. But this is still rather the proper and fitting accompaniment of the sacrament than the sacrament itself ; and when taken as the one and all in a manner of the service (as it plainly was from the time of Tertullian and onwards), the primary idea and end of the institution naturally fell into comparative abeyance, and the *commemoration* of a sacrifice became identified with the ever renewed *presentation* of it. This, beyond doubt, was the actual course which the matter took in the hands of the Fathers, though their language is not uniform or consistent. But the *commemorative* character of the ordinance, and

The writer referred to was Tertullian, who flourished at the close of the second and the beginning of the third century in North Africa.   Christianity had taken early root in that region, especially in the cities, where a vigorous race of Roman or Italian colonists formed the governing part of the population.   From the character of the people, the church there became peculiarly distinguished for its strength and moral earnestness, and, in many respects, exercised a formative influence over the government and polity of the church of Rome, and through her upon Christendom at large.   Tertullian was the first distinguished representative of this African church, and he brought into it the notions of order, and discipline, and stern administration, which he derived from his position and training as the son of a Roman centurion, and his education as a Roman lawyer—naturally, therefore, predisposed in a legal and ritualistic direction.   His writings, accordingly, contain much tending in this direction.   And in respect to the matter now immediately before us, he distinctly names the bishop the *summus sacerdos* or high-priest, though the dignity was still only in a provisional and fluctuating state—growing into definiteness and fixity rather than having actually attained to it.   In his treatise on baptism, and speaking of the right of administration, c. 17, he says, 'The high-priest, indeed, who is the bishop, has the right of giving it ; thereafter presbyters and deacons, not, however, without the bishop's authority, for the sake of the church's honour, by the preservation of which peace is secured.   Apart from this (*alioquin*), the right belongs also to laics ; for what is received on a foot-

---

that with reference to our common participation in the benefits of the great act commemorated (its sealing virtue or purport as a *communion*), this is preeminently its Scriptural aspect ; and in proportion as it departed from that view, the church lost the key to the ordinance.

ing of equality (*ex aequo*), on the same footing can be given. The word of the Lord should not be hid by any one : therefore also baptism, which is not less a thing of God, can be dispensed by all.' Elsewhere he applies the term *clerus* to denote the body holding ecclesiastical positions, with evident reference to the previous use of it in the Old Testament, as a collective designation of the priests and Levites, as the Lord's peculiar lot or heritage.[1] And for the same purpose he transfers the Roman official term *ordo* to the governing, the ecclesiastical body, while the laity are the *plebs*, but with the same kind of shifting flexibility as before.   Urging his favourite point of absolute monogamy,[2] he says, ' It is written, He has made us a kingdom and priests to God and our Father.   The authority of the church has made a difference between the order and the laity (*ordinem et plebem*), and a stamp of sacredness is set upon her honour by the meeting of the order.   Moreover, where there is no meeting of the ecclesiastical order, you both offer (*i.e.* dispense the communion) and baptize, and alone are a priest to yourself. But when three are present, though laics, there is a church ; for every one lives by his own faith, nor is there respect of persons with God.'

It was impossible, however, that matters could remain long in this kind of suspense—ecclesiastical orders with their appropriate functions, yet others on occasions taking their place—a priestly standing for some, yea, a high-priesthood, with sacrificial work to perform, rising out and apart from the common priesthood of believers, and yet, in the absence of those possessing it, the work allowed to be performed by unconsecrated hands.   Once acknowledge the distinction as the normal and proper one, and it was sure soon to develop into a regular and stereo-

---

[1] ' De Monog.,' chap. 12.   [2] ' De Exhort. Castitatis,' chap. 7.

typed, yea, indispensable arrangement ; as, indeed, we presently find it doing in the hands of Tertullian's immediate disciple—Cyprian of Carthage.   Bred, like the other, to the legal profession, and practising in the courts of law till within a comparatively short period of his elevation to the episcopate, Cyprian, even more than Tertullian, partook of the imperial impress, and carried into ecclesiastical life its regard for official distinctions and the observances of a regulated discipline.   Every thing, according to him, seemed to hang upon this.   Presbyters, as priests and bishops, still more as high-priests, held God's appointment ; His authority was with them ; by them His judgment was pronounced ; evils of every kind ensue if obedience is not paid to them ; and in their daily service at the altar 'they act in Christ's stead, imitating what Christ did, and offering a true and full sacrifice in the church to God the Father.' [1]   Such is the style of thought and speech introduced by Cyprian on this subject, in practice also vigorously carried out ; and here, still more than in the writings of those who preceded him, the affairs and incidents of Old Testament Scripture are in the roughest and most literal manner applied to those of the New, as if there were no characteristic difference between them.   The passages which describe the functions and services, the calling and privileges, of the priests and Levites, are transferred wholesale to the Christian ministry and diaconate : the rebellion of Korah, Dathan, and Abiram, has its exact counterpart in the deacon who treats his bishop with disrespect ; [2] and all sorts of external things are freely employed, which, from their colour or their use, presented any kind of likeness to the sacraments of the New Testament.   Even in the lamentable defection of Noah in his latter days—in the fact that

[1] Epp. 57, sec. 2 ; 63, sec. 11.   [2] Ep. 3, sec. 1.

he drank wine to excess, with all that followed, there was, according to Cyprian, 'exhibited a type of the future truth, since he drank not water, but wine, and so portrayed a figure of the passion of the Lord.'[1] Such a mode of interpretation, so singularly oblivious of the distinction between letter and spirit—carried, indeed, to peculiar excess in Cyprian, but in a great degree common to early Patristic writers generally—could not stop till it had assimilated the form of things in the new dispensation to that of the old; since it found, not the principle and germ merely of Christianity, but its very shape and lineaments in the rites and institutions of Judaism.

There was, however, another and a confluent stream of influence from the prevailing heathenism, which bore powerfully in the same direction, and in respect to nothing more than the Christian sacraments, around which the ritualistic tendency had been more peculiarly concentrating itself. For, besides what was ever flowing from the temples, the altars, the festal processions, and other public rites of idolatry, to beget and foster a sensuous spirit, there was the more specific and also more fascinating influence derived throughout the more cultivated portions of the Roman empire, from the celebration of the mysteries. Uncertain as these singular institutions were as to their origin and design, and associated, in the later periods of their history at least, with much that was disorderly and demoralizing, they still possessed a most powerful attraction to the popular mind, and, for ages after the introduction of Christianity, contributed immensely to deepen the hold which the existing religion had on men's imaginations and feelings. A sort of charmed virtue was ascribed to them, whereby the participants were supposed to be raised to a higher elevation—

[1] Ep. 63, sec. 2.

to become commingled in some mysterious way with the Divine. And by intensifying to the uttermost the sacerdotal element in the sacraments, especially in the celebration of the Supper, it came to be thought by the leaders of the Christian church, that an attractive and spell-like sway might be found within her pale, similar in kind to the other, but higher in character and aim. Hence, every distinguishing epithet applied to the heathen mysteries, with the view of heightening their sacredness and magnifying their importance, was transferred without limitation or reserve to the sacraments: they were called expressly the mysteries, and with every variety of designation (μυήσεις, τελετάς, τελειώσεις, ἐποπτείας), etc., the Eucharist, in particular, was *the mystery* by way of eminence, 'the great and terrible mystery;' to partake of it was to be initiated (μυεῖσδαι); the officiating priest was the initiator (μύστης, μυσταγωγός), who, in his action upon the elements, was said *conficere Deum* (to make God), or to make the body and blood of Christ, and, in respect to the initiated, to impart a kind of deification (Θείωσιν), or confer the vision (ἐποψίαν)—meaning such an insight into Divine things as the supernaturally illuminated alone can enjoy. The comparison might be, and has been, drawn out into the fullest circumstantiality of detail;[1]

---

[1] See the striking passage quoted from Is. Casaubon, in B. ii. p. 2 of 'Divine Leg. of Moses.' It is of no moment, for the point of view under consideration, whether the priestly act in the sacrament was considered as actually transubstantiating the elements, or in some mysterious way changing their character, so as to make them in power and efficacy the body and blood of Christ. Dr Goode has adduced apparently conclusive arguments, in the work previously referred to, for shewing that it was the latter, not the former, that was meant ; but he has not, we think, made due account of the priestly and sacrificial representations of the ordinance given by the Fathers, which were such as to render their view of it, in practical effect, scarcely less sensuous, and equally fitted to minister to superstitious uses as the Roman mass ; so that, in spite of all explanations, the Anglo-Catholic ritualists can claim the great body of Patristic writers, from the middle of the third century, as, at least, virtually on their side.

but 'the thing (as Warburton says) is notorious;' the Fathers, who at first denounced in unmeasured terms the heathen mysteries, afterwards adopted 'the fatal counsel' of bringing the most sacred Christian ordinances into the closest formal resemblance to them. So that, far asunder as Judaism and Heathenism were in their spirit and aims, there still was a class of things in which they wrought together with disastrous influence on the course of events in the Christian church. What the one, when applied at an earlier period to the institutions of the Gospel, began, the other, at a more advanced stage, consummated and crowned as with a super-earthly glory. The Christian ministry, under the one class of influences, passed into a vicarious priesthood, having somewhat of its own to effect or offer; and this priesthood, yielding to the seductive power of the other, became transformed into a kind of magic hierophants, in whose hands the symbolical ordinances of the Gospel exchanged their original simplicity for the cloudy magnificence of potent charms and indescribable wonders. A *formal* gain in the external show and aspect of things, but purchased at an incalculable loss as to their *real* virtue! For it was the loss of the truth in its Scriptural directness and power; and in comparison of this, the most attractive influences of an outward ceremonialism (even if it had borne the explicit sanction of Heaven) must ever prove a miserable compensation.

But if the legal and ritualistic elements of this new discipline might be said to concentrate itself here, it could not, in the nature of things, be confined to one department of the religious life; it was sure to spread, and actually did spread, in all directions. Baptism, for example, was accompanied with a whole series of symbolical services, preceding and following the rite itself;—the disrobing of the shoes and the ordinary garments; the turning to the west with a formal renunciation of the devil; the exorcism, and sanctification both of the subject of baptism, and the water; the three-fold immersion; then, after the action with water, the anointing with oil, the administration of milk and honey, etc.,—the greater part of which, though confessedly without any warrant in Scripture, are testified by Tertullian to have been traditionally observed in his time, and the prevailing custom is pleaded in their behalf as having virtually won for them the force of law.[1] Cyprian presses several of them as indispensable.[2]   In like manner, postures in devotion for particular times and seasons were religiously practised, the signing of one's forehead or breast with the mark of the cross (which already, in Tertullian's time, seems to have reached its height), the observance of days of fasting and prescribed seasons of watching and prayer, as necessary, to some extent, for all who would lead the Christian life, and, in the case of those who aspired to be religious in the stricter sense, growing into a regular and enforced system of discipline.   And the sad thing was, that while this new and complicated legalism was everywhere in progress, the leading minds in the church, overlooking the fundamental agreements between it and the things they were bound to reject, deemed themselves sufficiently justified in countenancing the course pursued, on account of certain superficial differences.   It was true that, after having been abolished, a vicarious, sacrificing priesthood had found its way again into the church; but then it differed from the Jewish in being held, not by fleshly descent, but by ecclesiastical ordination, and having to do directly with Christian, not with typical, events and objects.   The observance of Easter on the part of the Asiatics was characterized as Jewish, in contradistinction to that of the

[1] De Cor., c. 3, 4.   [2] Ep. 70.

church at large, which was Christian—not because the
services in the former partook more, in the latter less, of
a ritualistic and sacrificial character, but merely because
the mode of determining the day coincided with the
Jewish in the one case, and in the other somewhat
differed from it.[1]

And so, in other things, Tertullian, when contending
with the Psychical (as he called them), in behalf of more
frequent fastings than either New Testament Scripture or ecclesiastical usage had sanctioned, vindicates his
view on the ground of the same sort of circumstantial distinctions. 'We, therefore,' says he, 'in observing times
and days, and months and years, plainly galatianize (*i.e.*
imitate the folly of the Galatians), if, in doing so, we
observe Jewish ceremonies, legal solemnities ; for the
apostle dissuades us from these, disallowing the continued
observance of the Old Testament, which has been buried
in Christ, and urging that of the New.   But, if there is a
new condition in Christ, it will be right that there should
be new solemnities.'[2]   And then he goes on to press, not
only the now universal observance of Easter, but of fifty
days of exuberant joy after its celebration, and certain
stated fasts, as a proof that the church had already conceded the principle of the matter, and needed only to
proceed farther in the same line to reach a higher perfection.   So that, in the estimation of Tertullian, it was

[1] So the merits of the question are exhibited on the occasion of its final settlement at the council of Nicaea, in the letter addressed, in the name of the council,
by Constantine to the Asiatic churches : 'It seemed, in the first place, to be
a thing unworthy and unbecoming, that, in the celebration of that most holy
solemnity, we should follow the usage of the Jews, who, being persons that
have defiled themselves with a most detestable sin, are deservedly given up to
blindness of mind.   Let nothing, therefore, be common to us with that most
hostile multitude of the Jews' (Euseb. ' Vit. Const.,' iii. 18).

[2] ' De Jejunio,' c. 14.

enough to escape the condemnation pronounced by the
apostle on the Galatians, and to save the imposition of a
new yoke of carnal services from the charge of Judaism,
if only fresh periods and occasions were fixed for their
observance ; that is, if, in respect to the mere accident of
time, they underwent a change :—as if the apostle had
said that he was afraid of the Galatians, and regarded
them as imperilling the interests of the Gospel, not simply
because they made their resort to fleshly ordinances, and
observed times and days, and months and years, but
because the resort was to precisely *Jewish* things of this
description !   What the apostle really condemned was
the commingling with the Gospel of a law of carnal ordinances (no matter whence derived), as inevitably tending
to cloud the freeness of its salvation, and bring the filial
spirit proper to it into bondage.   Chrysostom saw a
little further into the matter than Tertullian ; and yet
did not see far enough, or possess sufficient strength of
conviction, to pierce to the root of the evil.   While, therefore, not unconscious of the aspect of legalism which had
been settling down upon the church, he rather sought to
throw a gloss over it, than rouse his energies to resist and
expose it.   Contending against the Jews, and endeavouring to shew how, though the Christians had been discharged from observing times and seasons, they should
yet celebrate Easter with a true oblation, and should have
their minds prepared and purged for it by exercising
themselves for forty days beforehand 'to prayers, and alms,
and vigils, and tears, and confession, and other such things,'
it is all only that the soul may get free from consciousness of sin—not as if any observation of days were in
itself necessary or commendable.   ' If, therefore (he
counsels), a Jew or a Greek should ask you, Why do you
fast ?   Do not say, on account of the Passover [*i.e.*, the

Christian oblation], nor on account of the cross, since thus
you would give him a great handle. For we do not fast
because of the Passover, nor because of the cross, but
because of our sins, since we are going to approach the
mysteries.' [1] But for what other purpose, one might
justly ask in reply, were the times and seasons of the Old
Covenant, with their confessions, purgations, and sacrifices, appointed ? Was it not also because of sin, and, in
the absence of the more perfect way of deliverance from it,
to have the minds of the people exercised aright concerning it ? And should the same be substantially continued
now—yea, greatly increased and intensified (for Judaism
knew of nothing like such a regularly recurring forty
days of penitence and mortification),—after this new and
better way has come ? Such a mode of procedure was
neither more nor less than the Galatian policy of seeking to perfect in the flesh what had been begun in the
spirit. It virtually said, 'These *are* legalisms, indeed, if
you regard them as absolutely tied to particular times,
or indispensable to the actual accomplishment of Christ's
salvation in the soul : you *would* judaize if you so
observed them.' What then ? Reject the impositions as
fraught with danger to your spiritual good ? as sure to
take off the regard of your soul from Christ, and find, at
least, a partial saviour in your prolonged asceticism ?
No ; the Fathers (says Chrysostom), 'have seen it meet
to enjoin such things ; it is wise and dutiful for you to
keep to the appointed order ; only, see that you do not
lose sight of the great realities of the faith, and feel as if
you might do every day what you more systematically do
in the course of these special solemnities.' [2]

[1] 'Adv. Jud.,' iii. 4.

[2] *See* also Origen, Hom. xi. in Lev. sec. 10—who draws well the distinction
between the new and the old in regard to fast days, but practically drops the
difference when he comes to the now stated and customary observances.

All this shews but too plainly, that the light of the church had become grievously darkened. The men of might, if in certain respects they had not lost their hands, had here, at least virtually, lost their eyes. They did not perceive that there might be the essence of Judaism—a bondage even surpassing the bondage of its necessary symbolism and prescribed ritual of service—though not a day might be kept, nor a rite observed, in exact conformity with the ancient institutions. It was the return to observances the same in kind, however differing in the accidents of time and mode, with those of the Old Covenant— it was the overshadowing of Christ and His blessed Gospel by a long procession of penitential exercises and awe-inspiring solemnities, regulated by the canons of an approved ecclesiastical order—it was this which constituted the essentially legal element, and therewith the anti-evangelical, perilous tendency of such a line of things —the very same substantially, only in a more developed form, which, at the beginning of the Gospel, crept into the churches of Galatia, and drew forth the earnest expostulation and warning of the apostle. This is no mere conjecture. We can appeal in proof of it to the testimony of the very greatest of the Fathers, though in giving it he might be said to bear witness against himself. Augustine was plainly conscious of a misgiving about the vast multiplication of rites and ceremonies in his day, as tending to the reproduction, in its worst form, of a spirit of legalism, while still he conceded to mere usage the virtual right of perpetuating and enlarging the burden. Take as an example his two letters to Januarius.[1] He is there returning an answer to certain questions, which had been proposed to him by his correspondent concerning the propriety, or otherwise, of observing some fasts and ordi-

---

[1] 'Classis,' ii. ; Epp. 54, 55.

nances, in which the practice of the church was not uniform ; and in doing so he sets out with a broad enunciation
of the principle, which he wished Januarius to hold by—
namely, that our Lord Jesus Christ, according to His own
declaration in the Gospel, placed His people under a
gentle yoke and a light burden, binding the community
of the New Testament together by sacraments very few
in number, quite easy of observance, in their purport
altogether excellent, and relieving them of those things
which lay as a yoke of bondage on the members of the
Old Covenant. These sacraments, of course, He would
have everywhere observed—yet not these alone, but what
things besides ecclesiastical councils and long continued
usage had sanctioned, though without any authority in
Sacred Scripture ; nay, even the special usages of particular localities, if they had obtained a settled footing—
such as fasting on the Sabbath (viz., Saturday, the Jewish
Sabbath) at Rome or Carthage, but not at Milan and
other places, where the practice had not yet established
itself—thus leaving the door open for the entrance of a
state of things very different from what he declared to be
the manifest design and appointment of Christ in the Gospel. And so the Christian feeling in his bosom expresses
itself before he reaches the close of his second epistle.
'But this (says he, sec. 35) I very much grieve at,
that many salutary prescriptions which are given in the
Divine Scriptures are too little heeded ; and all things
are so full of manifest prejudices, that if one have but
touched the ground with his naked foot during his octaves
(the week of holidays succeeding the Easter baptisms), he
is more severely reprimanded than one who has buried his
soul in intemperance. Therefore, all such ceremonies as
are neither enjoined by the authority of Sacred Scripture,
nor have been decreed by the councils of bishops, nor have

been confirmed by the usage of the church universal, should in my judgment be cut off, where one has the power to do so.   For, although it could not be discovered in what respects they are contrary to the faith, yet they oppress with servile burdens the religion which the mercy of God wished to be free, with very few and simple observances ; so that the condition of the Jews was more tolerable, since though they knew not the time of liberty, yet they were subjected only to legal burdens, not to human impositions.   But the church of God (he plaintively adds), having in her constitution much chaff and many tares, is tolerant of many things, without, however, approving or doing what is directly at variance with the faith or a good life.'

We have here a right apprehension of the evil which had been making way, but by no means a right conception of the proper mode of dealing with it.   It was not by such a temporizing policy, and such a faint resistance, that the swelling tide of ritualism was to be checked then, any more than now.   The question should have been boldly raised : Since the effect of yielding to usage and ecclesiastical councils has been to load the church with impositions, which have marred its primitive simplicity, and brought in upon it a worse than Judaic bondage, why not withstand and reject whatever has not its clear warrant or implied justification in Scripture ?   This position, however, was not taken, in regard to the points now under consideration, either by Augustine, or by any of the more prominent guides of the church in the centuries succeeding the apostolic age.   On the contrary, they allowed the untoward influences which were at work to fashion, by gradual and stealthy advances, a yoke of order and discipline, which, by connivance first, then by authoritative enactment, acquired the force of law, and stopt not till the

whole spirit and character of the new dispensation had
been brought under its sway.   The principle of Augustine,
that in respect to those things on which Scripture is silent,
‘ the custom of the people of God, or the appointments of
our ancestors, must be held as law ’—a principle substantially enunciated nearly two centuries before by Tertullian,
and systematically carried out by Cyprian and others[1]—
had not failed even under the legal economy to introduce
certain things that were at variance with its fundamental
scope and design ; but with the comparative freedom
which exists in the New Testament from detailed enactments and formal restraints, the entire field in a manner
lay open to it, and it was impossible to say how far, in
process of time, and with external circumstances favouring
its development, it might go in multiplying the materials
of the church’s bondage to form and symbol.   The practical result has been, that Rome has found in it a sufficient
basis for her mighty mass of ritual observance and ascetic
discipline.   Bellarmine’s principle here is little else than a
repetition of Augustine’s,[2] ‘ What are properly called
ecclesiastical traditions are certain ancient customs, originating either with prelates or the people, which by degrees,
through the tacit consent of the people, *have obtained the
force of law.*’   And so the legalizing tendency proceeded,
gathering and consolidating its materials, till it reached
its culmination in the edifice of the Tridentine Council,
which has been justly said to rest on the two great

[1] *See* Aug.’s ‘Ep. to Casulanus,’ sec. 2. ‘ In his rebus de quibus nihil certi
statuit Scriptura divina, mos populi Dei, vel instituta majorum pro lege tenenda
sunt.’   Also Ep. ad Januarium ; Tertul. de Corona, sec. 3 ; ‘ Observationes,
quas sine ullius Scripturae instrumento, solius traditionis titulo, et exinde
consuetudinis patrocinio vindicamus.’

[2] ‘De Verbo Dei,’ L. iv. c. 2. ‘ Ecclesiasticae traditiones proprie dicuntur
consuetudines quaedam antiquae, vel a praelatis vel a populis inchoatae, quae
paulatim, tacito consensu populorum, vim legis obtinuerunt·’

pillars—that Christ is a lawgiver in the same sense in which Moses was, and that the Gospel is a new law presenting, in a spiritualized form, the same features which the old did [1]—the same, indeed, in kind, though far surpassing them in its multifarious and irksome character, and operating also after the same disciplinary style, as the very eulogies of its adherents indicate.   In the church, they tell us, ' we are placed, as it were, under the discipline of childhood—God having constituted an order which shall bear rule over His people, and shall bring them under the yoke of obedience to Himself.' [2]   What is this but in effect to say of the Romish church, that she has brought back her people, through the carnal elements she has infused into her worship and polity, to the condition out of which it was the declared purpose of Christ's mission to raise and elevate the members of His kingdom? —not her glory, therefore, but her reproach.   The new in her hands has relapsed into the old ; what was begun in the Spirit, she has vainly sought to perfect in the flesh, and has only succeeded in displacing a religion of spirit for a religion of forms and ceremonies, and getting the dead works of a mechanical routine, for the fruits of a living faith and responsive love.

This were itself bad enough.   For it completely inverts the proper order and relation of things as set forth in New Testament Scripture—makes more account of external rites than of essential truths—and, while all-solicitous for the rightful administration of the one, provides no effectual guarantee for the due maintenance and inculcation of the other.   The primary aim of the church comes to be the securing of *legitimate* dispensers of ordinances, who may, at the same time, be teachers of heretical doctrine, and

---

[1] Litton ' On the Church,' p. 122.

[2] Manning ' On the Unity of the Church,' p. 254.

abettors of practical corruption—and in reality have often been such.   But this is by no means the whole of the evil. For, while avowedly designed to render salvation sure to those who keep to the prescribed channel of external order and ritualistic observance, it really brings uncertainty into the whole matter; and places New Testament believers not only under a more complicated service than was imposed on those of the Old Testament, but under a great disadvantage as regards the assurance of their heart before God.   The ancient worshipper, as regards the mediating of his services and their acceptance with Heaven, had to do only with objective realities, about which he could, with comparative ease, satisfy himself. There was for him the one well-known temple with which Jehovah associated His name—the one altar of burnt-offering, also perfectly known and obvious to all—the officiating priesthood, with their local habitations and carefully preserved genealogies, descending from age to age, and excluding almost the possibility of doubt; and the confession of sin which required to be made, and the offerings on account of it which were to be presented, in order to the obtaining of forgiveness, both had their explicit ordination from God, and were directly rendered to Him : they depended in no degree for their success on the caprice or the intention of him who served the altar. But the spiritual element, which it has been impossible to exclude from the new law of ordinances, has, in the ritualistic system, changed all this, and introduced in its stead the most tantalizing and vexatious uncertainty. The validity of the sacraments depends on the impressed character of the priesthood, and this, again, on a whole series of circumstances, of none of which can the sincere worshipper certainly assure himself.   It depends, first of all, on the ministering priest having been canonically ordained, after having been himself baptized and admitted to deacons' orders ; and if, as will commonly happen, several priests have to be dealt with, then the same conditions must be found to meet in each.   But these are only the earlier links.   The validity of ordinances depends not less upon the *spiritual pedigree* of the priesthood, who must have received ordination from a bishop, and he again have been consecrated by at least three bishops, none of whom has been without baptism, or deacons' and priests' orders, nor at the time under excommunication, or in deadly heresy and sin ; and so also must it have been with their predecessors, up through all the ages of darkness, ignorance, and disorder, to the time of the apostles.   ' The chance of one's possessing the means of salvation is (upon the ritualistic theory) just the chance of there having been no failure of any single link in this enormous chain from the apostles' time to ours.   The chance against one's possessing the means of salvation is the chance of such a failure having *once* occurred.   And is it thus that the Christian is to give diligence to make his calling and election sure ?   Is it thus he is to run not as uncertainly, and to draw near to God in full assurance of faith ?'[1]   It is easy to affirm, as Dr Hook does, ' There is not a bishop or priest or deacon, among us, who may not, if he please, trace his spiritual descent from Peter and Paul.'   But where is the proof of the assertion ?   ' It is probable,' says Macaulay, ' that no clergyman in the church of England can trace up his spiritual genealogy from bishop to bishop so far back even as the time of the Conquest.   There remain many centuries during which the history of the transmission of his orders is buried in utter darkness.   And whether he be a priest by succession from the apostles, depends on the question, whether

[1] ' Cautions for the Times,' p. 312.

X

during that long period some thousands of events took place, any one of which may, without any gross improbability, be supposed not to have taken place. We have not a tittle of evidence for any of these events.'[1] It is therefore justly concluded by the preceding authority, that ' there is not a minister in all Christendom who is able to trace up with any approach to certainty his own spiritual pedigree. Irregularities could not have been wholly excluded without a perpetual miracle ; and that no such miraculous interference existed, we have even historical proof.'[2] Even this, however, is not the end of the uncertainties. For, in this new, man-made law of ordinances, there is required the further element of the knowledge and intention of the parties—those of the worshippers in confessing to the priest, receiving from him absolution and the sacraments ; and those again of the priest in administering the rites—the utter want, or essential defect of which, on either side, vitiates the whole. And who can tell for certain, whether they really exist or not ? The poor penitent is at the mercy of circumstances, connected with the character and position of his spiritual confidant, which he not only cannot control, but which, from their remote or impalpable nature, he cannot even distinctly ascertain : he must either refuse to entertain a doubt, or be a stranger to solid peace.

On every account, therefore, this retrogressive policy, this confounding of things which essentially differ, is to be condemned and deplored as the source of incalculable evils. It is a disturbing as well as an enslaving system, shackles the souls which Christ has set free, and robs the Gospel of its essential glory as glad tidings of great joy to mankind. Men may disguise it from themselves ; they

---

[1] Essay on Gladstone's ' Church and State.'

[2] ' Cautions,' etc., p. 302.

may resolutely shut their eyes on its more objectionable features, or refuse to make full application of its more distinctive principles; but its native tendency and working unquestionably are to place the believer under the Gospel in much closer dependence than even the disciple of Moses on the carnal elements of a merely external polity and human administration; and, were it left to his choice, he might well exchange the fuller knowledge he has obtained of the eternal world for the larger freedom from arbitrary impositions, and the more assured possession of peace with God, which were enjoyed by those who lived in the earlier periods of the Divine dispensations.

SUPPLEMENTARY DISSERTATIONS.

I.

THE DOUBLE FORM OF THE DECALOGUE, AND THE QUESTIONS TO WHICH IT HAS GIVEN RISE.

IT is to the Decalogue, as recorded in Ex. xx. 1-17, that respect is usually had in discussions on the law ; and in the lecture directly bearing upon the subject (Lect. IV.), it has been deemed unnecessary to notice the slightly diversified form in which the ten words appear in a subsequent part of the Pentateuch (Deut. v. 6-21). It were improper, however, in so full an investigation as the present, to leave the subject without adverting to this other form, and noticing the few variations from the earlier which occur in it— variations which, however unimportant in themselves, have given rise to grave enough inferences and conclusions, which we hold to be erroneous. The differences are the following :—The fourth command begins with 'keep (שָׁמוֹר) the Sabbath day to sanctify it, as the Lord thy God commanded thee,' instead of simply, as in Exodus, ' Remember the Sabbath day to sanctify it ;' also, in the body of the precept, we have, ' nor thine ox, nor thine ass, nor any of thy cattle, nor thy stranger that is within thy gates, that thy man-servant and thy maid-servant may rest as well as thou,' instead of ' nor thy cattle, nor thy stranger that is within thy gates ;' then, at the close, instead of the reference to God's work at creation in Exodus, ' For in six days the Lord made heaven and earth,' etc., as the primary ground and reason of the command, there is merely an enforcement, from the people's own history, of the merciful regard already enjoined toward the servile class, ' And remember that thou wast a servant in the land of Egypt, and that the Lord thy God brought thee out thence, through a mighty hand and by a stretched out arm ; therefore the Lord thy God commanded thee to keep the Sabbath day.' In the fifth command there is, precisely as in the fourth, a formal recognition of the previous announcement of the command, 'Honour thy father and thy mother, as the Lord thy God commanded thee ;' and in the annexed promise, after ' that thy days may be long (or prolonged),' it is added, ' and that it may go well with thee' in the land which the Lord thy God giveth thee— both of the additions existing only in Deuteronomy. In the last four commands, there is used at the commencement the connecting particle *and* (*vau*), which is wanting in Exodus (for which, in the English Bible, there is used the disjunctive *neither*). Finally, the last precept, which in Exodus runs, ' Thou shalt not covet thy neighbour's house, thou shalt not covet thy neighbour's wife, nor his man-servant, nor his maid-servant, nor his ox, nor his ass, nor any thing that is thy neighbour's,' stands thus in Deuteronomy, ' Thou shalt not covet (תַחְמֹד) thy neighbour's wife, and thou shalt not desire (תִתְאַוֶּה)[1] thy neighbour's house, his field, nor his man-servant, nor his maid-servant, his ox, nor his ass, nor any thing that is thy neighbour's.'

1. Now, it is clear first of all, in respect to the whole of these alterations in the form of the Decalogue, that in no case do they affect the substance of the things enjoined : the commands are the same throughout, and stand in the same order in both the records. So that, viewed simply in the light of law, there is properly no difference between the earlier and the later form. For we must distinguish between what is commanded in God's moral law, and the considerations by which, in whole or in part, it may be enforced : the one, having its ground in the nature of God, must remain essentially the same ; the other, depending to a large extent on the circumstances of the people, and God's methods of dealing with them, may readily admit of variety. It is chiefly in regard to the law of the Sabbath that, even in this respect, any notable change has been introduced—the more general reason derived from the Divine procedure at creation being altogether unnoticed in Deutero-

---

[1] The renderings of the two verbs are unfortunately inverted in the authorized version.

nomy, and stress laid only on what had been done for Israel by the redemption from bondage, and what in turn they were bound to do for those among themselves whose condition somewhat resembled theirs in Egypt. Why there should have been, in this later record, so entire an ignoring of the one kind of motive, and so prominent an exhibition of the other, no definite information has been given us, and we are perhaps but imperfectly able to understand. The one, however, is no way incompatible with the other, and no more in this case than in many others are we entitled to regard the special consideration adduced as virtually cancelling the general, and narrowing the sphere of the obligation imposed. It is always dutiful, and is only a specific branch of the great law of brotherly love, to deal justly toward the stranger, the fatherless, and the widow, and beware of defrauding them of their rights : yet such duties are expressly charged upon the Israelites in the book of Deuteronomy, on the ground that they had been redeemed from the condition of bondmen in Egypt (chap. xxiv. 17, 18). In other cases, the general duties of compassion to the poor and help to the needy are in like manner enforced, and are said, on this special account, to have been commanded (chap. xv. 15, xvi. 12, xxiv. 19-22). Yet surely no one would think of asserting that duties of such a description had been imposed upon the Israelites merely because they had been so redeemed, and had not both a prior and a more general ground of obligation. All that is meant is, that from what God had done for them as a people, and the relation in which they stood to Him, they were in a very peculiar manner bound to the observance of such things—that, if they failed to do them, they would disregard the special lessons of their history, and defeat the ends of their corporate existence. And nothing more, nothing else, than this is the legitimate interpretation to be put on the similar reference to Israelitish history in the case before us. The primary ground of the Sabbath law lay still, as before, in the primeval sanctifying and blessing of the day at the close of creation, as indicative of man's calling to enter into God's rest, as well as to do His work, and to make 'the pulsation of the Divine life in a certain sense his own.' But now that Israel had become not only a free and independent people, but, as such, were already occupying a prominent place, having laid several powerful tribes at their feet, and were presently to rise to a still higher position, it was of the

greatest importance for them to feel that the power and the opportunities thus given them were to be used in subservience to the
great ends of their calling, and not for any carnal interests and
purposes of their own. As masters, with many helpless captives
and needy dependants subject to their control, it behoved them to
remember that they had themselves escaped from servitude through
God's merciful interposition, that as such they stood under law to
Him, and so were specially bound, alike for His glory and for the
common wellbeing of themselves and their dependants, to keep that
ever-recurring day of sacred rest, which, when observed as it was
designed, brings all into living fellowship with the mercy and goodness of Heaven. By this there was no narrowing of the obligation,
but only, in respect to a particular aspect of it, a special ground of
obedience pressed upon Israel—the same, indeed, which prefaced
the entire Decalogue.

It is scarcely necessary, perhaps, to refer to the slight addition
made to the reason employed in enforcing the observance of the
fifth precept ; for nothing new is introduced by it, but only an
amplification of what had been originally presented. That their
days might be prolonged in the land which the Lord had given them
is the promise connected, in Exodus, with the honouring of parents ;
and this was evidently all one with having a continued enjoyment
of the Lord's favour, or of being prospered in their national affairs.
It was virtually to say, that a well-trained youth, growing up in
reverent obedience to the constituted authorities in the family and
the state, would be the best, and, in the long run, the only effective
preparation for a well-ordered and thriving community. And this
is just a little more distinctly expressed by the additional clause in
Deuteronomy, ' that it may go well with thee :' thus and thus only
expect successive generations of a God-fearing and blessed people.

2. But allowing the fitness of such explanations, why, it may be
asked, should they have been necessary ? Why, when professing
to rehearse the words which were spoken by God from Sinai, and
which formed the basis of the whole legal economy, should certain
of those words have been omitted, and certain others inserted ? Do
not such alterations, even though not introducing any change of
meaning, seem to betray some tampering with the original sources,
or at least militate against the plenary inspiration of the Scriptures ?
So it has been argued by some modern critics ; but with no solid

ground, if the matter is contemplated from the true Scriptural point of view. For it is clear that Moses, in the rehearsal he made on the plains of Moab of what had been said and done nearly forty years before at Sinai, intended only to give the substance of the past, but not the exact reproduction, not the identical words with the same fulness, and in precisely the same order. A rhetorical element pervades the book, mingling with and to some extent qualifying the use made of historical data. The expression, twice repeated in the rehearsal of the Decalogue, 'As the Lord thy God commanded thee,' was alone sufficient to shew, that while Moses was giving afresh the solemn utterances of God, he was doing so with a certain measure of freedom—intent rather upon the object of reviving wholesome impressions upon the minds of a comparatively untutored people, than of presenting to critical ears an exact and literal uniformity. The same freedom also appears in other rehearsals given by him of what passed in his interviews with God.[1] And if the general principle be still pressed, that, on the theory of plenary inspiration, every word of God is precious, and any addition to it or detraction from it must tend to mar its completeness or purity, we reply that this is applicable to the case in hand only when there is an interference with the contents of Scripture by an unauthorized instrument, or beyond certain definite limits. Slight verbal deviations, while the sense remains unaffected, or such incidental changes as serve the purpose of throwing some explanation on the word, while substantially repeating it, and so as to give it a closer adaptation to existing circumstances, are of frequent occurrence in Scripture, and perfectly accord with its character and design.[2] For this also is of God. In the cases supposed, it is He who employs the second instrumentality as well as the first, and thereby teaches the church, while holding fast by the very word of God as revealed in Scripture, to use it with a reasonable freedom, and with a fitting regard to circumstances of time and place. It should also be remembered, that such slight alterations as those now under consideration have an exegetical value of some importance: they

[1] Compare, for example, Deut. x. 1, 2, with Ex. xxxiv. 1, 2; Deut. x. 11, with Ex. xxxiii. 1.

[2] See, as specimens, the manner of quoting Old Testament Scripture in such passages as Matt. ii. 6, xi. 10; Rom. xi. 26, 27; Heb. viii. 8-10, etc.

strongly corroborate the Mosaic authorship of the book of Deuteronomy. For, is it conceivable, as Hävernick justly asks,[1] 'that a later author would have permitted himself in such an alteration of what he himself most expressly attributes to Moses, and with the sacredness and inviolability of which he is deeply impressed, and not rather have observed the most conscientious exactness in the repetition of the Mosaic form?' Nothing, he adds, would be gained by the supposition of some simple forms of the commands traditionally preserved; for as soon as any form was committed to writing, we may be certain that, in the case especially of so very peculiar and fundamental a piece of legislation, that form would become identified in the popular mind with the thing itself. So that the alterations in question, which could not but be regarded as improper if coming from any one except the Mediator Himself of the Old Covenant, lend important confirmation to the Mosaic authorship of the book in which they occur.

3. The most important alteration, however, in the later form of the Decalogue, has yet to be noticed—one, also, which has given rise to considerable discussion respecting the structure of the Decalogue itself. It occurs at the commencement of what, in the Protestant church, is usually designated the tenth command. The insertion, somewhat later, of the *field* of one's neighbour, immediately after his *house*, as among the things not to be coveted, calls for no special remark; as it is in the same line with a similar addition in the fifth command already noticed—being only a further specification, for the sake of greater explicitness. But the change at the commencement is of a different sort; for here the two first clauses are placed in the inverse order to that adopted in Exodus. There it is: 'Thou shalt not covet thy neighbour's house, thou shalt not covet thy neighbour's wife;' but in Deuteronomy, 'thou shalt not covet thy neighbour's wife, thou shalt not desire thy neighbour's house'—there being, along with a different order, a different verb, expressive of the same general import, but of a less intensive meaning, in regard to house and other possessions, than that employed in regard to wife. And occasion has been taken, partly at least from this, to advocate a division of the Decalogue, which makes here two separate commands—one, the ninth, 'Thou shalt not covet thy neighbour's wife,' and another, the tenth, 'Thou

[1] 'Introd. to Pent.,' c. 25.

shalt not desire (so as to covet) thy neighbour's house, his field,' etc. The view in question can only be partly ascribed to this source; for Augustine, who is the earliest representative of it known to us (though he speaks of it as held by others in his day), and from whom it has descended to the Roman Catholic, as also to the Lutheran church, was evidently influenced in its favour fully as much by doctrinal as by exegetical considerations. By splitting the command against coveting into two, and throwing the prohibitions against the introduction of false gods and the worship of the true God by means of idols into one, a division was got of the Decalogue into three and seven—both sacred numbers, and the first deemed of special importance, because significant of the great mystery of 'the Trinity.' 'To me, therefore,' says Augustine,[1] 'it appears more fitting that the division into three and seven should be accepted, because in those things which pertain to God there appears to more considerate minds (*diligentius intuentibus*) an indication of the Trinity.' It was quite in accordance with his usual style of interpretation, which found intimations of the Trinity, as of other Divine mysteries, in the most casual notices; in the mention, for example, of the three water-pots at Cana, the three loaves which the person in the parable is represented as going to ask from his friend, etc. Stress, however, is also laid by Augustine, as by those who follow him, on the twofold prohibition, 'Thou shalt not covet,' in both forms of the Decalogue, though coupled in the one with the house first, and in the other with the wife—as apparently implying that the coveting in the one case belonged to a different category from that in the other; and he thinks there is even a greater difference between the two kinds of covetous desire, as directed towards a neighbour's wife and a neighbour's property, than between the setting up of other gods beside Jehovah, and the worshipping of Jehovah by idols.

But this view, though it has recently been vindicated by some writers of note (in particular, by Sonntag and Kurtz), is liable to several, and in our judgment quite fatal objections. In the first place, it is without any support from Jewish authority, which, in such a matter, is entitled to considerable weight. A measure of support in its behalf, has, indeed, been sought in the *Parashoth*, or sectional arrangement of the Heb. MSS. In the larger proportion

---

[1] 'Quæst. in Exodium,' 71.

of these MSS. (460 out of 694 mentioned by Kennicott) the Decalogue is divided into ten *Parashoth*, with spaces between them
commonly marked by a *Sethuma* (ס); and one of these does stand,
in the MSS. referred to, between the two commands against coveting, while it is wanting between the prohibition against having
any other gods, and that against worshipping God by idols. But
the principle of these *Parashoth* is unknown, and has yet found no
satisfactory explanation. For it is at variance with the only two
divisions of the Decalogue, which are certainly known to have
prevailed among the Jewish authorities—an older one, which is
found alike in Philo[1] and Josephus,[2] the only one, indeed, mentioned by them, making the division into two fives, the first closing with the command to honour father and mother; and a later
one, adopted by the Talmudical Jews, according to which there
still remain the two fives, and in the second only one command
against coveting, but in the earlier part the command against
images is combined with that against false gods, and the first command is simply the declaration, 'I am Jehovah thy God.' This
last classification is certainly erroneous; for in that declaration, as
Origen long ago objected,[3] there is nothing that can be called a
command, but an announcement merely as to who it is that does
command (*quis sit, qui mandat, ostendit.*) Without, however,
going further into Jewish sentiment or belief upon the subject,
it may justly be held as an argument of some weight against the
Augustinian division of the command about coveting into two
separate parts, and still more against the division as a whole into
three and seven, that it appears to have been ignored by both
earlier and later Jews, that it has also no representative among
the Greek Fathers, nor even among the Latins till Augustine.

Another reason against the view is, that it would oblige us to
take the form of the tenth command in Deuteronomy—that which
forbids the coveting of a neighbour's *wife* first, and his *house* afterwards—as the only correct form of the command; consequently, to
suppose the different order presented in Exodus to be the result of
an error in the text. For, were both texts held to be equally
correct, then, on the supposition of the command against coveting
being really twofold, there would be an absolute contrariety:

---

[1] 'Quis rerum div. haer.,' sec. 35.   [2] 'Ant.,' iii. c. 6, sec. 5.

[3] 'Hom. in Ex.' 8.

according to the one text, 'Thou shalt not covet thy neighbour's house,' would be the ninth in order, while, according to the other, it would be, 'Thou shalt not covet thy neighbour's wife.' If, however, all the objects of covetous desire were embraced in one command, it becomes a matter of no moment in what precise order they are placed: standing first, as it does in Exodus, the house is a general name for all that belongs to a man in his domestic relationship, and wife, man-servant, maid-servant, which follow, are the more prominent particulars included in it; while in Deuteronomy, the second place only being assigned to house, and wife standing first, the latter has an independent position of her own, and house must be understood as comprising whatever else of a domestic nature is dear and precious to a man. So understood, there is only a slight diversity in the mode of representation, but no contrariety; and such a view is, therefore, greatly to be preferred to the other, which requires, without any support from the evidence of MSS., that there is a textual error in one of the accounts, and that in this respect that which professes to be the later and is obviously the freer account of the matter, is to be held as the more exact representation of the original utterance: —both of them extremely improbable and entirely hypothetical.

Besides, while there undoubtedly is a specific difference between evil concupiscence as directed toward the wife of another man, and the same as directed toward his goods and possessions—sufficient to entitle the one to a formal repetition after the other—there still is no essential diversity; nothing like a difference in kind. The radical affection in each case alike is an inordinate desire to possess what is another's—only, in the one case with more of a regard to sensual gratification, in the other to purposes of gain. Hence, also in the more distinct references made to it in the New Testament, it is evidently presented as a unity.[1] It is quite otherwise, however, with the commands to have no God but Jehovah, and to make no use of images in His worship; for here there is a real and an easily recognised distinction—the one having respect to the proper object of worship, and the other to its proper mode of celebration. True, no doubt, from the very intimate connection which in ancient times subsisted between the use of idols in worship, and the doing homage to distinct deities, the two are not unfrequently identified in Old

[1] Rom. vii. 7 ; James i. 15, iv. 5.

Testament Scripture — being indeed but different stages in one course of degeneracy;[1] still, when formal respect is had to the two phases of evil, a very marked distinction is drawn between them, as when the sin of Jeroboam is spoken of as a light thing compared with that of Ahab, in avowedly setting up the worship of Baal, and thereby supplanting the worship of Jehovah.[2] The one was a corrupting of the idea of God's character and service, the other was an ignoring of His very existence.

On every account, therefore, the use which has been made of the concluding portion of the Decalogue, as given in the book of Deuteronomy, in the interest of a particular division of its contents, is to be rejected as untenable. A more obvious and palpable ground of distinction between the commands must have existed to lay the basis of a proper division. And if this may be said of the distinction attempted to be drawn between one part and another of the command against coveting, still more may it be said of the supposed reference in the Decalogue at large to the sacred numbers of three and seven, which has from the first chiefly swayed the minds of those who favour the division introduced by Augustine. It is of too inward and refined a nature to have occurred to any one but a contemplative, semi-mystic student of Scripture; while in things pertaining to the form and structure of a popular religion, it is rather what may commend itself to the intelligence of men of ordinary shrewdness and discernment, than what may strike the fancy of a profound thinker in his closet, which is entitled to consideration. Contemplated from this point of view, no distribution of the commands of the Decalogue can be compared, for naturalness and convenience, to that which comes down to us, on the testimony of Philo and Josephus, as the one generally accepted by the ancient Jews, which has also received the suffrage, in modern times, of the great body of the Reformed theologians; nor does any appropriation for the two tables so readily present itself, or appear so simple, as that of the two fives—though probable reasons can also be alleged for the division into four and six. But the difference in the latter respect is of no practical moment.

[1] Ex. xxxii. 32; 2 Cor. xiii. 8.　　　　[2] 1 Kings xvi. 31.

II.

THE HISTORICAL ELEMENT IN GOD'S REVELATIONS OF TRUTH AND DUTY, CONSIDERED WITH AN ESPECIAL RESPECT TO THEIR CLAIM ON MEN'S RESPONSIBILITIES AND OBLIGATIONS.

THE fact that a historical element enters deeply into God's revelations of Himself in Scripture, and exercises a material influence as well in respect to the things presented in them, at different periods, to men's faith and observance, as to the form or manner in which it was done, has been throughout assumed in our discussions on the law, but not made the subject of direct inquiry. The fact itself admits of no doubt. It is one of the most distinguishing characteristics of Scripture as a Divine revelation, and as such is prominently exhibited at the commencement of the Epistle to the Hebrews, in the words, ' God, who at sundry times, and in divers manners, spake in time past unto the fathers by the prophets, hath in these last days spoken unto us by His Son.' God's voice has been sounding through the ages, now in this manner, now in that, and with varying degrees of perspicuity and fulness, but culminating in the appearance and mission of the Son, as that wherein it found its deepest utterance and its most perfect form of manifestation. The simple fact, however, no longer satisfies; it comes at certain points into conflict with the critical, individualizing spirit of the age. But, to have the matter distinctly before us, we must first look at the consequences necessarily growing out of the fact with regard to the character it imparts to Divine revelation, and then consider the exceptions taken against it in whole or in part.

I. First, in respect to the fact, we have to take into account the extent to which the characteristic in question prevails. There is not merely a historical element in Scripture, but this so as even to impart to the revelation itself a history. Though supernatural in its origin, it is yet perfectly natural and human in its mode of working and its course of development. It stands associated with human wants and emergencies, as the occasions which called it forth; human agencies were employed to minister it; and, for transmission to future times, it has been written in the common tongues and dialects of men, and under the diversified forms of composition with which they are otherwise familiar. So little does this revelation of God affect a merely ideal or super-earthly style— so much does it let itself down among the transactions and movements of history, that it has ever been with outstanding and important facts that it has associated its more fundamental ideas. In these, primarily, God has made Himself known to man. And hence, alike in the Old and the New Testament Scriptures, the historical books stand first; the foundation of all is there; the rest is but the structure built on it; and just as is the reality and significance of the facts recorded in them, such also is the truth of the doctrines, and the measure of the obligations and hopes growing out of them.

But since revelation thus has a history, it necessarily has also a progress; for all history, in the proper sense, has such. It is not a purposeless moving to and fro, or a wearisome iteration, a turning back again upon itself, but an advance—if at times halting, or circuitous, still an advance—toward some specific end. So, in a peculiar manner, is it with the book of God's revelation; there is an end, because it is of Him, who never can work but for some aim worthy of Himself, and with unerring wisdom subordinates every thing to its accomplishment. That end may be variously described, according to the point of view from which it is contemplated; but, speaking generally, it may be said to include such an unfolding of the character and purposes of God in grace, as shall secure for those who accept its teachings, salvation from the ruin of sin, practical conformity to the will of God, and the bringing in of the everlasting kingdom of righteousness and peace, with which both the good of His people and the glory of His own name are identified. This is the grand theme pursued throughout; the different parts and stages of revelation are but progressive developments of it, and, to be rightly understood, must be viewed with reference to their place in the great whole. So that the revelation of God in Scripture finds, in this respect, its appropriate image in those temple-waters seen in vision by the prophet—issuing at first like a little streamlet from the seat of the Divine majesty, but growing apace, and growing, not by supplies ministered from without, but as it were by self-production, and carrying with it the more—the more it increased in volume and approached its final resting-place—the vivifying influences which shed all around them the aspect of life and beauty.

Now, this characteristic of Divine revelation, as being historically developed, and thence subject to the law of progress, has undoubtedly its dark side to our view; there are points about it which seem mysterious, and which we have no means of satisfactorily explicating. In particular, the small measures of light which for ages it furnished respecting the more peculiar things of God, the imperfect form of administration under which the affairs of His kingdom were necessarily placed till the fulness of the time had come for the manifested Saviour, and still in a measure cleaving to it—such things undoubtedly appear strange to us, and are somewhat difficult to reconcile with our abstract notions of wisdom and benevolence. Why should the world have been kept so long in comparative darkness, when some further communications from the upper Sanctuary might have relieved it ? Why delay so long the forthcoming of the great realities, on which all was mainly to depend for life and blessing ? Or, since the realities have come, why not take more effective means for having them brought everywhere to bear on the understandings and consciences of men ? Questions of this sort not unnaturally present themselves; and though, in regard at least to the first of them, we can point to a wide-reaching analogy in the natural course of providence (as has been already noticed at p. 62), yet, in the general, we want materials for arriving at an intelligent view of the whole subject, such as might enable us to unravel the mysteries which hang around it. It behoves us to remember, that in things which touch so profoundly upon the purposes of God, and the plan of His universal government, we meanwhile know but in part; and instead of vainly agitating the questions, why it is thus and not otherwise, should rather apply our minds to the discovery of the practical aims, which we have reason to believe stand associated with the state of things as it actually exists, and as we have personally to do with it.

Looking at the matter in this spirit, and with such an object in

view, we can readily perceive various advantages arising from such
an introduction of the historical element as has been described into
the method of God's revelation of His mind and will to men.   First
of all, it serves (if we may so speak) to *humanize* the revelation—
does, in a measure, for its teachings of truth and duty what, in a
still more peculiar manner, was done by the Incarnation.   The
Divine word spoken from the invisible heights, out of the secret
place of Godhead, and the same word uttered from the bosom of
humanity, linked on every side to the relations and experience of
actual life, though they might perfectly coincide in substance, yet
in form how widely different !   And in the one how greatly more
fitted than in the other to reach the sympathies and win the
homage of men !   It is, indeed, at bottom, merely a recognising
and acting on the truth, that man was made in the image of God,
and that only by laying hold of what remains of this image, and
sanctifying it for higher uses, can the Spirit of God effectually disclose Divine things, and obtain for them a proper lodgment in the
soul : the rays of the eternal Sun must reach it, not by direct
effulgence, but ' through the luminous atmosphere of created minds.'
Then, as another result, let it be considered how well this method
accords with and secures that fulness and variety, which is necessary to Scripture as the book which, from its very design, was to provide the seed-corn of spiritual thought and instruction for all times
—a book for the sanctification of humanity, and the developing in
the soul of a higher life than that of nature.   An end like this could
never have been served by some general announcements, systema-
tized exhibitions of doctrine, or stereotyped prescriptions of order
and duty, without respect to diversities of time, and the ever-varying evolutions of the world's history.   There was needed for its
accomplishment precisely what we find in Scripture—a rich and
various treasury of knowledge, with ample materials for quiet
meditation, the incitement of active energy, and the soothing influences of consolation and hope—and so, resembling more the freedom and fulness of nature than the formality and precision of art.
Hence, as has been well said, ' Scripture cannot be mapped or its
contents catalogued ; but, after all our diligence to the end of our
lives, and to the end of the church, it must be an unexplored and
unsubdued land, with heights and valleys, forests and streams, on
the right and left of our path, full of concealed wonders and choice

treasures.'[1]   One may readily enough master a system of doctrine,
or become conversant with even a complicated scheme of religious
observance ; but a history, a life, especially such lives and memorable transactions as are found in Scripture, above all, what is
written of our blessed Lord, His marvellous career, His Divine works
and not less Divine discourses, His atoning death and glorious resurrection—who can ever say he has exhausted these ?   Who does not
rather feel—if he really makes himself at home with them—that
there belongs to them a kind of infinite suggestiveness, such as is
fitted to yield perpetually fresh life and instruction to thoughtful
minds ?   And this, not as in the case of human works, for a certain
class merely of mankind, but for all who will be at pains to search
into its manifold and pregnant meaning.   Hence the Word of God
stands so closely associated with study, meditation, and prayer,
without which it cannot accomplish its design—cannot even make
its treasures properly known.   And on this account, ' the church
and theology must, while they are in the flesh, eat their bread by
the sweat of their brow ; which is not only not a judgment, but,
for our present state, a great blessing.   If the highest were indeed
so easy and simple, then the flesh would soon become indolent and
satisfied.   God gives us the truth in His word, but He takes care
that we must all win it for ourselves ever afresh.   He has therefore with great wisdom arranged the Bible as it is.'[2]   Still further,
in the actual structure of revelation, there is an interesting exhibition of the progressive character of the Divine plan, and of the
organic connection between its several parts—in this a witness of
the general organism of the human family, and, for individual
members thereof, a type of the progress through which the divinely
educated mind must ever pass, as from childhood to youth, and
from youth to the ripeness and vigour of manhood.   It thus has, as
it could no otherwise have done, its milk for babes and its meat for
strong men.   And the scheme of God for the highest wellbeing of
His people, is seen to be no transient or fitful conception, but a
purpose lying deep in the eternal counsel of His will—thence
gradually working itself into the history of the world—proceeding
onwards from age to age, rising from one stage of development to
another, the same grand principles maintained, the same moral aims

[1] Quoted in Trench's ' Hulsean Lectures,' p. 94.
[2] Auberlen ' On Divine Revelation,' p. 237, Eng. Trans.

pursued, through all external changes of position and varying forms
of administration, till the scheme reached its consummation in the
appearance and kingdom of Christ.   How assuring such a pre-
arranged and progressive course to the humble heart of faith, which
desires in earnest to know its God! And how instructive also to
mark the organic unity pervading the external diversity, and to
learn, from the earlier and simpler manifestations of the truth,
the lessons of wisdom, which are equally applicable, but often
more difficult of apprehension, under its higher and more spiritual
revelations! So that, for those living now in the ends of the world,
there is a rich heritage of instruction, counsel, and admonition laid
up for them in the Word of God, associated with every period of
the church's progress : Jehovah, the unchangeable One, speaks
to them in all; all has been 'written for *their* learning, that
through patience and comfort of the Scriptures they might have
hope.'

II. If the account now given of the matter, and the conclusion
just drawn as to its practical bearing—drawn in the language of
Scripture—be correct, then the historical and progressive character
of revelation, the circumstance of God's mind and will being communicated, in the first instance, to particular individuals, and
associated with specific times and places in the past, does not
destroy its application or impair its usefulness to men of other
times : we, too, are interested in the facts it records, we are bound
by the law of righteousness it reveals, we have to answer for all its
calls and invitations, its lessons of wisdom and its threatenings of
judgment.   But here exception is taken by the representatives and
advocates of individualism, sometimes under a less, sometimes
under a more extreme form ; in the one case denying any direct
claim on our faith and obedience, in respect to what is written in
Old Testament Scripture, but yielding it in respect to the New ;
in the other, placing both substantially in the same category,
and alleging, that because of the remoteness of the period to which
the Gospel era belongs, and the historical circumstances of the
time no longer existing, the things recorded and enjoined also
in New Testament Scripture are without any binding authority
on the heart and conscience.   It may be the part of wisdom to
accredit and observe them, but there can be no moral blame if we

should feel unable to do that, if we should take up an unbelieving and independent position.

1. Persons of the former class, who claim only a partial exemption from the authoritative teaching of Scripture—from the binding power of its earlier revelations—speak after this fashion : We were not yet alive, nor did the economy under which we live exist, when the things were spoken or done, through which God made revelation of Himself to men of the olden time—when Abraham, for example, at the Divine command, left his father's house, and was taken into covenant with God, or when Israel, at a subsequent period, were redeemed from the land of Egypt, that they might occupy a certain position and calling; and however important the transactions may have been in themselves, or however suitable for the time being the commands given, they still can have no direct authority over us; nor can we have to do with them as grounds of moral obligation, except in so far as they have been resumed in the teaching of Christ, or are responded to in our Christian consciousness. Of late years this form of objection has been so frequently advanced, that it is unnecessary to produce quotations; and not uncommonly the reasons attached especially to the fifth command in the Decalogue, and also to the fourth as given in Deut. v. 15, pointing, the one to Israel's heritage of Canaan, and the other to their redemption from Egypt, are regarded as conclusive evidences of the merely local and temporal nature in particular of the commands imposed in the Decalogue.

The mode of contemplation on which this line of objection proceeds is far from new; in principle it is as old as Christianity. For the view it adopts of Old Testament Scripture was firmly maintained by the unbelieving Jews of apostolic times, though applied by them rather to the blessings promised than to the duties enjoined. They imagined that, because they were the descendants of those to whom the word originally came, they alone were entitled to appropriate the privileges and hopes it secured to the faithful, or if others, yet only by becoming proselytes to Judaism, and joining themselves to the favoured seed. Fierce conflicts sprung up on this very point in subsequent times. Tertullian mentions a disputation of great keenness and length, which took place in his neighbourhood, between a Christian and a Jewish proselyte, and in which the latter sought 'to claim the law of

God for himself' (*sibi vindicare dei legem instituerit*). Conceiving the merits of the question to have been darkened, rather than otherwise, by words without knowledge, Tertullian took occasion from it to write his treatise against the Jews, in which he endeavoured to shew that God, as the Creator and Governor of all men, gave the law through Moses to one people, but in order that it might be imparted to all nations, and in a form which was destined, according to Old Testament Scripture itself, to undergo an important change for the better. Nearly two centuries later we find Augustine resuming the theme, and, after adducing various passages from Moses and the prophets about the redemption God had wrought for men, and the greater things still in prospect, the Jews are introduced as proudly erecting themselves and saying, ' *We* are the persons; this is said of us; it was said *to* us; for *we* are Israel, God's people.'[1] Thus the historical element in revelation, from the time it became peculiarly associated with the family of Abraham, was turned by them into an argument for claiming a kind of exclusive right to its provisions—as if Jehovah were the God of the Jews only; just as now it is applied to the purpose of fixing on the Jews an exclusive obligation to submit to its requirements of duty—except in so far as the matter therein contained

---

[1] ' Adv. Judæos,' sec. 9. Both Augustine and Tertullian have sharply exhibited, in their respective treatises, the substantial identity of the calling of believers in Christian and pre-Christian times. But in respect to the general principles of duty, they both except the law of the weekly Sabbath ; with them, as with the Fathers generally, this was a prominent distinction between the believing Jew and the believing Christian—the Sabbath being viewed, in common with many of the later Jews, as a day of simple rest from work—a kind of sanctimonious idleness and repose—hence, no further related to the Christian than as a prefiguration of his cessation from sin, and spiritual rest in Christ. All the precepts of the Decalogue they regarded as strictly binding but this (so expressly Aug., ' De Spiritu et Lit.,' c. xiv.; also Tert., ' De Idolatria,' c. 14 ; ' Adv. Jud.,' c. 4); or this only in the sense now specified. It was a branch of the Patristic misconceptions respecting Old Testament subjects, and one of the most unfortunate of them. Had they rightly understood the law of the Sabbath, they would undoubtedly have spoken otherwise of it. Those who dispute my assertion of this will perhaps judge differently when they hear what Ewald has to say of it. In his remarks on the Decalogue, he speaks most properly of the design and tendency of the Sabbath (though wrong, as I conceive, in ascribing its origin to Moses) : ' It was necessary (he says) for the community to have had such a pause in the common lower cares and

may be coincident with the general principles of moral obligation. The ground of both applications is the same—namely, by reason of the historical accompaniments of certain parts of Divine revelation, to circumscribe its sphere, and confine its authoritative teaching within merely local and temporary channels.

Now, as this is a point which concerns the proper bearing and interpretation of Scripture, it is to Scripture itself that the appeal must be made. But on making such an appeal, the principle that emerges is very nearly the converse of that just mentioned : it is, that the *particular* features in revelation, derived from its historical accompaniments, were meant to be, not to the prejudice or the subversion, but rather for the sake, of its *general* interest and application. They but served to give more point to its meaning, and render more secure its preservation in the world. So that, instead of saying, in respect to one part or another of the sacred volume, I find therein a word of God to such a person, or at such a period in the past, therefore not strictly for me ; I should rather, according to the method of Scripture, say, Here, at such a time and to such a party, was a revelation of the mind and will of Him who is Lord of heaven and earth, made to persons of like nature and calling with myself—made, indeed, *to* them, but only that it might *through* them be conveyed and certified to others ; and coming, as it does to me, a component part of the Word, which reveals the character of the Most High, and which, as such, He delights most peculiarly to magnify, I also am bound to listen to it as the voice of God speaking to me through my brother-man, and should make conscience of observing it—in so far as it is not plainly of a local and temporary nature, and consequently unsuited to my position and circumstances.

avocations of life, that they might collect their energies with the greater zeal for the life of holiness.' He thinks ' no institution could be devised which could so directly lead man both to supply what is lost in the tumult of life, and effectually to turn his thoughts again to the higher and the eternal. Thus the Sabbath, though the simplest and most spiritual, is at the same time the wisest and most fruitful of institutions, the true symbol of the higher religion which now entered into the world, and the most eloquent witness to the greatness of the human soul which first grasped the idea of it.' However, Tertullian in one place, ' Adv. Marcionem,' iv. 12, reasons with substantial correctness as to our Lord's treatment of the Sabbath, and His views regarding it, maintaining that it allowed certain kinds of work.

There are, no doubt, things of this latter description in the Word of God—things which, in their direct and literal form, are inapplicable to any one now; for this is a necessary consequence of the play that has been given to the historical element in Scripture. But then it is in a measure common to *all* Scripture—not wanting even in its later communications. Our Lord Himself spake words to His disciples, addressed to them both commands and promises, which are no longer applicable in the letter, as when He called some to leave their ordinary occupations and follow Him, or gave them assurance of an infallible direction and supernatural gifts. And how many things are there in the epistles to the churches, which had special reference to the circumstances of the time, and called for services which partook of the local and temporary? But such things create no difficulty to the commonest understanding; nor, if honestly desirous to learn the mind of God, can any one fail to derive from such portions of Scripture the lessons they were designed to teach—on the supposition of the requisite care and pains being applied to them. It is, therefore, but a difference in degree which in this respect exists between the Scriptures of the New and those of the Old Testament; there is in the Old Testament merely a larger proportion of things which, if viewed superficially, are not, in point of form, applicable to the circumstances, or binding on the consciences of believers in Christian times; while yet they are all inwrought with lines of truth, and law, and promise, which give them a significance and a value for every age of the church. Nay, such is the admirable order and connection of God's dispensations, so closely has He knit together the end with the beginning, and so wisely adjusted the one to the other, that many things in those earlier revelations have a light and meaning to us which they could not have to those whom they more immediately concerned: the *ultimate* aim and object of what was done was more important than its *direct* use. Read from the higher vantage-ground of the Gospel, and lighted up by its Divine realities, Moses and the prophets speak more intelligibly to us of God, and the life that is from Him, than they could do to those who had only such preliminary instructions to guide them.

From the time that God began to select a particular line as the channel of His revealed will to man, He made it clear that the good of all was intended. A special honour was in this respect to be conferred on the progeny of Shem, as compared with the other branches of Noah's posterity; but it was not doubtfully intimated that those other branches should participate in the benefit.[1]   When, however, the Divine purpose took effect, as it so early did, in the selection of Abraham and his seed, the end aimed at was from the first announced to be of the most comprehensive kind—namely, that in Abraham and his seed ' all the families of the earth should be blessed.'   It was but giving expression in another form to this announcement, and breathing the spirit couched in it, when Moses, pointing to the destiny of Israel, exclaimed, ' Rejoice, O ye nations, with His people ;'[2] and when the Psalmist prayed, ' God be merciful to us and bless us, that thy way may be known upon earth, thy saving health among all nations'[3]—the true prosperity of Israel being thus expressly coupled with the general diffusion of God's knowledge and blessing, and the one sought with a view to the other.   Hence also the temple, which was at once the symbol and the centre of all that God was to Israel, was designated by the prophet ' an house of prayer for all peoples.'[4]   And hence, yet again, and as the proper issue of the whole, Jesus—the Israel by way of eminence, the impersonation of all that Israel should have been, but never more than most imperfectly was—the One in whom at once the calling of Israel and the grand purpose of God for the good of men found their true realization—He, while appearing only as a Jew among Jews, yet was not less the life and light of the world—revealing the Father for men of every age and country, and making reconciliation for iniquity on behalf of all who should believe on His name, to the farthest limits of the earth and to the very end of time.

Looking thus, in a general way, over the field of Divine revelation, we perceive that it bears respect to mankind at large; and that what is special in it as to person, or time, or place, was not designed to narrow the range of its application, or render it the less profitable to any one for ' doctrine, for reproof, for correction, and for instruction in righteousness.'   And when we turn to particular passages of Scripture, and see how God-inspired men understood and used what came from Heaven, in other times and places

[1] Gen. ix. 26, 27.   [2] Deut. xxxii. 43.
[3] Ps. lxvii.   [4] Isa. lvi. 7.

than those in which themselves lived, the same impression is yet
more deepened on our minds—for we find them personally recognising and acting on the principle in question.   In the Book of
Psalms, for instance, how constantly do the sacred writers, when
seeking to revive and strengthen a languishing faith, throw themselves back upon the earlier manifestations of God, and recal what
He had said or done in former times, as having permanent value
and abiding force even for them !   ' I will remember the works of
the Lord, surely I will remember thy wonders of old.   Thou art
the God that doest wonders : Thou has declared thy strength among
the people.   Thou hast with thine arm redeemed thy people, the
sons of Jacob and Joseph.'   It was virtually saying, Thou didst it
all, that we might know and believe what Thou canst, and what
Thou wilt do still.   The principle is even more strikingly exhibited
in Hosea xii. 3-6, ' He (namely, Jacob) took his brother by the
heel in the womb, and by his strength he had power with God : yea,
he had power over the angel, and prevailed ; he wept, and made
supplication unto Him : he found Him in Bethel, and there He
(God) spake with us—even Jehovah, God of hosts, Jehovah is His
name.'   That is, Jehovah, the I am, He who is the same yesterday,
to-day, and for ever, in speaking ages ago with Jacob at Bethel, and
at Peniel giving him strength over the angel, did in effect do the
same *with us :* the record of these transactions is a testimony of
what He is, and what He is ready to do in *our* behalf.   And so,
the prophet adds, by way of practical application, ' Therefore turn
thou to thy God : keep mercy and judgment, and wait on thy God
continually.'   Passing to New Testament times, the principle under
consideration is both formally vindicated, and practically carried
out.   Not only does our Lord generally recognise as of God whatever was written in the Law and the Prophets, and recognise it as
what He had come, not to destroy, but to fulfil—not only this, but
He ever appeared as one appropriating, and, in a manner, living on
the word contained in them.   Thus, when plied by the tempter
with the plausible request to turn the stones of the desert into
bread, the ready reply was, ' It is written, Man liveth not by bread
only, but by every word which proceedeth out of the mouth of
God'—*man* does it ; man, namely, as the humble, docile, confiding
child of God—he lives thus ; so it was written ages ago in the
ever-living Word of God—written, therefore, also for Him, who is

pre-eminently such a man, as much as if it had been immediately addressed to Himself. And the same course was followed in the other temptations: they were successively met and repelled by what was written aforetime, as equally valid and binding at that time as when originally penned. To say nothing of the other apostles, who freely quote Old Testament Scripture, St Paul both formally sets forth and frequently applies the same great principle :—sometimes in a more general manner, as when he affirms, that 'the things written aforetime were written for our learning;'[1] or, more particularly, when speaking of the dealings of God with Israel in the wilderness, he states that 'they happened unto them for ensamples (types), and are written for our admonition;'[2] or, again, when identifying believers under the Gospel with Abraham, he asserts that 'they who are of faith are blessed with faithful Abraham'[3]— the blessing pronounced upon him being regarded as virtually pronounced also upon those in later times who exercise his faith. And still more striking is another exposition given of the principle, as connected with the Abrahamic blessing, in the Epistle to the Hebrews (chap. vi.), where, referring to the promise and the oath confirming it, it is said, God thereby shewed 'to the heirs of promise the immutability of His counsel,' so that 'by two immutable things, in which it was impossible for God to lie, we might have a strong consolation who have fled for refuge to the hope set before us'—not that *he* merely, to whom it was directly given, but that *we* too might have it. Therefore, the promise of blessing and its confirmatory oath were, according to the author of the epistle, designed as well for believers in Gospel times as for the father of the faithful; and why? Simply because they reveal the character and purpose of God in respect to the covenant of salvation, which, in all that essentially pertains to them, are independent of place and time, like their Divine Author changing not, but perpetually entitled to the faith and confidence of those who seek an interest ·in their provisions.

Such is the spirit or principle in which we are taught, on inspired authority—by Psalmists and Prophets of the Old Testament, by Christ and His apostles in the New—to regard and use that revelation of truth and duty, which comes to us bound up with the history of God's dispensations. If any thing can be deemed certain

[1] Rom. xv. 3.   [2] 1 Cor. x. 11.   [3] Gal. iii. 9.

regarding it, it is that we must look through the external accompaniments of what is revealed to its heart and substance; in other words, that we must not allow what is merely circumstantial in the Divine communications to interfere with that which is essential, and which, from the organic unity pervading those communications, is properly of no age or time. The false principle, which in various forms has from early to present times been put forth, is to invert this relation—to employ the circumstantial as a lever to undermine or drive into abeyance the essential. Had such been our Lord's method of interpreting ancient Scripture, what would it have availed Him to remember, in His hour of temptation, that man liveth not by bread only, but by every word of God, since that was written of Israel as redeemed from Egypt and fed with manna, while He was a stranger to both? Or, had it been Paul's, how should he ever have thought of transferring such special transactions and assurances of blessing as those connected with the faith of Abraham and the offering of Isaac, to believers generally of subsequent times? In acting as they did, they looked beyond the mere form and appearances of things, and entered into the faith of God's elect, which ever penetrates beneath the surface, and rather desires to know how much it is entitled to derive or learn from the written word of God, than to find how much it is at liberty to reject. But if there be any portion of Old Testament Scripture which more than another should be dealt with after this manner, it is surely that master-piece of legislation—the ten words proclaimed from Sinai—in which the substance is so easily distinguished from the accessories of time and place, and the substance itself is so simple, so reasonable, so perfectly accordant in all it exacts with the dictates of conscience and the truest wellbeing of mankind, that there seems to be needed only the thoughtful and earnest spirit of faith, to say, Lord, here is the manifestation of thy most just and righteous will toward me—incline my heart to keep these thy laws.

And here, indeed, lies the root of the whole matter—whether we have this spirit of faith or not. The possession and exercise of this spirit makes all, even the earliest parts of God's revelation to men, instinct with life and power, because, connecting the whole in our minds with the ever-abiding presence and immutable verity of God, it disposes us to feel that we have to do with the evolution of an eternal purpose, which step by step has been conducting fallen man to the righteousness and blessing of Heaven. *Nothing in such a case properly dies.* Whatever may be the aspect of God's word and ways we more immediately contemplate—whether the doom pronounced on the ungodliness of men, and the judgments inflicted on their impenitence and guilt—or the deliverances wrought for the children of faith in their times of danger and distress—or, finally, the fiery law issued as from the secret place of thunder, and prescribing the essential principles of a holiness which is the reflection of God's own pure and blessed nature—whichever it may be, the more profoundly we regard it as a still living word, 'for ever settled in the heavens,' and apply ourselves in earnest to have its teaching realized in our experience, the more do we appreciate its true character, accord with the design for which it was given, and illustrate the wisdom and goodness of Him who gave it.

2. But there is another and more extreme class of objectors, who make no distinction in this respect between New and Old Testament Scripture—who, as regards every thing of a supernatural kind that has a place in the sacred records, disallow any strict and proper obligation either to accredit what is testified, or to comply with its calls of duty. They were not personally present when the things so marvellous, so remote from one's every-day observation and experience, are reported to have taken place ; and no evidence of a simply historical kind can give them a claim upon their conscience. A divinely inspired attestation might, indeed, carry such a claim, did we certainly possess it ; but then inspiration belongs to the supernatural, and itself requires confirmation. So Mr Froude, for example : ' Unless the Bible is infallible, there can be no moral obligation to accept the facts which it records ; and though there may be intellectual error in denying them, there can be no moral sin. Facts may be better or worse authenticated ; but all the proofs in the world of the genuineness and authenticity of the human handiwork, cannot establish a claim upon the conscience. It might be foolish to question Thucydides' account of Pericles, but no one would call it sinful. Men part with all sobriety of judgment when they come on ground of this kind.'[1]

The objection is very adroitly put, and, if the alleged parallel instance from Grecian history were a fair one, the conclusion would

[1] Essay on 'Theological Difficulties.'

be inevitable, that it were the height of absurdity to think of establishing on such a basis a claim of moral responsibility. One is only disposed to wonder that so palpable an absurdity did not suggest to such a writer as Mr Froude the possibility of some hitch in his own reasoning on the subject, and that it was scarcely probable the whole race of Christian apologists (comprising many of the most thoughtful and sagacious intellects of past as well as present times) should have committed themselves to positions which bespoke an utter absence of sobriety of judgment. The argument is really one-sided and sophistical ; it proceeds on the supposition of there being only one element requiring to be taken into account in the cases represented as parallel—the one, namely, that is, or might be, common to them both ; while others, in which they differ, are thrown entirely into the background. The account of Pericles in Thucydides, and the evangelical narratives of Christ's person and work on earth, could easily be conceived to be alike genuine and authentic ; but it would not thence follow that they stood upon a footing as regards their claim on men's moral responsibilities. For as men occupy no specific moral relation to the life and transactions of Pericles, they might be true, or they might be false, for any thing that concerns the conduct we have to maintain in this world, or the expectations we are warranted to cherish respecting the next ; they might even remain to us a total blank, without materially affecting the course we pursue in respect either to God or to our fellow-men. Therefore, let the facts themselves be ever so certain, and the account transmitted of them beyond the slightest shade of suspicion, they still do not in the least touch our conscience ; we could at most be but somewhat less intelligent, if we refused to read or to accredit what is told of them, but we should not be one whit less happy or virtuous. It is entirely otherwise, however, with the recorded life and works of Jesus Christ. These carry on the very face of them a respect to every man's dearest interests and moral obligations ; if true, they bear in the closest manner on our present condition, and are fraught with results of infinite moment on our future destinies. And, unless the accounts we have of them present such obvious and inherent marks of improbability or imposture, as *ipso facto* to relieve us of all need for investigation, we are bound—*morally* bound by the relation in which the course of providence has placed us to them, as well as by the possible results to our own wellbeing—to consider the evidence on which they claim our belief, and make up our minds either to accredit or reject them.

There are undoubtedly persons who do assume the position just noticed, who hold the supernatural character of the events of Gospel history as alone sufficient to warrant their peremptory rejection of its claims to their belief. With them the miraculous is but another name for the incredible. This, however, is not the aspect of the question we have here to deal with. Mr Froude's exception is taken against the facts of Christianity, as connected with our moral obligations, not because they are miraculous, but simply because they are facts—reported to be such—matters of historical statement, which, as such, he alleges, however authentically related, cannot bind the conscience, or constitute, if disowned, a ground of moral blame. Is it really so in other things? Do the properly parallel instances in the transactions of human life bear out the position? Quite the reverse. A great part of men's obligations of duty, in the actual pursuits and intercourse of life, root themselves in facts, of which they can have nothing more than probable evidence. The whole range of filial duties, and those belonging to the special claims of kindred, are of this description; they spring out of facts, for which one can have nothing more than probable evidence, and evidence which sometimes, though fortunately not often, requires to be sifted in order to get assurance of the truth. In the department of political life, what statesman, or even comparatively humble citizen, can act in accordance with the spirit of the constitution—vindicate his own or his country's rights, provide against emergencies, devise and prosecute measures for the common good—without taking account of things near or remote, which he can only learn through the probabilities of historical testimony? And in the ordinary pursuits of business or commercial enterprise, every thing for men's success may be said to turn on their industry and skill in ascertaining what the probabilities are of things supposed to have emerged, or in the act of emerging—yea, in threading their way often through apparently competing probabilities; duty to themselves and their families obliges them to search thus into the facts they have to deal with, and to shape their course accordingly. Is not this, indeed, the very basis of Butler's conclusive argument in behalf of the *kind* of evidence on which all Christian obligation

rests ? 'Probable evidence' (he says), 'in its very nature, affords
but an imperfect kind of information, and is to be considered as
relative only to beings of limited capacities. For nothing which
is the possible object of knowledge, whether past, present, or future,
can be probable to an infinite intelligence ; since it cannot but be
discerned absolutely as it is in itself, certainly true, or certainly
false. But to *us*, probability is the very guide of life.'[1] And, as
he elsewhere states in the application of this principle, ' no possible
reason can be given why we may not be in a state of moral probation, with regard to the exercise of our understanding upon the
subject of religion, as we are with regard to our behaviour in
common affairs.' And the circumstance, ' that religion is not in-
tuitively true, but a matter of deduction and inference ; that a
conviction of its truth is not forced upon every one, but left to be,
by some, collected with heedful attention to premises—this as
much constitutes religious probation, as much affords sphere, scope,
opportunity for right and wrong behaviour, as any thing whatever
does.'[2]

Mr Froude, in his ' Short Studies on Grave Subjects,' has too
evidently not found leisure to make himself acquainted with the
principles of Butler's argument ; else he could scarcely have written
in the style he has done. But as we fear there are many in the
same position, and others in some danger of being carried away by
the false *gnosis* of the school to which he belongs, it may not be
improper to give the subject the benefit of the sharp and characteristic exposition of Mr Rogers. ' The absurdity, if anywhere, is in
the principle affirmed, namely, that God cannot have constituted it
man's duty to *act* in cases of very imperfect knowledge ; and yet
we see that He has perpetually compelled him to do so ; nay, often
in a condition next door to stark ignorance. To vindicate the
wisdom of such a constitution may be impossible ; but the fact
cannot be denied. The Christian admits the difficulty alike in
relation to religion and the affairs of this world. He believes, with
Butler, that probability is the guide of life ; that man may have
sufficient evidence in a thousand cases to warrant his action, and a
reasonable confidence in its results, though that evidence is very
far removed from certitude :—that, similarly, the mass of men are

[1] ' Analogy,' Introduction.   [2] *Ibid*., P. II. c. 6.

justified in saying, that they know a thousand facts of history to be true, though they have never had the opportunity or capacity of thoroughly investigating them; that the statesman, the lawyer, and the physician, are justified in acting, when they yet are compelled to acknowledge that they act only on most unsatisfactory calculations of probabilities, and amidst a thousand doubts and difficulties : all which, say we Christians, is true in relation to the Christian religion, the evidence for which is plainer, after all, than that on which man, in ten thousand cases, is necessitated to hazard his fortune or his life. . . . Those whom we call *profoundly* versed in the more difficult matters, which depend on moral evidence, are virtually in the same condition as their humbler neighbours. When men must act, the decisive facts may be pretty equally grasped by all; and as for the rest, the enlargement of the circle of a man's knowledge is, in still greater proportion, the enlargement of the circle of his ignorance; for the circumscribing periphery is in darkness.   If, as you suppose, it cannot be our duty to act in reference to an " historical religion," because a satisfactory investigation is impossible to the mass of mankind, the argument may be retorted on your own theory [that, namely, of F. Newman, which, as with Mr Froude, would place its chief reliance on the inner consciousness]. You assert, indeed, that in relation to religion we have an internal spiritual faculty, which evades this difficulty; yet men persist in saying, in spite of you, that it is doubtful, first, whether they have any such; second, whether, if there be one, it be not so debauched and sophisticated by other faculties, that they can no longer trust it implicitly; third, what is the amount of its genuine utterances; fourth, what that of its aberrations; fifth, whether it is not so dependent on development, education, and association, as to leave room enough for an auxiliary external revelation—on all which questions the generality of mankind are just as incapable of deciding as about any historical question whatever.'[1]

It is clear from such considerations, that certainty in religion cannot be attained by attempting to remove it from an historical to an internal, or strictly spiritual foundation; and also that the kind of certainty demanded to constitute the ground of moral obligation, is different from what is universally regarded as constituting such a ground in the common affairs and relations of life.

[1] 'Eclipse of Faith,' pp. 254-6.

Z

Besides, the principle against which we argue, were it valid, would render a general and progressive scheme of revelation impracticable —since such a thing could be possible only by the historical element entering into the dispensation of religion, and the historical developments of one age becoming the starting-point of the next. Even in the more general field of the world's progress it would evacuate, for all essentially moral purposes, the principle, acknowledged also by the more thoughtful and observant class of theists, that 'God is in history'—for this implies, that, as in the facts of history God reveals Himself, so it is the duty of His rational creatures both to take cognizance of the facts, and to mark in them the character of the revelation. Much more must such be man's duty with the higher revelation which God gives of Himself in Scripture, and which man needs for the relief of his profoundest wants, and the quickening of his moral energies. For this, the history of God's kingdom among men has an important part to play, as well as the direct teaching of truth and duty. And for the greater and more essential acts of that history, the genuineness and authenticity of the sacred records must of necessity form the more immediate evidence and the indispensable guarantee. Not, however, as if this were the whole ; for the facts which constitute the substance of the Gospel, and form the ground of its distinctive hopes and obligations, are commended to our belief by many considerations, which strengthen the direct historical evidence—in particular, by a whole line of prophetic testimonies, of which they were the proper culmination ; by the high moral aim of the writings which record them, and of the witnesses who perilled their lives in attestation of them ; by their adaptation to the more profound convictions of the soul, and the spiritual reformation which the sincere belief of them has ever carried in its train. But the misfortune is, this varied and manifold congruity of evidence receives little patient regard from the literary, self-sufficient individualism of the age. And here also there is some ground for the complaint, which has been uttered by a late writer of superior thought and learning, in respect to the rationalistic criticism of Germany : 'Men of mere book learning, who have never seen what the Spirit of God is working in the church, and who know little of life in general, take it upon themselves to pronounce final judgment upon the greatest revelations of spirit and life the world has ever seen ; upon the greatest of men, and the greatest outward and inward conflicts ; upon events which, more than all others, have moved the world ; upon words and writings which, more than all others, have been productive of life. What does not occur in our days, or at least what is not seen by certain eyes, cannot (it is thought) have happened in an earlier age, the products of which yet lie before us the greatest in the world, and to which we have nothing even remotely similar.'[1] Too manifestly, as the writer adds, there is in such things the evidence of an inward opposition to the truth, and hostility to the church of God.

[1] Auberlen, ' The Divine Revelation,' p. 274. Trans.

III.

WHETHER A SPIRIT OF REVENGE IS COUNTENANCED IN THE WRITINGS OF THE OLD TESTAMENT.

WHEN a spirit of revenge has been charged upon the morality of the Old Testament, the charge has usually been associated with passages in the Psalms and the Prophets, rather than with the precepts of the law. Superficial writers have sometimes, indeed, endeavoured to find it also in the latter, but without any proper warrant in the law itself. This, we trust, has been satisfactorily established at the proper place.[1] But there are portions of the Psalms, and occasional passages in the prophetical writings, which are very commonly regarded as breathing a spirit of revenge, and, as such, not unusually have the term *vindictive* applied to them. The lyrical character of the Psalms, which not only admitted, but called for, a certain intermixture of personal feeling with the thoughts appropriate to the particular theme, naturally afforded larger scope for utterances of a kind which might with some plausibility be viewed in that light, than could well be found in the writings of the Prophets. In the Psalms, the train of thought often runs in such a strain as this : the Psalmist finds himself surrounded with enemies, who are pursuing him with bitter malice, and are even plotting for his destruction ; and in pouring out his heart before God with reference to his position, he prays, not only that their wicked counsels might be frustrated, and that he might be delivered from their power, but that they might themselves be brought to desolation and ruin—that he might see his desire upon them, in the recoil of mischief upon their own heads, and the blotting out of their memorial from the land of the living. In a few Psalms, more particularly the 69th and the 109th, imprecations of this nature assume so intense a form, and occupy so large a space, that they give a quite distinctive and characteristic impress

[1] Lec. IV., pp. 98, 103.

to the whole composition.   In others, for the most part, they burst forth only as brief, but fiery, ebullitions of indignant or wrathful feeling, amid strains which are predominantly of a cheerful, con- solatory, or stimulating description :—as in Ps. 63, one of the most stirring and elevated pieces of devotional writing in existence, which yet is not brought to a close without an entreaty in respect to those who were seeking to compass the Psalmist's destruction, that they should fall by the sword, and become a portion for foxes ; Ps. 139, in which, after the most vivid portraiture of the more peculiar attributes of God, and the closest personal dealing with God in reference to them, the Psalmist declares his cordial hatred of the wicked, and asks God to slay them ; or Ps. 68, written in a predominantly hopeful and jubilant tone, yet opening with the old war-note of the wilderness, ' Let God arise, and let His enemies be scattered,' and identifying the future prosperity and exaltation of the Lord's people with their wounding the head, yea, dipping their feet in the blood, of their enemies, and the tongue of their dogs in the same.   Somewhat corresponding passages are to be found in Jer. xi. 20, xviii. 23, xx. 12, where the prophet asks the Lord that he might see his vengeance on those who sought his life ; also in Micah vii. 9, 10.

The late author of ' The Spirit of the Hebrew Poetry,' having referred to passages of this description, says : ' Undoubtedly we stay the course of our sympathy at such points as these.   It could only be at rare moments of national anguish and deliverance that expressions of this order could be assimilated with modern feelings.'[1] He so far, however, vindicates them as to hold them consistent with genuine piety in the writers, and suitable to their relative position. ' These war-energies of the Hebrew mind, in a past time, were proper to the people and to the age ; and would continue to be so until that revolution in religious thought had been brought about, which, in abating *national* enthusiasm, and in bringing immortality into the place of earthly welfare, gave a wholly new direction to every element of the moral system.'   This explanation may be said to point in the right direction, though, if taken alone, it would go far to antiquate such portions of Old Testament Scripture as no longer suitable, and even appears to concede to the force of circum- stances a power of determination in respect to what is right or

---

[1] Isaac Taylor, ' The Spirit of the Hebrew Poetry,' p. 152.

wrong in spiritual feeling, which it is scarcely proper to allow. The explanation, however, is partial and defective rather than incorrect; and, did the choice necessarily lie between them, it were greatly to be preferred to that often adopted in the more popular class of commentaries, which would silence objection by turning the imprecations into predictions. So Horne, for example : ' The offence taken at the supposed uncharitable and vindictive spirit of the imprecations, which occur in some of the Psalms, ceases immediately if we change the imperative for the future, and read, not, "Let them be confounded," etc., but, " They shall be confounded" —of which the Hebrew is equally capable. Such passages will then have no more difficulty in them than the other frequent predictions of Divine vengeance in the writings of the prophets, or denunciations of it in the Gospels.' In a grammatical respect, the explanation will not stand ; for the Hebrew imperative is not so interchangeable as it supposes with the future, and is not so regarded either by the ancient translators or by the more exact of modern scholars. But even if it were, what would be gained by it ? The real difficulty would be only shifted from one position to another ; and, indeed, from a lower to a higher, because placed in more immediate connection with the mind and will of God. Acute rationalists have not been slow to perceive this ; and one of them (Bauer), proceeding on the moral ground assumed in it, though with a different intent, asks, ' How could David think otherwise, than that he had a perfect right to curse his enemies, when he had before him, according to his conviction, the example of God ?' Bauer saw well enough that if the matter stood so with reference to God, there was no need for any change of mood in the verb ; since it could not be wrong for the Psalmist to desire and pray for what he had reason to believe God was purposed to do. Grant that to curse, or take vengeance on, one's enemies is known to be the will of God, and how can it be supposed otherwise than proper to pray that it be done ? The only room for inquiry and discrimination must be, on what ground, and with respect to what sort of persons, can such a line of desire and entreaty be deemed justifiable and becoming ? Considered with reference to this point, the language in question will be found to have nothing in it at variance with sound morality.

First of all, a strong consideration in favour of another view of the passages than one that would find in them the exhibition of a spirit of revenge, is the circumstance already noticed, that such a spirit is expressly discouraged in the precepts of the law. For it was thus stamped as unrighteous for those who lived under that economy; and to have given way to it in those writings which are intended to unfold the workings of a devout and earnest spirit in its more elevated and spiritual moods, would have been a palpable incongruity. One great object of the Psalmodic literature was to extract the essence of the law, and turn it into matter both for communion with God and practical application to the affairs of life. Nothing, therefore, that jars with the morality or religion inculcated in the law could find a place here; and the less so on this particular point, as in other passages there is a distinct response to the teaching of the law regarding it, and a solemn repudiation of the contrary spirit. In the Proverbs, which stand in close affinity with the Psalms, there are various passages of this description;[1] and one so explicit and full, that when St Paul would recommend such an exercise of love as might triumph over all hostile feelings and repay evil with good, he could find nothing better to express his mind than the language thus provided to his hand.[2] In like manner, in the Book of Job, which partly belongs to the same class, the patriarch is represented as declaring, that he would allow his friends to hold all his calamities sufficiently accounted for if he had rejoiced over the misfortune of an enemy, or had so much as wished a curse to his soul.[3] Similarly, also, the royal Psalmist— who goes so far as to invoke the Divine vengeance on his head, if he had done evil to him that was at peace with him, or had spoiled him that without cause was his enemy (for so the words should be rendered in Ps. vii. 4); and once and again, during the course of his eventful history, when by remarkable turns in providence it came to be in the power of his hand to avenge himself in a manner that would at once have opened for him the way to freedom and enlargement, he put from him the thought with righteous indignation.[4] He even expressed his gratitude to Abigail, and to the restraining hand of God through her interposition, that he had been kept from avenging himself on Nabal, and thereby doing what he

---

[1] Prov. x. 12, xvi. 32, xix. 11, xxiv. 17, 18.
[2] Prov. xxv. 21, 22 ; Rom. xii. 19, 20.   [3] Job xxxi. 29, 30.
[4] 1 Sam. xxiv. 5, 6 ; xxvi. 8-10.

knew, in the inmost convictions of his soul, to be evil.[1]   Is it, then, to be imagined that the spirit which David, as an individual believer, and in the most critical moments of his life, rejected as evil, should yet have been infused by him into his Psalms—the writings which he composed in his holiest seasons, and destined to permanent and general use in the sanctuary of God ?   This is against all probability, and can only be believed when it is forgotten what the real position of David was, whether as a servant of God, or as one supernaturally endowed for the purpose of aiding the devotions and stimulating the faith and hope of the covenant people.   In both respects he would have acted unworthily of his calling, had he given expression to revengeful feelings.

This, however, is only the negative aspect of the matter; we turn now, in the second place, to the positive.   David, and other men of faith in former times, could neither teach nor practise revenge ; but they could well enough ask for the application of the law of recompense, as. between them and those who sought their hurt—on the supposition that the right was on their side, that their cause was essentially the cause of God.   And this supposition is always, in the cases under consideration, either distinctly made or not doubtfully implied.   If the Psalmist speaks of hating certain persons and counting them his enemies, it is because they hate God and are in a state that justly exposes them to His wrath.   If he expects to see his desire upon his enemies, their counsels defeated, their mischievous devices made to return upon their own heads, it is because God was upon his side and against theirs—because he was engaged in doing God's work, while they were seeking to impede and frustrate it.   So, also, with the prophet Jeremiah, and other servants of God ; it was as wrestlers in the cause of righteousness, and in a manner identified with it, that they besought the retributions of judgment upon their keen and inveterate opponents. The question, therefore, between the contending parties must of necessity come to an issue on the law of recompense ; and so the Psalmist sometimes formally puts it, as in Ps. xviii. 23-27, 'I was upright before Him, and I kept myself from mine iniquity.   Therefore hath the Lord recompensed me according to my righteousness, according to the cleanness of my hands in His eyesight.   With the merciful thou wilt shew 'thyself merciful ; with an upright man

[1] 1 Sam. xxv. 31-33.

thou wilt shew thyself upright ; with the pure thou wilt shew thy-self pure ; for thou wilt save the afflicted people, but wilt bring down high looks.' To the same effect also in the history.[1]

This law or principle of recompense is merely an application of the Divine righteousness according to the parts men take in the conflict between good and evil. It is confined, therefore, to no particular age, but, like every other distinguishing characteristic in the Divine procedure, has its fullest manifestation in the work and kingdom of Christic. . Hence we find our Lord taking frequent opportunities to unfold it, as well in its benign aspect and operation toward the righteous, as in its contrary and punitive bearing upon the wicked ; and not merely in respect to these two parties con-sidered individually and separately, but also in their relation to each other. As regards individuals, some very striking and pro-minent exhibitions are given of it,—first, in the form of encourage-ments to the good, in such passages as the following, Matt. v. 7-10, x. 40-42, xix. 28, 29 ; Luke xii. 37 ; then, also, by way of warning to the careless and impenitent, in the terrible woes and judgments pronounced by Jesus upon the cities of Galilee, which heard His words and saw His mighty works, yet knew not the day of their merciful visitation ; in the like judgments and woes that were gathering to alight upon the Scribes and Pharisees, upon Jerusalem, and the Jewish people generally, or more generally still, in the aggravated doom declared to be the portion of those who (like the unforgiving servant in parable[2]) have acted with severity or injus-tice toward their fellow-men. On the law of recompense in this form, however, we are not called at present to remark ; we have to do with it only as bearing on the relative position of parties, who have espoused antagonistic interests—the one hazarding all for the truth and cause of God, the other setting themselves in determined array against it. In such cases, the triumph of the one interest inevitably carries along with it the overthrow of the other ; and though it is a sad alternative, yet the heart that is true to its principles cannot but wish for it. The ungodly world must perish, if Noah and the faithful remnant are to be saved ; at a later period, the Egyptian host must be drowned in the sea, if the ransomed of the Lord are to reach a place of safety and enlargement. And so still onwards—the discomfiture of the enemies of God is the indispens-

---

[1] 1 Sam. xxiv. 12-15.   [2] Matt. xviii.

able condition of security and wellbeing to His elect—whose cry
to Heaven in their times of trial and conflict must ever in substance
be, that God would revenge their cause.[1] Why should not David
and other ancient wrestlers in that cause have sought such a vindication when the claims of righteousness demanded it ? Why should
they not have wished and prayed that the good should prevail, by
confusion being poured on the bands of evil who had brought it into
peril ? Indeed, as matters then stood, no other course was left for
them. There was proceeding a trial of outward strength between
spiritual light and darkness—a contest between forces essentially
antagonistic, in which, if the right should be able to maintain its
position and carry out its designs, the contrary part, with all its
adherents, must be driven from the field. And who can for a
moment hesitate on which side the wishes and prayers of God's
people should have run ?

With this agreement, however, in the main between the things
relating to this subject in the past and present dispensations of
God, there is to be noted, thirdly, a difference in outward circumstances, which necessarily involves also a certain difference in the
mode of giving effect to the principle of recompense. It is not that
now—since life and immortality have been brought to light by the
Gospel—recompenses of evil as well as good in the cause of God
have ceased to have a place in the present administration of the
Divine kingdom, and that God will do in eternity what He cannot
do in time ; but that every thing respecting the kingdom has taken
a higher direction ; the outward is relatively less, the inward more ;
God's favour and the wellbeing it secures are no longer to be
measured, to the extent they once were, by national prosperity or
temporal distinctions of a palpable kind. Both for individual
believers and for the church at large, the conflict with the powers
of evil has lost certain of its grosser elements ; it has now greatly
less to do with weapons of fire and sword, more with such as
directly affect the reason and conscience ; and it is the special duty
of Christ's followers to strive that the means of this latter description placed at their command should be employed so as to subdue
the corruption of ungodly men—to destroy them as enemies, in
order that as friends they may pass over into the ranks of God's
people. But in desiring and pleading for such spiritual results, the

[1] Luke xviii. 7, 8.

Christian now, as the Psalmists of old, must pray for the discomfiture of all adverse influences, and of all interests, personal or national, which have linked themselves to the principles of evil. The prayer of the church must still be, ' Let all thine enemies perish, let them that hate thee flee before thee :'—only in pressing it, one may, and indeed should, have respect to a change for the better in the *spiritual* relation of the parties concerned, rather than in what concerns their *temporal* condition and their *secular* resources. For in the existing state of the world, it is usually by the one much more than by the other that the cause of truth and righteousness will be affected, and the tide of battle most effectually turned.

Finally, it must not be forgotten, in regard to the portions of Old Testament Scripture in question, that while the change of circumstances has necessarily brought along with it a certain change in the application of the principle embodied in them, their employment for religious culture and devotion has by no means lost either its reason or its importance. It serves to keep alive a right sense of the sins prevailing in the world, as dishonouring to God and deserving of His righteous condemnation ; of the calling, also, of the church to wage with these a perpetual warfare, not the less real and earnest that it has immediately to concern itself with matters of a spiritual nature. A corrective of this sort is needed very particularly in the present age, when loose views of holiness and sin are ready from so many quarters to press in upon the minds of those who are but partially established in the truth. And it can only be found in revelations which teach that there is severity as well as goodness, justice as well as mercy, in the character of God, which must have its manifestation in a measure even here, but shall have it pre-eminently in the final issues of His kingdom ; and this for the good of His people, not less than the glory of His own name. Hence, as justly remarked by Lange,[1] ' Christ recognises, in the fact of His crucifixion having been determined on,[2] the certain advent of the great day of wrath which is to bring the visitation of fire upon all the world. And indeed this inseparable combination stands in no contrariety to the reconciliation accomplished through the death of Christ; for as His death provides for the world the redemption which could meet all its necessities, so is the day of wrath the consummating act of redemption for all

---

[1] In Hertzog, 'Zorn Gottes.'   [2] Matt. xxiii. 39, xxiv. 1, *seq.*

believers ;[1] and the judgment of fire, which with the day of wrath
falls on the impenitent, is grounded in this very circumstance,
that they had not accepted the salvation of God in the death of
Christ, but in this death had sealed the judgment of God upon
their blindness. They have turned the Gospel into a savour of
death unto death.'

[1] Luke xxi. 28 ; 1 Thess. i. 7 ; 2 Pet. iii. 7-10.

EXPOSITION

OF THE

MORE IMPORTANT PASSAGES ON THE LAW IN ST PAUL'S EPISTLES.

IT was St Paul more especially who, among the apostles of our Lord, was called to discuss the subject of the law, as well in its remoter as its more immediate bearings—in its relation to New as well as Old Testament times. There is hence a very considerable variety in the mode of treatment given to it in his epistles, according to the specific point of view from which it is contemplated; and, at times, an apparent contrariety, when the passages are isolated from the context and the occasion, between what is said respecting it in one place, as compared with what is said in another. It is necessary, therefore, in order to ground securely the exhibition of doctrine contained in the Lectures, to give an exegesis of the passages in question, and to do so as nearly as possible in the order of time in which they proceeded from the pen of the apostle; for we thus more readily perceive how the matter grew upon the mind of the apostle, and developed itself in the history of his apostolical career. I have, therefore, begun with the passage in the Second Epistle to the Corinthians, which has all the appearance of a general outline or first draft of his views upon the economy of law, and its relation to that of the Gospel—an outline which is filled up in the Epistles to the Galatians and the Romans. According to the common chronology, the Epistle to the Galatians dates earlier than the Second to the Corinthians. But Dr Lightfoot, I think, has made the inverse relation appear more than probable;[1] and even were the actual succession otherwise, the passage in Corinthians must still be held to go first in the order of nature. In the other cases, the succession is sufficiently ascertained.

---

[1] *See* his Comm. on the Epistle, Introd., sec. iii.

I deem it unnecessary to preface the exposition by an inquiry respecting the different meanings of the term νόμος (law), as used by the apostle, and whether any appreciable difference is made on the meaning, according as it has or wants the article.   Much time might be, and often has been, expended to little purpose in general investigations of this sort; for the actual sense in each case must be ascertained by an analysis of the particular passages.   There can be no doubt that the term is used by St Paul in a considerable variety of senses, and in the same senses sometimes with, sometimes without, the article.   In respect to many of these, such as when it is used of the writings or books containing the law, or part of the Old Testament Scriptures generally,—or when employed by a sort of figure to designate any thing which works like a rule or principle of action, as in the expressions, *what sort of law, law of faith, law of sin, law in one's members, law of sin and death, law of the spirit of life*, etc.,—there is only a popular form of speech, which can scarcely occasion any serious difficulty even to unlettered readers.   But when, as not unfrequently happens, the question to be determined is, whether the law meant by the apostle is moral law in the abstract, or that law as embodied in the Decalogue, or the ceremonial law of the Old Covenant as contradistinguished from the moral, or, finally, these two conjointly in their economical adjustment, there is no way of reaching a safe conclusion but by a careful examination of the context.   For the most part, even in these uses of the term, no great difficulty will be experienced by an intelligent and unbiassed mind in determining which sense is to be preferred.—For the sake of precision, an exact rendering has been given of all the passages, which occasionally differs from that of the authorized version.

2 COR. III. 2–18.

' Ye are our epistle written in our hearts, known and read by all men, 3. Manifested as being an epistle of Christ ministered by us, written not with ink, but with the Spirit of the living God; not in tables of stone, but in tables of flesh, those of the heart.   4. But such confidence have we through Christ toward God : 5. Not as if we were sufficient as of ourselves to think any thing of ourselves, but our sufficiency is of God; 6. Who also has made us sufficient [to be] ministers of the new covenant, not of letter, but of Spirit : for the letter killeth, but the Spirit giveth life.   7. But if the ministration of death in the letter, engraven on stones, came in glory, so that the children of Israel were not able steadfastly to look on the face of Moses because of the glory of his face, [though a glory that was] to vanish away ; 8. How shall not rather the ministration of the Spirit be in glory? 9. For if the ministration of condemnation was in glory, much more does the ministration of right-eousness abound in glory. 10. For even that which has been made glorious has not had glory in this respect, by reason of the glory that excelleth. 11. For if that which vanisheth away was in glory, much more is that which abideth in glory. 12. Having then such hope, we use great boldness of speech; 13. And not as Moses put a veil on his face, in order that the children of Israel might not steadfastly look to the end of that which was to vanish away : 14. But their understandings were blinded; for until this very day the same veil remaineth at the reading of the old covenant, without having it unveiled (or discovered), that it is vanished away in Christ. 15. But unto this day, whenever Moses is read, a veil lies upon their heart. 16. But whenever it shall have turned to the Lord, the veil is taken away. 17. Now the Lord is the Spirit; but where the Spirit of the Lord is, there is liberty. 18. But we all, with unveiled face, beholding in a mirror the glory of the Lord, are transformed into the same image from glory to glory, as from the Lord the Spirit.'

This section has at first sight a somewhat parenthetical appearance, and introduces, in a manner that seems quite incidental, a subject not elsewhere discussed in either of the Epistles to the Corinthians—the difference in certain respects between the ministration of law and the ministration of the Gospel. Closer examination, however, shews that it was not done without reason, being intended to meet the unworthy insinuations, and incorrect or superficial views of the teachers, who by fair speeches, recommendatory letters or otherwise, had been seeking to supplant the apostle's authority at Corinth. That a certain Judaistic leaven existed also among some of these, may not doubtfully be inferred from their calling themselves by the name of Cephas or Peter (1 Cor. i. 12). And though the apostle had reason to conclude that the influ-ence of those designing teachers had already received its death-blow from the effect produced by his first epistle, we cannot wonder that he should still have deemed it needful—though only as it were by the way —to bring out the higher ground which he had won for himself at Corinth, and the practical evidence this afforded of the Divine power of his ministry, being in such perfect accordance with the spiritual nature of the Gospel dispensation, and the superior glory that properly belonged to it. This, then, is the apostle's starting-point—his own fitness or sufficiency as a minister of Christ: this, as to power and efficiency, is of God; it is proved to be so by the life-giving effects which it had pro-

duced among the Corinthians themselves, these having become like a
living epistle of the truth and power of the Gospel; and this, again, the
apostle goes on to shew, is the best of all testimonials, as being most
thoroughly in accordance with the character of the new covenant,
which in this very respect differs materially from the old.

Ver. 6. Passing over the two or three earlier verses which, for the
purpose we have more immediately in view, call for no special consideration, the apostle, after stating at the close of ver. 5 that his
sufficiency ($i\varkappa\alpha\nu\acute{o}\tau\eta\varsigma$) was of God, adds, 'who also has made us sufficient
to be ministers' ($i\varkappa\acute{\alpha}\nu\omega\sigma\varepsilon\nu$—not, as in the authorized version, ' made us
able ministers'), that is, has qualified us for the work of ministers, ' of
the new covenant.' The $\varkappa\alpha\acute{\iota}$ must be taken in the sense of *also*, or *thus
too*: our sufficiency in general is of God, who thus too has made us
sufficient—in this particular line has given proof of His qualifying grace,
by fitting us for the ministry of the new covenant. It is here first
that the term 'new covenant' is introduced, suggested, however, by
what had been said of the effects of the apostle's ministry in ver. 3, as
having constituted the members of the church at Corinth his recommendatory letter, written neither with ink, nor on tables of stone, but
by God's Spirit on the heart. The mention of tables of stone on the
one side, and Spirit on the other, naturally called up the thought of the
two covenants — the old and the new — the old, that which was
established at Sinai, and which, as to its fundamental principles or
terms, stood in the handwriting of the two tables; the new, that indicated by Jeremiah (xxxi. 31-34), according to which there was to be a
writing of God's law upon the hearts of men, an engraving on their
inward parts. Of this new covenant the apostle speaks as a thing
perfectly known and familiar to the minds of his readers: hence simply
new covenant, without the article, not to be rendered ' a new covenant,'
with Meyer, Stanley, and others, as if of something indeterminate, and
there was still room for inquiry which new covenant. This cannot be
supposed; it is rather assumed, that the readers of the epistle knew
both what covenant the expression pointed to, and what was the specific
character of the covenant. The definite article, therefore, may be quite
appropriately used, *the* new covenant. But then, standing related as
ministers to this new covenant, the apostle goes on to say, they were
ministers (for $\delta\iota\alpha\varkappa\acute{o}\nu o\upsilon\varsigma$ must be again supplied), not of letter, but of
Spirit (not of $\gamma\rho\acute{\alpha}\mu\mu\alpha$, but of $\pi\nu\varepsilon\tilde{\upsilon}\mu\alpha$). The expression is peculiar, and
can only be understood by a reference to the state of things then
existing; for in themselves there is no necessary contrast between
letter and spirit. The apostle himself elsewhere uses the word *letter* in

the plural, in connection with sanctifying and saving effects : the τὰ ἱερὰ γράμματα, the sacred letters, or writings, he says to Timothy—meaning the Scriptures of the Old Testament—' are able to make thee wise unto salvation.'[1]　And as letters are but the component parts of words, we may apply here what our Lord Himself affirmed of His words or sayings (ῥήματα), ' The words which I have spoken to you are spirit and life.'[2]　Hence, without pointing to any contrast between old and new, or outward and inward, we find Justin Martyr, or the author of ' Expositio Fidei,' denoting by the term a passage of Scripture, saying, in proof of the essential divinity of the Son and Spirit, ' Hear the passage' (ἄκουε τοῦ γράμματος, sec. 6); and Cyrill Alex. applies it specifically to the Scriptures of the New Testament, speaking of what is fitting ' according to the scope of the New Scripture (κατὰ τὸν τοῦ νέου γράμματος σκοπὸν) and ecclesiastical usage.'[3]　Paul might, therefore, in perfect accordance with Greek usage, have spoken of himself as a minister of letter or word, if he had so qualified and used the expression as to shew that he merely meant by it the oral or written testimony of God in Christ, which he elsewhere characterizes as ' the sword of the Spirit,' and as ' quick and powerful, and sharper than a two-edged sword.'[4]　But putting, as he here does, letter in contrast with spirit, it is quite clear that the apostle had respect to the written testimony or law of God, *considered by itself, and taken apart from all the spiritual influences with which, as given by Him, it was meant to be associated.*　And he was naturally led to this use of the term, with reference especially to Old Testament Scripture, by the undue, and, in many cases, exclusive regard paid, at and long before the Gospel era, by the Jewish authorities to the bare terms, or precise letter, of the written word. Their scribes (γραμματεῖς) had become very much men of the letter (γράμμα), as if every thing which a Divine revelation had to aim at might be accomplished by an exact and proper adherence to the terms in which it was expressed.　Hence arose a contrariety between Rabbinism, the system of the scribes, and Christianity, but which might equally be designated a contrariety to the true scope and spirit of the old covenant itself : the aim of each was substantially one, namely, to secure a state of things conformable to the revealed will of God ; but the modes taken to accomplish it were essentially different, according to the ·diversity in the respective modes of contemplation.　' Christianity demanded conversion, Rabbinism satisfied itself with instruction ; Christianity insisted on a state of mind, Rabbinism on legality ; Chris-

---

[1] 2 Tim. iii. 15.　　　　　　　　[2] John vi. 63.
[3] ' De Ador.,' L. xii.　　　　　　[4] Eph. vi. 17 ; Heb. iv. 12.

tianity expected from the communication of the Holy Spirit the necessary enlightenment, in order to discern in all things the will of God, Rabbinism thought it must go into the minutest prescriptions to shew what was agreeable to the law; Christianity expected from the gift of the Holy Spirit the necessary power to fulfil the Divine will, Rabbinism conceived this fulfilment might be secured through church discipline.'[1] The inevitable result was, that 'by the external position thus given to the law, there was nothing Divine in the heart; no repentance, faith, reformation, and hope, wrought by God's Spirit; no kingdom of God within, but all merely external;' and, in like manner, the prophets were viewed in a superficial manner, as if pointing, when they spake of Messias, to a mere worldly kingdom, no true kingdom of Heaven. But this senseless adherence to the letter was at variance, as we have said, not merely with Christianity, but with the teaching of the prophets, and the design of the old covenant itself (when taken in its proper bearing and connection). And hence (as Schöttgen long ago remarked, in his 'Hor. Heb.,' on the passage before us), by *the letter* is not to be understood the literal sense of the Divine word (in which sense many things in the Gospel were equally liable to abuse with those in the law, as the call of Christ to follow Him, to bear His cross, etc.), for that word, as having been given by the Spirit for the direction, not so much of man's body as his soul, is mainly spiritual, and the law itself is expressly so called by the apostle in Rom. vii. 14. But by *letter* must be understood the outward form merely of what is taught or commanded in the word, as contra-distinguished from its spiritual import or living power—the shell apart from the kernel; and, in this sense, neither the apostles nor any true messengers of God, in earlier any more than later times, were ministers of the letter. Not even circumcision, Paul elsewhere says, was of this description, that is, as designed by God, and properly entered into on the part of the people : ' Circumcision is of the heart, in the spirit, not in the letter ; '[2] and the same might, of course, be said of all the precepts and ordinances of the law ; none of them were intended to be taken and observed in what he calls ' the oldness of the letter.'[3] So that it is utterly to mistake the apostle's meaning here, to suppose that he draws a distinction betwixt the old and the new in God's revelations ; the distinction intended has respect mainly and primarily to a right and wrong understanding of these revelations, no matter when given ; and only hints, though it cannot be said distinctly to express, a difference between law and Gospel in this respect—that letter or formal prescription had a more prominent place in

---

[1] 'Rabbinismus,' in Hertzog, by Pf. Pressel.   [2] Rom. ii. 29.   [3] Rom. vii. 6.

the one than it has in the other. The meaning was given with sub-stantial correctness by Luther in his marginal gloss—greatly better than by many later expositors—' To teach letter is to teach mere law and work, without the knowledge of God's grace, whereby every thing that man is and does becomes liable to condemnation and death, for he can do nothing good without God's grace. To teach spirit is to teach grace without law and works [*i.e.*, without these as the ground of peace and blessing], whereby men come to life and salvation.'

' For the letter killeth, but the spirit giveth life (quickeneth).' This the apostle assigns as a reason why he and his fellow-labourers were ministers of the new covenant, in the sense just explained, not of letter but of spirit; when done otherwise, it is but a ministration of death. And this, whatever the nature of the word ministered, whether carrying the aspect of law or of Gospel. More obviously, the result took place with a ministration of law, since this consisted of requirements which were opposed to the natural tendencies of the heart, and which, when seriously looked into, demanded what man was not able of himself to perform; hence not peace and life, but trouble and death, were the inevitable consequence—although the law itself, if viewed in its proper connection, and taken as designed by God, as the apostle elsewhere testifies, ' was ordained for life.' [1] But the Gospel, too, when similarly treated, that is, when turned either by preacher or hearer into a letter or form of requirement concerning things to be believed and done with-out any higher agencies being called into play, in reality achieves nothing more; it is, in such a case, as the apostle had stated but a few verses before,[2] ' a savour of death unto death;' for to take up the yoke of Christ, to repent and be converted, to become new creatures and lay hold of everlasting life, is as far above nature as any thing in the law, and if isolated from the grace with which it ought ever to be associated, and in its bare terms pressed on men's responsibilities and obligations, or by men themselves so taken, the result can only be deeper condemna-tion, death in its more settled and aggravated forms.[3]

From the preceding exposition, it will be seen that we cannot, with the older expositors (also Bengel, Meyer, Alford), identify *letter* with the old covenant, and *spirit* with the new; nor altogether hold, with Stanley, that *letter* here denotes ' not simply the Hebrew Scriptures, but the more outward book or ordinance, as contrasted with the living power of the Gospel :' we take it generally of outward book or ordi-nance, whether pertaining to Old or New Testament times. Only, as from the ostensible and formal character of the two dispensations,

[1] Rom. vii. 10.   [2] Rom. ii. 16.   [3] Matt. xi. 25 ; John i. 5, v. 40, vi. 44, &c.

there was more of letter in the one, more of spirit in the other : what he says of the letter, and of its tendency to kill, admitted of a more ready and obvious application to the things of the old covenant, than to those of the new—an application the apostle proceeds immediately to make. The kind of killing or death (we may add) ascribed to the letter is certainly not, with some, and, among others, Stanley, to be understood of physical death, the common heritage of men on account of sin, but of the spiritual death, which consists in a painful sense of guilt, and the agonies of a troubled conscience. What is here briefly indicated in this respect is more fully developed in Rom. vii., and the one passage should be taken in connection with the other.

Ver. 7. ' But if the ministration of death in the letter,[1] engraven on stones, came in glory.'—(The authorized version is unfortunate here.) We adopt, as stated in the note below, the reading γράμματι (instead of that of the received text, γράμμασιν) *in the letter,* and couple this immediately with what precedes, not with what follows. The first clause is, ' If the ministration of death in the letter'—it being in this respect alone that the apostle is going to speak of it ; to speak, that is, of the Decalogue in its naked terms and isolated position, as contemplated by a spirit utterly opposed to the Gospel—the spirit of Rabbinism already described. The law itself, so contemplated, is called a ministration of death, because, in its native tendency and operation, certain to prove the occasion of death ; and there can be little doubt that it was from overlooking the peculiar or qualified sense in which the apostle thus spake of the law, that some copyists substituted the plural for the singular, and, instead of ' ministration of death in the letter,' took the meaning to be ' ministration of death engraved in letters'—leaving the subsequent expression, ' in stones' (λίθοις), as a mere appendage to

---

[1] Here there is a diversity in the copies, which are about equally divided between the singular and the plural form of the word : B D F G exhibit γράμματι, and ℵ A C E K L γράμμασιν, the latter outweighing the others somewhat in number, but not much in authority, as the last three (E K L) belong to the ninth century ; and the natural tendency was to change from γράμματι to γράμμασι, as affording a more obvious sense when coupled with ἐντετυπωμένη, since it would hardly do to say of the ten commandments, ' engraven in letter,' while ' engraven in letters' was quite simple. Hence also, in D, while at first hand it presents γράμματι, afterwards has this changed into the plural ; and, both in its later form, and in E K L, ἐν is inserted before λίθοις, to help out the sense, which had been injured by joining ἐντετυπωμένη to ἐν γράμμασιν. This also accounts for the versions following this later form. But the whole has arisen from adopting an obvious and superficial, in preference to the real and only proper sense. It is of a revelation, not in letters, but in *the letter* that the apostle is speaking throughout, and the change to the plural here brings confusion into the whole passage. Lachmann and also Alford adopt γράμματι.

the engraving. The change was altogether unhappy; for, first, it loses sight of that which renders the law a ministration of death—namely, its being viewed merely in the letter—and then the sense is weakened by a needless redundancy about the engraving : engraved in letters ! how could it be engraved otherwise, if engraved at all ! This was to be understood of itself, and adds nothing to the import; but the engraving in stones does add something, for it was the distinctive peculiarity of the ten commandments to be so engraved, as compared with the other parts of the Mosaic legislation. We therefore get the proper sense only by reading, ' If the ministration of death in the letter, engraven on stones, came in glory.' To speak of a ministration being engraven sounds somewhat strange ; but it is to be understood as a pregnant expression for, ' the law as ministered by Moses being engraven.' And when said to have come in glory (ἐγενήθη ἐν δόξη), the meaning more fully expressed is, came into existence in glory, had its introduction so among the covenant-people. What sort of glory is meant, the apostle, before going further, explains by pointing specifically to the radiance which shone from the face of Moses when he returned from the mount with the two tables of the covenant, and which, though not actually the whole, might yet justly be regarded as the symbol of the whole, of that glory which accompanied the formal revelation of law. This glory was such that ' the children of Israel were not able steadfastly to look on the face of Moses, because of the glory of his face [though a glory that was] to vanish away.' The corresponding statement in the history is, that when ' Aaron and all the children of Israel saw Moses, behold, the skin of his face shone ; and they were afraid to come nigh him.'[1] Dazzled with the supernatural appearance, it seemed to them as if something of the majesty of Heaven now rested upon Moses, and they durst not approach to fix their eyes intently on the sight—though still the glory was but transient. The original record does not directly state this, but plainly enough implies it, as it associates the shining of Moses' face only with his descent from the mount, and afterwards with his coming out from the Lord's presence in the tabernacle : the children of Israel, it is said, saw it then, but not, we naturally infer, at other times—the shining gradually vanished away, till brightened up afresh by renewed intercourse with Heaven. The train of thought, then, in this case, is, that the law written upon tables of stone, which was the more special and fundamental part of the legislation brought in by Moses, was, when taken apart and viewed as a scheme of moral obligation, a ministration of death, because,

---

[1] Ex. xxxiv. 30.

while requiring only what was good, requiring what man could not perform; that still there was a glory connected with it as the revelation of God's mind and will—a glory partly expressed, partly symbolized, by the radiance that occasionally shone from the face of Moses, dazzling and affrighting the Israelites, but, at the same time, a glory which was not abiding, one that, after a little, again disappeared.

Ver. 8. Having stated this respecting the glory of the law, which formed, in the sense explained, a ministration of death, the apostle asks, ' How shall not rather the ministration of the Spirit be in glory?' Why does he not say, the ministration of *life*, which would have been the more exact counterpart to the ministration of *death?* The chief reason probably was, that this might have created a false impression: a ministration of law taken in the letter, or simply by itself, can be nothing else for fallen man than a ministration of death; but there is no ministration in New Testament times which, with like regularity and certainty, carries life in its train. No doubt, if *spirit* here were to be understood directly and simply of the Holy Spirit (as Chrysostom, ' He no longer puts what is of the Spirit, viz., life and righteousness, ἀλλ' αὐτὸ τὸ πνεῦμα, but the Spirit itself, which makes the word greater'), it might well enough be held to involve life—life would be its inseparable accompaniment, as death of unmitigated law; for in so far as the Spirit ministers, the result can only be in life and blessing. But the apostle could not thus identify his apostolic agency with the third person of the Godhead, and call it absolutely a ministration or service (διακονία) of the Holy Ghost—as if ministration of the Spirit were all one with dispensation of the Spirit. In popular language they are often so confounded, but not in Scripture; and the expression in Gal. iii. 5, ' He who ministereth (ἐπιχορηγῶν) to you the Spirit,' points not to the apostle as a minister of the new covenant, but to God or Christ: it is He alone who can minister, in the sense of bestowing, the Holy Spirit. The ministration or service here meant is undoubtedly the evangelical ministry of the apostles and their followers—the teaching-function of the Gospel, as Meyer terms it, and called, he thinks, the ministration of the Spirit, because it is ' the service which mediates the Holy Spirit.' Strictly speaking, it is a ministration of word and ordinance, but such as carries along with it, in a quite peculiar degree as compared with former times, the regenerative, life-giving power of spiritual influence (the working of the Holy Ghost); and, named from this as its most distinctive feature, it is characterized as the ministration of the Spirit—much as a man is often called a soul, because it is from that more especially he derives what gives him his place and being in

2 COR. III. 2-18.

creation:—the Spirit, therefore, not hypostatically considered, but as a Divine power practically operative through word and ordinance in bringing life and blessing to the soul.

Vers. 9, 10. 'For if the ministration of condemnation was in glory, much more does the ministration of righteousness abound in glory.' This is substantially a repetition of the same idea as that expressed in the immediately preceding passage—only with this difference, that the law in the letter is here presented in its condemnatory, instead of its killing, aspect—condemnatory, of course, not directly, or in its own proper nature, but incidentally, and as the result of men's inability to fulfil its requirements. Accordingly, on the other side, righteousness is exhibited as the counterpart brought in by the Gospel: what the one requires, and from not getting becomes an occasion of condemnation, the other, through the mediation and grace of Christ, actually provides. A far greater thing, assuredly—hence in connection with it a surpassing glory; such, the apostle adds in ver. 10, that the glory which had accompanied the one might be regarded as nothing in comparison of the other.

Ver. 11. A still further aspect of the subject is here presented, one derived from the relative place of the two ministrations in respect to stability or continuance: 'for if that which vanisheth away was in glory, much more is that which abideth in glory.' In this form of the comparison, reference is had to what had been already indicated in the mention of the new covenant, implying that, with the introduction of this, there was a superseding or vanishing away of what went before. The two tables —the law in the letter, which is all one with the service or ministration of Moses—formed the material of a covenant, which was intended to last only till the great things of redemption should come; when a new covenant, and along with that a new service or form of administration should be introduced, adapted to the progression made in the Divine economy. The former, therefore, being from its very nature transitory, could not possibly be so replete with glory as the other; the higher elements of glory must be with the ultimate and abiding.

Here properly ends the apostle's contrast between the ministration of letter, and the ministration of spirit—for what follows is rather an application of the views unfolded in the passage we have been considering, than any additional revelation of doctrine. From the pregnant brevity of the passage, and the peculiar style of representation adopted in it, mistaken notions have often been formed of the apostle's meaning—as if the contrast he presents were to be understood of the Old and New Testament dispensations generally, of all on the one side that was connected with the covenant of law for Israel, and what on the other is provided and accomplished for mankind in the Gospel of Christ. So understood, the passage becomes utterly irreconcilable both with the truth of things and with statements elsewhere made by the apostle himself. If the law as given by God, and intended to be used by the covenant people, was simply a service of condemnation and death, it could have had no proper glory connected with it, and Moses, instead, of being entitled to regard and honour as the mediator that introduced it, would have been the natural object of repugnance and aversion. If also the doing or vanishing away spoken of had respect to the law in its substance, as a revelation of moral truth and duty, where could be the essential oneness of God's moral character? and how could the apostle here assert that to be done away, the very thought of doing away with which he elsewhere rejects as an impiety? ' Do we then,' says he, ' make void ($\varkappa\alpha\tau\alpha\rho\gamma o\tilde{v}\mu\varepsilon\nu$, put away, abolish, the very word in ver. 11 here) the law through faith? God forbid, yea, we establish the law' ($i\sigma\tau\acute{\alpha}\nu o\mu\varepsilon\nu$, give it fixed and stable existence).[1] The apostle, we may be sure, could not involve himself in such inconsistencies, nor could he mean to speak so disparagingly of the revelation of law brought in by Moses, if viewed in its proper connection, and kept in the place designed for it by the lawgiver. Moses himself, also, is a witness against the view under consideration; for he expressly declared that, if the people hearkened to the voice of God, they should live, and that he set before them life as well as death, blessing as well as cursing.[2] But, certainly, he could not have said this, if he had had nothing to point to but the terms of a law, which required perfect love to God, and the love of one's neighbour as one's-self. This law branched out into the ten commandments, which were engraved on the tables of stone, and were by Moses ministered to the people at Sinai, taken apart and read in the letter of its requirements, could never be for fallen men the pathway to life, and could only, by reason of their frailty and corruption, be the occasion of more certain and hopeless perdition. And here lay the folly of so many of the Jews, and of some Judaizing teachers also in the Christian church, that they would thus take it apart, and would thus press it in the letter, as a thing by which life and salvation might be attained. It is against this that the apostle is here arguing. He is exposing the idea of Moses being taken for the revealer and minister of life through the law he introduced, and as such the author of a polity which was destined to perpetuity. No, he in effect says, Moses, as the in-bringer of the law, did but shew what constituted life,

---

[1] Rom. iii. 31.   [2] Ex. xix. 5, 6 ; Deut. xxx. 15-19.

but could not give it; he exhibited the pattern, and imposed the obligations of righteousness, but could not secure their realization; this was reserved for another and higher than he, who is the Life and the Light of men; therefore, only condemnation and death can come from understanding and teaching Moses in the letter—while still, his ministration of law, if considered as an ordinance of God, and with due regard to its place in the economy of Heaven—that is, in its relation to the antecedent covenant of promise, and its subservience to the higher ends of that covenant—has in it a depth, a spirituality and perpetual significance for the church, which constitute the elements of a real glory—a glory that was but faintly imaged by the supernatural brightness on the face of Moses. This is in truth what the apostle presently states, when shewing, as he proceeds to do, what the carnal Jews missed by their looking at the ministration of the old covenant merely in the letter, instead of finding in it, as they should have done, a preparation for the better things to come, and a stepping-stone to the higher form of administration which was to be brought in by Christ.

Ver. 12. 'Having then such hope, we use great boldness of speech.' He had said before, ver. 4, that he had such, or so great *confidence* toward God—on account of the grace and power which were made to accompany his ministrations; he knew and felt that he was owned by God in his work. Now, he says he has such *hope*—such, namely, as arises out of the surpassing greatness of the blessing and glory connected with the Gospel and its ministration of spirit, and this not passing away, but abiding and growing into an eternal fulness and sufficiency of both; so that hope, as well as confidence, here has its proper scope. And having it, he could be perfectly open and bold in his speech, as one who had nothing to conceal, who had nothing to gain by the ignorance or imperfect enlightenment of the people, who also needed to practise no reserve in his communications, because the great realities being come, the clear light was now shining, and the whole counsel of God lay open.

Ver. 13. 'And not'—he adds, as a negative confirmation of what he had just stated, and also as an introduction to the notice he is going to take of the culpable blindness and carnality of the Jews—'And not as Moses put a veil on his face (an elliptical form of expression for, and we do not put a veil on our face, or mode of manifestation, as Moses put a veil on his face), in order that the children of Israel might not steadfastly look to the end (or cessation) of that which was to be done away.' The fact only, as already noticed, is mentioned in the history of the transaction, that Moses put a veil over his face, but not the

purpose for which it was done—which is left to be inferred from the
nature of the act, and the circumstances that led to its being done.
Nor is it very distinctly indicated either here or in Exodus, whether the
veil was put on by Moses while he addressed the people, or after he
had done speaking with them.   The authorized version, at Exodus
xxxiv. 33, expresses the former view, 'And *till* Moses had done speaking with them, he put a veil on his face ;' but there is nothing in the
original corresponding to the *till;* it merely states that he finished
speaking with them, and put a veil on his face, which seems to imply,
regarding that first discourse at least, that the veiling was subsequent
to the speaking.   And so the ancient versions give it (Sept. ἐπειδὴ κατέ-
παυσε λαλῶν ἐπέθηκεν ἐπὶ τὸ πρόσωπον αὐτοῦ κάλυμμα ; Vul. *Impletisque
sermonibus posuit velamen super faciem suum*).   But as to the future, it is
merely said that Moses took the veil off when he went in to speak with
the Lord 'until he came out ;' and when he came out and spake, the
children of Israel perceived that his face shone :   'And he put the veil
upon his face again until he went in to speak with Him' (vers. 34, 35).
The natural impression, however, is, that the method adopted at first
was still followed (though Meyer still takes the other view), namely,
that Moses did not veil his countenance quite immediately when he
came out, but only after he had spoken what he received to say to the
people; and that the direct object of the veil was to conceal from the
view of the people the gradual waning and disappearance of the supernatural brightness of his skin.   But viewing this brightness as a symbol
of the Divine mission of Moses, the apostle ascribes to him a still further intention in the veiling of it—namely, that the children of Israel
might not, by the perception of its transience, be led to think of the
transitory nature of the service or ministration of Moses itself—for this,
I think with Meyer, whom Alford follows, must be held to be the natural
sense of the words, 'in order that they might not steadfastly look
(πρὸς τὸ μὴ ἀτενίσαι-πρὸς τὸ, with the infinitive always denoting the purpose in the mind of the actor),[1] to the end of that which was vanishing
away (transitory).'   The vanishing away or transitory (τοῦ καταργου-
μένου) here is a resumption of the same (τὸ καταργούμενον) in ver. 11 ; and
which, as we there explained, was the service of Moses as the bringer
in of objective, written law.   There was a glory connected with this,
indicated by the shining of his skin (the seal, in a manner, of his Divine
authority), but as the symbol of the glory was transient, so also was
the ministration itself ; and Moses, the apostle would have us to understand, was aware of this ; but lest the children of Israel should also

---

[1] Matt. v. 28, vi. 1, xiii. 30 ; Eph. vi. 11 ; 1 Thess. ii. 9, etc.

perceive it, and at the very time the service was introduced might begin to look forward to its cessation, he concealed from them the fact of the passing away of the external glory by drawing over it a veil.[1] Many commentators have rejected this view, because appearing to them to ascribe something derogatory, a kind of dissimulation, to Moses, as if, while legislating for the people, he wished to hide from them the provisional nature of that legislation, and its relation to the future coming and kingdom of the Messiah. But this is to extend the object of the concealment too far: what Moses did in respect to the veil, he doubtless did under the direction of God; and what is affirmed by the apostle concerning it is, that the service of Moses as the minister of law engraven on stones (with all, of course, that became connected with this), was to be thought of as *the* service which they were specially to regard and profit by, according to its proper intent, without needlessly forestalling the time when it should be superseded by another service or ministration, that of the Gospel. For the former was the kind of service meanwhile adapted to their circumstances; and to have shot, as it were, ahead of it, and fixed their eyes on the introduction of a higher service, would have but tended to weaken their regard to that under which they were placed, and rendered them less willing and anxious to obtain from it the benefits it was capable of yielding. But this did not imply that they were to be kept ignorant of a coming Messiah, or were not to know that a great rise was to take place in the manifestations of God's mind and will to men; for Moses himself gave no doubtful intimation of this,[2] and it was one of the leading objects of later prophets, to make still more distinct announcements on the subject, and foretell the greater glory of the dispensation which was to come. But even with these, a certain concealment or reserve was necessary; and though a mighty change was indicated as going to take place, and the passing away of the old covenant itself into another, which, in comparison of it, was called new, yet so carefully was the ministration of Moses guarded, and so strongly was its authority pressed during the time set for its administration, that one of the very last words of ancient prophecy to the members of the old covenant was, ' Remember the law of Moses my servant, which I commanded unto him in Horeb for all Israel, with the statutes and judgments.'[3]

[1] I take the concealing to be the whole that is indicated by the veil, as most indeed do. Alford would find also the idea of suspension or interruption; but this seems fanciful; for no ministry is perfectly continuous. St Paul's was liable to suspension as well as that of Moses.

[2] Deut. xviii. 15-18.   [3] Mal. iv. 4.

Ver. 14. At the same time, the language used by the apostle implies that this was not what should have been ; it was an imperfect state of things, and involved a measure of blame ; but the blame lay with the people, not with Moses.   He could not make use of such boldness of speech, regarding Divine things, as was now done by apostles and preachers of the Gospel ; he was even obliged to practise a kind of disguise, with the view of concealing the transitory nature of the ministration with which he was more peculiarly charged.   And this for the sake of the spiritual good of the people themselves ; because, considering their state of mind, more of insight in that particular direction might have turned to evil ; and the ultimate reason follows : ' But their understandings were hardened (νοήματα, *thoughts* = thinking powers, understandings).'   The connection is not, I conceive, that given by Stanley : ' Nay, so true is this, that not their eyes, but their thoughts were hardened and dulled '—substantially concurred in by Alford, who takes ἀλλά in the sense of *But also*, and regards it as introducing a further assertion of their ignorance or blindness—blindness in respect to things not purposely concealed from them, but which they might be said to see : such modes of connection are somewhat unnatural, and scarcely meet the requirements of the case ; for something is needed as a ground for what precedes as well as for what follows. I take it to be this : Moses practised the concealment and reserve in question, not as if it were what he himself wished, or thought abstractedly the best ; but he did so because the understandings of the people were hardened, they had little aptitude for spiritual things, perfectly free and open discourse was not suited to them.   And the apostle goes on to say, it was not peculiar to that generation to be so —it was a common characteristic of the covenant people (so Stephen also says [1]), ' for until this day the same veil remains at the reading of the old covenant (that is, the book or writings of the covenant), without having it unveiled (discovered) that it (viz., the old covenant) is vanished away in Christ.'   Such appears to be the most natural construction and rendering of this last clause—ἀνακαλυπτόμενον being taken as the nominative absolute, and the vanishing or being done away being viewed, in accordance with the use of the expression in the preceding context, as having respect, not to the veil, but to the old covenant, or the ministration of Moses.   Having been so used once and again, it manifestly could not, without very express warrant, be understood now of something entirely different.   It is not, therefore, as in our authorized version, the veil which is done away in Christ, but the old covenant ;

[1] Acts vii. 51.

and the evidence of the veil being still spiritually on the hearts of the Jews, the apostle means to say, consists in their not having it unveiled or discovered to them that the old does vanish away in Christ. This was a far more grievous sign of a hardened understanding in the Jews of the apostle's time, than the hardening spoken of in the time of Moses; for now the disguise or concealment regarding the cessation of the Mosaic service was purposely laid aside; the time of reformation had come; and not to see the end of that which was transitory, was to miss the grand design for which it had been given.

Vers. 15, 16. ' But unto this day, whenever Moses is read, a veil lies upon the heart.' This is merely to be regarded as an explanation of what was meant in the preceding sentence by the want of discernment, as to the cessation of the old covenant in Christ. It arose from a veil being, not upon Moses, or upon the book of the covenant (for the advance of the Divine dispensations had taken every thing of that sort out of the way), but upon their own heart. *There* was the real seat and cause of the blindness. ' But (adds the apostle) whenever it shall have turned to the Lord, the veil is taken away' (περιαιρεῖται, a different word from that in the preceding verse, and confining the application there made of καταργεῖται to the old covenant, not to the veil). There is a certain indefiniteness in the statement, and opinions differ concerning the subject of the turning—some taking it quite generally: when any one shall have done so; some supplying Moses as the symbol or representative of the old covenant: when application is made of this covenant to the Lord; others, and, indeed, a much greater number, understand Israel; with substantial correctness—though it seems better, with Meyer and Alford, to find the subject in the ' their heart' of the immediate context: when the heart of the people, whether individually or collectively, shall have turned to the Lord, then the veil as a matter of course is taken away, it drops off. The language undoubtedly bears respect to what is recorded of Moses when he went into God's presence—as often as he did so putting off the veil; but it cannot be taken for more than a mere allusion, as the actions themselves were materially different.

Ver. 17. ' Now the Lord is the Spirit.' This is undoubtedly the natural and proper construction, taking *spirit* for the predicate, not (as Chrysostom, Theodoret, and several moderns) *Lord;* and the apostle is to be understood as resuming the expression in the preceding verse, and connecting it with what had been said before of spirit; *q. d.*, Now the Lord, to whom the heart of Israel turns when converted, is the spirit which has been previously spoken of as standing in contrast to the letter, and the ministration of which has been given as the distinctive characteristic apostolic agency. By *spirit*, therefore, must here be understood, not the Holy Spirit hypostatically or personally considered—for in that case it could not have been so identified with the Lord (by whom is certainly meant Christ), nor would it properly accord with the sense of spirit, in verses 6 and 8—but the Spirit in His work of grace on the souls of men —or Christ Himself in His divine energy manifesting Himself through the truth of His Gospel to the heart and conscience, as the author of all spiritual life and blessing. So that it is the inseparable unity of Christ and the Spirit in the effect wrought by the ministration of word and ordinance, not their hypostatical diversity, which here comes into consideration : Christ present in power, present to enlighten and vivify,—*that*, as here understood by the apostle, is the Spirit (in contradistinction to the mere ' form of knowledge and of truth in the law ') ; ' but (the apostle adds—δὲ as the particle of transition from an axiom to its legitimate conclusion) where the Spirit of the Lord is, there is liberty '—not *there* in the local sense (for ἐκεῖ is wanting in the best authorities, א A B C D, also in the Syriac and Coptic versions, nor is its employment in such a manner quite in accordance with the usage of the apostle) ; but merely as, along with the substantive verb, declarative of a certain fact : the man who is spiritually conversant with Christ, who knows Him in the spirit of His grace and truth, there is for such an one a state of liberty— he is free to commune with Christ himself, and to deal with the realities of His work and kingdom, as at home in the region to which they belong, and possessing, in relation to them, the spirit of sonship.[1] Not merely is the hardened understanding gone which prevents one from seeing them aright, but a frame of mind is acquired, which is in fitting adaptation to them, relishing their light and breathing their spirit.

Ver. 18. A still further deduction follows, the climax of the whole passage, rising from the matter discoursed of to the persons in whom it is realized : ' but we all with unveiled face beholding in a mirror the glory of the Lord, are transformed into the same image from glory to glory, as from the Lord the Spirit.' The *but* at the beginning indicates a certain implied contrast to the state of others —the bondmen of the house of Israel, who knew not the Lord as the Spirit, and the spiritual liberty such knowledge brings, but it is otherwise with us. *We* all—that is, we who are Christians, not apostles merely, or Christian ministers and evangelists, for the expression is purposely made quite general, in order to comprehend, along with himself, the whole of those whose case the apostle is now

[1] Rom. viii. 15.

handling—' We all with unveiled face behold.' The last reference to the veil had represented it as being upon the heart of the Israelites ; for it was as *hearers* of the law that he then contemplated them ; but now, as it is in connection with the sight that he is going to unfold the privilege of New Testament believers, he returns to the thought of the face in relation to the veil—the face of Moses having been veiled, indeed, to the people, but unveiled in the presence of the Lord, whence it received impressions of the glory that shone upon it from above. So we all—after the manner of Moses, though in a higher, because more spiritual, sense, but unlike the people for whom the glory reflecting itself on his countenance was veiled—' behold in a mirror the glory of the Lord.' I adhere to this as the most natural and also the most suitable sense of the somewhat peculiar word κατοπτριζόμενοι, as opposed to that of ' reflecting as in a mirror,' adopted by Chrysostom, Luther, Calov, also by Olshausen and Stanley. There is no evidence of the word having been employed in this sense. In the active, it signifies to ' mirror,' or shew in a glass ; in the middle usually, to ' mirror one's-self,' or ' look at one's-self in a mirror,' of which examples may be seen in Wetstein on the passage, but which is manifestly out of place here ; and to turn the seeing one's-self in a mirror, into reflecting one's likeness from it, is to introduce an entirely new and unwarranted idea into the meaning. Nor could it, if allowable, afford an appropriate sense ; for the mention of the unveiled face undoubtedly presents a contrast to the representation in vers. 14-16, and has respect to the free, untrammelled seeing of the Divine glory. There is also in Philo one undoubted use of the word in this sense (' Leg. Allegor.,' III. 33, μηδὲ κατοπτρισαίμην ἐν ἄλλῳ τινὶ τὴν σὴν ἰδέαν ἢ ἐν σοί τῷ Θεῷ, neither would I see mirrored in any other, etc.) The plain meaning, therefore, is, ' We all with unveiled face (the veil having been removed in conversion) beholding in a mirror (or seeing mirrored) the glory of the Lord.' The apostle does not say where or how this mirrored glory is to be seen, but he supplies the deficiency in the next chapter, when at ver. 4 he speaks of the light, or rather ' shining forth of the Gospel of the glory of Christ' (which Satan prevents natural men from perceiving), and at ver. 6 (when speaking of the contrary result in the case of believers), he represents God as ' shining in their hearts to the illumination of the knowledge of the glory of God in the face of Jesus Christ.' The glory, therefore, in so far as it is now accessible to the view of believers, is to be seen mirrored in the face or person of Jesus Christ, or, as it is otherwise put, in the Gospel of the glory of Christ—that is, the Gospel which reveals what He is and has done, and thereby unfolds

His glory. This is now freely opened to the inspection of believers, and by beholding it with the eye of faith, ' we are transformed into the same image' (τὴν αὐτὴν εἰκόνα μεταμορφούμεθα, the accusative, according to some, to be explained as that of nearer determination ; but better, perhaps, with Bernhardy, Meyer, and others, to be regarded as expressive of the form implied in the action of the verb, and so indirectly governed by it ; but either way capable of being rendered into English only by the help of the preposition, ' transformed *into* the same image'), the image, namely, of Christ's glory seen in the mirror of His Gospel, the living impression of which on our hearts is all one with having Christ formed in them;[1] hence, a deeper change than that which passed upon the skin of Moses, and indicative of a more intimate connection with the Lord; for it is now heart with heart, one spiritual image reproducing itself in another. And this ' from glory to glory'—either from glory in the image seen, to glory in the effect produced, or rather perhaps from one stage in the glorious transformation to another, till coming at last to see Him as He is, we are made altogether like Him.[2] Very different, therefore, from an impression of glory, which was evanescent, always ready to lose its hold, and tending to vanish away. ' Even as (the apostle adds) from the Lord the Spirit'—so, I think, the words should be rendered with Chrysostom, Theodoret, Luther, Beza, and latterly Stanley, Alford, seeing in them the same kind of identification of Lord and Spirit as in ver. 17; not, with Fritzsche, Olshausen, De Wette, Meyer, ' from the Lord of the Spirit,' which would introduce at the close a new idea, and one not very much to the purpose here, for, in the only sense in which the expression can be allowed, the Lord has ever been the Lord of the Spirit—as much in Old Testament times as now. The English version, ' from the Spirit of the Lord,' is inadmissible, as doing violence to the order of the words. The meaning of the apostle in this closing sentence is, that the result is in accordance with the Divine agency accomplishing it—it is such as comes from the operation of Him who makes Himself known and felt through the vital energy of the Spirit—whose working is Spirit upon spirit—therefore penetrating, inward, powerful—seizing the very springs of thought and feeling in the soul, and bringing them under the habitual influence of the truth as it is in Christ. This is a mode of working far superior to that of outward law, because in its very nature quickening, dealing directly with the conscience, and with the idea of spiritual excellence, giving also the power to realize it in the heart and conduct.

[1] Gal. iv. 19.   [2] 1 John iii. 3.

GAL. II. 14-21.

' But when I saw that they were not walking uprightly, according to the truth of the Gospel, I said to Cephas in the presence of all, If thou, being a Jew, livest after the manner of the Gentiles, why constrainest thou the Gentiles to live as do the Jews? 15. We by nature Jews, and not sinners of the Gentiles, 16. Knowing, however, that a man is not justified by the works of the law, [not justified] except through the faith of Jesus Christ, we also put our faith in Christ Jesus, that we might be justified out of the faith of Christ, and not out of the works of the law, because by the works of the law shall no flesh be justified. 17. But if, while seeking to be justified in Christ, we ourselves also were found to be sinners, is Christ therefore a minister of sin? God forbid. 18. For if the things which I pulled down, these I again build up, I prove myself to be a transgressor. 19. For I through the law died to the law, in order that I might live to God. 20. I have been crucified with Christ; but no longer I that live, but Christ liveth in me; and that which I now live in the flesh I live in faith—that [namely] of the Son of God, who loved me and gave Himself for me. 21. I do not make void the grace of God; for if righteousness [come] through the law, then Christ died without cause.'

There is not much of difficulty in this passage considered exegetically, nor will it call here for any lengthened exposition; but it is of importance as being, in point of time, the first recorded statement of a mode of representation by the apostle, respecting the relation of believers to the law, which was afterwards more than once repeated, and with greater fulness brought out. The historical occasion of it, as related in the preceding verses, was the vacillating conduct of Peter during a temporary sojourn at Antioch, of uncertain date, but probably not long after the council which met at Jerusalem concerning circumcision.[1] At first he mingled freely with Gentile believers, in food as well as other things, in token that all legal distinctions in this respect were abolished; but on the arrival of some of the stricter party of Jewish Christians from Jerusalem, he again withdrew, as afraid to offend their religious scruples and meet their censure. For this he was generally condemned (καταγνωσμένος ἦν, ver. 11); and St Paul, with Christian fidelity, brought the charge distinctly against him, and, in the verses just cited, shewed how fitted his conduct was to prejudice the truth of the Gospel.

In this he, first of all, points to what, by their very position as

[1] Acts xv.

Christians, they had acknowledged as to the way of salvation—that they had attained to it, not by what properly belonged to them as Jews, but by having become believers in Christ. By assuming even for a time the Gentile mode of life, assuming it as a thing in itself perfectly proper and legitimate for a Christian, Peter had confessed that salvation had come to him otherwise than by conformity to the Jewish law; and how, then, asks Paul, 'dost thou constrain the Gentiles to live as do the Jews?' (literally, to Judaize). He uses a strong expression—ἀναγκάζεις, constrain—to indicate the moral force which the conduct of one so high in authority as Peter was sure to carry along with it. With many it would have the weight of a Divine sanction—while yet, as he goes on to shew, it was in the very face of their Christian profession and hope: ' We by nature Jews, and not sinners of the Gentiles '—that is, not sinners after such an extreme type, the expression being used much as in the phrase ' publicans and sinners ' in the Gospels; their birth within the bonds of the covenant had saved them from such a state of degradation. ' Knowing, however (such plainly is the force of δέ here, introducing something of a qualifying nature, materially different, though not strictly opposite, Winer, sec. 53, b), that a man is not justified by the works of the law, except (ἐὰν μή, the two particles, have no other sense, but, as εἰ μή in Matt. xii. 4, Rev. ix. 4, perhaps also Gal. i. 19, refer only to the predicate in the preceding clause, which must be again supplied, ' not justified except') through the faith of Jesus Christ, we also put our faith in Christ Jesus, that we might be justified.' The meaning is, that though they were not sinners like the Gentiles, still they were sinners, and as such conscious of the impossibility of being justified with God on the ground of any works of law; hence had sought their justification by simply believing in Christ. By the works of the law here, as at Rom. iii. 20, and elsewhere in Paul's writings, are undoubtedly to be understood the works required generally by the law of the old covenant—not ceremonial as contradistinguished from moral, nor moral as contradistinguished from ceremonial—but whatever of one kind or another it imposed in the form of precept—the law, in short, as a rule of right and wrong laid in its full compass upon the consciences of men; but pre-eminently, of course, the law of the ten commandments which lay at the heart of the whole, and was, so to speak, its pervading root and spirit. By deeds of conformity to this law they knew they could not be justified, because they had not kept it; they could be justified only through the faith of Jesus Christ. The apostle purposely varies the prepositions—not ἐξ ἔργων, out of works as the ground, or formal cause of justification, but διὰ πίστεως, through faith, as the instrument or medium by which it is accepted.   Coming through faith, it is acknowledged and received as God's gift in Christ, whereas, had it been of works of law, it had possessed the character of a right or claim.   In the closing part of the passage, however, he uses the same preposition in respect to both modes of justification: ' that we might be justified out of (ἐκ) the faith of Christ, not out of the works of the law.'   The words resume, with a personal application to Peter and Paul, what had just been affirmed of men at large; they knew the general truth, and for themselves had sought justification in this way—the *out of* or *from* being here put in both cases alike, either as a formal variation, or rather perhaps because faith and works are contemplated merely as the diverse quarters from whence the justification might be looked for.   And the reason of their seeking it simply of faith follows, ' because by the works of the law shall no flesh be justified.'   Neither here, nor at Rom. iii. 20, where it is again repeated, is this weighty utterance given as a quotation from Old Testament Scripture—though substantially it is so, being to a nearness the words of the Psalmist,[1] ' For in thy sight shall no man living be justified;' and there can be little doubt, that the apostle uses it in both places as a word which all who knew Scripture would readily acknowledge and acquiesce in.   The no flesh (οὐ . . . πᾶσα σάρξ) in the one passage is, according to a common Hebrew usage,[2] substantially equivalent to the no one living (οὐ . . . πᾶς ζῶν) of the other.   So that here we have the great truth of the Gospel as to the way of salvation announced both in its positive and its negative form: through faith because of grace—not of works of law, because then necessarily on the ground of merit, which no one, be he Jew or Gentile, possesses before God.

Ver. 17. The apostle now proceeds to draw a conclusion from the preceding, taken in connection with what was involved in the inconsistent conduct of Peter : ' But if, while seeking to be justified in Christ (ἐν Χριστῷ, to be taken strictly, in mystical union with Him, as the ground or element into which faith brings us), we ourselves also were found to be sinners (that is, found still to be such; the fact of our seeking justification in Christ implied that we knew ourselves to be sinners prior to our coming to Him; but if still found to be so, and therefore failing—as your conduct would seem to betoken—to get justification, left as before in the condition of sinners, and needing to resort again for a ground of justification to works of law), is Christ therefore a minister of sin?'   Is this really the character in which we contemplate Him, and are going to present Him to the view of men?   Such appears to be the natural sense of the words, and the train of

---

[1] Ps. cxliii. 2.   [2] Gen. vi. 12 ; Num. xvi. 22 ; Ps. lxv. 2 ; Isa. xii. 5, etc.

thought they suggest.   The apostle brings out, with a kind of ironical
surprise in the mode of doing it, what was fairly involved in Peter's
behaviour, and would be its inevitable impression upon others ; namely,
that having gone as a sinner to Christ for justification, and still finding
himself in the condition of a sinner, he had fallen back again upon
observances of law for what was needed.   Could Christ possibly in
such a way be a minister of sin? for, if failing thus to remove its
guilt, in the behalf of those who trusted in Him, He necessarily
ministered to its interests.   The question is indignantly answered by
the apostle, 'God forbid:'—the thought is abhorrent, and nothing
must be done which would tend in the least degree to countenance
such an idea.   The expression (μὴ γένοιτο), as used by the apostle,
always imports this, and is always, too, preceded by a question; so
that the ἄρα of the received text is rightly accented, and must be taken
interrogatively.   In substance, the view now given is concurred in by
the best recent commentators—Meyer, Alford, Ellicott, Lightfoot, and
indeed by the great majority of commentators of every age, with only
such minor shades of difference as do not affect the main ideas.

Ver. 18. In this verse the apostle confirms what was involved in the
denial (μὴ γένοιτο) in respect to Christ, and shews where the real
ministration of sin in such a case lies : ' For if the things which I
pulled down, these I again build up, I prove myself to be a transgressor.'
It is Peter's doing that is actually described, but out of delicacy Paul
speaks in his own name.   In repairing to Christ, he virtually pulled
down the fabric of law as the ground of justification (formally did so,
under the Divine direction, in the house of Cornelius) ; but in now
returning to its observance as a matter of principle, he was again
building it up ; and in this he proved himself to be a transgressor—
but how?   Was it merely by the inconsistency of his conduct, which,
if right in the first instance, must have been wrong in the second?
Or, if right in the building up, involved his condemnation for previously
pulling down?   This is all that some commentators find in it (among
whom are Alford and Lightfoot), and who regard the act of transgression as chiefly consisting in the previous pulling down—that is,
deemed to be such by the person himself, as proved in his again
attempting to build up.   This seems to be an inadequate view of the
matter, and to fix the idea of transgression on the wrong point—on the
pulling down instead of, as the context requires, on the building up
again ; it would make the proving or constituting of the person a
transgressor turn on his own mistaken view of the law, not on the
relation in which he actually stood to the law.   The conduct in ques-

tion, however, was plainly chargeable as an act of transgression under two aspects—one more general, and another more specific: first, such vacillation, playing fast and loose, in so palpable a manner, with the things of God, was itself a grave error, a serious moral obliquity; and secondly, in the retrogression complained of, there was involved a misapprehension of or departure from the very aim of the law, which was (considered in its preparatory aspect) to lead men to Christ. The law was not given to form the ground of men's justification, but to make them see that another ground was needed; and, after this had come, to return again to the other was, in a most important particular, to defeat the intention of the law, to act toward it the part of a transgressor. That this last idea was also in the view of the apostle may be inferred, not only from the nature of the case, but also from what immediately follows, in which this very idea respecting the law is brought prominently into view.

Ver. 19. 'For I through the law died to the law, in order that I might live to God'—the emphatic position of the ἐγὼ at the commencement is evidently intended to individualize very particularly the speaker, 'I for myself;' it is Paul's own experience that he relates, and relates for the purpose of shewing how the law, when rightly apprehended, recoils as it were upon itself, renders an escape from its dominion necessary for the sinner. And the proof contained in this declaration, for the purpose more immediately in hand, lies, as noted by Meyer, specially in the result being said to have been reached διὰ νόμου; 'for he who through the law has been delivered from the law, in order that he might stand in a higher relation, and again falls back into the legal relation, acts against the law.' There can be no reasonable doubt, that the law through which the death is accomplished, is the same as that to which the death is represented as taking place—not, as Jerome, Ambrose, Erasmus, Luther, Bengel, etc., the Gospel law, the law of the spirit of life in Christ in the one case, and the Mosaic law in the other; for even if it were admissible to take the term *law* in such different senses, the point of the apostle's argument would be lost. It was the law itself in its accusing, condemning power upon his conscience, which made him die to it as a ground of justification and hope; so that it was in the interest of the law that he died to it (νόμῳ ἀπέθανον, dat. *commodi*),[1] the object and result being that he might live to God. It is the same thought which, at greater length, is unfolded, also in connection with Paul's own experience, in Rom. vii. But the process is briefly indicated also here, in what follows.

[1] *See* Ellicott here, and Fritzsche on Rom. xiv. 7.

Ver. 20. ' I have been crucified with Christ'—συνεσταύρωμαι, the perfect, pointing therefore to the past, but extending also to the present time, and so may be understood indifferently of the one or the other. It gives the explanation of his death to the law without defeating, but rather promoting the law's interests. Realizing that through sin he had fallen under the curse of the law, and that Christ died to bear its curse for them that believe on Him, he entered in the spirit of faith into Christ's death, and became partaker in the benefits of His crucifixion. As put by Chrysostom, ' When he said *I died*, lest any one should say, How then dost thou live ? he subjoined also the cause of his life, and showed that the law, indeed, killed him when living, but that Christ taking hold of him when dead quickened him through death ; and he exhibits a double wonder, both that He (Christ) had recalled the dead to life, and through death had imparted life.' This higher kind of life, growing out of his fellowship with Christ's crucifixion, the apostle describes as one not properly his own, not belonging to his natural self, but flowing into him from Christ his living Head. It is difficult to render his words here, so as to give them the precise point and meaning of the original. The authorized version, adopting a punctuation formerly common (ζῶ δὲ· οὐκέτι ἐγὼ, ζῇ δὲ ἐν ἐμοὶ Χρ.), translates, ' Nevertheless I live, yet not I but Christ liveth in me,'—which, however, would have required an ἀλλά before οὐκέτι, and is now, therefore, wisely abandoned. The apostle assumes that his crucifixion with Christ was, as in Christ's case, but the channel to a higher life, and so he does not simply tell us that he lives, but whence he has the source and power of life : ' I have been crucified with Christ ; but no longer is it I who live (or, a little more paraphrastically, thus : but as for living, it is no longer I that do so), but Christ liveth in me.' It is the appropriation of Christ's own words : ' I am the living bread that came down from heaven ; if any man eat of this bread he shall live for ever ; and the bread that I will give is my flesh, which I will give for the life of the world.' ' As the living Father hath sent me, and I live by the Father, so he that eateth me, even he shall live by me ;'[1] it is expressed also by others of the apostles, as by John,—' He that hath the Son hath life.'[2] Christ dwelling by faith in the heart has become the principle of a new life—a life hid with him in God, from which, as an inexhaustible fountain-head, the believer ever draws to the supply of his wants and his fruitfulness in well-doing. And so, the apostle adds, ' that which I now live in the flesh (so far, that is, as I now live in the flesh) I live in faith—that of the Son of God who loved me and gave Himself for me.'

[1] John vi. 51-57.   [2] 1 John v. 12 ; compare 1 Pet. i. 2, 3.

What he now regards as his life in the flesh, what properly distinguishes and makes it what it is, is its being in the faith of Christ, finding in such faith its proper element, and being thereby kept in perpetual fellowship with the fulness of life and blessing that is in Him. And recognising again the great truth, that it was as the dying and atoning Saviour that Jesus thus became the new source of life for mankind, he allows his faith to run out into the touching expression of appropriating confidence, ' who loved me and gave Himself for me.'

Ver. 21. ' I do not make void (ἀθετῶ, set at nought, or rather, render nought) the grace of God,'—namely, as manifested in the gift and death of Christ, for our deliverance from sin and justification by faith in His blood ; then follows the reason, ' for if righteousness [come] through the law (through this, that is, as the ground or medium of attaining to justification), then Christ died without cause :' not in vain, or to no effect (for δωρεὰν never bears that sense, but always that of the Latin gratis), though this too might have been said ; but the exact meaning is, there would have been no occasion for his death, or, as Chrysostom expresses it, the death of Christ would have been superfluous (περιττὸς ὁ τοῦ Χριστοῦ θάνατος). Thus ends the argumentation, which throughout magnifies the grace of God in the salvation of men through the sacrificial death and risen life of Christ, and depreciates, in comparison of it, works of law—but depreciates them simply on the ground that they are, in the proper sense, unattainable by fallen man—that the law's requirements of holiness only reveal man's sin and ensure his condemnation—and that, consequently, obedience to these can never be made the ground of a sinner's confidence and hope toward God, but to his own shame and confusion.

GAL. III. 19-26.

Ver. 19. Τί οὖν ὁ νόμος ; etc. ' Wherefore, then, the law ? It was added because of the transgressions, until the seed shall have come to whom the promise has been made, being appointed through angels in the hand of a mediator. 20. Now a mediator is not of one ; but God is one. 21. Is the law then against the promises of God ? God forbid ! For if a law were given which could have given life, verily righteousness should have been of the law. 22. But, on the contrary, the Scripture shut up all under sin, in order that the promise by faith of Jesus Christ might be given to them that believe. 23. But before the faith came we were kept in ward, shut up under the law for the faith which was going to be revealed. 24. So that the law has become our pedagogue in respect to Christ, in order that we might be justified by faith.   25. But now that the faith has come, we are no longer under a pedagogue.   26. For ye are all sons of God through the faith in Christ Jesus.'

This section respecting the law comes in as a natural sequel to the line of argumentation which had been pursued by the apostle from the beginning of the chapter.   In that his object was to prove that salvation or blessing was now, and had always been, of promise—of promise as unfolding the free grace of God to sinful men, and by them apprehended and rested on in faith ; it had been so in the case of Abraham hundreds of years before the law was given at Sinai—nor for Abraham as an individual merely, but as the head of a family, of Gentile as well as of Jewish origin, who were all destined along with himself, and in the same manner, to receive the blessing ; and the law, which came so long after, could not by possibility disannul the provisions thus secured by promise to the believing ; least of all could they be secured by the law, which carries with it a curse to as many as are under its dominion, because they have all violated its precepts (v. 10, 11).   But if the promise did so much, it might seem as if the law were disparaged ; hence the question that follows.

Ver. 19. ' Wherefore then the law ? '   Literally, ' What then the law ? ' viz., What does it do ?   What is its place and object ?   The τί, therefore, may be taken in its usual sense, and the passage regarded as elliptical ; but, as to the import, it is all one as if it were put for διὰ τί, *wherefore*.   The answer is, ' It was added because of the transgressions'—τῶν παραβάσεων χάριν.   Does this mean *in their interest, for their sake ?*   So Hilgenfeld, Meyer, Jowett, Alford, Lightfoot (Meyer, ' It was added in favour, *zu Gunsten*, of transgressions ;' Lightfoot, still more strongly, ' to create transgressions').   But to this view, Ellicott justly objects, that ' it ascribes a purpose [viz., in respect to the existence of transgressions] directly to God ;' it would imply not the fact merely, that by means of the law, and, as Paul elsewhere states, by reason of the weakness or perversity of the flesh,[1] transgressions were multiplied, but that the production of these was one of the purposes for which it was given—which seems to come very near making God the intentional author of sin.   Alford explains, that St Paul is here treating of the law in its propaedeutic office, as tending to prepare the way for Christ, and says that this office consisted in ' making sin into transgression, so that what was before not a transgression might now become one'—surely a somewhat arbitrary distinction, as if sin

---

[1] Rom. vii. 5, 8, viii. 3.

(ἁμαρτία) and transgression (παράβασις) differed materially from each other, and what were the one might not also be the other. Neither Paul's writings generally, nor the statements in this particular section, afford any ground for such a distinction; for what is here called *transgression*, and as such is associated with the law, is presently called sin (ver. 22), as it is also elsewhere.[1] And the apostle John expressly identifies sin and transgression: ' He that committeth sin, transgresseth also the law (τὴν ἀνομίαν ποιεῖ, does lawlessness, violation of law=transgression); for sin is transgression' (violation of law).[2] To speak of the law as creating either sin or transgression, is to present moral evil as something arbitrary or factitious; consequently something that might, and, but for the creative power of formal law, should, not have come into existence. The earliest extant interpretation, the one adopted by the Greek commentators, and by the Fathers generally, takes the expression of the apostle in a quite opposite sense, that the law was added for the purpose of preventing or restraining the spirit of transgression. Thus Chrysostom, ' The law was given because of transgressions; that is, that the Jews might not be allowed to live without check, and glide into the extreme of wickedness, but that the law might be laid on them like a bridle, disciplining, moulding them, restraining them from transgression, if not in regard to all, yet certainly in regard to some of the commandments; so that no small profit accrues from the law.' To the same effect Jerome, ' Lex transgressiones prohibitura successit,' referring to 1 Tim. i. 9; also Occum. Theoph., with a great multitude of modern commentators—Erasmus, Grotius, Morus, Rosenmuller, Olshausen, De Wette, etc. This view, however, is rejected by recent scholars, as attributing to χάριν a sense which is without support—a kind of practically reversed meaning of the natural one—importing, not in favour, but in contravention of, opposed to. It is further alleged, that the sense thus yielded, if it were grammatically tenable, would not suit the connection; as the apostle's object in the whole of this part of the epistle is to shew, not what benefit might be derived from the law in the conflict with sin, but rather what power sin derives from the law. There is, undoubtedly, force in both of these objections—though, in regard to the former, the readiness and unanimity with which the Greek expositors ascribed such an import to χάριν, may fairly be taken to indicate, that the sense was not altogether strange to them, and, if rarely found in written compositions, may have been not unknown in colloquial usage. But it appears better, with Ellicott and others, to take χάριν in the

---

[1] Rom. v. 13, 20, vii. 7, etc. [2] 1 John iii. 4.

somewhat general sense of *propter, causa, on account of*—a sense it un-questionably bears.[1] The sense of the passage will then be, the law was given on account of the proneness of the people to transgress; pointing merely to the fact, but with a certain implication in the very manner of expression, that the evil would not thereby be cured, that transgressions would become but the more conspicuous. For the law of itself could not repress the tendency, or diminish the number of transgressions; on the contrary, its tendency was to render them both more palpable and more aggravated—while still, if contemplated and used according to the design of God, as an handmaid to the covenant of promise, it would have helped most effectually to promote the cause of holiness, and consequently to repress and limit the manifestation of sin. But the apostle is here viewing it, as the Jews of his day generally viewed it, and as the Judaizing teachers in Galatia were evidently doing, in its separate character and working—as a great institute commanding one class of things to be done, and the opposite class not to be done—an institute, therefore, taking to do with transgressions, on account of which it actually came into being, but which it served rather to expose and bring to light, than to put down. Thus the law was given on account of transgressions.

And the apostle subjoins a definition of the period up to which the law in this objective and covenant form was to continue : 'until the seed shall have come to whom the promise has been made'—the form of the sentence to be explained from the circumstance, that the apostle puts himself in the position of one at the giving of the law, and from that as his starting-point looks forward to the moment in the future, when the seed shall have appeared in whom the promise was to reach its fulfilment. The meaning is, that while the covenant of promise was in a provisional state, travelling on to its accomplishment, the law was needed and was given as an outstanding revelation; but when the more perfect state of things pointed to in the promise entered, the other would cease to occupy the place which had previously belonged to it. A clause of some difficulty is added as to the spiritual agencies entrusted with its introduction, ' being ordained through angels (ordered or enjoined through the medium of angels), in the hand of a mediator.' Very much the same thought is expressed by Stephen on his trial, when he says the Israelites received the law εἰς διαταγὰς ἀγγέλων, at the ordination (according to the arrangements) of angels; and again in Heb. ii. 2, where the law is characterized as ' the word spoken by angels.' It is rather singular that in these passages such prominence

<hr>

[1] *See* Liddell and Scott, Rost and Palm, on the word.

should have been given to the ministration of angels at the giving of the law, while in the history no notice is taken of them, nor any allusion even to the presence of angels in connection with the law, except the passing one in the blessing of Moses on the tribes: 'The Lord came from Sinai, and rose up from Seir unto them; He shined forth from mount Paran, and He came with ten thousands of saints (literally, from amid myriads of holiness); from His right hand went a fiery law for them.'[1] The presence of myriads at the giving of the law is referred to also in Ps. lxviii. 17; and their mediating agency is more distinctly expressed by Josephus (ἡμῶν δὲ τὰ κάλλιστα τῶν δογμάτων καὶ ὁσιώτατα τῶν ἐν τοῖς νόμοις δι᾽ ἀγγέλων παρὰ τοῦ Θεοῦ μαθόντων, Ant. V. 5, sec. 3), and by Philo ('De Somn.,' p. 642, M.). But how this change in the mode of representation came about, or what might be its precise object, we are unable to say. The passages in Old Testament Scripture referred to, speak merely of the presence of angelic hosts as attendants on the Lord at Sinai, but say nothing of their active service in communicating the law to Moses; throughout Old Testament Scripture it is simply from the Lord that Moses is said to have received the law; and the introduction of an angelic ministry as mediating between the two, could scarcely have been thought of for the purpose of enhancing the glory of the law, since it appeared to remove this a step farther from its Divine source. Accordingly, in the Epistle to the Hebrews, the ministration through angels is regarded as a mark of relative inferiority, when compared with the direct teaching of the Lord Jesus Christ; but when not so compared, as in the speech of Stephen, or in the passages of Philo and Josephus, it is fitly enough associated with the ideas of peculiar majesty and sacredness. Here, I am inclined to think with Meyer and Alford, that the mention of angels cannot justly be understood in a depreciatory sense; for the covenant of promise itself, as established with Abraham, which is the more immediate object of comparison with the law, was also connected with angelic administration—more expressly so connected than the giving of the law.[2] The fact alone of an angelic medium is stated by the apostle, as a matter generally known and believed—though how it should have been worked into the beliefs of the people, while Old Testament Scripture is so silent upon the subject, we have no specific information; all we can say is, that it had come somehow to be understood. As to the mediator, in whose hands the law was established at Sinai, there can be no reasonable doubt that Moses was meant; he literally bore in his hand to the people, from the mount, the tables that contained its fundamental

[1] Deut. xxxiii. 2. [2] Gen. xxii. 11.

principles.[1] Philo and the Rabbinical Jews so regarded Moses;[2] the Fathers (Basil and Theodoret excepted) mistook the meaning of the apostle when, under mediator, they understood him to point to Christ; and they are followed by several modern interpreters of note—Calvin, Pareus, Calov, etc. But the other view is so much the more natural one, and is now so generally acquiesced in, that there is no need for enlarging on it. In the mention of a mediator, however, I see no ground for discovering (with Ellicott) an intentional note of inferiority in the law as compared with the covenant of promise. A mark of difference it certainly formed, but we have no reason to think of any thing more.

Ver. 20. This point of difference is here more distinctly exhibited: 'Now a mediator is not of one; but God is one.' The passage is somewhat famous for the variety of interpretations to which it has given rise.[3] A very considerable number, however, are manifestly fanciful and arbitrary; and among recent commentators of note there has been a substantial agreement in regard to the leading thoughts presented in the words, a difference chiefly discovering itself in the application. 'A mediator is not of one'—a general proposition; the office from its very nature bespeaks more than one party, between whom it is the part of the mediator to negotiate—hence (though this is left to be inferred, suggested rather than indicated), involving a certain contingency as to the fulfilment of the contract, since this depends upon the fidelity of both parties engaging in it. 'But God is one,'—the God, namely, who gave to Abraham the promise; He gave it of His own free and sovereign goodness, therefore it depends for its fulfilment

---

[1] Ex. xxxi. 18, xxxii. 15.   [2] *See* Schöttgen and Wetstein here.

[3] This circumstance, however, has been very loosely stated, and in a way fitted to produce erroneous impressions. Ellicott notes that it is said to have received interpretations 'which positively exceed 400.' Jowett is more explicit, and affirms, 'It has received 430 interpretations;' but in what sense or on what authority nothing is indicated. Lightfoot, however, is more moderate, and speaks of only 250 or 300 ; but he, equally with the others, conveys the impression that the interpretations all differ from each other, which is by no means the case. It is apparently a remark of Winer, in his Excursus on the passage, which has occasioned this manner of speech. He says that some had set forth, in separate publications, varias et antiquorum et recentiorum theologorum explicationes (ducentae fere sunt et quinquaginta); and he refers in a note particularly to a person of the name of Keil who had done so, and Weigaud, who had brought together 243 interpretations. But these various expositions were not all different ; there were so many interpreters, but nothing like so many interpretations. Winer himself coincides with Keil; and among English interpreters, a great many are substantially agreed. If the same mode were adopted with other passages, there is scarcely a text of any difficulty in the New Testament, on which hundreds of interpretations might not be produced.

solely on Him, and as such is sure to the seed, since the oneness which belongs to His being, equally belongs to His character and purposes. That sort of distance, or diversity of state and mind, implied in the work of mediation, is totally awanting here; every thing hangs on the will and efficient power of the God of the promise. But then the thought naturally arises, that to bring in, subsequent to the promise, a covenant requiring mediation, and consequently involving dependence on other wills than one, is fraught with danger to the promise, and renders its fulfilment after all uncertain. This is the thought which the apostle raises in the form of a question in the next verse, and answers negatively by pointing to the different purposes for which law and promise were respectively given.

Ver. 21. ' Is the law then against the promises of God? (*promises* in the plural, wiht reference, not only to the frequent repetitions of the word of promise, Gen. xii. 7, xv. 5, 18, xvii., xxii., etc., but also to the different blessings exhibited in it). God forbid! for if a law were given which could have given life, verily righteousness should have been of the law.' The expression, νόμος ὁ δυνάμενος (the article with a participle following the noun serving to define and limit the sense in which the idea in the noun is to be understood, Winer, Gr., sec. 20, 4), means precisely *a law which could*, or, *a law such as could*, possess the power of giving life. The apostle had already said that the covenant of grace or promise bestowed life (ver. 11), and in the previous chapter had enlarged upon it with special reference to his own experience ; and he now adds, that if this inestimable boon for a perishing world could have been obtained by a legal medium, this would certainly have been chosen ; for in that case man would only have been enjoined to do what lay within the reach of his capacities and powers, and the humiliation, and shame, and agony of the cross had been unnecessary. But the thing was impossible ; to give life to a sinful, perishing world is essentially Divine work ; if it comes at all it must come as the fruit of God's free grace and quickening energy. Whatever ends, therefore, the law might be intended to serve, this could not possibly be one of them ; and to look to it for such a purpose was entirely to mistake its design, and seek from it what it was powerless to yield. Not, however, after the fashion of Jowett, who represents the meaning thus : ' The powerlessness of the law was the actual fact; in modern language it had become effete ; it belonged to a different state of the world; nothing spiritual or human remained in it.' What the apostle means is, that, for the object here in view, it never was otherwise : as regards life-giving, the law in its very nature was powerless.

Ver. 22. ' But on the contrary (ἀλλά, a strong adversative, and requiring more than a simple *but* to bring out its force) the Scripture shut
up all under sin'—συνέκλεισεν, not shut *together*, as remarked by Meyer,
Ellicott, Alford, against Bengel, as if the συν had respect to the numbers embraced in the action, and whom it coerced into one and the
same doomed condition. It merely strengthens the meaning of the
verb, so as to indicate the completeness of the action—the closing in,
or shutting up under sin was, so to speak, on every side. And this is
further strengthened by the τὰ πάντα, in the neuter, as if he would say,
men and all about them. (Elsewhere, however, he uses the masculine,
in a very similar declaration.)[1] The act is justly represented as done
by the Scripture, not by the law—for the law by itself merely required
holiness, and forbade or condemned sin ; but the Scriptures of the Old
Testament, or God in these, had (as already indicated, ii. 16, iii. 10, 11)
pronounced all to be guilty of sin, and so had, in a manner, shut them
up without exception under this, as their proper state or condition—
marked them off as violators of law. Not, however, for the purpose of
leaving them there, but ' that the promise by faith of Jesus Christ
might be given to them that believe.' The word *promise* is here evidently used concretely for all that the word of promise contained—the
blessing of life and salvation ; which is again said to be ' of faith, ἐκ
πίστεως, out of this as the source whence it is derived, but of faith as
related to Jesus Christ, and finding all its sufficiency in Him. And to
render the matter still more explicit, to shut out the possibility of the
good being supposed to come through any other channel than faith, it
is added, ' to them that have faith,' or believe—faith's promised blessing is realized simply through the exercise of faith.

Ver. 22. ' But before the faith came'—faith, that is, in the specific
sense just mentioned, but with reference more particularly to its objective reality in Christ, with which it is in a manner identified—' we
were kept in ward (such is the exact and proper meaning of ἐφρουρούμεθα,
Vulg. *custodiebamur*, kept ὥσπερ ἐν τειχίω τινί, Chrysostom), shut up
under the law for the faith which was going to be revealed.' The
apostle here associates himself with believers in legal times, personifies
the entire body and succession of such, and represents them as in the
hands of a sort of jailer, who by reason of their transgressions had
them at his mercy, or rather in strict and jealous surveillance, waiting
the time of their deliverance, when it should be given them to believe
in the Lord Jesus Christ. So far from being able to set them free
from their guilt and liability to punishment, the law was their perpetual

---

[1] Rom. xi. 32.

monitor in respect to these—bound these upon them, but only that they might the more earnestly and believingly look for the mercy of God in Jesus Christ, as the only way of escape. The εἰς, *for*—for the faith which was going to be revealed—is to be taken ethically, denoting the aim or destination which the law, in this respect, was intended to serve : 'to the intent, that we should pass over into the state of faith.'[1] And the μέλλουσαν, as Meyer also notes, stands before the πίστιν, an inversion of the usual order, because the subsequent manifestation of faith in the future was set over against the existing state, in which it was still wanting.

Ver. 24. The apostle now draws the proper conclusion from this wardship under law, 'so that the law has become (γέγονεν) our pedagogue for (in respect to) Christ, in order that we might be justified by faith.' The rendering in the authorized version, 'our schoolmaster,' does certainly not give the exact idea of παιδαγωγός; for it suggests simply teaching or instruction, which was not properly the part of the ancient pedagogue, but that rather of the slave, who had to take charge of the boy on his way to and from the school, and to watch over his behaviour when at play. The pedagogue was the guardian and moral trainer of the boy till he arrived at puberty. And this corresponds to the office of the law, which, in the respect now under consideration, was not so much to teach as to discipline, to restrain, and direct to the one grand aim—namely, Christ, 'the end of the law for righteousness.'[2] The old Latin translation, however, gave the same sense as our English Testament ; and Ambrose refers to it with approbation : Paidagogus enim, sicut etiam interpretatio Latina habet, doctor est pueri; qui utique imperfectae aetati non potest perfecta adhibere praecepta, quae sustinere non queat.[3] Such a rendering, and the comment founded on it, may fairly be regarded as evidence, that a certain amount of instruction was not unusually communicated by the pedagogue to the boy under his charge—for Ambrose could scarcely be ignorant whether such was the case or not ; but this was certainly not the predominant idea ; and, as applied by Ambrose, it serves to give a wrong turn to the allusion here. Instruction, of course, respecting moral truth and duty, was inseparable from the law ; but it is the strict, binding, and imperative form in which this was given that the apostle has in view, and, consequently, not so much the amount of knowledge imparted, as the restraining and disciplinary yoke it laid upon those subject to it. The law would not have men to rest in itself, but to go on to Christ, where alone they could get what they needed, and enjoy the liberty which is suitable to persons in the maturity of spiritual life.

[1] Meyer.   [2] Rom. x. 4.   [3] 'Ep. Classis,' II. lxxi. 2.

Vers. 25, 26. 'But now that the faith has come, we are no longer under a pedagogue ; for ye are all sons of God through faith in Christ Jesus,'—the advance from the nonage state, which required the services of a pedagogue, to that of comparative maturity, in which the youth is able to take charge of himself. Ye are sons, *vioí*—not *τέκνα* merely, not even *παίδες*, in a mere boyish condition—but *sons*, with the full powers and privileges that belong to such ; and this ' through the faith in Christ Jesus,' that is, through the faith which rests in Christ, and brings the soul into living fellowship with Him. In plain terms, the law as an external bond and discipline is gone, because as partakers of Christ we have risen to a position in which it is no longer needed—the Spirit of the law is within.

GAL. IV. 1–7.

Ver. 1. ' Now I say that the heir, as long as he is a child, differs in nothing from a bond-servant, though he be lord of all ; 2. But is under guardians and stewards, until the time appointed of the father. 3. Even so we, when we were children, were kept in bondage under the rudiments of the world. 4. But when the fulness of the time came, God sent forth His Son, born of a woman, born under the law, 5. That He might redeem them that were under the law, that we might receive the adoption of sons. 6. But because ye are sons, God sent forth the Spirit of His Son into your hearts, crying, Abba Father. 7. So then thou art no more a bond-servant, but a son ; and if a son, an heir also through God.'[1]

It is unnecessary to enter into a detailed explanation of these verses, for they are merely a fresh illustration (under a slightly diversified figure) of the thought expressed in vers. 24-26 of the preceding chapter. In this respect, however, they are important, as they unfold more distinctly how the transition is made from the legal to the Christian state, not only without any danger to the moral condition of those who make it, but to their great gain. The figure is still that of a child ($νήπιος$), but a child with reference to the inheritance to which he has been born, not to his personal liberty. However sure his title to the inheritance, and however direct his relation to it, he is still kept from the proper fruition of it, during the period of his childhood, because wanting the mind necessary to make the proper use of it : therefore, placed under

---

[1] The correct text here seems to be *κληρονόμος διὰ Θεοῦ*, which is the reading of ℵ A B C, Vulg., Cop., and many of the Fathers.

guardians and stewards, in a virtual position of servitude, till the time set by his father for his entering on the possession. Of a quite similar nature, the apostle affirms, was the state of men in pre-Christian times: 'We too,' says he, identifying himself with them, 'when we were children, were kept in bondage under the rudiments of the world'— τὰ στοιχεῖα τοῦ κόσμου. It is a strong mode of expression, but intentionally made so, for the purpose of shaming the Galatians out of their backsliding position. The term στοιχεῖον originally signifies a *pin* or *peg*, then a *letter*, a component part or element of a word, then an element of any sort—whether physically, in respect to the composition of material nature, or morally, in respect to what goes to constitute a system of truth or duty. Once only in New Testament Scripture is the word employed with reference to the physical sphere of things— namely, in 2 Peter iii. 10, where 'the elements' are spoken of as melting with fervent heat under the action of that purifying fire which is one day to wrap the world in flames. Misled by this passage, and by the common use of the word in this sense, most of the Fathers took it here also in a kind of physical sense, as pointing to the festivals, such as new moons and sabbatical days, which are ruled by the course of the sun and moon (Chrysostom, Theodoret, Ambrose), or to the worship of the stars and other objects in nature (Augustine), in which they have been followed by a few moderns. But this is unsuitable to the connection which, however it may include a respect also to heathenish forms of worship, undoubtedly has to do mainly with the observances of Judaism, which had no immediate relation to the powers or elements of nature, but were strictly services of God's appointment. It is necessary, therefore, to take the word here in an ethical sense, and to understand it of the elementary forms or rudiments of a religious state—the A, B, C, in a manner, of men's moral relationship to God. The apostle says, the *world's* rudiments, not simply those of the covenant people; for, while the ritual of the old covenant was specially for the seed of Israel, it was never meant to be for them exclusively; others also were invited to share in its services, and blessings; and, such as it was, it formed the best, indeed, the sole divinely authorized form of religious homage and worship for the world in pre-Christian times. In it the world had, whether consciously or not, the style of worship really adapted to its state of spiritual non-age. Besides, as it was not merely, nor even chiefly, to Jewish Christians that the apostle was writing, but to those who are presently said to have formerly done service to false gods (ver. 8), an allusion is made, in the very form of the expression, to the religious rites of heathendom, which, in their prevailing carnality and outwardness, had a point of affinity with those of the law. The mode of speech is purposely made comprehensive of heathen as well as Jewish ceremonialism. And though, as Meyer notes, Paul had to do only with backslidings of a Judaistic nature, yet this does not prevent him, with the view of making his readers more thoroughly ashamed of the trammelled condition to which they had returned, from designating it in such a manner as to bring it under one idea, and place it in the same category, with the worship of heathendom. While there was a spiritual element in the one which was wanting in the other, it was not on this account that the Galatians had fallen back upon it, but rather for the sake of that outwardness which was common to both (ver. 10) —a palpable proof, therefore, of their still low, childish tone of thought and feeling. The expression στοιχεῖα τοῦ κόσμου is found much in the same sense at Col. ii. 8.

Having noticed this proof of inferiority or servitude in pre-Christian times, the apostle proceeds (ver. 4) to speak of the time and mode of deliverance : ' When the fulness of the time was come (τὸ πλήρωμα, what filled up, or gave completeness, namely, to the preparatory period of the world's history, parallel therefore to ἄχρι τῆς προθεσμίας τοῦ πατρός, in ver. 2), God sent forth from Himself (ἐξαπέστειλεν, denoting both pre-existence in Christ and close proximity to the Father) His Son, born of a woman, born under law.' *Born* is here the more exact equivalent to γενόμενον, rather than *made*—nothing being indicated by the expression but the fact of our Lord's coming into the world with the nature, and after the manner, of men. The birth, we know, was the result of an altogether peculiar, supernatural operation of Godhead ; but that belongs to an earlier stage than the one here referred to by the apostle, which has to do simply with Christ's actual appearance among men. *Born under law*—not become man merely, but become also subject to the bonds and obligations of law. The definite article is better omitted in English before *law*, as it is in the Greek (ὑπὸ νόμον) ; for, while special respect is no doubt had to the law as imposed on the Jews, yet the meaning is not, as too many (including Meyer, Alford, Ellicott) would put on it, that our Lord appeared as a Jew among Jews, and entered into the relations of His countrymen. For the whole nature and bearings of His work are here spoken of—His salvation in its entire compass and efficacy for mankind ; and so, not what was distinctly Jewish must have been contemplated in the bond which lay upon Him, but the common burden of humanity. All this, however, was in the law, rightly considered, which was revealed at Sinai ; the heart and substance of its requirements of duty, and (implied) threatenings against sin, relate to Gentile as well as Jew; they belong to man as man; and no otherwise was redemption possible for mankind than by our Lord's perfect submission, in their behalf, to its demands and penalties.[1] His atoning death, therefore, was, in this point of view, the climax of His surrender to the claims of law; as said in Heb. x. 10, 'By the which will (fulfilled even unto the bearing of an accursed death) we are sanctified through the offering of the body of Jesus Christ once for all.' The result, as stated in the words that follow here, has a threefold issue, 'in order that He might redeem ($\dot{\epsilon}\xi\alpha\gamma o\rho\dot{\alpha}\sigma\eta$, might buy off by paying what was due, as from a state of hopeless servitude) those that were under the law; [and this] in order that they might receive the adoption of sons. And because ye are sons (not, with Chrysostom, Theodoret, and not a few moderns, *that* ye are sons, or in proof and token of your being such, but because, or since ye are so, on the ground of your having received this place and privilege), God sent forth the Spirit of His Son into your hearts, crying Abba Father.' All follows by natural consequence from the spiritual union through faith of the soul with Christ: this brings, first, deliverance from the law's curse, which falls into abeyance by the removal of sin; then, it secures admission into the family of which Christ is the head, makes them sons after the pattern of His sonship; and, finally, because the soul and spirit here must correspond with the condition, the Spirit of sonship, with its sense of joyous freedom and enlargement, comes forth to rule in their hearts. Hence, as the apostle concludes in ver. 7, having risen to such a condition of sonship, and become endowed with the spirit proper to it, they could be no more bondmen; they were free, yet not to do what was contrary to, but only what was in accordance with, the spirit and tenor of the law. This latter point is brought out distinctly in another passage—the last we select from this epistle.

GAL. V. 13-15.

'For ye were called for freedom, brethren; only [use] not your liberty for an occasion to the flesh, but by your love serve (do the part of bondmen to) one another. For the whole law is fulfilled in one word, in this, Thou shalt love thy neighbour as thyself. But if ye bite and devour one another, take heed that ye be not consumed one of another.'

[1] Compare the comment on Rom. iii. 20, where there is noted a precisely similar fulness of reference in what is said of *law*.

The thought expressed in these words is much more fully unfolded in the epistle to the Romans, so that a few remarks here may suffice. The *for* at the commencement connects the passage with the wish expressed in the preceding verse, that the zealots of the law, who had been disturbing the Galatians, might be cut off, as tending to mar the very end of their Christian calling. '*For* ye were called for freedom' —ἐπ᾽ ἐλευθερίᾳ, the purpose or aim for this as your proper condition, called that you might be free.[1] Yet this freedom, from its very nature, involves a species of service—if free in one respect, bound in another—bound by love to serve one another, and, of course, also to serve God. He therefore defines the freedom: 'only not the liberty (μόνον τὴν ἐλευθερίαν) which is for an occasion to the flesh' —so the sentence might be construed, taking τὴν ἐλευ in opposition to the previous sentence, and explanatory of it; but it is better perhaps to regard this part of the verse as elliptical, supplying ποιεῖτε, or some such verb, and thus giving the sentence an independent, hortatory meaning, 'only use not your liberty,' etc. It is a liberty, the apostle would have them to understand, very different from an unrestrained license, or fleshly indulgence; and the reason follows, that though the external bond and discipline of the law is gone, its spirit ever lives, the spirit of love, which Christians are most especially bound to cherish and exhibit. In this respect, the law speaks as much as ever to the conscience of the believer, and can no more be set aside than the great principles of God's moral government can change. The explanation of Meyer here is excellent: 'The question, how Paul could justly say of the whole law, that it is fulfilled through the love of one's neighbour, must not be answered by taking νόμος to signify the *Christian* law (Koppe), nor by understanding it only of the *moral* law (Estius and others), or of the *second table* of the Decalogue (Beza and others), or of every divinely revealed law in general (Schott); for ὁ πᾶς νόμος can mean nothing else, from the connection of the entire epistle, than *the whole law of Moses*—but by placing one's-self on the elevated spiritual level of the apostle, from which he looked down upon all the other commands of the law, and saw them so profoundly subordinated to the law of love, that whosoever has fulfilled *this* command, is not to be regarded otherwise than as having fulfilled *all*. Contemplated from this point of view, every thing which does not accord with the precept of love, falls so entirely into the background,[2] that it can no more come into consideration, but the whole law appears to have been already fulfilled in love.' Brotherly love alone was mentioned by the apostle, because

[1] Winer, sec. 48, *c*. [2] Rom. xiii. 8-10.

what is here specially in view was the relation of Christians to each other—their imperative duty to serve one another by the mutual exercise of love, instead of, as he says in ver. 15, biting and devouring one another. But no one can fail to understand, that what holds of love in this lower direction, equally holds of it in the higher; indeed, rightly understood, the one, as stated by Meyer, may be said to include the other.

ROM. II. 13-15.

' For not the hearers of the law are just before God, but the doers of the law shall be justified. For when Gentiles, who have not the law, do by nature the things of the law (viz., the things prescribed in it), these, though they have not the law, are to themselves the law, being such as shew the law's work written in their hearts, their conscience jointly bearing witness, and their thoughts (or judgments) among one another accusing or also excusing.'

I take this to be a section by itself, and cannot concur with those commentators (including, certainly, some men of note—Calvin, Koppe, Harless, Hodge), who would connect what is said in vers. 14 and 15 about Gentiles doing the law, and being a law to themselves, not with the immediately preceding verse, but with the statement in ver. 12, that those who have been without the written law shall be judged without it, and those who have been under such law shall be judged by it. This seems arbitrary and unnatural, and could only be justified if the statement in the immediately preceding verse were obviously parenthetical, and incapable of forming a suitable transition to the assertions that follow. But such is by no means the case. The apostle's line of thought proceeds in the most regular and orderly manner. There are (he virtually says) grounds for judgment in the case of all, whether they have been placed under the written law or not, and ample materials for condemnation; for the mere privilege of hearing that law does not give any one a title to be called righteous in God's sight; this does not make the essential difference between one man and another, which turns mainly on their relation to the doing of what is required; the doers alone are justified, and though the heathen have not been hearers like the Jews, they may be viewed with reference to doing. It is no proper objection to this view of the connection, that it seems to bring in out of due place the subject of justification, and to represent the apostle as indicating the possibility of some among the heathen being justified by their works. Justification, in the full Gospel sense of the term, as acquittal from all guilt, and being treated as righteous, does not come into consideration here. The question contemplated is a narrower one—namely, what, in regard to particular requirements of the law, forms the proper ground of approval, or constitutes a good character? Is it hearing or doing? Doing, says the apostle; and then goes on to add that, on this account, Gentiles may justly be placed in the same category with Jews. ' For when '—here comes his matter of fact proof or reason—' Gentiles, who have not the law, do by nature the things of the law, these are to themselves the law.' It is not said of the Gentiles as a whole that they do this, but only when they do it, or in so far as any of them do it—implying, no doubt, that what is done by some may and should be done by others, yet this only as matter of inference. The want of the article, therefore, has its meaning—not τὰ ἔθνη, but merely ἔθνη; for, though the latter is sometimes undoubtedly used of the Gentiles in their totality (as at ch. iii. 29, ix. 24), yet this is only when the things affirmed are applicable to them universally, which is palpably not the case here. The statement is indefinite, both as to what proportion of the heathen might be characterized as doers of the law, and to what extent they were so. To do the things of the law is indeed to do what the law prescribes (x. 5; Gal. iii. 12); but (here we concur with Dr Hodge) ' whether complete or partial obedience is intended depends on the context. The man who pays his debts, honours his parents, is kind to the poor, does the things of the law; for these are things which the law prescribes. And this is all the argument of the apostle requires, or his known doctrine allows us to understand by the phrase, in the present instance.' Indeed, that such is his meaning, we have only to look to the examples which the apostle himself adduces a few verses afterwards, which include merely the law's precepts against stealing, adultery, and sacrilege; and the qualification which the whole current and tenor of his argument oblige us to put upon what he states here as to the doing of the law, confirms the perfectly similar qualification that we have shewn, ought to be put upon the justifying spoken of in the verse immediately preceding. It has respect simply to the actions which, in a legal point of view, are worthy of approval on the one side, or of condemnation on the other. And as regards the performance of what is ascribed to such heathen, the law-*making* (we are told) is of themselves—that is to say, it is the dictate of their own instinctive sense of right and wrong, forming, to a certain extent, a substitute for the written law; so also the law-*doing* is *by nature* (φύσει, causal dative, and undoubtedly to be coupled with the doing), it is such as arises from the impulse and energy of the moral faculty, naturally implanted in them, as contra-distinguished from the discipline of a formal legislation, or the gift of sanctifying grace.

The description in ver. 15 is to be taken as a further characterizing of the heathen in question, with reference to the power of being to themselves as the law, and observing it: ' They are such as shew,' in their behaviour outwardly exhibit, ' the law's work written in their hearts ;' so it is best to put the apostle's statement in English, rather than ' the work of the law written,' which leaves it doubtful whether what is said to be written is the law or the law's work. The con-struction in the original leaves no doubt that it is the latter—τὸ ἔργον τοῦ νόμου γραπτὸν, the law's work written. This, however, according to some, is all one with the law itself, ' the work of the law' being regarded as a mere periphrase for ' the law.' But this is not tenable ; nor is it quite correct to say with Harless,[1] that ' the work of the law is accusing and judging ;' so that the import of the apostle's state-ment respecting the heathen comes to be, ' They accuse themselves in their hearts and judge themselves, thereby shewing that what is the work of the positive law is written upon their hearts.' This is to make what ought to be regarded as but the incidental and secondary effect of the law, its primary and distinctive aim. Its more immediate aim, consequently its proper work, is to teach and command ; its work is done, if people know aright what they should do, and yield them-selves to the obligation of doing it—failing this, it of course becomes a witness against them, a complaining and judging authority. But when the law's work simply is spoken of, it is the direct aim and intention of the law that should be mainly understood : by doing the things of the law, they shew that they have prescribed for them-selves as right what the law prescribes, and imposed on themselves the obligation which the law imposes. And then, in fitting correspond-ence with this testimony without, the testimony of a morally upright conduct, is the testimony of conscience within—' their conscience co-testifying ' (so it is literally, συμμαρτυρούσης, testifying along with, viz., with the practical operation of the law appearing in the conduct), ' and among one another, their thoughts accusing or also excusing,' defend-ing. The μεταξὺ ἀλλήλων, as is now generally allowed, is most exactly rendered by ' among one another,' μεταξύ being taken as a preposition. But what is the reference of the ' one another ?' Does it point to the diverse sentiments and judgments, sometimes swaying one way,

[1] ' Ethik,' sec. 8.

sometimes another, in the minds of the individual? Or, to a like
diversity among different individuals? I am inclined, with Meyer, to
take it rather in the latter respect; both because, if the reference had
been to the thoughts in the same mind, the τῶν λογισμῶν would naturally have been placed before μεταξὺ ἀλλήλων (the natural order being
then, their thoughts among one another, or their thoughts alternately,
accusing and excusing); and also because the αὐτῶν, in the preceding
clause, and the ἀλλήλων, in this, appear to stand in relation to each
other—the former referring to those who do the works of the law, or
have its work written in their heart, conscience therein concurring and
approving; and the other to the heathen generally who, in their
thoughts and judgments, were ever passing sentence upon the things
done around them, and thereby shewed that they had a judging power
in their bosoms, according to which they accused what was wrong, and
excused or defended what was right. It is so put, however, that the
accusing was much more frequently exercised than the other—' accusing
or also (perhaps) excusing.' In other words, the moral sentiment,
when working properly, and exercising itself upon the doings of men
generally, found more materials for condemnation than for justification
and approval. This, however, is implied rather than distinctly stated;
and the leading purport of the apostle's announcement is that, beside
the approving verdict given by conscience, in the case of those who
understood and did what was required in the law, there was ever
manifesting itself a morally judging power among the heathen, condemning what was wrong in behaviour, and vindicating what was
right. But all, of course, only within certain limits, and with many
imperfections and errors in detail.

Rom. iii. 19, 20.

' Now we know, that whatsoever things the law saith, it speaks to
them who are in the law; in order that every mouth may be stopt, and
all the world become liable to punishment with God. 20. Because by
works of law shall no flesh be justified before Him; for through the
law is the knowledge of sin.'

We have here the more direct and immediate conclusions which the
apostle draws from the evidence he had furnished—that mankind at
large, Jews as well as Gentiles, are alike under sin. The later and
more specific evidence adduced had reference to the Jews; for, in
respect to them, proud as they were of their distinctive privileges, and

conscious of their superiority to the heathen, the difficulty was greatest in carrying the conviction he was seeking to establish. In their case, therefore, he did not rest satisfied with general charges of shortcoming and transgression, but produced a series of quotations from their own Scriptures, chiefly from the Psalms, but partly also from the prophets. And then he proceeds to draw his conclusion: 'Now we know (it is a matter on which we are all agreed), that whatsoever things the law saith (λέγει), it speaks (λαλεῖ) to them who are in the law.' There can be no reasonable doubt that the apostle here uses the term *law* as virtually comprehensive of the Old Testament Scriptures ; for it is on the ground of certain passages in these Scriptures that the inferential statement is now made; and the attempts of some commentators to take the expression in a narrower sense (Ammon, Van Hengel, Ward-law, etc.), have a strained and unnatural appearance. Yet there is no reason why we should not (as, with more or less clearness has been indicated by various expositors) regard the expression as indirectly referring also to the law in the stricter sense. For, those Scriptures were the writings of prophetical men, whose primary calling it was to expound and vindicate the law ; and hence, in the declarations they set forth respecting men's relation to the demands of law, they but served as the exponents of its testimony; virtually, it was the law itself speaking through them. Moses, in this respect, might be said to be represented by the prophets, not to stand apart from them.[1] What-ever, then, the law thus says concerning sin and transgression, it speaks or addresses to those who are in it; that is, who stand within its bonds and obligations. The law is regarded as the sphere within which the parties in question lived; and to these, as the parties with whom it had more immediately to do, it utters its testimony—primarily to them, though by no means exclusively; for, as there was nothing arbitrary in its requirements—as, on the contrary, they proceeded on the essential relations between God and man, the testimony admitted of a world-wide application. The argument, indeed, is here *à fortiori;* if the law could pronounce such charges of guilt on those who had the advantage of its light, and the privileges with which it was associated, how much more might like charges be brought against those who lived beyond its pale ! Hence, the apostle makes the next part of his con-clusion—the design or bearing of the law's testimony respecting actual sin—quite universal : 'in order that every mouth may be stopt (Jew as well as Gentile, and Gentile as well as Jew), and all the world become liable to punishment with God.' Such is the exact force of the expres-

[1] *See* at p. 198.

sion used here, ὑπόδιχος τῷ Θεῷ; it denotes one who, on account of mis-
demeanours, is in an actionable state, liable to be proceeded against with
a view to the infliction of deserved penalties, amenable to justice. The
general idea is expressed in the epithet *guilty* of the authorized version,
but *liable to punishment* is preferable, as giving more distinct expression
to it; and the liability is *to* God (as the dative τῷ Θεῷ implies); it is
He who has a right to exact the penalty; though, to avoid harshness in
the translation, we have put, liable to punishment *with* God.

The language of the apostle here has appeared somewhat too strong
to some commentators; they cannot understand how it should be spoken
of as the proper aim of the law in its announcements to stop every
mouth, as culprits who have nothing to say for themselves in the Divine
court of justice, and to bring all in as liable to punishment; therefore they
would soften the form of the expression, and render, not *in order that*
such might happen, but *so that*, as a matter of fact, it has come to be.
But this is to impair the natural import of the original (which has the
usual telic particle, ἵνα), and is also unnecessary; for, while the apostle
sets forth such universal conviction of guilt and liability to punishment
as the aim of the law, there is no need for understanding him to mean
more than its aim under one particular aspect—not its sole aim, nor
even its more immediate and primary aim as a part of Divine revelation,
but still an aim in the view of the Lawgiver, and, as the result very
clearly shewed, one which, so far as it remained unaccomplished,
rendered the work and mission of Christ practically fruitless. Where
the law failed to produce conviction of sin and a sense of deserved condemnation, there also failed the requisite preparation for the faith of
Christ, and still continues to do so.

In ver. 20 we have the ultimate ground or reason of the law's
deliverance upon the guilt of mankind, and their desert of punishment:
'Because by works of law shall no flesh be justified before Him; for
through the law is the knowledge of sin.' The διότι at the commencement has no other meaning in New Testament Scripture, nor elsewhere,
when used as an illative particle, than *because*, or for this reason. In
following Beza and some other authorities for the rendering *therefore*,
our translators have the great body of the more exact interpreters
against them—though they have also the support of some men of solid
learning (Pareus, Rosenmüller, Schöttgen, and others). But the
apostle is not here drawing a conclusion; he is grounding the conclusion he had already drawn: the law has brought in a verdict against
all men, and declared them amenable to the awards of Divine justice,
because by works of law shall no flesh be justified before God—not in

such a way is this great boon, as a matter of fact, attainable. The same sentiment was uttered by the apostle, and almost in the same form of words, in one of his earliest discussions on the subject, and has already been considered.[1] It is substantially, as we there remarked, a re-assertion of the Psalmist's declaration in Ps. cxliii. 2; and it undoubtedly had respect, in its Old as well as New Testament form, to men's obligations as made known in the revelation of law through Moses. It is of no moment, therefore, whether we put the expression simply, 'works of law,' as in the original, without the article, or with the article, 'works of the law;' for the works meant must be those which are required in the law, with which the apostle's readers were familiar, and to which, as contained in Old Testament Scripture, he had just been referring. But here, as elsewhere in his discussions on this subject, the apostle has pre-eminent respect to what had the place of pre-eminent importance in the law itself—namely, its grand summary of moral and religious obligation in the two tables. This is clearly enough proved—if any specific proof were needed—by the examples which he has already given of what he means by transgressions of the law (ch. ii. 21-24, iii. 10-18), and subsequently by the positive characteristics, both general and particular, which he connects with the law (ch. vii. 7, 12, 14, viii. 4, xiii. 8-10). This is the one distinction of any moment; all others seem at once unnatural and superfluous. As so contemplated, the law had nothing in it peculiarly Jewish; it was but the varied application and embodiment of the great principle of love to God and man; and, judged by these, as every man, be he Jew or Gentile, is destined to be judged, no mortal man, we are assured, can stand the test; justification by works of law is a thing impossible. And the reason follows—'for through the law is the knowledge of sin' ($\dot{\epsilon}\pi i\gamma\nu\omega\sigma\iota\varsigma$, is more than $\gamma\nu\tilde{\omega}\sigma\iota\varsigma$, accurate knowledge and discernment): the disclosures it makes to those who rightly understand and conscientiously apply it, is not their possession of the perfect moral excellence which it enjoins, but a manifold cherishing and exhibition of the sin which it condemns. The standard of duty which it sets up is never by fallen man practically realized; and the more thoughtfully any one looks into the nature of its claims, and becomes acquainted with the 'exceeding breadth' of its requirements, the more always does the conviction force itself upon him, that righteousness belongeth not to him, but guilt, and shame, and confusion of face. What is here announced only as a general principle is elsewhere formally taken up by the apostle, and at some length expounded.[2] But

---

[1] *See* on Gal. ii. 16.   [2] *See* at ch. vii. 7, *seq.;* also Gal. iii. 19, *seq.*

having now distinctly asserted the impossibility of obtaining justification by works of law, he goes on to shew how the grace of God has
provided for its being obtained without such works, through the mediation of Christ, in behalf of all who believe on Him; and then returns to
present, under other points of view, the different relations and bearings
of the law.

Rom. iii. 31.

' Do we then make void the law through faith? God forbid! on the
contrary, we establish the law.'

This important utterance respecting the law comes as a sequel to the
apostle's formal announcement of the great truth, that justification
before God is attainable for fallen men, not through the works of the
law, but only through faith in the propitiation of Christ. The law, he
had said, so far from affording a valid ground of justification, or a plea
of righteousness, brings the knowledge of sin. Then, turning from the
quarter whence salvation could not be found, to the manifested grace
of God, by which it had been freely provided and offered alike to Jew
and Gentile through faith in Christ, the apostle sees himself met with
the objection, coming as from the Jewish point of view, ' Do we then
make void (καταργοῦμεν, do away with, abolish) the law through faith?'
So it might naturally seem to one who had been wont to associate with
the law all his peculiar privileges and hopes. But the apostle indignantly rejects the idea, and says: ' God forbid! On the contrary
(ἀλλὰ, a strong adversative), we establish the law'—that is, we
confirm it, give effect to its authority and obligation.

But the question is how? In saying these words, does the apostle
utter an independent sentence, and give a deliverance on the subject,
without stopping to elucidate and prove it? Or is it rather the announcement of a general position, which he presently proceeds to make
good from passages and examples out of Old Testament Scripture?
The former view is implied in the present division of chapters, which
places this weighty sentence at the close of chapter third, as if it
formed a deliverance, provisional or ultimate, on the subject as already
considered, not the announcement of a theme to be handled in what
immediately follows. And such has been the prevailing view with a
large class of commentators—with all, indeed, who have understood by
law here, law in the stricter sense, and with reference more especially
to the great moral obligations it imposed on men, whether they be Jew

or Gentile. But several (Theodoret, Semler, Tholuck, etc.) would understand the term here of the Old Testament Scriptures generally ; and some recent commentators, while holding it to refer to the distinctively Jewish law, with all its rites and ordinances, expound in a way not materially different from the others. So, for example, De Wette, Meyer, the latter of whom says, 'This establishing is accomplished thus, that [1] the doctrine of Paul sets forth and proves how the justification of God's grace through faith was already taught in the law, so that Paul and his companions did not come into conflict with the law, as if they sought by a new doctrine to do away with this and put it in abeyance, but, through their agreement with the law and proof of their doctrine out of it, they certify and confirm its validity.' To the like effect, also, Alford, who thus presents the substance of the apostle's statement, 'That the law itself belonged to a covenant, whose original recipient was justified by faith, and whose main promise was the reception and blessing of the Gentiles.' He adds, 'Many commentators have taken this verse (being misled in some cases by its place at the end of the chapter) as standing by itself, and have gone into the abstract grounds why faith does not make void the law (or moral obedience) ; which, however true, have no place here ; the design being to shew that the law itself contained this very doctrine, and was founded in the promise to Abraham on a covenant embracing Jews and Gentiles— and therefore was not degraded from its dignity by the doctrine, but rather established as a part of God's dealings—consistent with, explaining, and explained by the Gospel.' One does not, however, see how this can be said to *establish* the law—unless by the law were understood the Old Testament Scriptures generally ; and yet both Meyer and Alford repudiate that : they alike hold that *law* here must mean the Mosaic law. The fact that the law given by Moses was founded in the promise to Abraham, might well enough be said to accord with the apostle's doctrine of justification by faith, and this doctrine might in consequence be affirmed not to invalidate the law, or not to interfere with the purpose for which it was given, but this does not come up to establishing the law. The apostle's doctrine by itself no more established the law than God's promise to Abraham did ; and unless one takes into account the moral grounds on which the plan of God in this respect proceeds—namely, the provision it makes for the vindication of the law in the work of Christ and the experience of His people— neither the one nor the other could with any propriety be said to establish the law ; they merely do not conflict with it, and provide

[1] *See* chap. iv.

what it was neither designed nor able to accomplish.   It is a further
objection to the same view, that the first verse of chap. iv., instead of
being connected with the last verse of the preceding chapter by a γὰρ,
for, as it naturally would have been if what follows had been a direct
continuation of that verse, begins with a τὶ οὖν, *what then ?*—a mode of
commencement very unlike the introduction of a proof of what immediately precedes, or a consequence deduced from it—one rather that
seems to point farther back, and to resume consideration of the leading
topic in the third chapter—the subject of justification by faith.   The
deliverance, on the other hand, respecting the law given in ver. 31, has
all the appearance of a passing declaration made to silence an obtrusive
objection, but left over meanwhile for its fuller vindication, till the
apostle had proceeded further in his course of argumentation.

Taking the passage, then, in what appears to be both its natural
sense and its proper connection, we regard the apostle as giving here a
brief but emphatic statement on the relation of his doctrine of justification to the law ; but, having still a good deal to advance in proof and
illustration of the doctrine itself, he again for the present resumes his
general theme, and leaves it to be gathered from the subsequent tenor
of his discourse how, or in what sense, the law is established by the
doctrine in question.   Referring to the portions which most distinctly
bear upon the point (ch. v. 12–viii. 4), we find the law established by
being viewed as the revelation of God's unchangeable righteousness—
the violation of which has involved all in guilt and ruin, the fulfilment
of which in Christ has re-opened for the fallen the way to peace and
blessing, and the perfect agreement of which, in its great principles of
moral obligation, with men's inmost convictions of the pure and good,
must ever impel them to seek after conformity to its requirements—
impel them always the more the nearer they stand to God, and the
more deeply they are imbued with the Spirit of His grace and love.
The law and the Gospel, therefore, are the proper complements of each
other ; and, if kept in their respective places, will be found to lend mutual
support and confirmation.   So, substantially, the passage is understood
by the great body of evangelical expositors, of whom we may take
Calvin as a specimen : ' When recourse is had to Christ, first, there is
found in Him the complete righteousness of the law, which, through
imputation, becomes ours also ; then sanctification, whereby our hearts
are formed to the observance of the law, which, though imperfect,
strives towards its aim.'

ROM. V. 12-21.

' Wherefore as by one man sin entered into the world, and by means of sin, death, and so death extended unto all men, because all sinned: 13. For until the law, sin was in the world; but sin is not reckoned where there is no law. 14. But death reigned from Adam to Moses even over those who sinned not after the similitude of Adam's transgression, who is a type (figure) of the future one. 15. But not as the offence so also is the gift of grace; for if by the offence of the one the many died, much more did the grace of God, and the gift in grace, which is of the one man Jesus Christ, abound toward the many. 16. And not as through one that sinned is the gift; for the judgment was by one to condemnation, but the free gift is by many offences unto justification. 17. For if by the offence of the one death reigned through the one, much more shall they who receive the abundance of grace, and of the gift of righteousness, reign in life through the one, Jesus Christ. 18. Therefore as through one offence [it came] upon all men unto condemnation, so also through one righteous act [it came] upon all men unto justification of life. 19. For as by the disobedience of one man the many were made sinners, so also by the obedience of the one shall the many be made righteous. 20. But the law came in besides, in order that the offence might abound; but where sin abounded, grace superabounded; 21. That as sin reigned in death, grace also might reign through righteousness unto life eternal, through Jesus Christ our Lord.'

It is only in part that this passage has respect to the law, and, as such, calls for special consideration here. The other portions, though in themselves of great moment, may be noticed only as having an incidental bearing on the subject now more immediately in hand. There is a certain abruptness in the transition here suddenly made to the case of Adam, and the comparative view instituted between him and Christ; for, though the general sinfulness and corruption of mankind had been already portrayed, nothing had as yet been indicated as to the primal source of mischief. The discourse of the apostle hence becomes somewhat involved; since, in order to explicate the points relating to the one side of his comparison, or prevent it from being misunderstood, he is obliged to introduce some explanatory statements, before proceeding to bring out what relates to the other side of the comparison. This necessarily breaks the continuity of the line of thought in the passage, while still the general meaning and drift of the whole admit of being quite definitely ascertained. The *wherefore* (διὰ τοῦτο) at the outset is best referred to the immediate context, vers. 9-11, in which the believer's state of reconciliation, peace, and hope, through Christ, had been stated, and which suggested to the apostle the thought of what had been lost in Adam, as a further mode of magnifying the grace of God; *wherefore*, since this unspeakable boon has been secured for us in Christ, we may justly compare, in order to see the wonderful riches of Divine grace, what comes to us of evil from Adam, with what comes to us of good through Christ—only, as already said, there is an interruption, after the announcement of the first member, of the comparison, to make way for some thoughts that were deemed necessary to complete it. *As by one man sin entered into the world, and by means of sin, death*—Adam is, of course, the one man; by his breach of the command laid upon him, or violation of the covenant of life under which he stood, sin entered into the world—entered, that is, not merely as a specific act, but as a dominant power—and in the train of sin, as its appointed recompense, death. There is nothing new in these announcements—the apostle, indeed, gives expression to them as matters too well known to require proof, being clearly exhibited in the history of the fall;[1] therefore, he goes on, *and so death extended to all men* (εἰς πάντας ἀνθρώπους διῆλθεν, passed through among, extended to, all men), *because all sinned.* The *and so* at the beginning is as much as *which being done*, or such being the case, Adam having died on account of sin, the evil diffused itself throughout the whole race of mankind, because all sinned—ἐφ᾽ ᾧ πάντες ἥμαρτον. Not *in whom*, with the Vulgate, Augustine, Estius, Beza, and others, as if the Greek had been ἐν ᾧ, but *propter id quod, because that* (see Fritzsche here); and, besides, the antecedent (the one man) is too far removed to admit of such a construction. Nearly all the better and more recent commentators are agreed in this mode of interpretation, which is that also of our common version; and the proper import of the clause cannot be more exactly represented than in the following exposition of Meyer (as given in the later, which here differs from the earlier, editions of his work): ' *Because all sinned*, namely (observe the momentary sense of the Aorist), when, through the one, sin entered into the world. Because, since Adam sinned, all men sinned in and with him, the representative of the entire race of mankind, death, by reason of the original connection in Adam between sin and death, has diffused

---

[1] Jowett seems entirely to ignore that history, when he says that 'the oldest trace of the belief common to the Jews in St Paul's time, that the sin of Adam was the cause of death to him, is found in the Book of Wisdom, ii. 24.' Certainly, Paul's mode of reading Old Testament Scripture furnished *him* with a greatly earlier trace of it. Compare with the passage here, 2 Cor. xi. 3; 1 Tim. ii. 13-15.

itself through all: All have become mortal through Adam's fall, because the guilt of Adam was the guilt of all.' Plainly, it is the relation of mankind to Adam in his sinfulness, not their own personal sin (according to the Pelagian view), which is asserted to be the procuring cause of death to mankind; and hence the absolute universality of death, the sin that caused it being in God's reckoning the sin of humanity, and the wages of that sin, consequently, men's common heritage.

Ver. 13. But this was a point which called for some additional explanation or proof; for it might seem strange, and even unjust, that that one sin, with its sad penalty, should involve all alike, if all were not in substantially the same state of sin and condemnation; particularly after what the apostle had himself declared but shortly before, that 'where no law is, there is no transgression' (iv. 15). Might it not, in that case, be held that those who lived before the law was given, were not chargeable with sin, and, consequently, not liable to its penalty? No, says the apostle—there is no room for such a thought to enter; 'for, until the law (ἄχρι νόμου, up to the time when it came), sin was in the world;' that is, not only were men involved in the one act of Adam's transgression, but sin, as a principle, continued to live and work in them onwards till the period of the law-giving at Sinai, as well as after it—shewing (for that is what it was needful to prove, and what the statement does prove) that sin in Adam was disease in the root, and that, as those who sprung from him ever manifested the same moral obliquity, they could not be placed in another category, or treated after another manner. They, too, were all sinners; but 'sin (the apostle adds) is not reckoned where there is no law;' sin and law are correlates of each other; hence, though not, like Israel afterwards, placed under *formal* law, those earlier generations must have been *virtually*, *really* under the obligations of law—as, indeed, all by the very constitution of their nature are (according to what had already been stated, ii. 9-16). This, however, was not the whole: 'But death reigned from Adam to Moses, even over those who had not sinned after the similitude of Adam's transgression;' that is, as I understand it, not only those who had themselves sinned, who by their violations of moral duty had given palpable evidence that actual sin was in the world from Adam to Moses, but even such as were not capable of sinning like Adam, sinning by any personal overt transgression (infants must be chiefly understood), these, as well as others, were during all that time subject to the penalty of sin—death. Relationship to Adam, therefore, renders all alike, from the first, partakers of a heritage of sin, and as such subject to condemnation; of which we have two proofs—first, that

2 D

throughout past generations, before the law as well as after it, sin has been ever manifesting itself in those who were capable of committing it, and that in the case of others who, by reason of age, were not so capable, death, which is the penalty of sin, still reigned over them—though they had not sinned like Adam, they nevertheless died like Adam. Vers. 13 and 14 thus contain a double proof of the general position laid down in ver. 12—the universal prevalence of sin (in such as were capable of committing it), and the universal dominion of death (whether there had been actual sin or not). And that the former—the prevalence of actual sin—is included in the apostle's proof, as well as the latter, seems clear both from the natural import of the words (sin *was* in the world, the world all through has been a sinful one), but also from the account made in the comparative view which follows of the actual sins or offences of mankind. These, along with the sin of Adam, constitute the mass of guilt from which deliverance had to be brought in by the second Adam, and out of which justification unto life eternal had to be imparted; while the sin of the one man wrought for all unto condemnation and death, the righteousness of the other prevailed, not only against that sin, but against numberless offences besides, unto justification and life (ver. 16).

Interpreted thus, every part of the apostle's statement is taken in a quite natural sense, and has its due effect given to it; but the other interpretations which have been adopted always fail, in one part or another, to give what seems a full or natural explanation. For example, the clause respecting the reckoning or imputing of sin, is understood by a large number of commentators (Augustine, Ambrose, Luther, Calvin, Beza, Stuart, etc.) as referring to men's own sense of sin; being without law, they did not charge guilt upon their consciences, did not take it to heart, or, as put by Usteri, Tholuck, and others, ' Man did not feel his sin as a punishment.' But this is to take the verb in an arbitrary sense, which plainly denotes a formal transaction, a legal reckoning, as of a matter that may or may not justly be placed to one's account; and it also introduces an irrelevant consideration; for the question here was not what men thought of themselves, but how they stood in reference to the judgment and procedure of God. The view of Meyer, Alford, and several recent commentators, appears equally untenable: they understand the passage to say, that while there was sin constantly existing in the world before Moses, yet it was not reckoned to men as formal transgression, or as deserving of punishment, because the law had not been given. According to Meyer, ' it was not brought into reckoning, namely, for punishment, and indeed by God—for it is of the Divine procedure, in consequence of the fall, that the whole context treats.' Alford modifies it a little, as if the representation of Meyer were somewhat too strong: ' In the case of those who had not the written law, sin (ἁμαρτία) is not formally reckoned as transgression (παράβασις) set over against the command; but in a certain sense, as distinctly proved, ch. ii. 9-16, it *is reckoned*, and they are condemned for it '—that is, reckoned, indeed, but reckoned as ' in a less degree culpable and punishable.' But this is to put a meaning on Paul's language, for which Paul himself gives no warrant; he is speaking, not of degrees of culpability, but of what might or might not be reckoned sin, and, as such, deserving of death. Besides, to distinguish between sin and transgression in this way, when the matter relates to actual guilt, is to make too much hang on a verbal difference; nor is it warranted by other passages of Scripture.[1] Un- questionably, before the giving of the law, men were not only spoken of as sinners, but formally reckoned such, judged, held deserving of the severest penalties;[2] and the apostle merely epitomizes this part of Old Testament history, when he states that sin was in the world up to the giving of the law, and consequently bespoke the existence of law (though not formally enacted as from Sinai) of which it constituted the violation. It is true, he does not ascribe the heritage of death to these actual violations of law, but only to the sin of Adam; this, however, does not prevent his seeing in them a proof, that all were held to have sinned in Adam, and in him to have fallen into a state of depravity and condemnation—the point immediately in hand. So far, I entirely con- cur with Dr Hodge: ' If there is no sin without law, there can be no imputation of sin. As, however, sin was imputed (or reckoned), as men were sinners, and were so regarded and treated before the law of Moses, it follows that there must be some more comprehensive law in relation to which men were sinners, and in virtue of which they were so regarded and treated.' Assuredly, but I see no reason for holding that this has reference simply to original sin, or to men's relation to the one sin of Adam—that they were regarded and treated as sinners, merely because they were viewed as having sinned in Adam; for this would be to put rather a forced inter- pretation on the clause, that sin was in the world till the law, making it to mean that the sin of Adam's first transgression was in the world. This were unnatural, especially just after that sin had been mentioned as a past act; and, besides, by fixing attention only on that one sin,

[1] *See* the remarks at Gal. iii. 19.

[2] Gen. iv. 8-12, vi. 3-7, 13, etc., ix. 6, xi. 1-8, xviii. 17, xix. 29, etc.

the thought of actual offences would be virtually excluded; while yet these, as we presently find, form an important item in the comparative view drawn by the apostle. Take the line of thought to be that which we have presented, and there is no ground for such objections. ' All sinned in Adam '—this is the general position; and the proof is, sin was in the world from Adam to Moses, as well as since, at once the fruit of Adam's sin, and the parent of numberless other sins ; but, apart also from these, death has reigned with undistinguishing equality over one and all, whether or not chargeable with personal transgressions.

Having made this explanation about sin and death in relation to Adam's fall, the apostle now begins to wend his course back to the comparison of the two great heads of humanity ; and first notices the resemblance, by saying of Adam, that he was ' the type of the future One '—of the Man, by way of eminence, that was afterwards to come. He was the type in regard to the great principle of headship—it being true alike of both, that their position in the Divine economy carried along with it the position of all who are connected with them—the one in nature, the other in grace. But with this general resemblance, the apostle goes on to say, there were important differences ; and more especially, first, in regard to the *kind* of results flowing from the connection—in the one case evil, condemnation, death ; in the other good, justification, life ; secondly, in regard to the mode and ground of procedure—one man's sin bringing upon the many such a heritage of evil, the righteousness of the other (because of its absolute perfection and infinite worth) prevailing over many sins to secure a heritage of good, greatly more than counterbalancing the evil ; hence, thirdly, the surpassing excellence of grace as manifested in the one line of operations, as compared with the actings of nature in the other.

Two points only, and these of a somewhat incidental kind, call for a brief notice. One is, as to the place where the explanatory matter ends, and the apostle formally concludes the comparison begun in ver. 12. It is, as all the better commentators now agree, at ver. 18, where there is a recapitulation of what had been previously stated, and a pressing of the formal conclusion : ' Therefore as through one offence [it came] upon all men to condemnation, so also through one righteous act (δι᾽ ἑνὸς δικαιώματος, pointing specially to the consummation of Christ's work on the cross) [it came] upon all men unto justification of life,' etc. The other point has respect to what is said of the law in its bearing on the subject, which was, not to provide the means of justification, but rather to increase the number of offences from which justification was needed : ' But the law came in besides ($\pi\alpha\rho\epsilon\iota\sigma\tilde{\eta}\lambda\theta\epsilon\nu$, subintravit, entered by the way as a kind of subsidiary element, therefore with power only to modify, not to alter essentially, the state of matters) in order that the offence might abound '—not, of course, in an arbitrary way to increase the number of sins, or strictly for the purpose of working in this direction, but with such a certain knowledge of its tendency so to work, that this might be said to have been its object. Prescribing to men the way of righteousness, and commanding them to observe it, the law did but shew the more clearly how far they had gone from it, and by its very explicitness as to duty, served to multiply the number and aggravate the guilt of transgressions. Substantially the same thought is expressed in Gal. iii. 19, so that it is unnecessary to enlarge on the subject here.

ROM. VI. 14–18.

' For sin shall not have dominion over you : for ye are not under the law, but under grace. 15. What then ? May we sin, because we are not under the law, but under grace ? God forbid ! 16. Know ye not, that to whom ye yield yourselves servants for obedience, his servants ye are whom ye obey, whether of sin unto death, or of obedience unto righteousness. 17. But thanks be to God, that ye were the servants of sin, but ye obeyed from the heart that form of instruction to which ye were delivered. 18. And being freed from sin, ye became servants to righteousness.'

This passage respecting the relation of believers to the law, forms part of a much longer section, in which the apostle handles the connection between justification and sanctification—shews how the doctrine of a gratuitous salvation through the faith of Christ, so far from leading to a life of sin, renders such a life impossible, makes holiness, not sin, the rule and aim of the believer's course. The fundamental ground of this result, as the apostle states at the outset (near the beginning of the chapter) lies in the believer's relation to Christ ; he becomes, by the very faith which justifies him, vitally united to Christ, and consequently participates in that death of Christ to sin, and that life to righteousness, which characterize Him as the spiritual Head and Redeemer of His people. This, therefore, is the security of the believer, and his safeguard against the dominion of sin in his soul, that the grace which saves him has, at the same time, transplanted him into a new state, has brought him into connection with holy influences, and changed the

current of his desires and purposes. Hence, the apostle exhorts those
who have undergone this blessed change to realize the great truth
involved in it, and give themselves in earnest to the life of faith and
holiness to which it called them. Sin had no longer any *right* to reign
over them, and they should not allow it, in fact, to do so. This is
what is meant in ver. 14, ' For sin shall not have dominion over you '
—ὑμῶν οὐ κυριεύσει, shall not domineer, or lord it over you ; the power
to do this was now effectually broken, and they should act under the
buoyant and joyous feeling, that they did not need to be in bondage,
that spiritual liberty-was secured for them. Then comes the reason or
ground of this freedom, ' for ye are not under the law, but under grace.'

In endeavouring to get at the precise meaning of this statement,
which has been variously understood, there is no need for raising any
question as to what is intended by *law*, whether the Mosaic, or some
other form of law. The proper explication cannot turn on any
difference in this respect ; for it is plainly of the law as a system of
requirements (no matter what these might specifically be), of the law
as contradistinguished from grace, God's system of free and unmerited
benevolence, that the apostle is speaking ; consequently, law is taken
into account merely as the appointed rule of righteousness, which men
are bound as rational creatures to keep, and which, for the subjects of
revelation, would naturally be identified with that of Moses. The law
so understood, and by reason of its very excellence as the revelation of
God's pure righteousness, so far from being the deliverer from sin,
is the strength of sin ;[1] for if placed simply under it, the condition
of fallen man becomes utterly hopeless ; it sets before him, and binds
upon his conscience, a scheme of life, which lies quite beyond his
reach, and he falls like a helpless slave under the mastery of sin.
But believers are otherwise situated ; they stand under an administration of grace, which brings the mighty power of redeeming love to
work upon the heart, and, freeing it from condemnation, inspires it
with the life and liberty of the children of God. This new and better
constitution of things supplants, for those who are interested in it, the
ground of sin's dominion in the soul, and opens for it the way to ultimate perfection in holiness.[2]

The apostle, however, was writing to those who were still but imperfectly acquainted with the operation of grace ; and readily conceiving how they would startle at the thought of believers being no longer
under the law, as involving a dangerous sort of licence, he turns as it
were upon himself, and asks, ' What then ? May we sin (the proper

[1] 1 Cor. xv. 56.   [2] The point is unfolded at much greater length in chap. vii.

reading is undoubtedly ἁμαρτήσωμεν, the subjunctive of deliberation, not the future ἁμαρτήσομεν) because we are not under the law, but under grace?' The question is asked only that an indignant disclaimer may be given to it: 'God forbid!' The thought is not for a moment to be entertained; and the moral contradiction, which the supposed inclination and liberty to sin would involve, is exposed by presenting sin and obedience (much as our Lord presented God and mammon[1]) as antagonistic powers or interests, to the one or other of which all must stand in a relation of servitude. There is no middle course, as the apostle states: one must either act as the servant of sin, and receive the wages thereof in death, or in the spirit of obedience (namely, to God), and attain to righteousness. 'Servants of obedience' is certainly a peculiar expression, and would probably have been put, as in ver. 18, servants of righteousness, but for the purpose of keeping up the parallel—on the one side sin unto death, on the other obedience unto righteousness. This personified obedience, however, involves the idea of God, as the One to whom it is due: the servants of obedience are those who realize and feel that they must obey God, and this by aiming at righteousness. And it is implied, that as the service of sin finds in eternity the consummation of the death to which it works, so also with the righteousness which is the result of obedience; it is consummated only in the life to come, when they who have sincerely followed after it shall receive 'the crown of righteousness from the Lord, the righteous Judge.'[2] Righteousness so considered is not materially different from eternal life. Further, it is clear, that as obedience implies objection to an authoritative rule, and the life of grace is here identified with obedience, the child of grace is not more freed from the prescription of a rule than those who are in the condition of nature. The life to which he is called, and after which he must ever strive, is conformity to the Divine rule of righteousness; just as, on the other side, all sin is a deviation from such a rule.

The apostle, in ver. 17, expresses his gratitude to God that those to whom he wrote had passed from the one kind of service to the other: 'But thanks be to God that ye were the servants of sin (the stress should be on the *were*, thanks that this is a thing of the past, and can be spoken of as such), but ye obeyed from the heart that form (τύπον, type, rather) of instruction into which ye were delivered.' The form of expression in this last member of the sentence is peculiar, εἰς ὃν παρεδόθητε τύπον διδαχῆς, literally, obeyed into what pattern of instruction ye were delivered; evidently a pregnant form of construction for

[1] Matt. vi. 24. [2] 2 Tim. iv. 8.

obeyed the pattern of instruction into which ye were delivered (τῷ τύπῳ τῆς διδ. εἰς ὄν παραδόθητε). The Christian instruction they had received is viewed as a kind of pattern or mould, into which their moral natures had been in a manner cast, so as to take on its proper impress, and give forth suitable manifestations of it. It is a question with commentators, whether this plastic sort of instruction is to be understood generally of the rule of faith and manners in the Gospel, or more specially of St Paul's mode of teaching the Gospel, as contradistinguished from the Judaistic type of Christian doctrine. De Wette, Meyer, and some others, would take it in the latter sense; but apparently without any sufficient reason, as it would involve a closer relationship on the part of the Romish community to St Paul's teaching than we have any ground for supposing. It is quite enough to understand by the expression, the Gospel of the grace of God in its grand outlines of truth and duty, through whatever precise channel it might have reached the believers at Rome; this they had not only received, but from the heart obeyed. 'Paul,' to use the words of Calvin, 'compares here the hidden power of the Spirit with the external letter of the law, as though he had said: "Christ inwardly forms our souls in a better way, than when the law constrains them by threatening and terrifying us." Thus is dissipated the following calumny, "If Christ free us from subjection to the law, He brings liberty to sin." He does not, indeed, allow His people unbridled freedom, that they might frisk about without any restraint, like horses let loose in the fields; but He brings them to a regular course of life.' It is the same truth substantially which is taught by our Lord when He says: 'Ye are clean through the word which I have spoken unto you;' and again, 'Ye shall know the truth, and the truth shall make you free.'[1] And finally, let there be noted here the beautiful combination in the apostle's statement of the action of Divine grace and of man's will. 'They obeyed the doctrine heartily; in this they were active: yet they were cast into the mould of this doctrine, and thereby received the new form of faith, obedience, and holiness, from another hand and influence. So that they were active in obeying the truth; and at the very same time were passive with regard to the superior influence.'[2]

The apostle adds, virtually repeating what had been said before, only with special application to the Christians at Rome: 'And being freed from sin, ye became servants to righteousness.' This is probably as fit a rendering of the words (ἐδουλώθητε τῇ δικαιοσύνῃ) as can be obtained. The rendering of Alford, 'Ye were enslaved to righteousness,' though

[1] Jo. xv. 3, viii. 32. *See* also 1 Pet. i. 22. [2] Fraser.

apparently nearer to the original, is in reality not so; for, to speak of enslavement in the spiritual sphere can scarcely fail to convey to an English reader the idea of unwilling constraint, a sort of compulsory service, which certainly was not what the apostle meant. It is merely a thorough, life-long, undivided surrender to the cause of righteousness. And he proceeds to unfold, to the end of the chapter, the blessed nature of the service to which they had thus given themselves, as contrasted with that from which they had been withdrawn, and to press the things which belonged to it on their regard, both from consideration of the present benefits to be derived from it, and the relation in which it stands to the eternal recompenses of blessing in God's kingdom.

ROM. VII.

' Know ye not, brethren (for I speak to them that know the law), that the law has dominion over a man so long as he lives? 2. For the married woman is bound by the law to her living husband; but if the husband have died, she is loosed (lit., made void) from the law of her husband. 3. So, then, while her husband lives, she shall be called an adulteress if she become another man's; but if her husband have died, she is free from the law, so as not to be an adulteress though she have become another man's. 4. Wherefore, my brethren, ye also were made to die to the law through the body of Christ, that you might become another's, even His who was raised from the dead, in order that ye might bring forth fruit to God. 5. For when we were in the flesh, the motions of sins which were through the law wrought in our members to the bringing forth of fruit unto death. 6. But now we have been delivered from the law, having died to that wherein we were held, so that we serve in newness of spirit and not in oldness of letter. 7. What shall we say, then? Is the law sin? God forbid! On the contrary, I had not known sin except through the law; for, indeed, I had not known lust, except the law had said, Thou shalt not lust. 8. But sin, taking occasion by means of the commandment, wrought in me all manner of concupiscence; for without the law sin is dead. 9. I was alive, indeed, without the law once; but when the commandment came, sin revived, and I died. 10. And the commandment which was for life, even this was found by me unto death. 11. For sin, taking occasion through the commandment, deceived me, and through it slew me. 12. So that the law is holy, and the commandment holy, and just, and good. 13. Did, then, the good become death to me? God forbid! [not that] but sin, in order that it might appear sin, through the good working in me death, in order that sin, through the commandment, might become exceeding sinful. 14. For we know that the law is spiritual; but I am carnal, sold under sin. 15. For what I effect I know not; for not what I wish do I perform; but what I hate, that do I. 16. But if I do that which I wish not, I consent to the law that it is good. 17. Now, however, it is no longer I that effect it, but sin that dwelleth in me. 18. For I know that in me, that is, in my flesh, good does not dwell; for to wish is present with me, but to perform that which is good is not; 19. For not the good which I wish, but the evil which I do not wish, that I do. 20. But if what I do not wish, that I do, it is no longer I that perform it, but sin that is dwelling in me. 21. I find, then, this law to me, when wishing to do good, that evil is present with me. 22. For I consent to the law of God after the inner man. 23. But I see another law in my members warring against the law of my mind, and bringing me into captivity with the law of sin that is in my members. 24. Wretched man that I am! who shall deliver me from the body of this death? 25. Thanks be to God through Christ Jesus our Lord. So, then, I myself with my mind indeed serve the law of God, but with my flesh the law of sin.'

The leading object of the apostle in this section is to bring out precisely the relation of the believer to the law, with the view at once of establishing the law, and of shewing that he is not under it (ch. iii. 31, vi. 14), but, on the contrary, is freed from it, or dead to it.[1] It is the latter point which comes first, and in treating it, he avails himself of the image of the marriage-tie, which, as every one acquainted with the law in such matters knows, holds so long as the contracting parties live, but when the husband dies, the wife is set free to become united to another spouse. In like manner, says the apostle, there has been a death in our experience which has dissolved our original connection with the law, and united us to the risen Saviour, that we may bring forth fruit of righteousness to God. This is the comparison in its essential

---

[1] The relation of this whole chapter to chap. vi. 14, is very well stated by Mr Owen in his note to the translation of Calvin on Romans, at ch. vii. 1 : 'The connection of the beginning of this chapter with the 14th verse of the former chapter deserves to be noticed. He says there, that sin shall not rule over us, *because* we are not under law, but under grace. Then he asks in ver. 15 : "Shall we sin because we are not under law, but under grace?" This last subject, according to his usual mode, he takes up *first*, and discusses it till the end of the chapter; and then, in this chapter, he reassumes the first subject—freedom from the law. This is a striking instance of the apostle's manner of writing, quite different from what is usual with us in the present day. He mentions two things; he proceeds with the last, and then goes back to the first.'

points of agreement; but as actually applied, there is a difference in detail. In the natural relation employed, as it is the woman that represents the case of believers under the Gospel, so it is not her death, but the death of her husband which dissolves the bond of her obligation, and sets her free to enter into a new alliance. But with believers it is their own death, that is, their fellowship with Christ in his death, which has changed their relationship to the law, and made them partakers of a life which it had no power to impart. It was, no doubt, to render the parallel more complete, that the received text, on the authority of Beza, adopted the reading ἀποθανόντος in ver. 6, instead of ἀποθανόντες, to convey the meaning that the death in question had passed upon the law, not upon us (against all the uncial MSS. א A B C K L, and other authorities). The apostle never speaks of the law as undergoing change or dying; but in ver. 4 he had expressly said of believers, that they had died—nay, had been put to death or slain (ἐθανώθητε) to the law through the body of Christ. The form of expression is purposely made stronger here than in the case of the natural relation, to indicate that the death in this case had to do with the infliction of a penalty, and an infliction in which the law itself might be said to have a part; for it has respect to Christ's crucifixion or death under the curse of the law, which is in effect also theirs; so that through the law they become dead to the law,[1] yet in such a sense dead as at the same time to pass into another and higher life. The comparison, therefore, only holds, and was only intended to hold, in regard to the fact of death in either party putting an end to the right and authority of law: with the intervention of death, the prior relation ceased, and it became competent to enter into a fresh alliance.

But what in this connection is to be understood by the law? and what by the marriage-like relation supposed to have been held to it? Here a certain diversity meets us among commentators—though, among the better class, less now than formerly. The Grotian school, including Hammond, Locke, and some others in this country, considered the law, as here used, to be meant chiefly of religious rites and judicial institutions, or the law in its distinctively Jewish aspect, as the ground and basis of the temporal economy under which Israel was placed. But such a view is entirely arbitrary and superficial, and as such has been generally abandoned. The whole tenor of the apostle's discourse is against it, which never once points to that part of the Old Testament legislation which was in its own nature provisional and temporary. The law of which he speaks is one that penetrates into

[1] Gal. ii. 19.

the inmost soul, comes close to the heart and conscience, is in itself spiritual, holy, just, and good (vers. 7, 12, 14), and one's relation to which determines the whole question of one's peace and hope toward God (vers. 24, 25). How any intelligent critics could ever have thought of finding what corresponded to such a description in the outward ritual and secular polity of the Hebrew commonwealth, it is difficult to conceive. There is no need, however, while rejecting this view, to go with some to the opposite extreme of maintaining that the language has respect exclusively to the moral law, and that what seemed to the Grotian school to be its one and all, must be altogether eliminated from it. Speaking, as the apostle does, without reserve or qualification of *the law*, and taking for granted the familiar acquaintance of those he addressed with what was implied in the term, we can here think of nothing else than the law of Moses—only, it is to be borne in mind here, as in passages already considered, that of that law the ten commandments occupied, not only the chief, but the properly fundamental place—the principle of the whole is there as to what it involved of moral obligation. When reasoning, therefore, of men's relation to the law, the apostle must be understood to have had this part of the Mosaic legislation prominently in view; and, consequently, while there is a direct reference in what he says to the law as ministered by the hand of Moses, it is of this substantially, as the rule of God's righteous government, that he speaks; the law as the sum of moral and religious duty. Hence, the term 'brethren,' by which he designates the persons whom he sought to instruct respecting the law, is to be taken in the full sense, not of the Jewish-Christians only at Rome, but of the whole body of believers; for all alike were interested in the law as here discoursed of, and stood essentially in the same relation to it. But of that relation in its earlier form, how are we to understand it? The comparison of the apostle implies, that it was somewhat like a marriage, and might be presented under that aspect—though he says nothing as to when or how such a relation was constituted. Indeed, it is not so properly the formation, or the existence of the relation in question, as its termination, on which the apostle seeks to fix the attention of his readers. 'Wherefore,' says he, after stating the law of marriage, or, ' So then, my brethren, ye also were made to die to the law through the body of Christ, that you might become another's.' Still, the dissolution of the one, that the other might be formed, bespoke a formal resemblance between the relations—a marriage to the law in the first instance; then, on the dissolution of that, a marriage to Christ. How, then, was that previous marriage formed, and when? Is it to be simply identified with the establishment of the covenant at Sinai? And shall we, with Macknight, explicate the apostle's meaning, by referring to those passages in which God represents his connection with the Jews as their king, under the idea of a marriage solemnized at Sinai[1]—a marriage 'which was to end when they, with the rest of mankind, should be put to death in the person of Christ?' But this was altogether to shift the ground assumed by the apostle—since to be married to God, and married to the law, are very different things; God being to His people the fountainhead of grace as well as of law, and, indeed, of grace more prominently than of law. This was recognised in the Decalogue itself, which avowedly proceeded from God in the character of their most gracious Benefactor and Redeemer. To identify their being married to Him, therefore, with being married to the law (in the sense here necessarily understood), were virtually to say, that they entered into covenant with God, or stood related to God, under only one aspect of His manifestations, and that for fallen men not the primary and most essential one. It were also at variance with the view, given by the apostle in another passage,[2] of the relation of Israel to the law, which was no more intended, on the part of God, to be *per se* a spouse and a parent of children to the covenant people, than Hagar in the house of Abraham: when contemplated in such a light, it was diverted from its proper purpose, and looked to for results which it was not given to secure.

We must, therefore, ascend higher in the order of God's dipensations for the proper ground of the apostle's representation here respecting the law. The marriage relation which he assumes to have existed between us and it, must be regarded as having its ground in the constitution of nature rather than of grace ; and it is associated with the law as given to Israel, not as if that law had been formally propounded as a basis on which they might work themselves into the possession of life and blessing, but because in its great principles of truth and duty it presents the terms which men are *naturally* bound to comply with, in order that they may warrantably expect such things, and because Israel, whenever they sought in themselves what they so expected, acknowledged their obligation to seek for it according to the terms therein prescribed : they sought for it, ' as it were by the works of the law.' Here, therefore, was the natural ground of such a relationship as that indicated by the apostle. Contemplated as in substance the revelation of that righteousness which God has inherently a right to demand of His rational creatures as a title to His favour, the law holds over men,

[1] Jer. ii. 2, iii. 14; Ezek. xvi. 8.   [2] Gal. iv. 21-31.

merely as such, an indefeasible claim to their fealty and obedience ;
they cannot, by any right or power of their own, shake themselves free
from it ; the bond of its obligation is upon their conscience, and they
are held by it, whether they will or not (ver. 6) : while yet, whenever
they look seriously into the height and depth of its requirements, and
consider the sanctions which enforce its observance, and the penalties
which avenge its violation, they necessarily die to all hope of making
good what it exacts at their hands to secure the blessing. *As children
of promise*, the covenant people were not called to stand in such a relation to the law ; to place themselves in it was to fall from the grace of
the covenant ; but with reference to the responsibilities and calling of
nature, it is the relation in which not only they, but mankind generally,
stood and must ever stand to it.

Vers. 5, 6. The statements in these verses are more especially
designed to confirm and illustrate what had been said immediately
before as to the advantage yielded by the new marriage relation over
the old—viz., that it is fruitful of good, while the other was not ; but
they also incidentally support the view just given of the first marriage
relation as one pertaining to the state of nature, as contradistinguished
from the state of grace. *For when we were in the flesh*—this stands
opposed to the being killed or crucified with Christ in the immediately
preceding verse, and so is much the same with being in the state of
fallen nature—subject to the law, yet with a frame of mind utterly
opposed to its pure and holy requirements. It is the state in which
the merely human element ($\sigma\acute{a}\rho\xi$) bore sway, and, according to its
native tendency, fretted against and resisted the will of God. To
understand it, with Grotius, Hammond, Whitby, etc., of subjection to
the ordinances of the Old Testament, which, as compared with those
of the New, are elsewhere called fleshly, carnal, beggarly,[1] is entirely
to mistake the meaning of the expression. For in that case it would
include God's true and faithful people, as well as others, since they also
were subject to the legal observances of the old covenant, and yet,
being men of faith and love, were endowed with the Spirit, and brought
forth fruit to God. The state of such is always substantially identified
by the apostle with that of believers under the Gospel, not set in
formal opposition to it. But to be in the flesh is to be in a state of
sin, working unto death—as he himself, indeed, explains in chap.
viii. 5-8, where ' having the mind of the flesh,' or ' walking after
the flesh,' is represented as being in a state of ungodliness, utterly
incapable of pleasing God, nay, in living and active enmity to Him.

[1] Gal. iii. 3, iv. 9.

So also at Gal. v. 17-21, where the lusting of the flesh and its natural results are placed in opposition to the life and Spirit of God. In all such expressions, *the flesh* indicates human nature in its present depraved state; so that 'to be in the flesh' is merely to be under the influence or power of human depravity. And this is all one with being under the law; for it is the universal condition of men, who have not received the Spirit of God,[1] and the Spirit does not come by the law, but by the faith of Christ. Had the true members of the old covenant stood simply under the law, this would necessarily have been their condition; but they were under the law as the heir, though a child, having also the covenant of promise;[2] and therefore were not left merely to the dominion of flesh and law, but were in a measure partakers of grace, and as such capable of doing acceptable service to God. Of men, so long as they are in the flesh, the apostle says, that *the motions* ($\pi\alpha\theta\eta\mu\alpha\tau\alpha$, affections, stirrings) *of sins which were through the law wrought in our members to the bringing forth of fruit unto death.* The idea of this passage again recurs and is more fully expressed in ver. 13. We, therefore, need not dwell upon it here. Its chief peculiarity consists in saying, that the sinful emotions which work in men's souls before they come under grace are through the law ($\delta\iota\grave{\alpha}\ \tau o\tilde{v}\ \nu\acute{o}\mu o\nu$), ascribing to the law some sort of instrumental agency in their production. This cannot be better stated than it was long ago by Fraser : 'It is just to say, that the precept, prohibition, and fearful threatening of the law do, instead of subduing sinful affections in an unrenewed heart, but irritate them, and occasion their excitement and more violent motion. Nor is this a strange imputation on the law of God, which is not the proper cause of these motions. These are to be ascribed to the corruption of men's hearts, which the apostle insinuates when he ascribes these sinful motions by the law to men in the flesh. The matter has been often illustrated by the similitude of the sun, by whose light and heat roses and flowers display their fine colours, and emit their fragrant smell; whereas by its heat the dunghill emits its unsavoury steams and ill smell. So the law, which to a sanctified heart is a means of holy practice, doth, in those who are in the flesh, occasion the more vehement motions of sinful affections and lustings, not from any proper causality of the law, but from the energy of the sinful principles that are in men's hearts and nature. There was great wrath and sinful passion in Jeroboam by the reproof of the prophet[3]— which was not to be imputed to the prophet, but to Jeroboam, a man in the flesh. In David, a man of very different character, Nathan's

[1] Gal. viii. 9.   [2] Gal. iv. 1-3.   [3] 1 Kings xiii. 4.

very sharp reproof had no such effect.'   In saying that there not only were such sinful emotions, stirred rather than repressed by the law, but that they brought forth fruit unto death—had this, as it were, for their aim and result—the apostle has respect to the natural design of marriage as to yielding fruit, but characterizes the fruit in this case as the reverse of what one desires and expects—a fruit not for life but for death—hence not to be hailed and rejoiced in, but to be mourned over and deplored as the just occasion of bitterness and grief.   The death, also, in such a case, must evidently be of a spiritual rather than of a corporeal nature.

'But now,' the apostle adds, giving the reverse side of the picture, 'we have been delivered ($\varkappa\alpha\tau\eta\rho\gamma\dot\eta\theta\eta\mu\varepsilon\nu$, made void, discharged) from the law, having died to that wherein we were held, so that we serve in newness of spirit, not in oldness of letter.'   The deliverance or freedom from the law here mentioned is that already explained—namely, release from it as the ground of justification and life.   We die to it in this respect when we enter through faith into the fellowship of Christ's sufferings and death; but not with the effect of getting free from any duties of service—with the effect rather of serving in a higher style of obedience—serving in newness of spirit (which is all one with bringing forth fruit to God), not in oldness of letter (bringing forth fruit to death).   These expressions have been virtually explained in the exposition of 2 Cor. iii. 6, and a few words here may suffice.   It is implied, that those who owned their relation to the law, and were conscious of no higher relationship, would endeavour after some sort of obedience. But then, with no power higher than human, and with tendencies in the human ever running in the opposite direction, the obedience could have no heart or life in it; it could be only such outward formal obedience as a fearful, slavish, mercenary spirit is capable of yielding—looking at the mere letter of the command, and trying to maintain such a conformity to it by a fair show in the flesh.   This is what is meant by serving in oldness of letter—the only kind of service which old corrupt nature is capable of rendering, and one that can bring no real satisfaction to the conscience, or receive any blessing from God.   Believers in Christ are freed from such service, because raised, through fellowship with Christ, above nature—brought into the region of the Spirit's grace and power, so that what they do is done under the influence of things spiritual and Divine, with a sincere and loving heart, and with an unaffected desire of pleasing God.   There is a newness in such service, and it is newness of spirit, as contradistinguished from the flesh's oldness—the mere formalism of a carnal and hireling service.   As to the things done, it may be the same service still (no change in this respect is here indicated), but it is service of quite another and higher kind.

Ver. 7. ' What shall we say then? Is the law sin?' etc. The apostle here formally states and answers a question, which naturally suggested itself from his apparent identification of the dominion of sin with subjection to the law. Was the law, then, the actual source and parent of sin? Is it in itself evil? He repels the idea with a μὴ γένοιτο, God forbid. But not satisfied with this, he proceeds to unfold, by a reference to his own experience, the true relation of the law to sin, and shews how, by reason of its very goodness, it tends to evolve the element of sin, and aggravate the sense of it in the soul. The *reason* for adopting this mode of representation is stated with admirable propriety and clearness by Alford: ' I ask, why St Paul suddenly changes here to the first person? The answer is, because he is about to draw a conclusion negativing the question, *Is the law sin?* upon purely subjective grounds, proceeding on that which passes within, when the work of the law is carried on in the heart. And he is about to depict this work of the law by an example which shall set it forth in vivid colours, in detail, in its connection with sin in a man. What example, then, so apposite as his own? Introspective as his character was, and purified as his inner vision was by the Holy Spirit of God, what example would so forcibly bring out the inward struggles of the man, which prove the holiness of the law, while they shew its inseparable connection with the production of sin? If this be the reason why the first person is here assumed (and I can find no other which does not introduce into St Paul's style an arbitrariness and caprice which it least of all others exhibits), then *we must dismiss from our minds all exegesis which explains the passage of any other*, in the first instance, *than of Paul himself:* himself, indeed, as an *exemplar*, wherein others may see themselves: but not himself *in the person* of others, be they the Jews, nationally or individually, or all mankind, or individual men.' Entirely concurring in this, which is substantially the Augustinian view of the passage—the view also which, with solid argument in the main, and sound evangelical feeling, was set forth and vindicated with great fulness in the last century by Mr Fraser in his work on Sanctification—we set aside as arbitrary and unnatural the view of the Grotian school, which regards Paul as personating here the Jewish people, before and after the introduction of the law of Moses; the view also of Meyer and many others, that Paul gives, in his own person, a kind of ideal history of humanity, first in its original state, then as under law, and lastly as redeemed in Christ; with various subordinate shades of difference under each of these general modes of representation. But holding the delineation of experience to be properly personal, and only as such representative, there is no need for supposing that it should in every part exhibit what is peculiar to the regenerate. The operation of law on the natural conscience will often, to a considerable extent, produce the same feelings and convictions as are experienced in a more intense and vivid form, as with more permanent results, by those who are the subjects of renewing grace. There is nothing here, however, which does not more or less find a place in the history of every one who has come under the power of the quickening Spirit—although some parts of the description belong more to the initiatory, others to the more advanced exercises of the believer, several again to those complex operations, those interminglings of the flesh and the Spirit of which all believers are at times conscious, and those always the most who are most sensitively alive to the claims of the Divine righteousness, and most watchful of the movements of their own souls in reference to these. A spirit of discrimination, therefore, is needed for the interpretation of the particular parts, even when there is a proper understanding of the general purport and bearing of the passage.

The principle with which the apostle sets out in this narrative of his inward experience, and which he keeps in view throughout, is one he had already announced, that ' by the law is the knowledge of sin ' (iii. 20) ; for, obviously, what discovers evil cannot be itself evil ; it must be the opposite of evil—good. In answer therefore to the question, whether the law is sin, after a strong negation, he says, ' On the contrary (ἀλλὰ, I cannot see why Alford should regard this simply adversative sense as not exactly suitable here—the apostle is going to state precisely the reverse of what an affirmative to the question would have implied), I had not known sin, except through the law '— literally, I was not knowing (οὐκ ἔγνων), I was in ignorance of sin, except through the law. This might be taken two ways, either that he did not know such and such a thing to be in its own nature sinful, unless the law had condemned it ; or he did not know the existence and operation of sin as a principle in his soul, unless the law had brought it to light. Both to a certain extent are true, though from the context it is clear that the latter is what the apostle has mainly, if not exclusively, in view. It only holds of some things, that they could not have been known to be sinful but through the law ; in regard to many, especially such as relate to breaches of the second table, the natural light of conscience is quite sufficient to pronounce upon their character (as the apostle, indeed, had already affirmed, ii. 14, 15). But it is not specific acts of sin, and their objective character, that the apostle here has in his eye ; it is the principle of sin in his own bosom, as a deep-rooted, latent evil, which was naturally at work there, but which he was not sensible of till the law, by its prohibition, discovered it.[1] And so he adds, in further explication of his meaning, ' For indeed I had not known lust except the law had said, Thou shalt not lust.' It is not something strictly new that is here introduced, but a particular example in illustration of the general statement made immediately before (τε γάρ, *denn-ja*, fortius est quam γάρ solum ; scilicet τε istud non copulat, sed lenius affirmat quam τοι, unde natum est, Fritzsche). The lusting (ἐπιθυμία, sometimes, desire generally, but here inordinate desire, concupiscence, so elsewhere 1 Tim. vi. 9 ; 2 Tim. ii. 22 ; 1 John ii. 17, etc.) is not to be confined to mere sensual appetite, but includes all the undue affections and desires of the heart, which, if carried out, might lead to the overt violation of any of God's commands. The closing prohibition, therefore, of the Decalogue spreads itself over all the other precepts, and includes, in its condemnation, every sort of lusting or concupiscence which tends to the commission of the acts forbidden in them. Hence it was that the consideration of this particular command let in such a flood of light upon the apostle's soul, as to his real state before God. ' He had been a Pharisee, and with great zeal and earnest effort serving in the oldness of the letter, as he understood it. His mind being biassed by corrupt teaching and sentiment, he thought himself chargeable with no sin, until the law struck at his heart within him, as subject to its authority and direction no less than the outward man. Until then he thought all his works were good. Now he sees all his works, taking into the account the evil principles, and the concupiscence which in various forms was set at the root of all his works, to be evil. Instead of keeping all the commandments from his youth up, he then saw he had truly fulfilled none of them.' We have, indeed, the same confession substantially from the apostle

[1] Of this use of ἁμαρτία to denote, not actual sin, but a habitual tendency and constitution of the inward life, Müller says, in his work on Sin (B. I. P. 1, chap. 3): ' In that passage which gives us the fullest and minutest instruction of sin and its development in man, Rom. vii., it cannot be doubted that ἁμαρτία is used in the signification of a power dwelling and working in man, including a sinful bias, a perverted constitution. So especially in Rom. vii. 8-11 : Sin, which before was dead, by the entrance of the law, revived, and took occasion, by the commandment, to put man to death ; this can have no meaning, unless the term *sin* means a power dwelling in man in a concealed manner.' He points to Matt. xii. 33, xv. 19 ; 1 John ii. 16 ; James i. 14, 15, as teaching the same truth, though the term ἁμαρτία is not always used.

as here, only more briefly unfolded, and with reference more to actual change of state than to the workings of inward experience, in Phil. iii. 6-10. There also the apostle expresses a perfect satisfaction with his condition at one time, as if all were right, and then represents this as giving way to an entirely opposite state of feeling, when he came to see into the reality of things. What before seemed good, now was found worthless; what was thought gain, came to be reckoned loss; what had looked like life, was but death in disguise, and the true life only found when confidence in the law was forsaken for confidence in Christ.

Ver. 8. ' But sin, taking occasion by means of the commandment, wrought in me all manner of concupiscence; for without the law sin is dead.' Sin here is still the principle of sin in the soul, which exists whether there is any sense or not of its contrariety to law, but only in a kind of unconscious or slumbering state, till it is confronted with the peremptory *nay* of the command. This rouses it into conscious and active opposition. The command here meant (ἡ ἐντολὴ) is not the law in general, but the specific precept referred to just before, ' Thou shalt not lust.' And the principle of the passage is very much the same with that of Prov. ix. 17, ' Stolen waters are sweet,' or with the *nitimur in vetitum semper cupimusque negata* of Ovid. So also Augustine: ' The law, though in itself good, yet, by forbidding, increases sinful desire; for somehow that which is desired becomes more pleasant simply by being forbidden.'[1] It is good, but ' weak through the flesh.' The ungodly heart chafes against the restraint laid on it, and the evil, comparatively latent before, rises into active opposition. But when the apostle says, that ' without the law sin was dead,' he can only mean dead in the sense and feeling of the soul; for sin not only exists without the law as a principle in the soul, but is ever ready also to go forth in active exercise on the objects around it; living, therefore, in reality, though not consciously known and realized as such.

Ver. 9. ' *I was alive without the law once, but when the commandment came, sin revived, and I died.*' Recognising the principle that sin, by inevitable necessity, is the source of death, it naturally follows that, according to the conscious presence and vitality of sin or the reverse, so should also be the sense of life or death in the soul. While ignorant of the depth and spirituality of the law, the apostle was unconscious of sin, and as a matter of course felt and acted as one in the enjoyment of life; but when the commandment entered with its penetrating light and Divine authority into the convictions of the inner man, it was like the opening of a new sense to him; sin sprung into conscious activity,

---

[1] ' De Sp. et Lit.,' sec. 6.

and the pains of death took hold of him. It could be but a relative thing in the one case, the slumber of sin and the enjoyment of life, and the quickening of sin into activity, with its production of death, in the other; for the commandment did not *create* the evil principle or its deadly fruit, only awoke the sense and realization of them in the soul. It is of this, therefore, that the apostle speaks, primarily in his own case, and indirectly in the case of others. Up to the time that the law, in its wide reaching import and spiritual requirements, takes hold of the heart, it is as if a man's life were whole in him : whatever errors and imperfections he may perceive in his past course, they appear but as incidental failings or partial infirmities, which can easily be excused or rectified ; they seem to leave untouched the *seat* of life. But with the right knowledge of the law, if that ever comes, there comes also a true insight into his case as a sinner ; and then all his fancied beauty and blessedness of life are felt to consume away; he sees himself corrupt at the core, and an heir of condemnation and death. Such an experience, of course, belongs to the very threshold of the Christian life, when the powers of regeneration are just beginning to make themselves known in the soul.

Ver. 10. ' And (or, so) the commandment which was for life, even this was found by me unto death '—a mere sequel to the preceding. The commandment was designed for, or had respect to life ; because making known that wherein life, in the higher sense, properly consists —the moral purity, rectitude, loving regard to God and man, which are essential to the harmonious action and blessed fellowship of the soul with God. But this delineation of life, when turned as a mirror in upon the soul, served but to bring to light the features and workings of a spiritual malady, which had its inevitable result in death.

Ver. 11. This is further explained by the statement, ' For sin, taking occasion through the commandment, deceived me, and through it slew me.' The indwelling principle of sin did with the apostle, by the law, much what the tempter did with Eve by the tree of the knowledge of good and evil. It gave rise to false expectations, and so entailed disastrous results. How should it have done so ? Simply by leading him to imagine that he should find life and blessing in another way than that prescribed by the commandment. Striving to resist the Divine call, it would have him seek his good in the gratification of forbidden desires, but only to involve him in the forlornness and misery of death, when the living force and authority of the commandment took hold of his conscience. Then experience taught him the hollowness of sin's promises, and the stern reality of God's prohibitions and threatenings.

Ver. 12. Now follows the legitimate inference in regard to the law:
' So that the law is holy, and the commandment holy, and just, and
good.' The distinction between the law and the commandment is
merely between the whole and a principal part : all is alike holy, and
that which more especially laid its bond on the desires and affections
of the soul, so far from being excepted, has even two additional epithets
applied to it (just and good), as if on purpose to shew how entirely
accordant even these more spiritual demands are with the claims of
rectitude and the truth of things. The experience of the apostle certified such to be the character of the law, as being in no proper sense
the cause of the death which he felt had come upon him, but only the
means of discovering the real nature and tendency of what the sinful
principle in his soul had prompted him to covet and seek after.

Ver. 13. ' Did then the good become death to me ? ' The question
might seem unnecessary after the statements already made ; but to
remove the possibility of misapprehension, and present the matter in
a little different light, the apostle puts it. The reply is very explicit
in meaning, but in form somewhat elliptical : ' God forbid ! [not the law
of God, which is good, was made death to me], but sin [was so] ; in
order that it might appear sin, through the good working death in me,
in order that sin through the commandment might become exceeding
sinful.' A twofold design—that sin might be exposed in its real character, and that the heinousness of its evil might appear in turning the
good itself into the occasion and instrument of bringing home to his
experience the pains and sorrows of death. It is here with life in the
spiritual precisely as in the natural sphere. When a deadly disease
has taken possession of the bodily frame, what is the class of things
that most conclusively prove the presence of such a disease? Not
those which are in themselves unfavourable to health, and tend to
impair bodily vigour—for, in that case, one naturally associates the evil
with these, to which no doubt they partly contribute. But let the
reverse supposition be made—let the circumstances of one's position be
altogether favourable—let the subject of disease have the benefit of the
most bracing atmosphere, the most nourishing diet, and of every thing
fitted to minister support and comfort : if still the frame continues to
languish, and the symptoms of death come on apace under the very
regimen of health, who can then shut his eyes to the fact, that a fatal
malady has seized the vitals of his constitution, since the good with
which it is plied, instead of mastering the evil, serves but to discover
its strength, and develop its working? So exactly with the good
exhibited in the law of God : when this is brought to bear on the cor-

rupt nature of man, the evil not being thereby subdued, but only rendered more clearly patent to the view, and more sensibly destructive of all proper life and blessing, it is then especially seen to be what it really is ; namely, sin—and, as such, hateful, pernicious, deadly.

Vers. 14-25. It is unnecessary here to go into a detailed exposition of these concluding verses ; for, with the exception of the first clause, ' We know that the law is spiritual '—which is also but another form of the statement in ver. 12, that the law is holy—the passage has respect, not properly to the apostle's relation to the law, but to his relation to indwelling sin. And the chief question it gives rise to is, whether the apostle, in the description he gives of the conflict between good and evil, represents what he, as a settled believer, and as an example of believers generally, was conscious of at the time he wrote the epistle, or what he merely, as a natural man, thought and felt, personating what natural men generally must think and feel, when awaking to a right knowledge of truth and duty, but still without the grace needed to conform them in spirit to it ?   Both sides of this alternative question have been espoused by commentators from comparatively early times, as they still are ; and it is quite possible to make the latter alternative, which is usually the one that commends itself to the less deeply exercised and spiritual class of minds, appear the more plausible and safe, by pressing one class of expressions to the uttermost, and passing lightly over another.   But undoubtedly the natural supposition is, that as the apostle had, in the verses immediately preceding, exhibited his own experience as one just awaking under the power of Divine grace to a right view of his own condition, so, continuing as he does still to speak in his own person, but in the present tense, he should be understood to utter the sentiments of which he was presently conscious.   Any view inconsistent with this, or materially differing from it, would require for its support very conclusive proof, from the nature of the representation itself.   This, however, does not exist. Certainly, when he describes himself as being ' carnal, sold under sin,' ' doing what he did not wish,' 'not having good dwelling in him,' 'brought into captivity by the law of sin in his members,'—if such declarations were isolated, and the full sense put upon them which, taken apart, they are capable of bearing, the conclusion would be inevitable that they cannot be understood of one who is in any measure a partaker of the Divine life.   But this would not be a fair mode of dealing with them, especially when they are coupled with statements that point in the opposite direction—statements which cannot with any propriety be applied to those who are strangers to the life and grace of the Spirit. The very first announcement is of this description : ' We know that the law is spiritual '—for who can be truly said to know this, except such as really have the discernment in Divine things which it is the part of the Spirit to bestow ?[1] In like manner, to wish sincerely what is spiritually good, to consent to it as good, to hate what is of an opposite nature, to hate it so truly and fixedly that it could be said when done not to be done by that which constituted one's proper personality as a man of God, to delight in the law of God, and with his mind to serve it, these are things which plainly distinguish the regenerated and spiritual man from one still remaining in the carnality and corruption of nature.   And pointing as they do to the state of thought and feeling in the higher region of his being, in what the apostle calls ' the inner man,' they necessarily include the more essential characteristics of the personal state—those which relate to the deeper springs of its moral being—and must ultimately determine its place and destiny.   What, therefore, the apostle says on the other and lower side must be taken in a sense not incompatible with those higher characteristics—must be understood, in short, of that other self, that old man of flesh or corruption, which, though no longer predominant, was still not utterly destroyed.   Indeed, the apostle himself furnishes the key to this interpretation, when he distinguishes so sharply between the me in one sense and the me in another (' in me, that is in my flesh,' ver. 18, ' I myself with my mind,' ver. 25), between the law in his members, working unto sin, and the law of his mind, consenting unto and desiring the good.   He is conscious of a sort of double personality, or rather a twofold potency in his person, the one derived from nature still adhering to him and troubling him with its vexatious importunities and fleshly tendencies, the other holding of the risen life of Christ, and ardently desirous of the pure and good.   And it is, it *can* only be, of the sinful emotions, and usually repressed, but sometimes also successful, workings of that old self, that he speaks of himself as destitute of good, carnal, and in bondage to the power of evil.

Entirely similar confessions of the dominancy of indwelling sin, and lamentations over it, have often been heard in every age of the church, from spiritually-minded persons ; and are to be regarded as the indication, not of the absence of grace, nor of the prevalence of sinful habit, but of that tenderness of conscience, that delicate perception of the pure and good, and sensitive recoil from any thing, even in the inner movements of the soul, that is contrary to the holiness of God, which is the

[1] 1 Cor. ii. 14.

characteristic of a properly enlightened and spiritual mind. So, in ancient times, for example, Job who, in his more advanced stage of enlightenment, confessed himself to be vile, yea abhorred himself, and repented in dust and ashes (xl. 4, xlii. 6); so in many places David;[1] and very strikingly the writer of Psalm 119, who, after unfolding in every conceivable variety the thoughts and feelings, the desires and purposes, of the devout Israelite in reference to the law and service of God, after repeatedly declaring how he loved the law of God, and delighted in His commandments, winds up the whole by what cannot but seem to the mere worldling or formalist a somewhat strange and inconsistent utterance: 'I have gone astray like a lost sheep: seek thy servant; for I do not forget thy commandments.' It is the same still. 'If one over-heard a serious, upright Christian saying, on some occasion, with much deep regret—as many such have done—Ah! what a slave am I to carnal affections and unruly passions! How do they carry me away and captivate me!—would he hastily say, that this complaint had no foundation at all in truth? Or, would he conclude, if it had, that this man was truly and absolutely a slave of sin, and still unregenerate? A person so judging, I should think, would not deserve to be favour-ably regarded.'[2] And in respect to the relative preponderance of the two counter-forces in the apostle's representation, the same judicious author observes: 'What here would strike my mind free of bias is, that this *I* on the side of holiness against sin, is the most prevailing, and what represents the true character of the man; and that *sin* which he distinguishes from this *I* is not the prevailing reigning power in the man here represented; as it is, however, in every unregenerate man.' So, also, Augustine happily of himself: 'I indeed in both, but more I in that of which I approved, than in that which I disapproved of as being in me.'[3]

We must not enlarge further in this line; but two points of great importance for our present investigation come prominently out in this disclosure of the apostle's experience. One is, that, though writing under the clear light of the Gospel, and a spiritual acquaintance with its truths, he has no fault to find with the law as a revelation of duty, or a pattern of moral excellence. What he misses in the law is not the perfect exhibition to our knowledge of moral goodness, but the power to communicate moral life. The only reason specified why it cannot help one to the possession of righteousness, is because of the prevent-ing flesh, or law of sin in the members, which works in opposition to

[1] Ps. xix. 12, 13, xii. 12, li. 3.   [2] Fraser.   [3] 'Confes.,' L. viii. 5.

the better knowledge derived from the law of God, and the better impulse implanted by grace.   So that, viewed as an exhibition of good, the law is represented as in unison with the desires of the regenerated moral nature, and simply by reason of its goodness, coupled with remaining imperfections in himself, giving rise to trouble and distress. The other point is, that so far from there being any contrariety between the scope of the law's requirements and the spirit of the new life, the apostle rejoiced in the higher powers and privileges of this life, chiefly because through these the hope had come to him of gaining the victory over the contrariety in his nature to the good in the law, and having it yet realized in his experience.   As thus replenished from above, his more settled bent and purpose of mind were now on the side of the righteousness exhibited and enjoined in the law—nay, with his mind he served it (ver. 25); or, as he expresses himself in the following chapter, his general characteristic now was to walk not after the flesh but after the Spirit, and, in proportion as this was the case, to have the righteousness of the law fulfilled in him (viii. 4).   Hence, also, in this epistle, precisely as in that to the Galatians, when he comes to the practical exhortations, he points to the law still as the grand outline, for Christian not less than earlier times, of moral obligation, and urges his readers to the regular and faithful exercise of that love, which is the heart and substance of its precepts, as *for them* also the sum of all duty (xiii. 8-10).   As regards men's relation to the law, therefore, in the sense meant by the apostle throughout this discussion, the difference between Old and New Testament times can have respect only to relative position, or to the form and mode of administration, not to the essentials of duty to God and man.

Rom. x. 4-9.

' For Christ is the end of the law for (or unto) righteousness to every one that believeth.   5. For Moses describes the righteousness which is of the law, that the man who has done those things shall live in them.[1] 6. But the righteousness which is of faith speaks thus, Say not in thine heart, Who shall go up into heaven? that is to bring Christ down.

---

[1] The reading here is a little different in three of the older MSS. ℵ A D and the Vulgate, which omit the ἀυτὰ (those things), and change (with the exception of D, but here B takes its place) the αὐτοῖς at the close into αὐτῃ.   But the sense is much the same, only, instead of those things, in the doing of which the righteousness consists, the righteousness itself becomes prominent; it then reads, 'the man who has done [it] shall live in it.'

7. Or, Who shall go down into the deep (abyss)? that is to bring Christ up from the dead. 8. But what saith it? The word is nigh thee, in thy mouth and in thy heart; that is, the word of faith which we preach; 9. That if thou wilt confess with thy mouth the Lord Jesus, and believe in thy heart that God raised him from the dead, thou shalt be saved.'

The subject which gave rise to this fresh statement respecting the law and its righteousness, as contrasted with the way of salvation by Christ, was the sad case of the unbelieving Israelites. They had sought righteousness, indeed, but sought it in the way which lies beyond the reach of fallen man—the way of their own goodness; hence they had not submitted themselves to, but strenuously resisted the righteousness of God. The statement implies, that what, in such a case, is of man, and what is of God, belong to quite different categories—they are mutually antagonistic. And this is confirmed by the declaration in ver. 4 as to God's method of making righteous, *For Christ is the end of the law for righteousness to every one that believeth.* The general meaning is plain enough; it affirms that Christ is set for righteousness as well as the law, and that for the believer in Christ this righteousness is made practically available—he actually attains it. But it is a matter of dispute in what sense precisely the *end* ($\tau \acute{\epsilon} \lambda o \varsigma$) of the law is to be understood. Does it denote simply the termination of the legal dispensation —its termination in the death of Christ, which provided the new method of justification? Or does it, along with this, indicate the aim and object of the law—as having found in the work of Christ its *destined* completion? There is no lack of authorities on both sides of this question (for the first, Augustine, Koppe, Rückert, De Wette, Olshausen, Meyer, Hodge, &c.; for the other, Chrysostom, Therphylact, Beza, Grotius, Wetstein, Tholuck, Alford, &c.). I am inclined to agree with the latter class, on the ground that the simple fact of the law's termination in its provisional character as for a time forming an essential part in the revealed plan of salvation, scarcely comes up to what seems required for the occasion. Beyond all doubt, the law had an aim in this matter, as well as a period of service; nay, just because it had an aim, and that aim reached its accomplishment in Christ, in a way it never had done or could do of itself, it therefore ceased from the place it had occupied. And as the expression here quite naturally carries this idea, there seems no valid reason why it should not be included. The law, taken in its complete character, certainly aimed at righteousness; so also does Christ in His mission as the Redeemer; with this all-important difference, that what could never be properly accomplished by the one is accomplished by the other—hence, also, the provisional character of the one, while the other is permanent. The sense could scarcely be better given than it was by Chrysostom: 'If Christ is the end of the law, he who has not Christ, though he may appear to have it, has it not; but he who has Christ, though he have not fulfilled the law, has yet obtained all. So, too, the end of the medical art is health. As, therefore, he who has proved able to give health, though haply unskilled in medicine, has every thing, while he who is unable to cure, however he may seem capable of administering the art, has altogether failed. So also in respect to the law and faith; he who has this has also attained to the end of that; but he who is destitute of the former, is an alien from both. For what did the law seek? To make a man righteous; but it was not able to do so; for no one fulfilled it. . . . . This same end, however, is better accomplished by Christ through faith.'

The verses that follow give the proof of this proposition—give it out of Moses—the lawgiver himself being called as a witness against his misguided and foolish adherents in apostolic times. *For Moses describes the righteousness which is of the law, that the man who has done those things shall live in them.*[1] The passage referred to, and almost literally quoted, is Lev. xviii. 5; and the *those things* are the statutes and judgments mentioned immediately before; for the whole passage runs thus: ' Ye shall do my judgments, and keep mine ordinances, to walk therein; I am Jehovah your God. Ye shall therefore keep my statutes and my judgments; which if a man do, he shall live in them.' Taken in its original connection, the passage undoubtedly points to Israel's happy privilege as well as sacred calling. Their condition is contrasted with that of the Egyptians and Canaanites, whose ordinances and customs, especially in regard to the gratification of lust, are declared to be matters of horror and abomination before God (vers. 3, 30); they are solemnly charged to avoid these, and to keep the Lord's ordinances, statutes, and judgments, both because Jehovah is their God, and because by doing them they should find life in them, while practices of an opposite kind had brought judgment and destruction on the Canaanites. Such is the connection and the import of the original statement. And it seems, at first sight, somewhat strange, that the apostle should here refer to it in the way he does, as describing the righteousness which is obtained by *doing* in contradistinction to that which comes by *believing*, as if the way of attaining life for the members of the Theocracy were

[1] The same use is made of the passage in Gal. iii. 12, but without any formal citation of it.

essentially different from, and in some sort antagonistic to, that under the Gospel. He has so often asserted the reverse of that, and in this very epistle (ch. ii. 17-29, iii. 19, 20, iv., etc.), that it would certainly be to misunderstand the application to take it in that absolute sense. The life which Israel had, whether viewed with respect to the earthly inheritance, or to the everlasting kingdom of which that was but the shadow, unquestionably came from their relation to Jehovah in the covenant of promise, and not from what was imposed in the covenant of law ; the law, with its demands of holiness, its statutes of right, and ordinances of service, was no further ordained for life than as describing the moral characteristics in which life, so far as it existed, must exhibit itself, or, when these failed, appointed what was needed to obtain cleansing and restoration. The amplest proof has been already adduced of this (in the exposition of the passages in Corinthians, Romans, and Galatians, also in Lec. III.). Yet from the prominence of law in the Theocracy—which was such that even the things which pertained to forgiveness and the promise of blessing usually took a legal form—the language employed respecting the calling of the people and their prospects of good were naturally thrown in many cases into the same form. The people were told that they should live and prosper, only if they obeyed God's voice, or kept the statutes and ordinances imposed on them—but without intending to convey the impression, that they were actually placed under a covenant of works, and that they could attain to the good promised, and avoid the evil threatened, only if they did what was enjoined without failure or imperfection. On the contrary, those very statutes and ordinances had bound up with them provisions of grace for all but obstinate and presumptuous offenders ; by the terms of the covenant—that is, by the law in its wider sense—they were called to avail themselves of these, and to make their resort to God as 'rich in mercy, and plenteous in redemption.' Still, the language even in such parts carried a legal impress ; it linked the promised good to a prescribed ritual of service ; and if people were minded, in their pride and self-sufficiency, to lay the stress mainly on the legal element in the covenant—if they should imagine that every thing was to be earned by the completeness and merit of their obedience, then it must be meted to them according to their own principle, and they should have to face the sentence uttered from the sterner side of the covenant: ' Cursed is every one that continueth not in all things that are written in the book of the law to do them.' [1]

Now, keeping these considerations in mind, it is not difficult to

Deut. xxvii. 26 ; Gal. iii. 10.

understand how St Paul should have singled out the brief passage
under examination as being, when looked at merely by itself, descriptive of the righteousness which is won by obedience to precepts of law,
while yet it was not meant that Israel were expected to attain to such
righteousness, or were, in the strict and absolute sense, dependent on
the attainment of it for life and blessing. It set before them the ideal
which they should earnestly endeavour to realize—which also to a
certain extent they must realize as partakers, if only in an incipient state,
of the Divine life; but not unless they were minded (as the unbelieving
Jews of the apostle's day certainly were) to stand simply upon the
ground of law, and be in no respect debtors of grace, was a complete
and faultless doing to form the condition of receiving the promised
heritage of life. In this case, it assuredly was. The words must then
be pressed in the full rigour and extent of their requirement; for life
could only be ministered and maintained on a legal basis, if the condition of perfect conformity to law had been made good. That Moses,
however, no more than the apostle, intended to assert for Israel such a
strictly legal basis as the condition of life, is evident, not only from
the connection in which that particular declaration stands, but also
from other parts of his writings, in which the evangelical element comes
distinctly into view, in his words to the covenant people. To one of
these, the apostle now turns (vers. 6-9) for a proof of the righteousness of faith; for it must be held with Meyer, Fritzsche, and others,
that it is Moses himself who speaks in the words contained in these
verses. 'The δὲ in ver. 6 places the righteousness of faith over
against the just-mentioned righteousness of the law, for *both* of which
kinds of righteousness the testimony of the lawgiver himself is
adduced. The expression, " for Moses describes," in ver. 5, does not
merely apply to the word in that verse, but also stretches over vers.
6-8; and so the objection is not to be urged against our view of the
want of a citation formula at these verses.'[1] The passage quoted,
though with some freedom, is in Deut. xxx. 10-14. And it is to be
noticed, as a confirmation of the explanation we have given of the
preceding passage from Leviticus, that this also, though embodying
the evangelical element, and for that very purpose quoted, also carries
the form of law. In the original it stands thus, ' For this commandment which I command thee this day, it is not hidden from thee, neither
is it far off. It is not in heaven that thou shouldst say, Who shall go
up for us to heaven, and bring it unto us, that we may hear it and do
it ? Neither is it beyond the sea, that thou shouldst say, Who shall

[1] Meyer.

go over the sea for us, and bring it unto us, that we may hear it and
do it? But the word is very nigh unto thee, in thy mouth and in thy
heart, that thou mayest do it.' The general import is here again quite
plain; namely, that the way of peace and blessing had been made
alike clear and accessible; no one could justly say it was difficult to
be understood, or mocked their efforts with impossibilities, as if, in
order to reach it, heaven had to be scaled, or the boundless ocean to
be crossed :—no, the word was nigh them, and every thing provided
to their hand which was needed to secure what it set before them. But
commentators are divided on the points, whether the passage as spoken
by Moses properly bears the spiritual sense put upon it by the apostle,
or has this sense infused into it by giving it a kind of secondary prophetical bearing—whether the questions, also, considered with regard to
this spiritual sense, are questions of unbelief, questions of embarrassment,
or questions of anxiety. It is not necessary for our immediate purpose
to go into the examination of such points; and for any purpose of a
strictly expository nature, it appears to me that very little depends
on' them. A somewhat too specific or realistic view is taken of the
words by those who chiefly raise the questions. The description, in
itself, is so far general, that it might be applied to the calling of the
church of God in every age. Moses applied it, in the first instance, to
the members of the old covenant; Paul, on the ground of this original
application, points to Moses as a witness of the way of salvation by
faith; but in doing so, intersperses comments by way of guiding its
application to Christian times. He takes for granted that those to
whom he wrote looked for salvation, or the righteousness connected with
it, only in Christ; to them, if Christ was near or remote, salvation would
be accessible or the reverse. And the original import of the word, with
this fresh application of it, amounts to nothing more than the following:
God's method of salvation is such, so easy, so accessible, that no one
needs to speak about climbing heaven on the one hand, or diving into
the lowest depths on the other, in order to have the Saviour brought
near to him—He is already near, yea, present, with all His fulness of
life and blessing, in the word of His Gospel; and all that is necessary
for the sinner is to receive this word with an implicit faith, and give
evidence of his hearty appropriation of it, in order to his finding righteousness and salvation. Between the case of believers, in this respect,
under the old, and that of believers under the new covenant, there is no
other difference than that now the way of salvation by faith is more
gloriously displayed and more easily apprehended by those who are in
earnest to find it.

ROM. XIV. 1-7.

' Now, him that is weak in the faith receive ye, but not for judgments of thoughts. 2. One believes he may eat all things ; but he that
is weak eateth (only) herbs. 3. Let not him that eateth despise him
that eateth not ; and let not him that eateth not judge him that eateth ;
for God has accepted him. 4. Who art thou that judgest the servant
of another ? To his own master he stands or falls ; but he shall be
made to stand, for the Lord is able to make him stand. 5. One esteems
one day above another [lit., day above day] ; another esteems every
day : let each be fully persuaded in his own mind. 6. He that regards
the day, to the Lord regards it ; and he that eats, to the Lord eats, for
he gives God thanks ; and he that eats not (viz., flesh), to the Lord
eats not, and gives God thanks. 7. For none of us lives to himself,
and none dies to himself ; for if we live, we live to the Lord, and if we
die, we die to the Lord,' &c.

The subject handled in these verses, as in the chapter generally
from which they are taken, is the treatment that should be given
by Christians of enlightened understandings and ripe judgment in
Divine things to those whom the apostle calls weak in the faith—
persons who, while holding the faith of Christ, were restrained by
some scruples of conscience, or some apprehensions of evil, from
using the liberty in certain respects to which they were called in
Christ. But from the imperfect description which is given of their
case, it is extremely difficult to arrive at an intelligent view of
their religious position, and consequently to determine the precise bearing of the apostle's remarks concerning them on questions of legal
obligation or Christian duty in present times. The general principle
announced at the commencement, that persons weak in the faith
should be received, that is, acknowledged as of the brotherhood of
faith, must be understood as implying, that the weakness did not
touch any vital doctrine, or commonly recognised Christian duty ;
for in that case it had been the part of the more intelligent and
steadfast believers to endeavour to convince them of their error, and,
till this was accomplished, keep them at some distance, lest others
should become infected with their leaven. So much is plain ; and
hence the negative prescription given in connection with the receiving
of them, that it should not be *for judgments of thoughts* (εἰς διακρίσεις
διαλογισμῶν)—that is, for doing the part of censorious critics and judges
on the views peculiar to the persons in question. This, certainly, is

the meaning of the expression—not, as in the English Bible, *to doubtful disputations*, which the original words will not strictly bear, and which also, in its natural import, seems to point rather in the wrong direction. For the apostle could not mean to say, that it was doubtful which of the two parties occupied the right position, since he characterized the one as relatively weak, and as such, of course, falling below the mark, which they should have aimed at and might have attained. But he means to say, that the specific weakness having its seat in the thoughts of the mind, and these thoughts exercising themselves about matters of no great moment to the Christian life, no harsh judgments should be passed upon them; the persons should be treated with forbearance and kindness.

But to what type or class of early Christian converts shall the persons spoken of be assigned? On this point there has been a considerable diversity of opinion, and the materials apparently are wanting for any very certain conclusions. They could not be, as some have supposed, Jewish-Christians, who stood upon the legal distinctions respecting meat and drink; for these distinctions said nothing about total abstinence from flesh, or the ordinary use of wine. Nor, with others, can we account for those self-imposed restraints, by supposing that it was flesh and wine which had been used in heathen offerings that the persons in question would not taste; for no limitation of this sort is so much as hinted at in the apostle's words, nor, if that had been the precise ground of their refusal, would he have characterized it as simply a weakness; in another epistle he has at great length urged abstinence from such kinds of food as a matter of Christian duty.[1] Then, in regard to the distinguishing of days, so as to make account of some above others, it is difficult to understand how this could be meant of a scrupulous adherence to the Jewish observances as to times and seasons, as if any thing depended on such observances for salvation; for, in the case of the Galatians, the apostle had characterized such adherence to the Jewish ritual, not as a tolerable weakness, but as a dangerous error—a virtual departure from the simplicity of the faith. That the parties are to be identified with Christians of the Ebionite school (according to Baur), who were tinged with the Gnostic aversion to every thing of a fleshly and materialistic nature, while they retained their Jewish customs, is altogether improbable—both because there was no such distinctly formed Ebionite party at the time this epistle was written, and because, if there had, they could certainly not have been treated so indulgently by Paul, whose teaching stood in

[1] 1 Cor. viii.-x.

2 F

such direct antagonism to their views.[1] And though there is a nearer approach to the apparent circumstances of the case in the supposition of others (Ritschll, Meyer, etc.), that the weak Christians of our passage were a class of supra-legal religionists, believers probably of the Essene sect, who brought with them into Christianity some of their rigid observances and ascetic practices, yet there is no proper historical evidence of such converts to the faith of Christ existing anywhere, and particularly at so great a distance from the seat of the Essene party, at the early period to which the epistle to the Romans belongs. Besides, as the ascetic and ritualistic peculiarities of the Essenes were essentially of that type, against which Paul, in other places,[2] so earnestly protested, and in which he descried the beginnings of the great apostasy, one is at a loss to understand how, on the supposition of its representatives being found at Rome, he should have made so little account of the fundamentally erroneous principles interwoven with their beliefs.

Amid this uncertainty as to the specific position of the persons referred to, it is necessary to proceed with caution in the interpretation of what is written, and to beware of deducing more general inferences from it than the expressions absolutely warrant. It was one of the exhibitions given, the apostle tells us, of weakness of faith, that one believed he should eat simply vegetables or herbs, while the relatively strong was persuaded he might partake of whatever was edible ; and it is implied, in ver. 21, that the weakness also shewed itself with some in a religious abstinence from wine. But on what grounds the abstinence was practised—whether as a species of fasting, with a view to the mortifying of the flesh, or as a protest and example for the good of others in respect to prevailing excesses in meat and drink, or, finally, from lingering doubts, originating in ascetic influences, as to the Divine permission to use such articles of diet—on such points nothing is here indicated, and we are entitled to make no positive assertion. The personal incident mentioned by Josephus, that, after having in early life sought to make himself acquainted with the distinctive Jewish sects, he took up for a time with one Banos, who lived in the desert, and scrupulously abstained from any clothing but what grew on the trees, and ate no food but the spontaneous products of the earth ; and the additional fact given in the same direction, that two priests, whom he describes as excellent men, and whom he accompanied to Rome to plead their cause, chose for their food only figs and nuts,[3] clearly shew that peculiarities of this sort were not of infrequent occurrence at that

---

[1] *See* Neander, ' History of Planting of Christian Church,' B. iii. c. 7.

[2] Col. ii. ; 1 Tim. iv.   [3] ' Life,' secs. 2, 3.

time among the Jews, though they were probably of too irregular and arbitrary a character to come under any common religious definition. Of the persons here referred to by the apostle, we merely know that, for some conscientious reasons (adopted by them as individuals, not as belonging to certain sects), they had thought it their duty neither to eat flesh nor to drink wine ; and the apostle's advice respecting them was, that they should not on this account be treated with harshness or contempt. It was a weakness, no doubt, but still one of a comparatively harmless nature ; it had approved itself to their own conscience ; let the matter, therefore, be left to Him who is Lord of the conscience, and who would not fail to sustain and guide them, if their hearts were right with Him in the main.

It is scarcely possible to be more particular in regard to the other form of weakness specified ; it is not even very definitely indicated on which side the weakness lay, or how far there was a weakness. Two facts only are stated : 'One man esteems one day above another ; another esteems every day' (the *alike* added in the authorized version is better omitted). We naturally infer, from the mode of putting the statement, that the weaker was he who made the distinction of day above day ; but then how was the distinction made ? Wherein did he shew his esteeming of it ? Could this have consisted only in his considering it proper to devote one day in the week more especially to religious employments and works of mercy ? This had surely been a strange manifestation of weakness, to be marked as such by the apostle, who himself was wont, along with the great body of the early Christians, to appropriate the first day of the week to such purposes, and to style it emphatically the Lord's day.[1] Nor has the experience of the past shewn it to be a weakness, but, on the contrary, to be at once a source and an indication of strength, to avail one's-self of those statedly recurring opportunities to withdraw from worldly toil, and have the soul braced up by more special communion with itself and Heaven for the work of a Christian calling. Wherever such opportunities are neglected, and no distinction of days is made as to religious observance, the result that inevitably ensues is a general decay and gradual extinction of the religious sentiment. This is admitted by all thoughtful men, whether they hold the strictly Divine institution of the Lord's day or not. It is impossible St Paul could be insensible to it, or could wish to say any thing that tended to such a result. If, therefore, the esteeming of one day above another is represented as a weakness, one may suppose that some specific value was attached to the day *per se*,

[1] Acts xxi. 17 ; 1 Cor. xv. 2 ; Rev. i. 10.

as if it had 'the power of imparting some virtue of its own to the things done on it, apart from their own inherent character.   To attach such ideas, either to the Jewish weekly and other Sabbaths, or even to the Christian Lord's day, might be regarded as a weakness ; since, while the setting apart of such days for special exercises had important ends to serve under both economies, it was only as means to an end ; the time by itself carried no peculiar virtue ; and, in contradistinction from any feeling of this description, every day should be esteemed.   But no day should, in that case, be disesteemed, or regarded as unfit for religious and beneficent action.   Nor does the apostle say so, when the correct form of his statement is given, as by Lachmann (approved also by Mill, Griesbach, Meyer[1]).   The words run thus : ' He that regards the day to the Lord regards it ; and he that eats (viz., flesh), eats to the Lord ; for he gives God thanks ; and he that eats not, to the Lord eats not, and gives God thanks.'   The negative, as well as the positive side is exhibited as regards the eating ; for both alike eat, and give thanks for what they eat, only the one in his eating confines himself to a vegetable diet.   But in the other case, the positive alone is exhibited ; for while one may, with a true religious feeling, regard one day more than another, and even carry this to a kind of superstitious extreme ; yet not to regard the day can scarcely be represented as a thing done to the Lord.   Not the regarding of no particular day is the counter-position indicated by the apostle, but the regarding of every day—this, it is implied, would bespeak the strong man, if so be the other betrayed something of weakness ; and the strength in that case would necessarily consist in giving one's-self to do every day what others deemed it enough, or at least best, to do more especially on one—to do, that is, what may more peculiarly be called works of God.   So to employ one's-self would put all the days on a kind of equality ; but, certainly, not by depriving them alike of regard, or by reducing them to the same worldly level ; on the contrary, by raising them to a common elevation, devoting them to the special service of Heaven, and the best interests of humanity.   So did our Lord, the highest exemplar of healthful and sustained energy in the Divine life ; His works were all works of God, proper therefore for one day as well as another ;[2] so that it might be

---

[1] These authorities omit the clause in ver. 6, καὶ ὁ μὴ φρονῶν τὴν ἡμέραν, κυρίῳ οὐ φρονεῖ, with all the best MSS., ℵ A B C D E F G, the Italic, Vulgate, Aeth. Copt. versions, Jer., Aug., and other authorities.   To admit a text with such evidence against it, and only one uncial MS. L. of no great antiquity for it, were to violate all the established canons of criticism ; besides that, it makes no proper sense ; at least not without some considerable straining.   [2] John v. 17.

truly said of Him, He regarded every day. And yet it was deemed by Him no way incompatible with this, that He should shew His regard to the seventh day in a somewhat different manner from what He did in respect to the other days of the week. In principle, the works done on this and other days were alike, yet they took, to some extent, their distinctive forms of manifestation. So that, however often the passage before us has been held by certain interpreters to argue something at variance with the religious observance of a Christian Sabbath, this is found rather by ascribing to it an imaginary sense, than by evolving its legitimate and proper import.

EPH. ii. 11-17.

' Wherefore remember, that once ye, Gentiles in the flesh, who are called Uncircumcision by that which is called Circumcision in the flesh wrought by hands; 12. That ye were at that time without Christ, alienated from the commonwealth of Israel, and estranged from the covenants of promise, not having hope, and without God in the world. 13. But now in Christ Jesus, ye who once were far off were brought nigh in the blood of Christ. 14. For He is our peace, who made both one, and broke down the middle wall of the partition—(15) the enmity— in His flesh, having done away the law of commandments in ordinances, that he might make the two in Himself into one new man, making peace; 16. and that He might reconcile both of us in one body to God through the cross, having slain on it the enmity. 17. And having come, He preached peace to you who were far off, and peace to them that were nigh; 18. For through Him we have our access, both of us, in one Spirit to the Father.'

This passage has obviously a monitory aim, and is chiefly designed to awaken a sense of gratitude in the minds of the Ephesians on account of the wonderful change which, through the mercy of God in Christ, had been made to pass over their condition. Their elevated state, as participants in the benefits of Christ's death and the glory of His risen life, had been described in the preceding verses ; and now the apostle calls upon them to remember how far otherwise it was with them in their original heathenism, and how entirely they were indebted for the change to the work of reconciliation accomplished by Christ. The first two verses delineate in dark colours their position prior to their interest in Christ. *Remember that once ye* (ποτὲ ὑμεῖς, the ποτὲ before ὑμεῖς with the best MSS. א A B D), *Gentiles in the flesh* (a compound expression denoting the category or class to which they belonged—Gentiles, or heathen, as contradistinguished from Jews, and this ἐν σαρκί—without the article, because forming one idea with the τὰ ἔθνη, Winer, Gr. 20, sec. 2—in their corporeal frame without the mark of covenant relationship to God, hence visibly in an unsanctified condition), *who are called Uncircumcision by that which is called Circumcision in the flesh wrought by hands.* This points to the hereditary antipathy cherished, or the sacred recoil felt toward them on the part of the covenant people, so long as they were in their heathenish state ; for to be called *Uncircumcision* by them was all one with being accounted reprobate or profane.   But when the apostle speaks of the Circumcision, who so called them being the Circumcision in the flesh wrought by hands, he insinuates that those who applied the reproachful epithet to the heathen, and cherished the feelings it expressed, might not themselves possess the reality which the rite of circumcision symbolized; it might be, after all, in *their* case but an outward distinction.   The apostle does not venture to say it was more, knowing well how commonly the rite had lost to his countrymen its spiritual significancy, and with how many circumcision was no more than a mere conventional sign or fleshly distinction.   But even so, it drew a line of demarcation between them and the Gentile world, and bespoke their external nearness to the God of the covenant : it constituted them, as to position and privilege, the chosen people, on whom God's name was called, while the others wanted even the formal badge of consecration.   In so far as the circumcision was only in the flesh, these who possessed it had of course little reason to boast it over the uncircumcised Gentiles, for in that case both alike needed the real sanctification which is required for true access to God; and while this thought could not but appear to aggravate the former degradation of these believing Gentiles, as having been counted profane by those who were themselves but nominally otherwise, it at the same time implied that, as regarded effectual rectification, both parties were substantially on a footing—what was needed for the one was needed also for the other.

Ver. 12. The apostle here resumes his interrupted sentence, commences afresh : *that ye were at that time* (corresponding to the ὅτι ποτέ ὑμεῖς in ver. 11) *without Christ;* that is, not only destitute of the actual knowledge of Him, but away from any real connection with Him or friendly relation to Him—so that the hope of a Saviour (which the Jews had) was as much wanting as the personal enjoyment of His salvation. What this separation implied, and how far it reached, is stated in what follows, *alienated from the commonwealth of Israel, and estranged from the covenants of promise, not having hope, and without God in the world.* By the πολιτεία, or commonwealth of Israel, is evidently meant the theocratic constitution and people of the old covenant, as those alone which had associated with them the elements of life and blessing—the one state and community in which fellowship with God was to be found. From this they were in their heathen condition alienated—ἀπηλλοτριω-μένοι—at the opposite pole, as it were, from the rights of citizenship, but without implying any thing as to a prior state of connection; for such an idea, which some would find in the description, would be out of place here; it is the actual state alone which the apostle characterizes. Further, they were *estranged from* (lit., *strangers of,* ξένοι τῶν, the ξένοι being put as a sort of antithesis to κληρόνομοι, heirs or possessors of) *the covenants of promise.* Under covenants of promise, the apostle could scarcely mean to include the covenant of law along with the covenant of Abraham, for the former is not of promise; so that we must either understand by the expression the successive and somewhat varied forms given to the Abrahamic covenant, or perhaps that covenant itself in conjunction with the new covenant of Jeremiah xxxi. 31, which was also justly entitled to be called a covenant of promise. As heathen, the Ephesians, in their unconverted state, were entirely out of the region of these covenants—strangers to the field they embraced with their blessed prospects of better things to come. And, as the necessary consequence of this unhappy isolation, they *had not hope*—that is, were devoid of this in any such sense as might properly meet the wants of their condition; hope, as the well-grounded and blessed expectation of a recovery from the evils of sin, was unknown to them; and they were *without God in the world,* unconscious of, and incapable of finding where they were, any spiritual link of connection with Him. 'They had not God, but only thoughts about Him; Israel, however, had God and the living word of His mouth. Hence there belonged to the covenant people what did not come from themselves, but from that which is greater than man's heart, the hope of the coming salvation. Heathenism, however, had but the product of its own state, hopes which had no better security than the uncertain [utterly inadequate] ground of personal piety.'[1]

Ver. 13. *But now in Christ Jesus ye who once were far off were brought nigh in the blood of Christ*—the contrast to the former state, and strikingly exhibited as a change that was once for all effected (potentially) in the atoning work of Christ—though actually experienced, of course, only when they came to a personal interest in His salvation. So, too, St Peter speaks of the resurrection of Jesus Christ as having begotten believers

[1] Harless.

to a lively hope (1 Pet. i. 3)—as if the accomplishment of the one carried the other also in its bosom. The blood of Jesus Christ, by making provision for the pardon of sin, lays open the way for all to the bosom of God's household, and of any individual who enters into the fellowship of this blood, or who takes up his standing in the faith of Jesus as the crucified for sin, it may be said he was brought nigh in the blood of Christ; in the shedding of that blood, he sees for ever removed the alienation caused by sin. And to mark very distinctly the efficacious ground or living source of the boon, the apostle designates the recipients as first 'in Christ Jesus,' and again as finding all 'in the blood of Christ.'

Vers. 14, 15. A further grounding and explanation of the statement follows : *for He is our peace, who made both one, and broke down the middle wall of the partition.* The language here also is very forcible and pregnant. The work of incorporation into God's blessed household is represented as done once for all in Christ—ideally, the reunion has attained to realization in Him. Hence, he is called ' Our Peace '—not simply as Bengel notes, our *Pacificator*, peacemaker, but the one who, by the sacrifice of Himself, has procured peace, and is Himself the bond of union to both (*ipse vinculum utrorumque*). He is such as regards Jew and Gentile, having made the twain (the divided parts, τὰ ἀμφότερα) one, not by acting directly upon their mutual antagonism, and applying Himself to heal the breach it occasioned, but by elevating both to a higher unity—effecting for them alike reconciliation with God through the blood of His cross. Brought through this one medium of reconciliation into a common relation to God, and recognising themselves as alike children of the one Father of a redeemed and blessed family, the cause of enmity and alienation as a matter of course fell away—both parties being lifted into a position where it no longer had room to operate. This is the apostle's solution of the difficulty, as to the existing separation between Jew and Gentile : he regards it as the offshoot of a higher and graver quarrel—the sinful departure and alienation of both from God; and the healing of the grand breach carries in its train the healing of the smaller one, by taking out of the way the circumstances that incidentally ministered to it. The apostle expresses the mode of accomplishing the result by saying that Christ *broke down the middle wall of the partition*, or the fence ; figurative language, proceeding on the assumption, that the two parties—the one of whom had been outwardly near, the other far off from, the region of life and blessing—were both in a manner fenced off from that region—the one more palpably so, indeed, than the other; separated and fenced off even from those who were comparatively near, because wanting the very appearance and formal badge of a consecrated condition. But the apostle sees in this only the outer line, as it were, or lower half of that partition-boundary which lay between men and the proper fellowship of love in God; for those who were called near, were still, while the old state of things existed, at some distance; they had not free access to the presence of God (as the veil in the temple, and the manifold restrictions of its appointed ritual, too clearly indicated), and were rather, for the time, tolerated in a measure of nearness, than frankly, and as of right, admitted into the joyous liberty of Divine communion and blessedness of life. For both parties, therefore, something had to be broken down, in order to have the way laid open into the holiest, and through this into the full brotherhood of love with each other. What it was, the apostle more distinctly expresses in the next term, *the enmity* ('broke down the middle wall of the partition—the enmity—in His flesh'—so the passage should be pointed and read). The enmity stands in apposition to the middle wall of partition in the preceding clause, and more exactly defines it. That this enmity has a certain respect to the hostile feeling and attitude subsisting between Jew and Gentile, seems clear from the reference going before to that antagonistic relationship and its abolition in Christ ('made both one,' ver. 14, though previously one stood aloof from the other as profane and outcast, ver. 11). But it seems equally clear, that no explanation can be satisfactory which would limit the expression to this lower sphere; for *the enmity*, which Christ destroyed in His flesh, or, as again said, which He slew through His cross, naturally carries our thoughts up to the great breach in man's condition, and the great work done by Christ to heal it. In other expressions, also, the apostle plainly identifies the removing of this enmity with the reunion of sinners to God; for it is in reconciling the parties spoken of to God that he describes the enmity as being slain; and, by the act of gracious mediation which effects this, Christ is represented as becoming the peace of those who were near, as well as those who were far off—implying that the one, as well as the other, notwithstanding their relative advantages, had in their condition an obstructive barrier to be thrown down, an enmity to be overcome. Both alike also are represented as partaking of the same regenerating process—raised together, so as to become not one man merely, but one *new* man, as contradistinguished from the old state of each. Throughout the passage, Christ is plainly described as doing substantially one and the same work for both, and that a work which bore directly on their relation to God, while it carried along with it also conciliatory and peaceful results in respect to their mutual relationship to each other.   There is no way of understanding this but by supposing that the apostle saw, in the one class of relations, the fruit and reflex of the other.   The mutual enmity which, like a partition-wall, shut off Jew from Gentile, had in his view no independent existence ; it was merely the shadow and incidental effect of that common alienation which sin had produced between man and God ; and it was, he would have his readers to understand, by striking an effectual blow at that tap-root of the evil (as it might be called) that Christ had become the medium of a proper reconciliation in regard to the other and merely consequential form of alienation.

That the destruction of the enmity, through the introduction and establishment of a state of blessed nearness to God, is said to have been done *in the flesh* of Christ, can only be regarded as a brief expres-sion for His great work in the flesh—virtually synonymous with the words ' in His blood' in ver. 13, and ' through His cross' in ver. 16. The expression itself might be coupled either with what precedes, or with what follows : we might either say [having destroyed] ' the enmity in His flesh,' or, ' in His flesh having abolished (made void) the law of commandments,' etc.   The latter is the connection adopted in the authorized version, ' having abolished in His flesh the enmity, even the law of commandments,' etc., including also in the sentence the τὴν ἔχθραν, and taking the enmity as parallel with the law of commandments. But this, though supported by many commentators, proceeds on a somewhat unnatural mode of construing the words ; and it better accords with the proper parallelism of the passage, and also with the general usage of the two verbs (as one can readily enough speak of dissolving or breaking down an enmity, but not so well of making it void, and so abolishing it).   But the general sense still remains much the same ; and certainly with the breaking down of the partition-wall, or dislodging the enmity, the apostle couples the annulling or doing away of the law of commandments in ordinances as either coincident with the other, or somehow essential to it.   How then was it so ? What precisely is meant by the law of commandments in ordinances ? And in what sense was the doing away of this in Christ necessary to the bringing about of the reconciliation and enmity ?   The law of com-mandments in ordinances is but another name for the Sinaitic legislation, or the old covenant.   This was, by way of eminence, the law, and as such composed of specific enactments ; these formed its contents ; and when further said to be ἐν δόγμασιν (the latter without the article, because expressive of one notion with τῶν ἐντολῶν, *commandments in individual ordinances* [1]), it points to the form of the contents as being of an imperative or decretory character, so that the expression may be fitly enough rendered, with Alford, ' the law of decretory commandments,' or of ' decretory ordinances,' with Ellicott. It comprised the whole system of precepts, moral and religious, which were introduced by Moses, and peremptorily enjoined on the covenant people : the law, in its economical character, as a scheme of enactments or form of administration, which was intended, indeed, to mediate the intercourse between God and man, but was perceived, even while it stood, to be imperfect, and declared as such to be transitory, destined one day to be supplanted by another and better.[2] The apostle had already, in various passages, given forth a similar judgment ; had affirmed it to be incapable of providing an effectual remedy for the evils adhering to human nature, fitted rather to make known and multiply transgression than deliver from its guilt and doom, hence done away in Christ who brings in the real deliverance.[3] So, here again, when setting forth Christ as the only true Peace of the world, the apostle represents the system of law, with its commands and ordinances, as done away, in order that humanity might, through faith in the incarnation and atoning death of Christ, be lifted out of its con- demned and alienated condition, might be formed into a kind of corpo- rate body with Himself, and participate in that fellowship of peace and blessing which He ever enjoys with the Father. But this, obviously, is a *kind* of doing away, or making void, which at the same time confirms. It loosens men's relation to the law in one respect, but establishes it in another ; releases them from it as a provisional arrangement for coming at the righteousness and life which are essential to an interest in God, but only that they might find the end it aimed at in this respect through faith in Christ [4]—find it as a gift brought to their hand through the infinite grace and prevailing media- tion of Christ. Thus, there is nothing arbitrary in the change here indicated by the apostle : it is a change of form, but not of substance, for the same great principles of truth and duty characterize both economies, only brought now to their proper establishment in Christ, and associated with results which, till then, had been but faintly appre- hended or partially experienced.[5]

[1] Winer, secs. 31, 10, obs. 1.   [2] Jer. xxxi. 31.
[3] 2 Cor. iii. 11, 14 ; Gal. iii. 19 ; Rom. v. 20, vii. 5-8.   [4] Rom. x. 4.
[5] The rendering of the two verses (vers. 14, 15), in the authorized version, is in several respects unfortunate—first, inserting *between us*, namely, Jew and Gentile, after the words, ' broken down the middle wall of partition,' thereby confining this to the earthly sphere ; second, separating between the middle wall and the enmity,

There is, it is proper to add, a certain difference in the doctrinal statements here made respecting the law, and those elsewhere given; but it is merely a formal one, and such as naturally arose from the nature of the subject. The point more immediately handled here has to do, not with justification before God, but with reconciliation and peace toward Him, and between one portion of the human family and another. These, however, are but diverse aspects of the same question; and the necessity of doing away with the decretory ordinances and precepts of the old covenant, in order to meet the wants of man's condition, and placing in its stead the atoning work of Christ, holds alike in both aspects of the matter. But in none of the passages can the doing away be understood in an absolute sense; it must be taken relatively. And here, in particular, the apostle, as justly remarked by Harless, indicating also the connection between this and other statements of the apostle, ' does not treat of the law as regards any part of its contents, but of the form, the legal externality of its demand, which, as unfulfilled, wrought enmity, because it pronounced the judgment of condemnation upon men's guilt, and hence is rendered without effect. This is done objectively without us, through the atoning death of Christ.[1] Subjectively, it is realized in us, when, as the apostle elsewhere expresses himself, the word of faith comes to be in the mouth and in the heart,[2] or, as stated presently here, when Christians, through the redemption in one Spirit, have access to the Father, and are built into an habitation of God in the Spirit. This is the subjective realization of

by throwing the latter into the next clause, and joining it to καταργήσας, instead of to the preceding λύσας; third, identifying the enmity with the law of commandments, ' the enmity, *even* the law of commandments.' In the general structure and connection of the passage, I follow Meyer, Ellicott, Alford, who, es ecially the two former, have clearly shewn the advantage in naturalness and grammatical accuracy of the mode preferred by them over others, also the inadmissibility of joining ἐν δόγμασιν with καταργήσας (with the Vulgate, Chrysostom, Theodore, also Grotius, Bengel, Fritzsche, Harless), as if the meaning were, having abolished, by means of Christian doctrines, the law of commandments, or, as Harless, abolished the law on the side of, or in respect to, the commanding form of its precepts. The New Testament usage will not admit of either mode of exposition. But the Greek commentators (Chrysostom, Theophylact, and Œcumenius) were substantially right in their general view of the passage, understanding the separation and enmity on the one side, and the reconciliation and peace on the other, to have respect, not merely to Jew and Gentile, but primarily and mainly to men's relation to God, and only subordinately to the other. Meyer, with many more, take the other view of the partition-wall and the enmity; the expositions of Calvin, and many of the earlier Protestant commentators, were by no means satisfactory in the treatment of the passage.

¹ Col. ii. 14.   ² Rom. x. 8.

the law's displacement. The apostle speaks of it in Rom. vii. 6, when he says, " We are delivered (κατηργήθημεν) from the law," as, inversely, they who would be justified by the law are delivered (κατηργήθητε) from Christ.'¹ All, therefore, depends upon the sense in which such expressions are understood, or the respect in which they are applied. They merely tell us that we have the law made of no force and effect to us, done away as the ground of justification before God, or as the means of obtaining a solid reconciliation and peace with Him : but this simply on account of the high and holy nature of the requirements it sets forth, which for fallen men made the good it aimed at practicably unattainable. Its relation to men's responsibilities as the revelation of God's righteousness, in the sphere of human life and duty, remains thereby untouched.

Vers. 16-18. These verses, which contain merely some further expansion and application of the principles exhibited in the preceding context, call for no lengthened remark here. *And that He might reconcile both of us in one body to God through the cross :* this was the higher end of Christ's work on earth—the lower having been mentioned just before, namely, the uniting of the divided human family into one new corporate body ; and the former, though the last to be named, the first in order, as being that on which the other depends. It is the reconciliation of both parties to God through the peace-speaking blood of Christ's cross, which carries them over the fence of earthly divisions and antipathies. And this being said to be done *in one body*, points— not, as some would understand it, to the corporeal frame of Christ, in which respect the idea of plurality was, from the nature of things, excluded—but to the compact society, the one corporate, mystical body which Christ forms for Himself out of the scattered and too often antagonistic members of the human family. Alike drawn through the cross to God,² their common enmity to Him, and their individual enmities one toward another, receive, in a sense, their death-blow ; they melt away under the redeeming love of the cross ; but only, of course, as regards men's personal experience, when this comes to be realized as a Divine power in the heart. To this the next clause refers, which says of Christ, '*And having come, He preached peace to you who were far off, and peace* (the εἰρήνην should be again repeated, with all the better MSS., and most of the ancient versions) *to them that were nigh.* This also is ascribed to Christ, for His agency was continued in that of the apostles, who, in preaching the tidings of salvation to Jew and Gentile, derived their authority from His commission, and their success from

¹ Gal. v. 4. ² John xii. 32.

His presence.[1]   So that to Christ belongs at once the effective means of reconciliation, and the bringing of these to bear on the personal state of mankind.   The relatively near (Jews) and the relatively far off (Gentiles) alike need the salvation provided, and they alike have it brought within their reach.   Then follows the ground or reason on which the proclamation and assurance of peace proceeds, *for through Him we have our access, both of us, in one spirit to the Father*—to (πρὸς) the Father as representing the Godhead, *through* (διὰ) the Son as Mediator, and *by* or *in* (ἐν) the Spirit as the effective agent—shewing clearly the pre-eminent regard had by the apostle in the whole matter, to the peaceful relationship of the parties to God.   It is this more especially that is mentioned here, because this is what is primarily and directly secured by the death of Christ; and the distinction between Jew and Gentile falls away, because, as component parts of one redeemed family, they are animated by one Spirit (the Spirit of life and holiness in Christ Jesus), and in that Spirit are enabled to draw near, and abide near, to God—equally inmates of His spiritual house, and alike free to participate in its blessed privileges and hopes.

COL. II. 11-17.

' In whom (Christ) ye also were circumcised with a circumcision not wrought by hands, in the putting off of the body of the flesh in the circumcision of Christ ; 12. Buried together with Him in your baptism, wherein also ye were raised up with Him through your faith in the operation of God, who raised Him from the dead. 13. And you who were dead in your trespasses and the uncircumcision of your flesh, He quickened together with Him,[2] having forgiven us all our trespasses ; 14. Having wiped out the handwriting in ordinances that was against us, which was contrary to us, and took it out of the way, nailing it to His cross ; 15. Having put off principalities and powers, He boldly made a show of them, while in it (viz., the cross) He triumphed over them.   16. Let no one, therefore, judge you in eating or in drinking, or in the matter of a feast, or of a new moon, or of Sabbaths ; 17. Which are a shadow of things to come, but the body is of Christ.'

The phase of false teaching which the apostle meets in this and other parts of the epistle to the Colossians, is somewhat different from any

---

[1] Matt. xxviii. 20 ; John xiv. 18 ; Acts iii. 26, xxiv. 23.

[2] The better authorities (א A C K L) have here a second ὑμᾶς, repeated for the sake of emphasis, ' you who were dead . . . He quickened you.'

thing that presents itself in his other epistles. That it contained a strong Judaistic element, is plain from the injunctions pressed against a return to the distinctive rites and services of Judaism ; but the parties espousing and propagating it cannot be regarded as simply Judaising Christians. For evidently a philosophical or Gnostic element mingled with the Judaistic, in this peculiar form of false teaching, laying an undue stress upon the possession of a speculative sort of knowledge, which sought to carry the mind beyond the province of Scripture, and to elevate the tone of the religious life by fancied revelations of the angelic world, and by the practices of an ascetic piety. Apparently, therefore, the false teaching warned against was a compound of Jewish and Gnostic peculiarities, somewhat after the fashion of what is reported to have become known at a later period as the doctrine of Cerinthus, or is associated with the Gnostic Ebionites, who were probably a sect of Christianized Essenes. Neither the time at which this epistle was written, nor the region in which it contemplates the false teaching in question to have appeared (Phrygia), admits of our connecting it with the heretical parties just referred to. But there were tendencies working in the same directions, which found a congenial soil in that part of Asia Minor, and which, notwithstanding the remonstrances and warnings here addressed to the church of Colossae, continued long to hold their ground and to prove a snare to believers. In one of the earliest councils of which the canons have been preserved, that of Laodicea, a place quite near to Colossae, it was found necessary to prohibit the practice of angel worship, and also of adherence to some Jewish customs.[1] So late as the fifth century, Theodoret makes mention, in his comment on this epistle, of oratories still existing in that quarter dedicated to the Archangel Michael.

In the passage more immediately before us, it is the Judaistic element in the false doctrine beginning to prevail about Colossae which the apostle has in view, and which he endeavours to expose by shewing how the design and object of the Jewish law, with its religious observances, had found their realization in the work and Gospel of Christ. Pointing first to the initiatory ordinance of the old religion, he declares circumcision, not in form, but in spirit, to belong to those who have heartily embraced the Gospel of Christ—the great truth underlying it, and for the sake of which it was appointed, having, in the most effective manner, become exemplified in their experience. *In whom ye also were circumcised with a circumcision not wrought by hands ;* that is, a work accomplished by the power of the operation of God upon the soul, as

[1] Neander, 'Planting of Christian Church,' B. iii. ch. 9.

contradistinguished from a mere fleshly administration, which is else-where characterized as a thing wrought by hands.[1] When applying the term *circumcision* in this way, the definite article should be wanting in the English, as it is in the Greek—for it could not be referred to as a thing familiarly known to the Colossians: it was not *the*, but *a*, circumcision, yet one which rose immensely in importance above the other, and could be made good only by a Divine agency.   It was nothing, however, absolutely new; for in Old Testament Scripture, also, it was spoken of as a thing that *should* have gone along with the external rite, though too frequently wanting in the outwardly circum-cised.[2]   So much was this the case, that the apostle, in describing circumcision according to its true idea, denies it of the act performed on the body, as apart from the spiritual change this symbolized, ' it is of the heart, in the spirit, and not in the letter,'[3] and what was merely in the letter he stigmatizes with the name of *the concision*—as if it were nothing more than a corporeal cutting.[4]   The spiritual act, the inward circumcision, is described as *the putting off of the body of the flesh in the circumcision of Christ*.   By the body of the flesh is undoubtedly meant the same as what is elsewhere called 'the old man which is corrupt,'[5] and by a still stronger term, ' the body of sin,'[6] and 'sinful flesh,' literally, 'flesh of sin;'[7] the bodily or fleshly part of our natures being viewed as the seat of the lusts, which are the prolific source of sin, and bring forth fruit unto death.   To have this put off, therefore, in a spiritual respect, is to be delivered from the dominion of sin, to die to sin as a controlling and regulating power, by the pure and holy principles of a Divine life taking root in the soul, and giving another tone and direction to the general procedure.   When this spiritual change is accomplished, the flesh is, so to speak, evacuated of its sinful quality—instead of domineering, it becomes subservient to the good ; and the change is wrought, the apostle says, in the circumcision of Christ, that is, in the spiritual renewal which a union to Him brings along with it.   We are not, with some, to think here of Christ's personal circumcision, which is entirely against the connection, since it would introduce an objective ground where the discourse is of a subjective personal operation.   The forming of Christ in the soul as the author of a new spiritual life—*that* is for the individual soul the circumcision of Christ, or, as we may otherwise call it, the new birth, which, by the Divine impulses of a higher nature, casts off the power of corruption.   Essentially, it is the action of Spirit

[1] Eph. ii. 11. [2] Deut. x. 16, xxx. 6 ; Ezek. xliv. 7. [3] Rom. ii. 29.
[4] Phil. iii. 2. [5] Eph. iv. 22, Col. iii. 9. [6] Rom. vi. 6. [7] Rom. viii. 3.

upon spirit; and the apostle elsewhere describes it as wrought by the Lord the Spirit,[1] or as the result of Christ dwelling in him by faith.[2] But here, in what immediately follows, he couples it with baptism, to shew that, in this higher style of things belonging to New Testament times, there is substantially the same relation of the inward reality to an outward ordinance that there was in the Old.

Ver. 12. *Buried along with him in your baptism, wherein also ye were raised through your faith in the operation of God, who raised him from the dead.* It is clear that baptism is viewed here, as in the corresponding passage of Rom. vi. 3, 4, in its full import and design, ' in the spirit and not in the letter,' as a practical and living embodiment of the great things which had already taken place in the experience of the believing soul. Baptism, in this sense, formed a kind of rehearsal of the believer's regeneration to holiness—solemnly attesting and sealing, both on his part and God's, that fellowship with Christ in His death and resurrection, on which all personal interest in the benefits of His redemption turns. Commentators very generally assume that a reference is made to the form of baptism by immersion, as imaging the spiritual death, burial, and resurrection of those who truly receive it. This is not, however, quite certain, especially as, at the passage in Romans, he couples with the burial a quite different image—that, namely, of being planted together with Christ. Nor is it really of any moment; for beyond doubt the meaning actually conveyed in the language has respect to the spiritual effect of baptism as sealing the participation of believers in the great acts of Christ's mediation—identifying them with Him in His death, burial, and resurrection. The apostle brings prominently out the latter point of this fellowship with Christ, because the other was but as the necessary channel to it: *wherein also* (ἐν ᾧ καὶ) *ye were raised up together with Him,* so I think it is most naturally rendered, taking the ἐν ᾧ as referring to the baptism. It might certainly be understood, with many commentators, of Christ (*in whom also*); but it seems more natural to confine the reference to the immediate antecedent, and to regard the apostle as indicating, that the whole process of a spiritual renovation—the rise to newness of life as well as the death to the corruption of nature—has its representation and embodiment in baptism. And to shew how the outward is here based on the inward, and derives from this whatever it has of vital force, he adds, *through the faith of the operation of God* (that is, as the great majority of the better commentators understand it, faith *in* God's operation, the genitive after πίστις being usually expressive of the object on which it

[1] 2 Cor. iii. 18.   [2] Gal. ii. 20, Eph. ii. 5-8.

rests); the spirit of faith in the baptized appropriates the act of God's mighty power in Christ when *He raised Him from the dead*, as an act which transmits its virtue to all who in faith realize and lay hold of it. Spiritually, they have thus already risen with Him; and therein have the pledge of a literal rising also, when the time for it shall have come.[1]

Vers. 13-15. In these verses, there is nothing properly additional to what has been already stated regarding the work of Christ in its effect upon the soul; but there is a specific application of this to the believing Gentiles whom the apostle was addressing, and a more detailed explanation of the matters involved in it. First, their personal quickening out of a state of spiritual death and defilement: *you being dead* (or when you were dead) *in your trespasses and the uncircumcision of your flesh;* that is, the uncleanness which attached to them as abiding in their still unsanctified fleshly natures; this as the root of the evil, though from his particular point of view placed last in the apostle's statement, and the other, the death in trespasses, the fruit that sprung from it, and gave evidence of its malignant nature; both alike were put away by the renewing and quickening energy which flowed into their experience from the risen life of Christ. Then, as the essential groundwork and condition of this quickening, there was the free pardon of their sins: *having forgiven us* (the apostle including himself, and making the statement general) *all our trespasses*—χαρισά-μενας, the indefinite past, indicating that the thing was virtually done at once, that forgiveness was secured through the vicarious work of Christ, as a boon ready to be bestowed on every one who might in a living faith appropriate the gift. Hence, thirdly, as the necessary condition of this, or its indispensable accompaniment, there was the removing of what stood in the way of their acquittal from guilt—the condemning power and authority of the law: *having wiped out the hand-writing in ordinances that was against us, which was contrary to us, and took it out of the way, nailing it to His cross.* What here is meant by the handwriting in ordinances (χειρόγραφον τοῖς δόγμασιν) must be the same with that which fastened on them the charge of guilt and condemnation, and, as such, formed the great barrier against forgiveness. This, there can be no doubt, was the law, not in part but in whole—the law in the

---

[1] All this, of course, is to be understood directly of adult baptism—the baptism of actual believers, or such as had the profession and appearance of believers. The application of it to the children of believers necessarily calls for certain modifications in the doctrinal aspect of the matter, as already stated in Lecture VIII. But it is unnecessary to enter on these here.

full compass of its requirements; called here *the handwriting*, with reference to the frequent mention of writing in connection with it ;[1] and this in, or with ordinances, namely, decretory enactments (the dative of instrument, as γράμμασιν at Gal. vi. 11, the enactments forming the material with which the writing was made), pointing to the peremptory form which the revelation of law assumed. The expression has already been under consideration at Eph. ii. 15. It cannot be limited to outward observances, though it is clear, from the use of the verb and its connection in ver. 20, that these were here specially in view. Of the law thus described, the apostle says, *it was against us*, and as if this were not explicit enough, he adds the separate statement, *which was contrary*, or hostile, *to us :* not meaning, of course, that it was in itself of a grievous or offensive nature (he elsewhere calls it ' holy, just, and good '[2]), but that it bore injuriously upon our condition, and, from its righteous demands not being satisfied, had come to stand over against us like a bill of indictment, or Divine summary of undischarged obligations. But Christ, says the apostle, or God in Him, *wiped out* the writing (ἐξαλείψας, precisely as in Acts iii. 19, with reference to sins, and in Rev. iii. 5, with reference to a name in a book) ; that is, in effect deleted it, and so *took it out of the way*, carried it from among us, namely, so far as, or in the respect in which, it formed an accusing witness against us. But, plainly, this could not be done by an arbitrary abolition of the thing itself ; moral and religious obligations cannot be got rid of in such a way ; they must be met by a just and proper satisfaction ; and this is what was stated by the apostle in the next clause under the figurative expression, *nailing it to His cross*. Ostensibly and really Christ's body was the only thing nailed there ; but suffering, as He did, to bear the curse of the law for sin, and actually enduring the penalty, it was as if the law itself in its condemnatory aspect toward men was brought to an end—its power in that respect was exhausted. ' Never,' says Chrysostom, ' did the apostle speak so magniloquently (but this applies also to ver. 15). Do you see what zeal he exhibits to have the handwriting made to disappear ? To wit, we were all under sin and punishment : He being punished, made an end both of sin and punishment ; and He was punished on the cross. *There*, therefore, He transfixed it (the handwriting), and then, as having power, He tore it asunder.' Did with it, in short, what the satisfied creditor does with his charge of debt, or the appeased judge with his bill of indictment ; cancelled it as a claim that could involve us any more in guilt and

---

[1] Ex. xxxi. 18, xxxiv. 1, 27 ; Deut. x. 4, xxvii. 3, etc.　　　[2] Rom. vii. 12.

condemnation, if we receive and trust in Him as He is there presented to our view.[1]

Finally, a statement is made respecting the relation of Christ's work for His people on the cross to what he calls the principalities and powers: the original is, ἀπεκδυσάμενος τὰς ἀρχὰς καὶ τὰς ἐξουσίας ἐδειγμάτισεν ἐν παῤῥησίᾳ, θριαμβεύσας αὐτοὺς ἐν αὐτῷ. The exact import of some of the words, and the proper mode of explicating the sentiment contained in them, have given rise to some difference of opinion, and are not quite easily determined. The *general* bearing of the statement, however, on the more immediate subject of discourse, is plain enough, and this, amid the diversity of opinion which exists in other respects, should not be forgotten. Obviously, it is intended in the first instance to convey an impression of the completeness of Christ's work on the cross as to the procuring of forgiveness for sin, and the effecting of a true cleansing or renewal of state in as many as believed: in this point of view, the scene of deepest humiliation had become the chosen theatre of Divine glory—the place and moment of victory over evil. Then, in token of this, we are told that whatever orders or powers of a higher kind had, or were anyhow supposed to have, an interest in retaining things as they were, and consequently in opposing this result, these, instead of triumphing, as might to the bodily eye have seemed to be the case, were themselves effectually overthrown on the cross—the ground and occasion of their power to carry it against men, being thereby taken out of their hand. So much seems plain ; no one can well fail to derive this amount of instruction from the words ; but when we go into detail, and ask, what precisely are to be understood by those principalities and powers, who are here said to have lost their ascendency and their means of strength, or how explain the specific acts to which the result is ascribed, there is some difficulty in arriving at a satisfactory answer. By far the commonest, as it was also the earliest,

---

[1] It was chiefly on the ground of this passage, including also Eph. ii. 13-17, that a mode of representation, once very common among a certain class of preachers in this country, was adopted—namely, that in respect to sinners generally 'all legal barriers to salvation have been removed by Christ.' The representation is perfectly Scriptural and legitimate, if understood with reference to the objective manifestation of Christ, and the exhibition of His offered grace to the souls of men. It is un-doubtedly under this aspect that the truth is here presented by the apostle ; and it is quite in accordance with his statement, to go to sinners of every name and degree, and tell them to look in faith to Christ, and to rest assured, if they do so, that, by His work on the cross, all legal barriers have been removed to their complete salva-tion. But the expression may be, and undoubtedly has sometimes been, used as importing more than this ; and consequently, if still employed, should be cleared of all ambiguity.

view of commentators regarding the principalities and powers, holds them to be demons, the spirits of darkness, who, as instruments of vengeance, ever seek to press home upon men the consequences of their sin, but who by reason of the satisfaction given to the demands of God's law through the death of Christ on the cross, have had the ground of their successful agency taken from them—the curse given them to execute has been fully borne—and, instead of now being at liberty to spoil, and ravage, and destroy, they are themselves, as regards believers in Christ, in the condition of spoiled and vanquished forces—their prey gone, their weapons of war perished. Some, however (Suicer, Rosenmüller, etc.), have conceived that the principalities and powers in question are to be sought for in the earthly sphere, and are none other than the authorities, priestly and secular, who arrayed themselves in opposition to Christ, and thought by crucifying Him to put an end to His cause. More recently, Hofmann,[1] Alford, and a few more, take the expression to refer to good angels, as having ministered at the introduction of the law, and thereby thrown around God a sort of veil, which hindered the free outgoing of His love, and shrouded His glory to the view of the heathen, and in a measure also to the covenant people—this, like an old vesture, being now rent off and cast aside through the atoning death of Christ, the angelic powers associated with it are said to be put aside along with it, exhibited as in a state of complete subjection to Christ, and made to follow, as it were, in the triumphal procession of Him who is the one Lord and Saviour of men. This last mode of explanation manifestly carries a strained and unnatural appearance, and represents the angels of Heaven as standing in a relation to Christ and His people, which is without any real parallel in other parts of Scripture. According to it, they did the part not of subordinate agents merely in God's earlier dispensation, but in some sense of antagonistic forces, and required to be exposed in no very agreeable aspect, nay, triumphed over, and driven from the field. There is nothing at all approaching to this in any other passage touching on the ministry of angels, and the endeavour to accommodate the language of the apostle so understood to the general doctrine of angels in Scripture, can only be regarded as a play of fancy. The second view, also, which has never met with much acceptance, has this fatal objection against it, that the terms, *principalities and powers*, always bear respect in St Paul's writings to spiritual beings and angelic orders;[2] whether of a good or of an evil nature, is left to be gathered from the context. Of the two passages just referred to in the Epistle to the

[1] 'Schriftb.' I. p. 350, *seq.*   [2] Eph. i. 21, vi. 12 ; Col. i. 16, ii. 10.

Ephesians, the first applies the terms to good, the second to malignant, spirits; and it can, therefore, be no valid objection to a like application in the latter sense here, that in two earlier passages of this epistle they have been used of the higher intelligences in the heavenly places. The things asserted of them in each case leave little room to doubt to what region they should be assigned, and with what kind of agency associated. And here, both the natural import of the language, and the very general consent among commentators of all ages in the interpretation of it, seem to shut us up to the first view specified, and oblige us to regard the principalities and powers, whose ascendency and influence for evil received a fatal blow on the death of Christ, as belonging to the empire of darkness, and not of light. It is no valid objection to this view, that the definite article is used before the terms in question, as if pointing to the kind of principalities and powers mentioned in preceding passages;[1] for at Eph. vi. 12 also, where the terms undoubtedly refer to hostile agencies, the definite article is employed, notwithstanding that, in the earlier passage where they occur, the words were used in a good sense. There can be no reason why the same peculiarity might not occur here; especially as the very nature of the subject implies a certain individualizing—the principalities and powers, not all such, but those who, from their antagonism to the good, occupied a hostile relation to Him who undertook the cause of our redemption. But allowing this to be the kind of intelligences referred to, there is still room for difference of opinion respecting the specific acts of dealing said to have been practised upon them. These are in our version *spoiled*, *made an open show of*, *triumphed over*. The diversity turns chiefly on the first, and whether it should be having *spoiled*, *divested them of*, or having *stripped off from himself*, *divested himself of*. The former is the rendering of the Vulgate, *expolians*, which has been followed by all the English versions, and by the great body of modern expositors: 'it contemplates the principalities and powers as having been equipped with armour, which God as their conqueror took from them and removed away.'[2] And this, as preparatory to their being exhibited in humble guise and carried off in triumph, undoubtedly presents a quite suitable meaning, and has hence met with general acceptance. But exception has been taken to it by some (Deyling, Hofmann, Ellicott, Alford, Wordsworth), on the ground that the verb ἀπεκδύω, in the middle, never bears that sense, and that the apostle himself very shortly after, in ch. iii. 9, uses exactly the same part of it as here, ἀπεκδυσάμενος, in the sense, not of having spoiled, but of having put off, or divested one's-self of, namely,

[1] Alford.   [2] Meyer.

the old man and his deeds. This also is the meaning ascribed to the word by Origen (*exuens principatus et potestates* [1]), by Chrysostom, who says the apostle speaks of diabolical powers here, 'either because human nature had put on these, or, since it had them as a handle, He having become a man, put off the handle;' and, to the like effect, Theophylact and others. Such, undoubtedly, is the more natural and best supported meaning of the expression'; and the exact idea seems to be that our Lord (whom, and not God, against Meyer and Alford, we take to be the proper subject), when He resigned His body to an accursed death, that He might pay the deserved penalty for our sin, at the same time put off, or completely reft from Him, and from as many as should share with Him in His work of victory, those diabolical agencies who, by reason of sin, had obtained a kind of right to afflict and bruise humanity ; this, as the house of their usurped dominion, or the victim they hung around with deadly and destructive malice, was now wrung from their grasp, and they were cast adrift like baffled and discomfited foes, their cause hopelessly and for ever gone. So that, by suffering for righteousness, Christ most effectually prevailed against the evil in our condition ; [2] and thus turned the shame of the cross into the highest glory,[3] made it the instrument and occasion of boldly (ἐν παρρησίᾳ, in an assured and confident manner) putting to shame the patrons and abettors of the evil, or exposing their weakness in this mortal conflict, and triumphing over them even amidst their apparent victory. Thus explained, though the radical idea is a little different, the general meaning is much the same as in the authorized version.

In vers. 16, 17, we have the practical inference from the view that had been given of the work of Christ : *let no one, therefore, judge you in eating or in drinking, or in the matter of a feast, or of a new moon, or of Sabbaths ; which are a shadow of things to come, but the body is of Christ.* The term βρῶσις is not exactly food, but *eating*, the act of taking food—as appears by comparing Rom. xiv. 17, 1 Cor. viii. 4, 2 Cor. ix. 10, with others in which the passive form, βρῶμα, is employed for the thing eaten, or the food itself.[4] But what, of course, is meant by the expression is the kind of food which one takes, and which was limited by express enactment in the law of Moses. And the same also in regard to drink (πόσις)—though here there was no general limitation under the ancient economy ; only in the case of the ministering priest, and of persons under the Nazarite vow, was a restraint laid in respect to the temperate use of wine.[5]

Hom. in Jos. 8.   [2] Heb. ii. 14 ; 1 Pet. iii. 18-22.   [3] Jo. iii. 14, 15, xii. 32.
[4] 1 Cor. iii. 2, vi. 13, x. 3, &c.   [5] Lev. x. 9 ; Num. vi. 3.

These cases, however, were so partial and peculiar, that some have supposed (in particular Meyer, Ellicott) that among the parties referred to additional practices of an ascetic kind had been introduced respecting drinks, of a theosophic or rabbinical origin. This is possible enough ; but no special account can be made of it here, as the distinctions in question are presently affirmed to stand in a definite relation to the realities of the Gospel, and, consequently, are contemplated as of Divine appointment. When he says, Let no one judge you on the subject of eating and drinking, he may be understood generally to refer to articles of diet ; in respect to these, the distinction as between clean and unclean was now gone ; and whatever one might take he must not on this score be judged, or held to act unsuitably to the true ideal of a Christian life. And, in like manner, with respect to, or in the matter of (for such undoubtedly is the meaning of ἐν μέρει[1]) a feast, a stated solemnity (such as the Passover or Pentecost), or of a new moon (not strictly a holy day, except the seventh, but one marked by a few additional observances), or of Sabbaths. That the latter include, and indeed chiefly designate, the weekly Sabbath of the Jews, can admit of no reasonable doubt, both from days of that description comprising by far the greater part of those bearing the name of Sabbaths, and also because nearly, if not all, the other days to which the term *Sabbath* was applied, were already embraced in the feasts and new moons previously specified. Thus the distinctively sacred days appointed in the Mosaic law, together with its stated festivals, its distinctions of clean and unclean in food, and, by parity of reason, other things of a like outward and ceremonial nature, are here placed in one category, and declared to be no longer binding on the consciences of believers, or needful to their Christian progress. And for this reason, that they were all only shadows of things to come, while the body is of Christ ; that is, they were no more than imperfect and temporary prefigurations of the work He was to accomplish, and the benefits to be secured by it to those who believe ; and as such, of course, they fell away when the great reality appeared. It might seem as if something further should have been concluded— not merely the non-obligatory observance of those shadowy institutions of the old covenant, but, as in the Epistle to the Galatians, the essential antichristianism of their observance. There is, however, a difference in the two cases ; the churches of Galatia had actually fallen back upon Jewish observances as necessary to their salvation, but the Colossians were as yet only exposed to the temptation of having in their neighbourhood persons whose teaching and practice lay in a similar direction.

[1] 2 Cor. iii. 10, ix. 3.

So far as yet appeared, correct views of the truth and of their liberty in Christ might be all that was required to guard against the danger.

But was there no danger from the apostle's own doctrine in another direction? In coupling Sabbath days with the other peculiar observances of Judaism, as things done away in Christ, does he not strike at the obligation of maintaining the observance of one day in seven for the more especial service of God, and break the connection between the Lord's day of Christians and the Sabbath of earlier times? So it has often been alleged, and, among others, very strongly by Alford, who says, 'If the observance of the Sabbath had been, *in any form*, of lasting obligation on the Christian church, it would have been quite impossible for the apostle to have spoken thus. The fact of an obligatory rest of one day, whether the seventh or the first, would have been directly in the teeth of his assertion here : the holding of such would have been still to retain the shadow, while we possess the substance.' To this Ellicott justly replies, that such an assertion ' cannot be substantiated. The Sabbath of the Jews (he adds), as involving other than mere national reminiscences, was a σκία (shadow) of the Lord's day : that a weekly seventh part of our time should be specially devoted to God, rests on considerations as old as the creation : that that seventh portion of the week should be the *first* day, rests on apostolical, and perhaps, inferentially, Divine usage and appointment.' Substantially concurring in this, I still deem it better to say, that in so far as the Sabbath was a *shadow* of any thing in Christian times, it was, with all of a like nature, abolished in Christ; and on that account particularly (though also for other reasons), the day which took its place from the beginning of the Gospel dispensation, and had become known and observed, wherever the Christian church was established, as emphatically the Lord's day, was changed from the last to the first day of the week. The seventh day Sabbath had been so long regarded as one of the more distinctive badges of Judaism, and had also, as an important factor, entered into many of the other institutions of the old covenant (the stated feasts, the sabbatical year, the year of Jubilee), that it necessarily came to partake, to some extent, of their typical character, and, in so far as it did so, must, like them also, pass away when the time of reformation came. But this is only one aspect of the sabbatical institution—not the original and direct, but rather a subsidiary and incidental one. As in a peculiar sense the day of God—the day, as Jesus Himself testified, which was made for man, and of which He claimed to be the Lord,[1] the Sabbath was essentially one with the Lord's day of the Christian church,

[1] Matt. xii. 8 ; Mark ii. 27, 28.

which, when the apostle wrote, was everywhere recognised and observed by believers. For in that respect there was nothing in the Sabbath of earlier times properly shadowy, or typical of redemption. It commenced before sin had entered, and while yet there was no need for a Redeemer. Nor was there any thing properly typical in the observance of it imposed in the fourth commandment; for this was a substantial re-enforcement of the primary institution, in its bearing on the general relation of men to God, and of members of society to each other. When associated with the typical services of the old covenant, the same thing virtually happened to it as with circumcision, which was the sign and seal of the Abrahamic covenant of grace, and had no immediate connection with the law of Moses; while yet it became so identified with that law, that it required to be supplanted by another ordinance of nearly similar import when the seed of blessing arrived, in which the Abrahamic covenant was to find its fulfilment. So great had the necessity become for the abolition of the one ordinance and the introduction of the other, that the apostle virtually declares it to have been indispensable, when he affirms (in his Epistle to the Galatians), of those who would still be circumcised, that they were debtors to do the whole law. At the same time, as regards the original design and spiritual import of circumcision, this he makes coincident with baptism [1] —speaks here (v. 11) of baptized believers as the circumcision of Christ; and so presents the two ordinances as in principle most closely associated with each other, differing in form rather than in substance. We have no reason to suppose his meaning to be different in regard to the Sabbath; it is gone so far as its outward rest on the seventh day formed part of the typical things of Judaism, but no further. Its primeval character and destination remain. As baptism in the Spirit is Christ's circumcision, so the Lord's day is His Sabbath; and to be in the Spirit on that day, worshipping and serving Him in the truth of His Gospel, is to carry out the intent of the fourth commandment.[2]

1 TIM. I. 6-11.

'In respect to which things [viz., love out of a pure heart and a good conscience, and faith unfeigned], some having gone astray, turned aside to vain talk; 7. Wishing to be teachers of the law, without

[1] Rom. ii. 28, 29, iv. 11.

[2] See 'Typology of Scripture,' Vol. II. p. 146, from which some of these later remarks are taken.

understanding either the things they say, or concerning what things they make asseveration. 8. Now we know that the law is good, if one use it lawfully ; 9. Knowing this, that the law is not made for a righteous man, but for lawless and unruly persons, for impious and sinful, for unholy and profane, for smiters of fathers and smiters of mothers ; 10. For fornicators, abusers of themselves with mankind, slave-dealers, liars, perjurers, and if there is any thing else that is contrary to the sound teaching ; 11. According to the Gospel of the glory of the blessed God, with which I was put in trust.'

This passage contains the last recorded statement of St Paul regarding the law ; and it is of importance, for a correct understanding of its import, and bearing on the Christian life, to have a distinct perception of the point of view from which the apostle is here contemplating it. This was determined by the class of errorists against whom he was now seeking to warn Timothy—a class differing materially from those whom he found it necessary to contend against in his other epistles (to the Galatians, the Romans, and the Colossians) on the subject of the law. The latter were sincere, but mistaken and superficial, adherents of the law in the letter of its requirements, and the full compass of its ceremonial observances—legalists of the Pharisaical type. But those here in the eye of the apostle were obviously of a quite different stamp. So far from being sincere and earnest in their convictions, they are represented as morally in a very degenerate and perverted condition ; entirely lapsed, or erring from (ἀστοχήσαντες), what must ever distinguish the genuine believer, whether altogether enlightened or not in his apprehensions of the truth—the love which springs from a pure heart, a good conscience, and faith unfeigned. They not only wanted this essential characteristic of a sound moral condition, but had, in a spirit of error and declension, gone into another direction, and for the exercise of a pure and elevating love had fallen into a kind of empty talk. Then as to the manner in which this empty talk exhibited itself, he tells us, that while it turned somehow upon the law, of which they wished to be more especially the teachers, yet so little were they qualified for the task, that they neither understood what they spake about it, nor had any proper acquaintance with the things on which they made asseveration, or delivered themselves with an assured confidence (διαβεβαιοῦνται). How could they, indeed, since they wanted the love which is the very essence of the law, and the purity of heart and conscience, which a real conformity to its demands must ever presuppose and require ? In such a case, if they continued to make any account of the law, they necessarily turned aside to some arbitrary or fanciful applications of it, which were fitted rather to gratify an idle curiosity or a vain conceit, than to promote its spiritual ends. What precisely, then, was the character of their perverted ingenuity? Baur has endeavoured to prove that it took the form of antinomianism; that the assumed teachers of the law were in reality opponents of the law; that they were in fact heretics of the Marcionite school, who repudiated the Divine authority of the law, and were anti-legalists of the most advanced type. But to call such parties 'teachers of the law' would be an abuse of terms, besides involving, as a matter of course, the spurious character of the epistle, since the school of Marcion belongs to a period considerably subsequent to the apostolic age. The view, therefore, has met with few supporters even in Germany; and, indeed, carries improbability on the face of it; for, not only are the parties in question represented as in some sort teachers of the law, but contemplating them as such, and conceding somewhat to them in that respect, the apostle begins his counter-statement by saying, 'Now we know that the law is good'—as much as to say, on that common principle we are agreed; we have no quarrel with them as to the excellence of the law. The parties, therefore, were legalists, yet not after the fashion of the Jewish-Christians of Galatia and Colossae, for the manner of meeting them here is entirely different from that adopted in the epistles to those churches; they are charged, not with pressing the continued observance of what about it was temporary, or with exalting it as a whole out of its proper place, but with ignorance of its real nature, and making confident assertion of things respecting it which had no just foundation.

Now, one can readily understand how well such a description would apply to persons of a dreamy and speculative mood—disposed formally to abide by the revealed law of God; but, instead of taking its prescriptions in their plain and natural sense, seeking to refine upon them, and use them chiefly as an occasion or handle for certain mystical allegorizings and theosophic culture. And this is precisely the form of evil which (as is now generally believed—for example, by De Wette, Huther, Ellicott, Alford) prevailed among a class of Jewish believers about Ephesus—a class combining in itself certain heterogeneous elements derived from an incipient Gnosticism on the one side, and a corrupt Judaism on the other. The parties in question would keep by the law, they would even make more of it than the apostle did; but then it was the law understood after their own fashion, lifted out of its proper sphere, and linked to airy speculations or fanciful conceits. In the works of Philo—probably the soberest, certainly the best surviving specimens of this tendency—we find the law to a large extent evacuated of its moral import, and much that should have been applied to the heart and conscience turned into the channel of a crude and ill-digested physics. But in the case of inferior men, morally as well as intellectually inferior, men of a perverted and sophistical cast of mind, both the fancifulness of the expositions given of the law, and its application to other than the moral and religious purposes for which it was revealed, would naturally be of a more marked description. There would now be wild extravagance, and, under lofty pretensions to superior wisdom, a mode of interpretation adopted which aimed at establishing a licentious freedom. And so, indeed, the corresponding passage in Titus distinctly informs us,[1] where the apostle, evidently referring to the same sort of pretensions and corrupt legalists, says, ' There are many unruly and vain talkers and deceivers, specially they of the circumcision, whose mouths must be stopt, who subvert whole houses, teaching things which they ought not for filthy lucre's sake.' He further characterizes them as persons who give heed to Jewish fables and commandments of men, which turn from the truth, in their actings abominable, and in their very mind and conscience defiled. So that their fanciful and perverted use of the law must have led them quite away from its practical aim, into purely speculative or allegorical applications. And in such writings of the apostle John, as were more immediately addressed to the churches in the same Asiatic region, but at a period somewhat later, we find indications of a perfectly similar state of mind, only in a more advanced stage of development. They make mention of the ' blasphemy of those who say they are Jews and are not, but are of the synagogue of Satan,' of persons who taught the doctrine of Balaam, who practised the seductions of Jezebel, who were familiar with the depths of Satan, etc. :[2]—statements which could only be made of such as had given way to foolish imaginations, and lost the right moral perception of things. To teach the law, therefore, as those persons did, must have been virtually to defeat its end, because keeping it apart from the practical designs and purposes which it aimed at securing.

Vers. 8, 9. In opposition to this misuse of the law, the apostle proceeds to indicate its proper use—which he makes to consist in a plain, direct, and peremptory repression of the corruption and vicious practices which are at variance with its precepts. *Now we know that the law is good;* so far we are perfectly agreed ; in itself, the law is unimpeachable, and can work only good, *if one use it lawfully ;* in other words, apply it to the great moral ends for which it was given. Then,

[1] Titus i. 10.　　　　[2] Rev. ii. 9, 14, 20, 24.

as regards this legitimate use, the apostle indicates just one condition, a single guiding principle, but this perfectly sufficient to check the pernicious errors now more immediately in view : *knowing this, that the law is not made for a righteous man.* Though the article is not used before νόμος, it must plainly be taken (as the great majority of expositors, Chrysostom, Theophylact, and latterly De Witte, Huther, Weisinger, Alford, Ellicott) in the specific sense of God's law—the law by way of eminence —the Decalogue.   While, grammatically, Middleton's explanation, ' No law is enacted,' might be adopted—understanding law in the general sense, but inclusive of the law of Moses—the connection and obvious bearing of the passage does not properly admit of such a comprehensive reference ; it is the law, emphatically so called, in the view of God's professing people, as is clear alone from the respect had in the enumeration of crimes (vers. 9, 10) to the successive precepts of the Decalogue. By the just or righteous person (δίκαιος), for whom the law is not made (κεῖται), that is, constitutionally enacted or ordained, must be understood not such merely, as in the estimation of the world, are morally correct, but those who, in the higher Christian sense, are right before God—very much the same with the class of persons described in ver. 5, as having attained to the end of the commandment, by the possession of love, out of a pure heart, and a good conscience, and faith unfeigned. This certainly includes their justification through faith in the blood of Christ, but it includes sanctification as well ; it is indeed their complex condition that is indicated, as persons in whose experience the great principles of righteousness had come to the ascendant and bore rule. As such, they already have what the law aims at producing ; they are moving in the way which it prescribes ; and so, for them it may justly be said not to have been enacted.   Then, on the other side, the apostle goes on to describe the different sorts of persons for whom it *is* enacted —those whom it is given to check and restrain, and bring to a better state ; beginning with designations of a more general 'kind, and afterwards employing the more specific.   There is no need for dwelling on them : they are, *the lawless and unruly,* persons of a self-willed, wayward, and rebellious spirit; *the ungodly and sinful,* the same characters again, only contemplated from a more distinctly religious point of view, as devoid of respect to the authority and will of God ; *the unholy and profane,* differing from the immediately preceding epithets, only as pointing to the more positive aspect of the ungodly disposition, its tendency to run into what is openly wicked and irreligious—all, though general in their nature, having respect to men's relation to God, and their contrariety to the things enjoined in the earlier precepts of the

Decalogue. Then follow a series of terms which, in regular succession, denote the characters in question, with reference to the later precepts of the Decalogue: *smiters of fathers and smiters of mothers*—breakers of the fifth command of the law, yet not perhaps strictly parricides and matricides, as the verb ἀλοάω, or ἀλοιάω, which enters into the composition of πατρολῴαις and μητρολῴαις, signifies merely to *thresh, smite*, and such like, so that the compound terms do not necessarily import more than the dishonouring in an offensive manner, the contemptuous and harsh treatment of parents; *men-slayers*, the violaters of the sixth command; *fornicators, abusers of themselves with mankind* (Sodomites, ἀρσενοκοίταις), the violaters of the seventh; *men-stealers*, kidnappers and slave-dealers, the most obnoxious class of transgressors in respect to the eighth; finally, *liars and perjurers*, the open and flagrant breakers of the ninth. But the apostle had no intention of making a full enumeration; he points only to the more manifest and palpable forms of transgression under the several kinds; and, therefore, he winds up the description by a comprehensive delineation, *and if there is any thing else that is contrary to the sound teaching*—that, namely, which proceeds from the true servants and ambassadors of Christ, and which is characterized as sound, healthful (ὑγιαίνουσῃ), in opposition to the sickly and unwholesome kind of nutriment ministered by the corrupt teachers of whom he had been speaking. This term, though used only in the two epistles to Timothy, is aptly descriptive of the persons referred to—a class of theosophists, who thought themselves above the ordinary teaching of the Gospel, and the plain precepts of the law, who, in their aspirations after what they deemed the higher kind of life, restrained themselves from things in themselves lawful and good; while, on the other hand, they were dealing falsely with their consciences as to the fundamental distinctions between right and wrong in their behaviour, and, under the cloak of godliness, were prosecuting their own selfish ends.

In ver. 11 a word is added to indicate the conformity of the apostle's view of the matter with the Divine commission he had received: *according to the Gospel of the glory of the blessed God with which I was put in trust*. The connection with what precedes is general rather than particular; and the utterance is not to be limited merely to the sound teaching going before (as if it had been διδασκαλίᾳ τῇ, or τῇ οὔσῃ, κατὰ τὸ εὐαγγέλιον), but must be taken as embracing the whole of the preceding statement. His view of the law, and of the classes of character against whom it was more especially directed, its use rather in repressing evil and convicting of sin than carrying the spiritual and good to the higher degrees of perfection, so far from being a doctrine of his own devising, was in accordance with that Gospel which is emphatically the revelation of God's glory. It was not therefore to be thought of or characterized as a low doctrine, but was in accordance with the essential nature of Godhead, and the high aims of redeeming love.

INDICES.

I.

PASSAGES OF SCRIPTURE MORE PARTICULARLY REFERRED TO AND EXPLAINED.

II.

AUTHORS AND SUBJECTS.